The Global Schooner

The Global Schooner

Origins, Development, Design and Construction ♦ 1695-1845

Karl Heinz Marquardt

CONWAY MARITIME PRESS

Frontispiece: Replica of the Australian merchant schooner *Enterprize* of 1830. In 1835 this small schooner carried a handful of pioneers from Tasmania to the shores of Port Phillip Bay where they founded a settlement that later became Melbourne. Reconstruction designed by the author. *(Courtesy of The Enterprize Trust, Melbourne)*

Title page: An American topsail schooner by Pierre le Comte, 1831.

Acknowledgements

I have the pleasure of saying a heartfelt thank you to the following people and institutions for their assistance in obtaining valuable materials during my research on schooners. Many of the drawings could only be prepared with the new research obtained:

Mr A Aleshin, Central Naval Museum, St. Petersburg; Mr B Braatz, Berlin; Mr A Degerström, Krigsarchivet Stockholm; Mr M A Edson, Jr. Bethesda, MD; Mr A Fisher and Ms S Haasum, Statens Sjöhistoriska Museum Stockholm; Mr H S Jensen, Rigsarkivet, Copenhagen; Dr P F Johnston, Peabody Museum, Salem, Mass; Mr D Marung, Bautzen; Mr H Menzel, Hamburg; Dr H H Meyer, Focke Museum Bremen; Captain S Moen, Marinemuseet Horten; Mr M Robinson, National Maritime Museum, Greenwich England; Mr S A Schlytchkow, St. Petersburg; Mr P Tamm, Wissenschaftliches Institut für Schiffahrts-und Marinegeschichte, Hamburg; Mr R Vorstman, Nederlandsch Historisch Scheep vaart Museum, Amsterdam; City of Überlingen; Mitchell Library, Sydney, NSW; National Library, Canberra, ACT; State Library of Victoria, Melbourne, Victoria; Teyler's Museum, Haarlem.

First published in Great Britain in 2003 by Conway Maritime Press, 9 Blenheim Court, Brewery Road, London N7 9NY
www.conwaymaritime.com

A member of Chrysalis Books plc

British Library Cataloguing in Publication Data
A record for this title is available upon request from the British Library

ISBN 0 85177 930 1

Designed by Stephen Dent
Printed and Bound in Spain

Contents

◆

Continued over:

Appendix 2: Mast and spar dimensions 1735–1858
Mast and spar dimensions of the schooner *St Ann* (1735)
Dimensions of masts and spars for the schooner *Sultana* (1767)
French eighteenth-century schooner specifications
1. Schooner from Brest Harbour (1769)
2. Masting of other eighteenth-century schooners of 21m in length
The proportional dimensions in direct measurements
Dimensions of masts and yards for a schooner of 110 tons (1794)
Table of masts and spars etc, for a US Navy schooner (1826)
Proportions for masts, yards, booms etc, of schooners (1829)
Tables in J Fincham's Treatise
Various proportions for the masting of schooners (1858)
Dimensions of masts and spars for brigantine and topsail schooner (1858)

Appendix 3: Rigging dimensions 1818–1864
Tables of the lengths and dimensions of the standing and running rigging, with the species, size and number of blocks, hearts, dead-eyes etc. (1818)
Standing rigging dimensions (1856)
Some linear measurements and weights as used in this book
A table showing the length and size of standing and running rigging for all classes of US Navy vessels (Extract: Schooner)
A table showing the size and description of the different blocks of all classes of US Navy vessels (Extract: Schooner)

Appendix 4: Furniture etc.
Anchor measurements for smaller vessels
Dimensions of oars for sloops, brigs, barges, lighters and ships' boats
Dimensions of oars and skulls for barges, wherries and skiffs
Building dimensions for boats
Mast and spar dimensions for boats

Introduction

———◆———

OUR maritime past harbours a multitude of ships and rigs and to know all types is a task too large to contemplate. However, the names of some of these ships have become part of our general vocabulary. One name in particular, schooner, has often been used liberally and quoted out of context.

There are two main questions that need to be answered about schooners: what is a schooner and what does the name mean? The first question can be answered relatively easily: a schooner can be any shape and size but must meet the criteria of a certain type of rig. That criteria was stipulated in 1769 by William Falconer in his *Universal Dictionary Of The Marine*, at a time when the term 'schooner' was still a relative newcomer to nautical language:

'A small vessel with two masts, whose main-sail and fore-sail are suspended from gaffs reaching from the mast towards the stern; and stretched out below by booms, whose foremost ends are hooked to an iron, which clasps the mast so as to turn therein as upon an axis, when the after-ends are swung from one side of the vessel to the other.'[1]

In later years one or two masts were added to the rig criteria and the term schooner began to be used for larger vessels. The three-masted, or tern, schooners, which were introduced around 1800, are an important development in the history of schooners and are therefore included here.

Answering the second question, of the name, is slightly more difficult. The term schooner first appeared in documents and newsprint about two decades after the type's inception and we can be reasonably sure that it is an American idiom. With the schooner evolving since the Revolution as the preferred coastal vessel in American waters, and the word being a household name in the United States for about a century, an American claim to the invention of the schooner rig seems natural. This claim is evident in the first American book on shipbuilding, where Lauchlan McKay, a brother of the famous clipper-builder Donald McKay, writes:

'When we look at the improvements made by ship-wrights in the United States, and know at the same time that they have been introduced by guess in many instances, we may well be surprised that so little true science and so few methodical rules have been understood; but when again we think of the many failures, of the clumsy, misshapen structures that have been produced, at all times and in all places among us, in the course of these very experimental efforts, it causes regret that

enterprise should not have been guided by better knowledge. The schooner is an American invention. The Baltimore clippers, as they are called from their fleetness, astonished and puzzled the British seamen in the last war. The writings of their naval officers are full of expressions of admiration and wonder at the feats of this species of craft upon the ocean.'[2]

Published in 1839, McKay's assumption of the schooner being an American invention was mainly based on the superior qualities of the Baltimore Clipper. Burgeoning national pride turned this type of vessel into an icon associated with nationhood, privateering, blockade running etc., in the American quarrels with England during the Revolutionary and Napoleonic Wars. From there it was only a short step to the schooner's birth being anchored into American folklore. A local historical study, *The History of the Town of Gloucester, Cape Ann* by John J Babson (Gloucester, 1860)[3], set the story in motion and only a few years later it was taken up by *Webster's Dictionary*. By 1874 the story appeared in Germany in an article by Friedrich Schüler, and in 1880 Henry Hall[4] named 1745 as the year in which the schooner was contrived. For the past century or more since Hall's assertion was published, every book and larger essay on schooners tells the story of how the ship came to be named:

The schooner *Enterprize* in the Bass Strait. Oil painting by the author.

in 1713 (or 1745 depending on the source), Captain Andrew Robinson from Gloucester, Maryland, watched the launch of his two-masted, square-sterned vessel; an onlooker, captivated by the faster than normal speed of the just-launched craft, called out 'See, how she scoons' and Robinson, still in search of a good name replied, 'A scooner let her be'. The honour of being the birthplace of the first schooner is therefore handed to Gloucester, one of the East Coast's most important schooner-building ports. It is unfortunate that the story's narrators cannot even agree on the year of this important occasion and have overlooked another consequential point: the term 'schooner' does not, and never has, implied a hull shape; only the rig turns a vessel into a schooner. Many dismissed this anecdote as a fable, but others still try to confirm it with supporting evidence. With no dialectic base of the word 'scoon' found in the English or Scottish language, as claimed by some, A H Clark[5] was probably close to the truth when he connected 'schooner' with the Dutch word *schoon* (translated as beautiful or handsome). Although no practical application of the word was discovered in nautical vocabularies, schooner remained an unresolved, but accepted, type name.

However, to explain the word 'schooner' we do not necessarily have to look for nautical connotations. By considering the evolution of the two seventeenth-century gaff rigs and their differing application, we may discover the key to this mysterious word. In a rough classification, one rig, evolved from the sprit rig of full-bodied cargo vessels, was called the standing gaff rig, while the other, deriving from the small spreader for hoisting a blunted shoulder of mutton sail on a smaller pleasure craft, was the running gaff rig with boom. One- or two-masted yachts using this latter rig, and with their smart lines, copious ornaments and eye-pleasing sail arrangements, would be called handsome vessels in anyone's language. The Dutch expression '*een schoone Schip*' refers to the beauty of two-masted yachts and must have been heard or read many times during the seventeenth and early eighteenth century, especially during the visits to Holland made by the British Royal yacht HMS *Royal Transport*. With no name for this and other new two-masted fore-and-aft rigs available in those early years, and seeing it set up on American small vessels, a Dutch settler's admiration for the beauty of those elaborate yachts could have seemed the perfect phrase in that multilingual climate of the early eighteenth-century American eastern seaboard. English-speaking listeners could have easily misinterpreted his elated cry '*Wat een schoone Schip*' for a type designation. In the English tongue 'sch' is almost always pronounced 'sk', while an 'e' at the end of a word is always expected to be followed by an 'r', which means that even today the Dutch word *schoone* would sound more like *scooner* to an English speaker. So *een schoone Schip* becomes 'a scooner ship', which habitually became shortened to a *scooner* or, in later years, a *schooner*. Registration of a cargo or fishing vessel rigged in that new two-masted fore-and-aft style as a Scooner or Schooner appears a plausible consequence. Although we will never know the true

origin of the word this is surely more realistic than the story offered by Robinson. This would not have been the first foreign word to enter the English language through misconception.

The schooner story is not only about a new rig; the unsung tale contains more than just the description of a small craft's new ropes and sails. It tells of a decision by the Russian Tsar Peter the Great to study shipbuilding, not only in Holland but also in England, where they build ships 'who sail against the wind'. It tells also of new innovations in headsail arrangement, which soon revolutionised the headgear of all ships, large and small. And it tells about the magnitude of duties performed by schooners, duties ranging from royal pleasure cruising to harvesting the sea, from mercantile ventures to a privateer's lust for bounty, from trading in opium and human cargo to exploration, and from fast sailing fleet tenders to the more cumbersome gunboats of coastal protection. That handy fore-and-aft rig of royal beginnings could be found everywhere and made 'schooner' a word adopted by several languages.

Many drawings of schooners are represented in this book, but five of them are extensively prepared for model building and follow the changes and developments made during the 150 years discussed here: the *Schooner For Port Jackson* and *Enterprize* represent common merchant schooners; *Elgen*, as coast-guard, and *Berbice*, as privateer, are two very different types of armed schooners; and *Axel Thorsen* depicts the robust gunboat. The tripartition of schooner types into schooners (unarmed merchant vessels), armed schooners and schooner-rigged gunboats (armed naval vessels) as listed in the Royal Navy was similarly reflected in the Continental fleets of Europe and in the newly formed United States Navy. The terms armed schooner and schooner-rigged gunboat may for the layman encapsulate one and the same type of vessel, but they were units of considerable difference. Armed schooners, often built for speed, derived in direct line from the first schooner and deployed small-calibre carriage and/or swivel guns and in later years carronades. Gunboats evolved as sturdily built products of military confrontation during the American and French Revolutions and were armed with one to three larger carriage guns, usually 18- or 24-pdr, and occasionally with some smaller armament.

———— ◆ ————

Notes:

1   Falconer, W, *An Universal Dictionary of the Marine* (London, 1769), edition of 1780 reprinted by David & Charles Reprints (Newton Abbot, Devon, 1970) p.257

2   McKay, Lauchlan, *The Practical Shipbuilder*, Collin, Keese and Co. (New York, 1839), repr. Macdonald and Jane's (London, 1974) p.8

3   Morris, E P, *The Fore and Aft Rig in America*, Yale University Press (New Haven, 1927), repr. Macdonald and Jane's (London, 1974) p.174

4   Hall, Henry, *Report on the Shipbuilding Industry in the U.S.*, Department of the Interior, Census Office (Washington DC, 1884), repr. Macdonald and Jane's (London, 1974) p.11

5   Clark, Arthur H, *The History of Yachting 1600-1815*, G P Putnam's & Sons (1904)

Chapter 1

♦

Origin of Schooners

How it began

Although the schooner rig as we know it did not appear before the declining years of the seventeenth century, its seeds were sown about one hundred years earlier on the waterways of that emerging nation around the estuaries of Rhine and Maas, the Netherlands. As it seems, they were seeds of an exotic nature indeed. Around 1600 a very simple, but alien, rig began to compete on smaller craft with the conventional square and spritsails of the Dutch fishing and coastal fleets. Consisting of one or two extremely aft raking masts, they had only a triangular sail laced to each. Neither yards nor booms were used, not even one rope of stabilising rigging, only a sheet to keep the sail's foot on the wind and a simple tye to set the sail.

The new rig appeared suddenly and its origins are difficult to trace. Dr A W Sleeswyk[6] offers a good explanation of its probable background in his 1987 article for the *Mariners Mirror*. The first European report of this simple rig on a balsa raft off the Peruvian coast came from the Andalusian pilot Bartolomé Ruiz in 1526. The earliest pictorial evidence is an engraving in a journal kept by Joris van Spilbergen, a Dutch navigator, who in 1615 encountered such raft in Payta Bay. With that rig, named by the Dutch *torentuig* (tower rig), already visible on H C Vroom's painting 'The arrival of the Elector Palatine Frederick V and his English bride in Flushing roadstead 1613', its actual introduction in the Netherlands was about two decades earlier than van

Torentuig-rigged Dutch boat from a picture by Adam Willaerts (1629).

Spilbergen's illustration. Sleeswyk argued that certain elements suggest the rig was first developed during the closing years of the previous century. In 1592 two Dutchmen in Portuguese service, Jan Huygen van Linschoten and Dirk Gerritszoon Pomp, returned to their homeland from India via the South American coast. It is plausible that these seafarers carried the knowledge of the ingenious triangular balsa-raft rig with them, thereby introducing it as a simple boat rig to Dutch waters. Those rafts, with their primitive centreboards for course and abdrift correction, could also have been an inspiration for the leeboards that appeared around the same time on Dutch small craft. The creation of the shoulder-of-mutton rig was an entirely new concept: raking masts and triangular sails without a boom. After being introduced to the Bermudas, probably by a shipwrecked Dutch ships carpenter[7] during the second decade of the seventeenth century, the rig later became known in England as Bermoothes or Bermudoes and in America as Bermuda rig.

Peruvian raft from a journal by Joris van Spilbergen (1615).

While Vroom painted the *torentuig* still in its original state, an earlier introduction of the rig can be assumed, since its next evolutionary step, the *speeljacht* rig, was already well established within a few years of the painting. An early picture of that variation, dated 1601, is 'The *Overtoomseweg* outside Amsterdam', which for a long time was accredited to Cornelis Claes van Wieringen. New research into the style and artistry suggests that the painting is more likely to be the work of Jan de Wet, with a revised date of post-1620. This lively pen, ink and watercolour drawing shows two relatively small, canal-based trading vessels fitted with the only recently introduced leeboards, which are so characteristic of Dutch craft. The vessels masts are stepped vertically, and while the foremast stood on the keel's forefoot, just aft of the stem, the mainmast was placed afore mid-ships. Laced to these straight masts were triangular sails, which had their head stick-secured peak hoisted on a halyard. Another innovation was a pivotal boom for that loose-footed, shoulder-of-mutton sail.

Dutch ingenuity transformed a primitive South-American-raft rig into an easy rig for small, inland-waterways craft. Unsupported by stays and shrouds, that improved but still rudimentary *toren* (tower) rig used only the aforementioned mast-lacing, a halyard and tack for the sail and a topping lift plus a sheet for the boom. The available pictorial evidence (with the exception of Jan de Wet's drawing) suggests that the burghers adopted the *toren* rig mainly for their leisure boats: seventeenth-century maritime artists such as Dirk Everson Lons, Salomon Savry, A D Willarts and Simon Vlieger, all depict the *speeljacht* (play or pleasure yacht). However, one must accept certain attempts

Speeljacht by Adam Willaerts (1642).

for its mercantile use, as shown by de Wet and several decades later in America, where these early tower-rig developments could be found on coastal-fishing craft such as the Block Island boat and the Fair Haven sharpie.

The *speeljacht* with her two-masted, fore-and-aft rig without bowsprit is the acknowledged forerunner of the schooner. Booms and mast trunks, to lower the masts when passing under bridges, are innovations accredited to this par-

'The *Overtoomseweg* outside Amsterdam', probably by Jan de Wet (after 1620).

Speeljacht reconstructed from an etching by Dirk Everson Lons (1629).

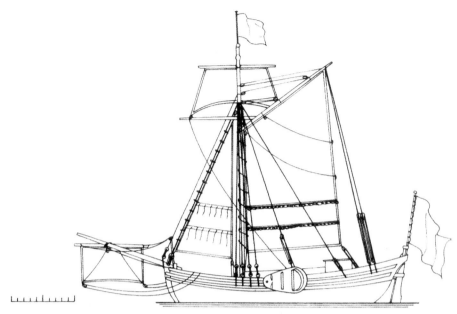

Boeijer reconstructed from an etching probably by Dirk Everson Lons (1629).

ticular rig. Not much larger than our weekend sailing boats, her mainmast was approximately one third of vessel length aft of the stem position. The foremast of seven-tenths the mainmast length stood at one-quarter of that length above the keel footing. *Speeljachts* were otherwise open boats, only decked between the masts; their sails were rigged as previously discussed, whereby two reef-point rows provided the means for sail reduction.

If the *speeljacht* is the most obvious visual link to the schooner, other less notable links were the single-masted,

standing-gaff-rigged Dutch *boeijers* and the running-gaff-rigged *bezaan jacht*, which emerged at similar times on the Dutch fishing and coastal scene. By about 1620–25 small mercantile and fishing craft, which before had only been square- or sprit-rigged, had a third rig – the halfsprit, later renamed standing gaff. With the cumbersome long sprit now half its previous length and pivoting with jaws on the upper mast, the halfsprit was a great improvement over the full-sprit rig and was soon widely accepted for full-bodied cargo vessels. By the middle of the seventeenth century it also replaced

'Man o' War and Fishermen off the coast' by Jan Porcellis (about 1625).

Bezaan-rigged mail
packet from an etching
by Joost van Geel
(1665).

Bezaan-rigged mail
packet from an etching
by Joost van Geel
(1665).

from the head stick, a boom very similar to the *speeljachts* and a near triangular mainsail with its sheet reaching to the outer end of the boom over the stern. Additional ropes were a fore stay and one or two pairs of shrouds. Smaller craft using the halfsprit rig also carried a fore staysail but very often had no bowsprit. The first images of *bezaan* rigs appeared during the mid-seventeenth century and show that pleasure yachts had a bowsprit but working craft did not. This is evident by comparing several etchings by Joost van Geel on his *Postal Map* of 1665, which depict a mail packet and a pilot boat without bowsprits, with Lieve Verschuier's painting 'The Fleet of Yachts with Charles II of England is passing Rotterdam, 24 May 1660' which shows probably the first bowsprit-carrying, *bezaan*-rigged pleasure yacht. G C E Crone[8] named that yacht as the Prince of Orange's *bezaan-jacht* and pointed out that this vessel was much smaller than the *paviljoenjachten* (transom yachts) and differently rigged. A similarly rigged yacht is illustrated in I Sailmaker's painting 'The Shipyard of the East India Company on the Thames', which dates from about 1670, and another appears in a sketch from 1679 in Dankaerts and Sluiter's *Journal of a Voyage to New York*[9].

These three fore-and-aft rigs emerging in the Netherlands during the seventeenth century laid the foundation for new developments. Various types of sloop rig blossomed concurrently in Northern European countries, for example the brigantine, which is probably French, and the schooner rig.

The Birth of the Schooner

There are two contrasting lines of thought about the beginnings of the schooner: one, advocated by A Laing[10], favours a story of evolutionary development using the evidence found in three contemporary engravings; the second believes the schooner was an individual design effort and that the new rig was created by taking components from known fore-and-aft rigs of that period.

The evolutionary theory, which stands on somewhat shaky ground, begins its argument with van Bremden's glorification of 'Capture of the Spanish silver fleet by Piet Hein off Havana in 1628'. A small two-master with a risen quarterdeck is shown near the event as a spectator vessel under bare poles. Looking at her in detail she carries a bowsprit, a forestay, a mainstay, a probable boom or sprit with a lift, and the downward-leading mainstay indicates a square sail for the foremast rather than a gaff sail. One vertical line on that sketchy craft could be interpreted as a shroud, which means that the assumed mainmast's fore-and-aft rig could only be defined as boom or sprit rig. If, however, this line is interpreted as a mast and the mast line as lift, the boom line transforms suddenly into a lowered, fore-and-aft-stowed square-sail-yard. This makes it much more likely that the vessel is actually a common early-seventeenth-century bark, similar to another small vessel to her left in the painting, which has an identical hull shape but is shown fully rigged under square sails.

The second piece of evolutionary evidence can be viewed on the left of Joan Blaeu's world map from 1648, in the Pacific just above the equatorial line. In a scene reminiscent

the sprit rig on royal and governmental transom yachts. The large gaff, combined with its traditional fore-and-aft sail could do without a boom but right from the outset a square-rigged topsail formed part of the rig. Jan Porcellis' (1584–1632) painting 'Man o' War and Fishermen off the Coast' depicts a gaff-rigged *boeijer* with a halfsprit rig.

With the simple *speeljacht* rig remaining an inland water rig, a single-masted *bezaan* rig developed in parallel with the halfsprit rig. In contrast to the latter with its bowsprit spritsail, one or two staysails and a square rigged topsail, the *bezaan* rig consisted of a short running gaff, which evolved

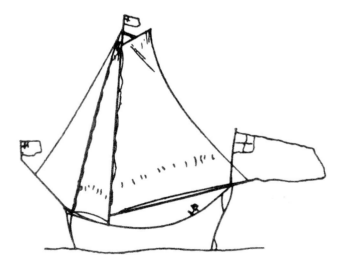

Sketch of a sloop in
Dankaerts and Sluiter's
*Journal of a Voyage to
New York* (1679–80).

Detail of an engraving by D van Bremden, 'Capture of the Spanish silver fleet by Piet Hein off Havana in 1628'.

Detail of Joan Blaeu's great world map of 1648.

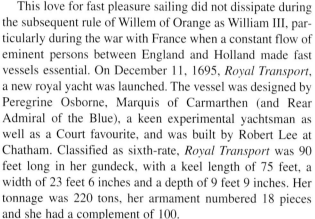

Detail of the picture 'Capture of Loki, Celebes in 1652' in Laurens van der Hem's *Secret Atlas* of about 1678.

of van Bremden's painting, a spectator vessel can be seen with the same bowsprit, forestay and mainstay configuration, but with the added difference of a *speeljacht* suit of sails.

The schooner from the 'Capture of Loki' in Laurens van der Hem's *Secret Atlas* from approximately 1678 is the third piece of evidence in the evolutionary theory. It has been said that Van der Hem relied strongly on Blaeu's great atlas, which might suggest that the vessel is only an elaborate repetition of the second piece of evidence. Van der Hem's 'schooner' is a more modern vessel than Blaeu's, which can be explained by the fact that his painting was created thirty years later, and the rig that he shows (with two added head-sails and a spritsail but without a mainstay) is not collaborated by any other contemporary evidence. Although Van der Hem is well known for his nautically correct ship drawings, the idea for this particular vessel could well have come from Blaeu's map. If rigs of that kind did exist in 1678 there would be further examples of it in the works of other seventeenth-century maritime artists. In its heyday Dutch maritime art provided a great many impressions of every rig used and although a number of *speeljachts* can be found, no schooner rig appears anywhere. With no further evidence supporting these three illustrations, one can only conclude that a bark probably inspired Blaeu to add a known set of sails to the bare-poled vessel and that van der Hem used artistic licence by modernising that vessel throughout. A new rig of such importance would not have gone unnoticed in Europe, especially by that keen yachtsman Charles II of England. The Crown owned no less than 26 yachts during the King's 25-year rule, at least 24 of which were developed and built for the Royal household by the best English shipwrights in accordance with the Dutch pattern used for the first two, the transom yacht *Mary* and the *bezaan*-yacht *Bezan*. To make them faster the later yachts were ketch rigged, rather than one-masted, which was an idea claimed by the king himself.

This love for fast pleasure sailing did not dissipate during the subsequent rule of Willem of Orange as William III, particularly during the war with France when a constant flow of eminent persons between England and Holland made fast vessels essential. On December 11, 1695, *Royal Transport*, a new royal yacht was launched. The vessel was designed by Peregrine Osborne, Marquis of Carmarthen (and Rear Admiral of the Blue), a keen experimental yachtsman as well as a Court favourite, and was built by Robert Lee at Chatham. Classified as sixth-rate, *Royal Transport* was 90 feet long in her gundeck, with a keel length of 75 feet, a width of 23 feet 6 inches and a depth of 9 feet 9 inches. Her tonnage was 220 tons, her armament numbered 18 pieces and she had a complement of 100.

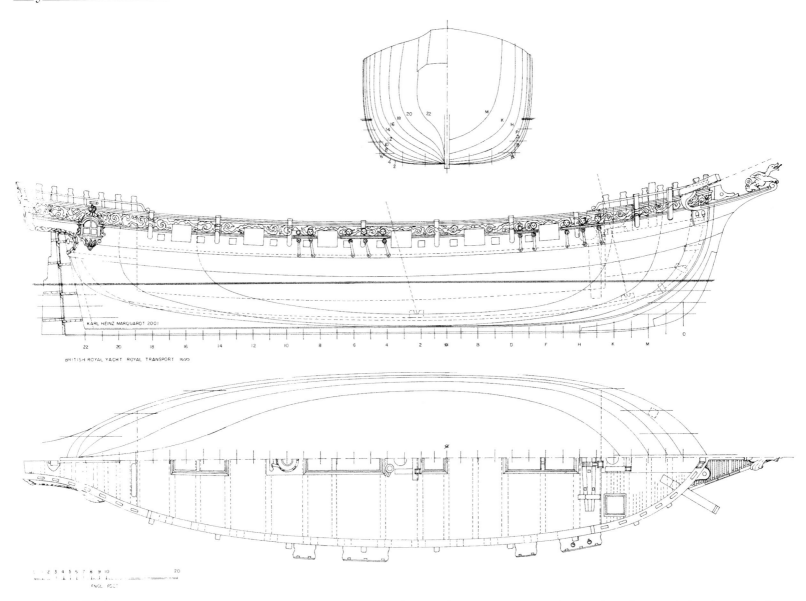

KARL HEINZ MARQUARDT 2001

BRITISH ROYAL YACHT 'ROYAL TRANSPORT' 1695

Lines of HMS *Royal Transport*, reconstructed from model photographs and known dimensions.

December 11, 1695, is without doubt a milestone in schooner development: it is the first schooner's birthday. Note that the date is not 1713 and the birthplace is not Gloucester, Massachusetts, as the American version of the tale goes. Although the term schooner was yet to be invented, the two-masted *Royal Transport* had a completely new mast arrangement with both fore and mainmast being gaff-rigged. It is certainly unfortunate that draughts of that remarkable vessel do not exist; yet we are not completely without evidence of her appearance and unusual rig design. An excellent contemporary model has survived the rigours of time and is today part of the Central Naval Museum in St. Petersburg. W F Ryan, who wrote about the yacht's connection with Tsar Peter the Great of Russia, has also unearthed further documentary material which supports the idea that HMS *Royal Transport* was not just another progressive step in the evolutionary theory.

If ships like *Royal Transport* were already known for decades in Holland could the Marquis of Carmarthen, without running the risk of being ridiculed and jeopardising the British wish for a tobacco monopoly in Russia, have claimed in a letter to Tsar Peter that his rig design was unique, and that this

'...small craft of my invention was designed not only for utility and comfort but also so that it should be faster and more powerful than other ships exceeding it in size...'? [11]

If the Tsar, with his great interest in sailing and naval matters and vast knowledge of Dutch shipbuilding, had come across a similar rig design before he would have dismissed that claim and stayed in Holland, but he was intrigued by the new vessel and came to England. Carmarthen was an experimenter with ships and not always looked on favourably by the Admiralty [12]. Yet in 1694, when the navy began to build their own boats, the Navy Board recommended his tender. Despite being described by Sir Cloudesley Shovell as 'an incomparable sailer', Carmarthen's prototype, the galley *Bridget*, was rejected by the Admiralty as being too expensive. Perhaps, though, the real problem was that the prototype was too revolutionary for its conservative members? Was she already an experimental schooner? Although these are questions that can never be answered it would be logical to think that Carmarthen would have tried his radically new concept on an inconspicuous vessel before fitting it to his monarch's yacht.

Contemporaries attested Camarthen of having created

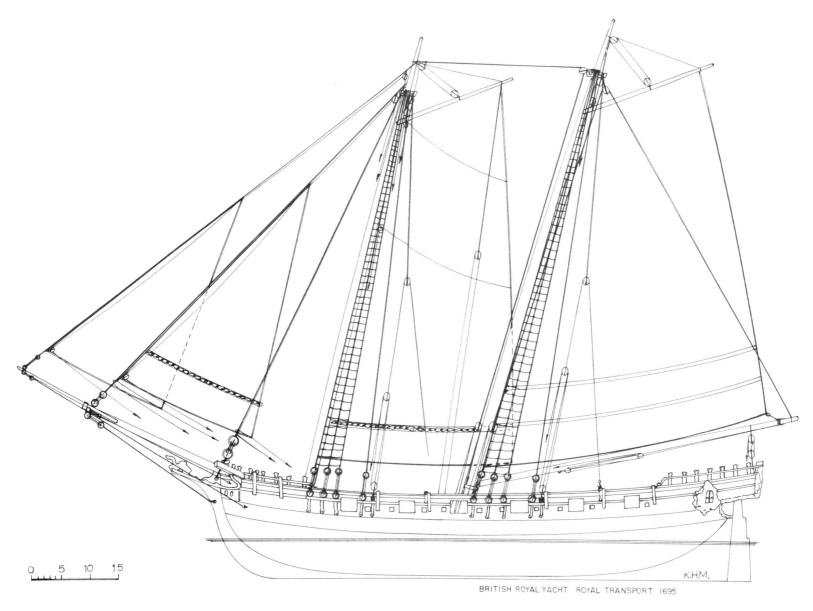

BRITISH ROYAL YACHT ROYAL TRANSPORT 1695

K.H.M.

0 5 10 15

something new and very successful. HMS *Royal Transport* was not only a yacht; she was the most modern ship in the fleet – fast and with a completely new rigging concept. Captain John Perry described *Royal Transport* in 1716:

'...as much the fastest and best yacht then in England, built frigate-fashion, carrying twenty-four guns and contrived by my Lord Marquis of Carmarthen on purpose for the King's own use for crossing the sea during the war.' [13]

The King himself requested that, as a successor to *Royal Transport* which was presented to the Tsar in 1698, another yacht or frigate of not more than 190 tons be built at the Chatham Dockyard under Carmarthen's direction. This ship, the galley *Peregrine,* was a sixth-rate of 190 tons, 32 guns and a crew of 58. She was renamed *Carolina,* then *Royal Caroline* before becoming *Peregrine* again. She was a very well known royal yacht indeed and a very fast sailer (a hallmark of Carmarthen designs). Another royal yacht, the *Royal Ann* galley, was launched in June 1709, '...of a new invention under the direction of the Marquese of Carmarthen, carrying 40 guns, being the finest that was ever built.' [14]

If one considers the *speeljacht* as the grandfather of all schooners, then nothing claims the role of father more than HMS *Royal Transport.* She not only had a noble beginning and was one of the finest and fastest vessels afloat, she also carried a number of innovations that soon revolutionised the headgear of all ships. Other curiosities were her flat bottom and near vertical sides. With the exception of a more rounded bilge, she had the very roomy main frame of a Dutch merchant craft. All this attracted Peter the Great to come to England and close the tobacco monopoly deal. After being presented with the yacht, he left England's shores in April 1698. Originally planning to sail in her to Archangel, he departed the ship at Helvoetsluys in Holland and travelled the quicker route overland to Russia. *Royal Transport* (known in Russia as *Transport Royal*) sailed then without the Tsar to Archangel, where she remained until 1715 as part of the White Sea Flotilla. Attempts to transport her overland to the Baltic Sea failed. Refitted in 1715, she set sail for the Baltic Sea in September and was wrecked in a storm off the Swedish coast. Her captain, Hutchinson, and twenty of her crew became prisoners of war in the ongoing struggle between Sweden and Russia.

Rigging of HMS *Royal Transport* based on the model, with sails indicated.

Contemporary model of HMS *Royal Transport* (1695), which was presented to Tzar Peter the Great during his stay in England in 1698. (*Courtesy of Central Naval Museum, St. Petersburg, Russia*)

Detail of Bow and deck
section of HMS *Royal
Transport* after a recent
restoration at the
Central Naval Museum,
St. Petersburg.
*(Courtesy of
Mr S A Schlytchkow,
St. Petersburg, Russia)*

Bow view from below.
*(Courtesy of
Mr S A Schlytchkow,
St. Petersburg, Russia)*

Deck view from the
mainmast aft of HMS
Royal Transport after
restoration. The steering
wheel seems to be a late
addition.
*(Courtesy of
Mr S A Schlytchkow,
St. Petersburg, Russia)*

The pinque stern of the
model. A rudder was
added during
restoration.
*(Courtesy of
Mr S A Schlytchkow,
St. Petersburg, Russia)*

First Seventy Years of Schooner Development in Europe and America

It is interesting to note that after 1695 a chain of records can be established that firmly lifts the schooner rig into maritime renown. A schooner rig would have been as important in Blaeu's time as it was fifty years later, which seems to suggest that schooners simply did not exist before 1695. Willem van der Velde, the Younger, supplies evidence of further utilisation of the new rig in the British fleet in a pencil sketch of the sloop *Bonetta*, one of eight built during the war with France in 1699. Only lightly armed with two guns and two swivels, she was of 66 ¾ tons and built at Deptford by Surveyor Miller. The sketch not only reveals the telltale signs of a fore-and-aft schooner rig (with only two or three dead eyes per mast) but also a main boom with a lowered gaff above, which definitely makes her an early schooner. The sketch shows at quarterdeck a kind of temporary flag-pole erected with a limp hanging ensign, which was probably only used when rowing.

Further evidence of schooner development in England before 1704 can be found in van der Velde's painting 'English Yachts at Sea in a fresh Breeze'. That painting was

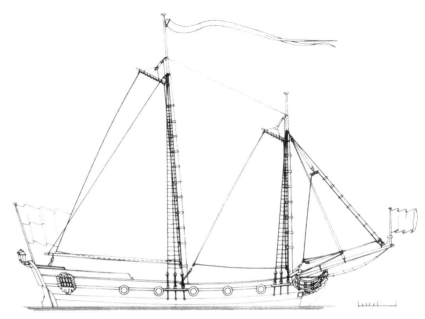

a popular theme and was copied several times by other artists. The English maritime art expert M S Robinson mentioned a few versions which, judging by the flags shown and the style of painting, were probably produced after the painter's death. They all show the same two yachts, rigged

British yacht about 1704, reconstructed from 'English Yachts at Sea in a fresh Breeze' by W van der Velde, the Younger.

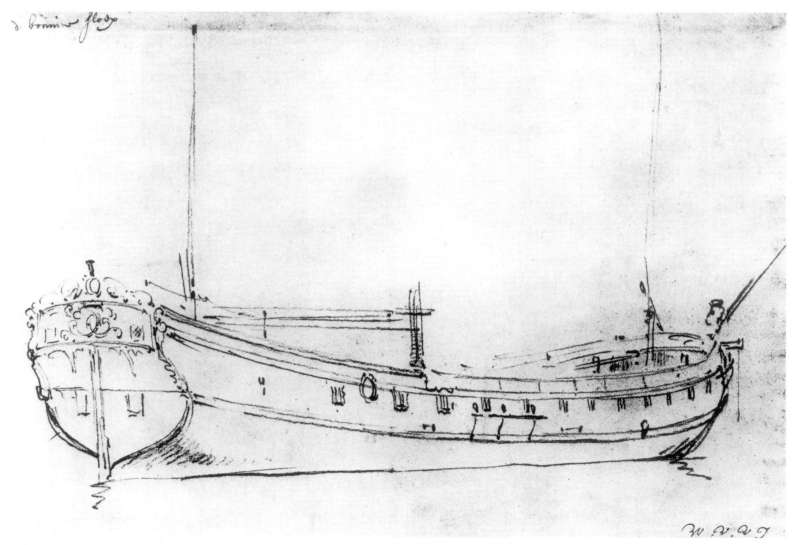

Sloop *Bonetta* (1699), by Willem van der Velde, the Younger. (*Courtesy of National Maritime Museum, Greenwich, England*)

Boat with schooner rig after J Kip (1697 or 1708–9).

with gaff sails on fore- and mainmasts, armed with broadsides of 5–6 guns and with a sail shape strongly resembling a *speeljacht*. These yachts were fitted with a bowsprit and carried a headsail and nearly all the rigging necessary to sustain a larger fore-and-aft vessel. When comparing these rigs with that of *Royal Transport,* a retrogressive step is obvious, as if Peregrine Osborne's concept was not fully understood, or another experiment had been tried. The schooner's mast was kept much shorter and stood like a *speeljacht*'s above the forefoot, with the boom's outer peak remaining inside the taffrail. No attempt was made to use the new jib boom invention and only one headsail is shown. Judging by the number of sail cloths in the foot of both gaff sails and considering main deck gun deployment (presumably 3-pdr by looking at widths of gun port, the minimum space between gun ports, etc.), these yachts were at least 70 feet over deck and approximately 130 tons. Two originally ketch-rigged yachts, *Fubbs* built in 1682 and *Isabella* built in 1683, were rebuilt in 1701 and 1703 respectively and compare favourably in their measurements with the yachts in the painting. *Fubbs* had a keel length of 63 feet, an over deck length of 73 feet 6 inches and was of 148 tons with 12 guns, while *Isabella* had a keel of 60 feet and was of 114 tons, carrying 10 guns. It is probable, after the excellent experience with *Royal Transport*'s new rig, that the refitted yachts were rigged similarly. Adding the sloop and these two yachts to the list of early schooners, we have during the first ten years of that rig's history at least four English schooners of 66–220 tons well documented.

Another early reference comes from Jan Kip, whose 1708 work '*Nouveau Théâtre de la Grande Bretagne*' provides a picture of an English shallop-like boat on the Thames. Fitted with two schooner-rigged masts, the boat also carries a bowsprit and a headsail. E P Morris[15] points to a separate copy of that illustration in the British Museum print room

with a pencil-marked date of 1697 on the margin. The pencilled date could hint at the boat's origin. At that time HMS *Royal Transport*, rigged in 1695 as a schooner, was still carrying VIPs to and from Holland and this miniature imitation could either have been a boat of the larger royal yacht, or as hinted by the flags flown, a boat owned by the Marquis of Carmarthen. Peregrine Osborne was, after all, an Admiral of the Blue and the dark flag at the stern may have been an indication of rank. Having been instrumental in designing the new rig, he could have applied it to his own personal river conveyance as well.

A fifth naval vessel can be counted as a possible candidate. At Deptford between 1709 and 1711 the *Jamaica* class of 117 tons was built, consisting of *Jamaica, Tryall, Ferrett* and *Sharke. Ferrett* was re-rigged with two masts in 1715–1716. There is no evidence to suggest what this two-masted rig was and it has been classed as a brigantine after an assumption made by R C Anderson[16] who looked at an engraving of the English sloop *Drake* of 1729. Due to the American claim of creating the first schooner in the early eighteenth century historians have placed many early two-masted sloops lacking documentary evidence into the brigantine or snow class. However, by looking at the evidence discussed earlier, the oldest of the two-masted, fore-and-aft rigs would be the schooner. An engraving by W Burgis 'A View of Boston', which dates from 1723 or 1725 and is therefore the earliest known picture of schooners in America, shows a Royal Navy sloop, rigged as a fore-and-aft schooner, which could well have been the aforementioned *Ferret.*

By looking again at early sloop draughts in the Admiralty collection of the National Maritime Museum in Greenwich two vessels seem to have been previously misclassified by modern historians. The 90–ton sloop *Swift*, built in 1721 at Woolwich, was classified as snow but the mainmast is not a snow mast, both masts are fitted in schooner position and her channels only have sets of two and three dead eyes each, which is not enough to rig a snow but is adequate for a fore-and-aft schooner. The dead-eye configuration for a slightly larger snow-rigged sloop (*Spy* of 1732) was five and seven. With contemporary literature considering a snow the largest two-masted vessel, some rigging interpretations of original draughts are just guesswork.

There are two other schooner candidates. The *Spence*, built at Deptford in 1730 of 206 $\frac{54}{94}$ tons and with a length of 87 feet, had masts that were set schooner fashion. The *Sharke* sloop of 1732, built at Portsmouth of 201 $\frac{13}{94}$ tons and with the dimensions of 80 feet overall length, 63 feet (keel) x 24 feet 6 inches x 9 feet 11 ¼ inches, is mentioned as ketch-rigged despite appearing otherwise on the draught: a fore-and mainmast with a certain (schooner) rake is indicated rather than a main and mizzenmast, and channels and dead eyes are not shown[17]. If some of the few surviving early plans and pictures of Royal Navy sloops suggest the schooner rig, there may be many more of which only the name and dimensions can be found.

It was merely a question of time before gaff/boom-rigged fast sailing yachts and other naval vessels influenced mercantile craft. W A Baker[18] discovered that in May 1716 the

Boston Port Records mentioned a scooner and that the Gloucester Town Records from August in the same year reported the loss of a new fishing scooner. Another American author, Merritt A Edson, Jr, refers to the Boston News-Letter issues of 4–11 February, 8–15 July and 10–17 November 1717 as the first published dates regarding the type designation 'schooner' [19]. One of these issues also mentions that pirates had captured two schooners, one from Boston and the other London-owned, off the North Carolina coast. This London-owned vessel provides another documented link in the chain of English schooner evolution at a time when American involvement was only first mentioned. This can be confirmed by looking at William Burgis' 1725 illustration 'A View of Boston', which not only shows three fore-and-aft-rigged merchant schooners, but also the aforementioned schooner-rigged Royal Navy sloop. Identified by the figurehead and the jack and pennant, this naval vessel is fore-and-aft-rigged but Burgis has drawn a boom on her schooner mast, providing the first known illustration of such a rig.

The Boston News-Letter also hinted at the commercial use of the schooner rig. In contrast to the rig's use on British navy vessels of a size up to 220 tons, the earliest American evidence of the rig, 21 years later than HMS *Royal Transport*, is of colonial schooners on a much smaller scale. W A Baker writes that in 1718 two fishing schooners hailing from Small Point Harbour in Maine were of 10 tons and a third of 8 tons, while E P Morris lists two schooners of 30 and 50 tons among 42 vessels registered in Connecticut in 1730. From the 94 vessels counted at Newport, Rhode Island in 1762, seven were schooners with an average displacement of 45 tons. According to these figures, there were less than ten schooner-rigged vessels in these American centres during the first few decades of the eighteenth century and they were of a much lower tonnage than their European cousins, perhaps providing further evidence that the schooner could not have been an American creation.

Throughout history humans have tried to push the limits of the two essentials of sea-borne commerce, speed and capacity, by constantly improving hull design and experimenting with rigging. Whilst certain naval vessels had a need for fast, close-hauled sailing, fishing and merchant craft had different requirements that could not be met by a pure fore-and-aft rig. A blending of both gaff rigs – the standing gaff with the additional square topsail for the fore or schooner mast and the running gaff with boom for the mainmast – created the topsail schooner. The available evidence suggests that this marriage took place between the late 1820s and early 1830s, although the location cannot be identified. Although Burgis' 'A View of Boston' shows only fore-and-aft-rigged schooners with short gaffs, the draughts of *Spence* and *Sharke* indicate an additional topsail. The draught of the Portuguese 36-ton schooner *St. Ann* of 1736 is the first to provide us with the written dimensions of masts and spars for her rig as a topsail schooner. In July 1736 *St. Ann* arrived in Britain from Lisbon and was taken off at Portsmouth dockyard in August.

F H af Chapman came across the *St. Ann* draught (which now resides in the archives of the Swedish Statens Sjöhistoriska Museum in Stockholm) whilst working as a ship's carpenter in England. The vessel is an important link in the chain of schooner development, which becomes easier to trace after the middle of the century. Her draught named the *St. Ann* 'a Portugal Scooner' and it has always been assumed, yet never proven, that she was American built, which is now very doubtful. With only limited documentation available of early colonial American craft, one cannot go outside the limits of small commercial vessels, and the *St. Ann* was not even a naval craft but a speedy yacht. Her extreme deadrise and tumblehome also suggest that there was no consideration given to freight carrying. In America a small fishing or merchant craft of her size would not have been built with a head, which in its shape and elaborate arrangement of head rails was typically English. Her overall design and general construction has a strong English influence, indicating that her shipwright must at least have

Detail of 'A View of Boston' (1725) by W Burgis.

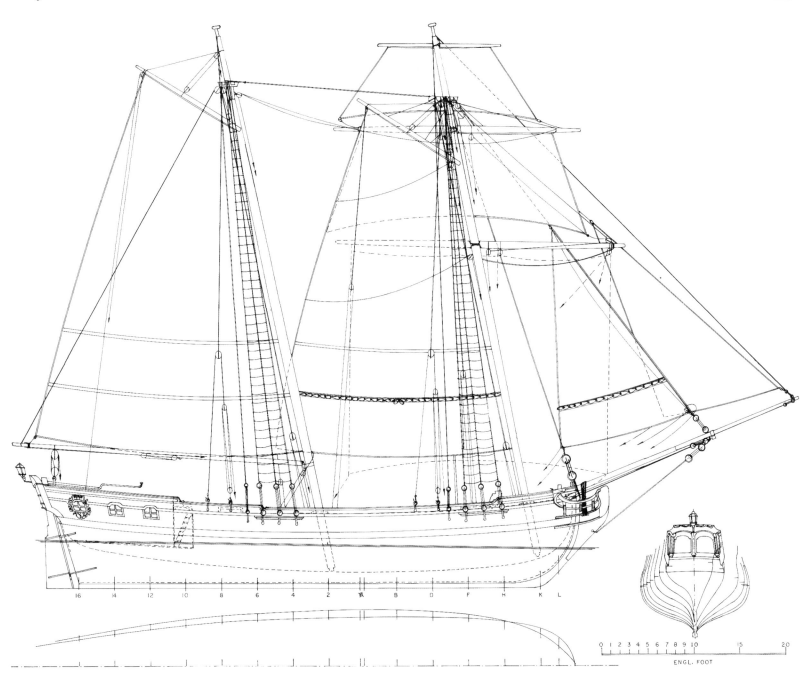

16 14 12 10 8 6 4 2 A B D F H K L

0 1 2 3 4 5 6 7 8 9 10   15   20
ENGL. FOOT

Portuguese schooner
St. Ann, **plan developed from an original draught.**
(*Courtesy of Statens Sjöhistoriska Museum, Wasavarvet, Stockholm, Sweden*)

been trained in England. With all these characteristics eminent and with European schooner development documented for four decades before her lines were taken off in 1736, this vessel could well be of European origin. The reasons for her being recorded by the Admiralty were certainly not the novelty of her rig (no rigging plan was given), but her narrow beam and fine lines, resulting in an impressive speed. She carried a temporary squaresail, a topsail and a topgallant sail on her foremast, with her mast and spar dimensions listing 'Topg'lt yard or Pidgeon each', both of which will be discussed later in Masting & Rigging (pages 155–189).

After such strong evidence it would be wrong to repeat glibly the assertion of an American schooner birth, and to presume the non-existence of schooners on the European scene for several decades. The evolution of the European schooner was a long and ongoing process, covered by other type designations and lost among the newly developing rigs of that period. Before 'schooner' was adopted into the nau-

tical language of several nations in the early sixties, the term 'sloop' was used for all British Navy vessels with less than three masts, which makes the rigging of many of these smaller vessels pure guesswork. The assumption that the schooner was a non-European rig, appearing no earlier than in the second decade of the 1700s, did not help either as the logic suggested that, if there was no pictorial or written evidence, the one- or two-masted sloops would be either sloop- or brigantine-rigged. Although there were two other two-masted rigs, these were easier to identify: the ketch stepped a main and mizzenmast, and the snow, as the youngest of those rigs, was fully rigged like a ship but her third mast stepped as an annex of the mainmast. This was known as snowmast or try-sail mast and mainly carried on merchant vessels, while sloops of war often fitted a vertical horse instead. All contemporary writers referred back to a similar description of the snow as Falconer did in his *Universal Dictionary of the Marine*: 'Snow, (senau, Fr.) is generally the largest of all two-masted vessels employed by Europeans, and the most convenient for navigation.'

The earliest evidence of the term 'snow' being applied to a rig comes from around 1730. The sloop *Spy* (1732–1745) of 200 $^{91}/_{94}$ tons is noted on the plans as being a snow, and the more upright masting in combination with the necessary dead eyes sustains that claim. Another contender for first snow-rigged naval vessel was the *Wolf* (1731–1741), a sloop of 244 $^{32}/_{94}$ tons. A German publication describes another snow (of 1705) under the French term *seneau*, but the description is very different: 'Seneau is a long barge, used by the Dutch for trekking/ can not carry more than 20 or 25 people.' [20]

These few words described what Dutchmen called a *treck-schuyt* and it suggests that the term 'snow' had as much to do with its special rig as had the seventeenth-century term 'brigantine'. Early evidence for the brigantine rig evolution from a two-masted, square-rigged vessel to a fore-and-aft-rigged vessel comes from the engravings by G Du Pas dated 1709 and those of Labat dated 1720.

In contemporary literature brigantine was not mentioned as a rig denomination before Falconer in 1769 and only then for merchant ships with two masts. When the term 'brigantine' became a synonym for a certain rig can only be guessed at. *Der Geöffnete See-Hafen* mentions a brigantine as a low-boarded vessel with 10–15 oars and often used by pirates. Thomas R Blanckley, whose work A *Naval Expositor* was published in 1750, acknowledges the vessel: 'Brigantines: Not now used, but were built light for rowing and sailing, and had two Masts and square Sails.' [21]

With this in mind one can say that not all of those early eighteenth-century sloops would have been only snow-, ketch- or brigantine-rigged, particularly as the schooner rig was so advantageous when introduced. If we consider again the main facts and the probabilities they suggest, then the schooner's European history looks more viable than the American claim.

1695–1715	HMS *Royal Transport*, English, later Russian
1699–1712	HMS *BONETTA*, English sloop, W van de Velde the Younger
1704 approx.	'English Yachts in a fresh Breeze', W v d Velde the Younger
1697 or 1708	'Schooner rigged Boat on the Thames', J Kip
1717	London-owned schooner captured by pirates off the North Carolina coast, Boston News-Letter
1721–1741	Draught of English sloop *Swift*
1725	Royal Navy schooner in 'A View of Boston', W Burgis
1730–1749	Draught of English sloop *Spence*

1732–1755	Draught of English sloop *Sharke*	Snow rig by F H af Chapman.
1736	Draught of *St. Ann*, A Portugal Scooner	

So, by the year 1736 there are already ten possible pieces of evidence for the schooner and at this time the only difference between a brigantine and a topsail schooner was the fore course, which was yard-rigged on a brigantine and gaff-rigged on a schooner, with neither rig denomination yet an official nautical term. This is a very small difference indeed if one considers that only the lowering of the fore gaff and the hoisting of a temporary squaresail could transform a topsail schooner into a brigantine. By comparing dead-eye

Brigantine by G Du Pas (1709).

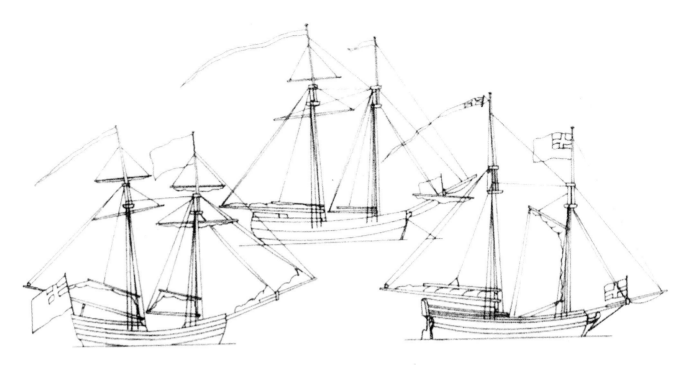

numbers of schooner-rigged vessels in Chapman's *Architectura Navalis Mercatoria* with British Admiralty sloop draughts we recognise a similarity in numbers for both rigs. One can therefore not dismiss all of these draughts as brigantine classifications. From what is known, the later brigantine-, or brig-, rig developed from existing fore-and-aft rigs. As neither topsail schooner nor brigantine were officially accepted terms, such vessels were generally classified as sloops. In his 1750 work Blanckley also presented a shallop with a very simple schooner rig, similar to Kip's rig but without bowsprit and headgear. In his description he used the term 'lugg sails' for the boom-less, short gaff sails, a term repeated in his next entry:

'Sloops: are sailed and masted as Mens Fancies lead them, sometimes with one Mast, with two, and with three, with Bermudoes, Shoulder of Mutton, Square, Lugg, and Smack Sails; they are in Figure either square or round Stern'd.'

When dissecting this statement quite a few rigs emerge: bermudoes were large quadrilateral sails with a short gaff and a long boom; shoulder of mutton were triangular sails mostly rigged without boom; square sails were quadrilateral sails on yards, hoisted at the middle; lugg sails were quadrilateral sails on yards, hoisted at one-third of their length; smack sails were halfsprit or standing gaff sails without a boom. These sails relate to the different rigs in a number of ways: sloops with two masts and bermudoes-rigged would have been fore-and-aft schooners, as with bermudoes and smack-sail topsail schooners; the brigantine was a combination of square sails and bermudoes; the snow had squaresails and a smack-sail. Adding Blanckley's explanation to our ten pieces of evidence, the sudden influx of schooners in the European navies in the 1760s appears to be nothing more than an official adoption of the term 'schooner' in European nautical language.

In 1769 Falconer considered that a lug-sail was not a boomless, short-gaff sail as Blanckley had described it, but a boat sail:

'Lug-Sail, treou, Fr.) a square sail, hoisted occasionally on the mast of a boat, or small vessel, upon a yard which hangs nearly at right angles with the mast. These are more particularly used in the barca longa, navigated by the Spaniards in the Mediterranean.' [22]

With the British schooner development amply documented in model, navy draughts and paintings, early American schooners are not so well covered. William A Baker[23] wrote in 1975 that within a decade of the first mention of fishing schooners most of the ketch-rigged fishing vessels were converted and that until the 1760s only little definite information can be found. He also quoted from an 1853 fishery report by L Sabine that, in 1741, the average size of these vessels was 50 tons, and that Marblehead owned 160 fishing vessels while Gloucester alone sent 70 schooners to the Great Banks. If Baker admits that very little definite information was available before the 1760s, Sabine's statement of about 100 years earlier could also only be an assumption based on hearsay. After W Burgis' 'A View of Boston' of 1725 the next known pictorial evidence of American schooners survives in *The Journals of Ashley Bowen (1728–1813) of Marblehead* [24]. It contains sketches of eight schooners on which he served between 1747 and 1780, the oldest being the *Peter & Mary*.

Draughts of American eighteenth-century schooners are rare and without the determination of the British Admiralty to have ships purchased or captured by the Royal Navy drawn up, no detailed evidence of American schooners of that period would exist. Only through those efforts do we know of the lines of Marblehead- or Virginia-built schooners. Evidence of American-built schooners for the Royal Navy can also be obtained through Naval documentation. Several schooners were built on the Great Lakes during

Barque longue by Jouve (1679).

the fifties and bought for the Royal Navy.

By looking at two nautical works printed in 1768 and 1769 it can be assumed that the term 'schooner' must have been anchored into nautical language long before its official adoption. The printing of such books is usually, even today, a long, time-consuming act of collecting, sorting and preparing before the final act of editing and printing takes place. Therefore, the initial writing or drawing of an item could be done several years ahead of printing. To have W Falconer describe the schooner in a way not foreign to the English reader presumes that such vessels must have been around for a reasonable time. Looking from that angle into Chapman's *Architectura Navalis Mercatoria*[25], we not only notice schooners as generally accepted in Europe in 1768, we also recognise a variety of schooner-rigged vessels from 34–195 tons. These vessels are not created in the American mould but along European lines and are in some instances larger than the average American tonnage of that time. It becomes obvious that Chapman did not include the schooner in his foreign section 'Several Kinds of Vessels Used by Different Nations', although he did include the Bermuda sloop, English cutter, French tartane and Dutch flyboat. There was no American schooner, as one would expect if the schooner rig were a novelty in the Europe of the 1760s. On the contrary, he applied the schooner rig to a frigate hull, a bark, two packet boats, two pleasure craft and two privateers, not only in a manner of great personal familiarity with that rig, but in a way that general Swedish acceptance of rig and name was assumed. On plate LXII, 'Several Figures, Representing The Different Manners Of Rigging, Which Are Most In Use In The Northern Contrys', the schooner rig was placed in sixth posi-

tion. The observant viewer will recognise the rigs on this plate as situated according to their importance to the author and the Swedish public at large. Last but not least the work's time-frame must be considered. According to our previous belief knowledge about schooners in mid-century Europe could only be obtained in England. Chapman first stayed in England from 1741 to 1744, when, as a nineteen-year-old, he worked there as a ship's carpenter. After studies in Stockholm he moved again to London in 1750 to further his knowledge, then in 1754 moved to Holland, went to France in 1755, and a year later came back to England before going home to Sweden in 1757. He worked then as an assistant shipwright for the Government at Karlskrona, spent part of 1758 and 1759 in Finland, 1760 to 1762 in Stralsund and then until 1764 in Sveaborg, Finland, before taking a leave of absence in 1764 to compile his famous work. His seven years of work around the Baltic Sea virtually removed him from the acknowledged centres of schooner knowledge, but, despite this, his competence in schooner-design is outstanding.

It is reasonable to conclude, then, that the schooner rig was very well known in England between 1741 and 1757, at a level of use not even anticipated in America, and became a familiar sight for the young Chapman. Also, by 1764 the schooner must already have been a fully accepted rig in Sweden, with its application to various hull types known. Both conclusions contradict the 'sudden discovery' theory and are more in line with a continuing European acceptance and use of a rig that was first installed on HMS *Royal Transport* in 1695.

Chapman went on to design further schooner-rigged vessels for the Swedish Navy. Danish schooner construction is documented since 1769, French since 1767 and the earliest German reference to schooners is dated 1787. Considering these dates, the introduction of schooner rigs on mercantile craft could have been slower on the Continent than with the major sea powers of the time, or was it only the aforementioned introduction date of the term schooner that makes us think so?

J H Röding, writer of the eighteenth-century's major German maritime dictionary, spells this out when he writes: 'By the English, Americans and generally in West India are schooners very frequently used in trade and carry 50 to 100 and more lasts.'[26]

———— ◆ ————

Notes:

[6] Sleeswyk, A W, 'The Origin and Development of the Triangular Sail and the Gaff Sail in Seventeenth Century Holland', *Mariner's Mirror* (London, 1987), Vol.73(4), pp.377–383

[7] Morris, E P, *The Fore and Aft Rig in America*, Yale University Press (New Haven, 1927), repr. Macdonald and Jane's (London, 1974) quoting from Captain John Smith's *Generall Historie Vol. 5* in the chapter about Governor Butler of Bermuda (1619–1621) p.119: 'Having an excellent Dutch Carpinter he entertained of them that were cast away in the Dutch Frigot; he emploied him in building of Boats, whereof they were in exceeding great want'.

[8] Crone, G C E, *De Jachten der Oranjes*, NV Swets & Zeitlinger Boekhandel & Uitgevers-Mij (Amsterdam, 1937) p.75

[9] Morris, E P, op. cit. p.82

[10] Laing, A, *The American Sail*, E P Dutton & Co Inc (New York, 1961) pp.193–199

[11] Ryan, W F, 'Peter the Great's English Yacht, Admiral Lord Carmarthen and the Russian Tobacco Monopoly', *Mariner's Mirror* (London, 1983), Vol.69(1), p.68: Letter of Carmarthen to Tsar Peter, dated 9 November 1697 (only a Russian copy exists)

[12] Ibid., p.70, and Admiralty Office to the Lords Justice, PRO.Adm. 7/334, p.65: 'such experiments ought not to be made on any of His Majesty's ships of war… building His Majesty's ships according to the fancy and humour of particular persons will break through those wholesome Rules and Methods which have been found absolutely necessary for the performance of His Majesty's Service.'

[13] Ryan, W F, 'Peter the Great's English Yacht', *Mariner's Mirror* (London), Vol. 69/1 p.68: Captain John Perry on the State of Russia under the Present Czar, dated London 1716

[14] Ryan, W F, 'Peter the Great's English Yacht', *Mariner's Mirror* (London), Vol. 69/1, p.70

[15] Morris, E P, op. cit. p.176

[16] Anderson, R & R C, *The Sailing Ship*, G G Harrap & Co (London, 1926) p.170

[17] Lyon, D, *The Sailing Navy List*, Conway Maritime Press (London, 1993) pp.53, 55

[18] Baker, W A, 'Fishing under Sail in the North Atlantic' from *The Atlantic World of Robert G. Albion* edited by B W Labaree, Wesleyan University Press (Middletown, Conn, 1975) p.59

[19] Edson Jr, M, 'The Schooner Rig, A Hypothesis', *The American Neptune*, Vol.xxv/2 (1965)

[20] Unknown, *Der geöffnete See-Hafen* (Hamburg, 1705–1706) repr. E Kabel Verlag, (Hamburg, 1989) p.171: '*Seneau ist eine lange Barque, welche die Holländer zum Lauff gebrauchen / kan aber über 20 oder 25 Personen nicht einnehmen*'.

[21] Blanckley, T R, *A Naval Expositor* (London, 1750), repr. Jean Boudriot Publications (Rotherfield, 1988): entry on brigantines on p.148; entry on sloops on p.149

[22] Falconer, W, *An Universal Dictionary of the Marine* (London, 1769), 1780 edition reprinted by David & Charles Reprints (Newton Abbot, Devon, 1970) p.185

[23] Baker, W A, op. cit.

[24] Ph C F Smith, ed., *The Journals of Ashley Bowen (1728–1813) of Marblehead*, Colonial Society of Massachusetts & Peabody Museum (Salem, 1973)

[25] Chapman F H af, *Architectura Navalis Mercatoria* (Stockholm, 1768) repr. Hinstorff Verlag (Rostock, 1968)

[26] Röding, J H, *Allgemeines Wörterbuch der Marine* (Hamburg & Leipzig, 1794) Vol.2, p.522, repr. Uitgeverij Graphic Publisher (Amsterdam, 1969): '*Bey den Engländern, Amerikanern und überhaupt in Westindien werden die Schuner sehr häufig zur Handlung gebraucht und führen 50 bis 100 und mehrere Lasten*'.

Chapter 2

◆

Yachts, Navy Sloops and Privateers

THE schooner rig proved adaptable to many hull shapes during its early years as it had advantages that other rigs did not: it allowed a vessel to sail very close to the wind and needed a smaller handling crew. Whether the nobleman originally intended to provide his king's yacht with superior sailing qualities or not, these qualities soon found wider recognition. The rig was installed on small naval sloops, developed from the square-rigged *barques longues* or brigantines, which were rowed as well as sailed. Some larger sloops followed the same trend before the schooner concept inspired experimentation with new rigging combinations, such as the altered brigantine rig. During that period such a vessel would still be called a brigantine, even if she was schooner and not square-rigged. The only designations according to rig were 'ketch', the earliest rig, and 'schooner'; all other vessels were designated according to hull shape. For example, a bark or cutter could have a schooner rig, but a schooner could not have a bark or cutter rig. A combination of the proven old and the praised new could easily have developed into what we now know as a brigantine rig. The earliest brigantine-rig pictures (by G Du Pas and dated 1709) are French, which suggest that the rig could have been developed in France. Falconer described this schooner-inspired rig as a 'merchant-ship with two masts' and he did not acknowledge its use in the Navy at all. However, the term 'brig' has recently been discovered in his work, similar to Chapman's 'brigg'. Naval recognition was given to this type of rig in 1778 when the first batch of six brigs, the *Childers* class of 202 tons was built. The draught of that class carries the designation Brigantine, which was later altered to Brig Sloop.

The rig of an eighteenth-century two-masted draught could be determined by contemporary documentation, pictorial or otherwise, and one may very well try a rule of thumb. The number of sails in the various rigs, and their shape and size, require a different number of shroud pairs and dead eyes on their channels. Chapman's *Architectura Navalis Mercatoria* provides not only draughts of various vessels but also their proposed rig specifications. This unique collection of draughts offers comparable primary references for hull and rig, not for one particular vessel but for the whole spectrum.

By comparing this information with other contemporary sources, it can be ascertained that a topsail schooner would not carry more than four pairs of shrouds, and had one or, rarely, two back-stay pairs. *St. Ann* of 36 tons, which we have already considered to be a topsail schooner, was not fitted with the ship or cutter masts of later schooners, but had the stepped pole masts of earlier fore-and-aft rigged vessels and, like them, had only three shroud pairs to each mast. Pure fore-and-aft-rigged schooners, dependent on their size, were fitted with either two or three shroud pairs per mast.

As already stated, the very first schooner-rigged vessel was a yacht – the royal yacht *Royal Transport*, built in 1695 by Robert Lee at Chatham Dockyard. Classified as a sixth rate, she was of 220 tons and had a pinque stern with an ornamental quarter badge and a gilded dragon as a figurehead. A short poop deck over the large cabin covered the aft 20 per cent of the upper deck. According to the Admiralty Progress Book for 1695, her armament consisted of 18 guns, but her contemporary model indicates only 12 gun ports and 4 swivel posts in the bow. Willem van de Velde the Younger introduces a further two schooner-rigged yachts in his painting 'English Yachts at Sea in a fresh Breeze', which are assumed to be *Fubbs* and *Isabella* after their rebuilds in 1701 and 1703 respectively.

The first sloops with schooner rigs are also known from a sketch by William van der Velde the Younger. During the same war in which *Royal Transport* emerged as the fastest ship in the Royal Navy, the old square-rigged and oared brigantines were replaced by small, fast craft that patrolled the Scottish and Irish coasts, gathered intelligence and prevented French supplies from reaching the Jacobites. After a group of advice boats were built in 1694, another eight of about 65 tons and armed with two guns and two swivels came into service in 1699: *Bonetta, Fox, Merlin, Prohibition, Shark, Swallow, Swift* and *Woolfe*. A sketch of *Bonetta* shows her to be a schooner and, although no evidence is available, it seems likely that the other seven would

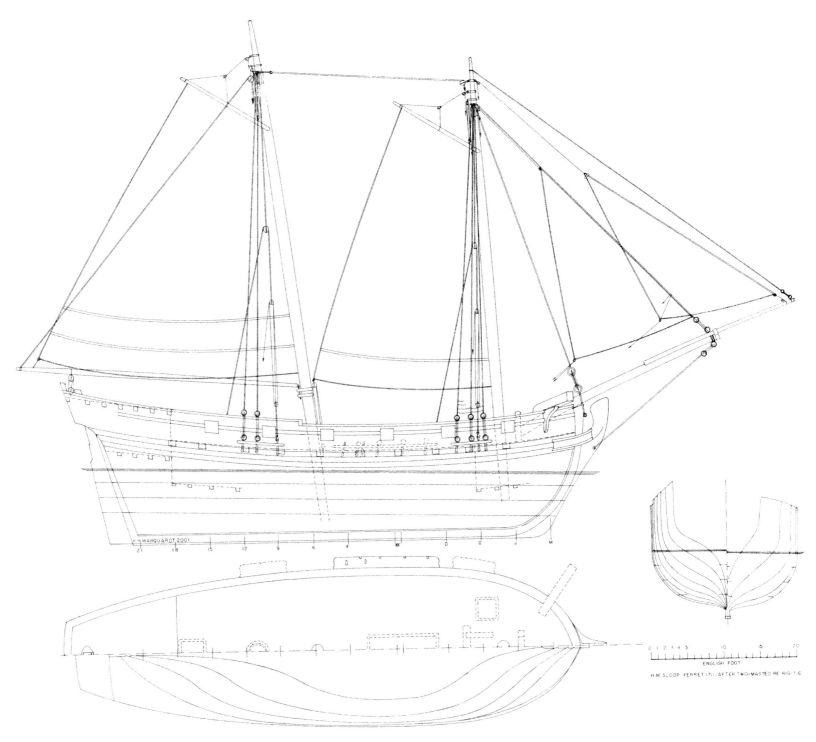

Sloop *Ferret* of 1711 as she may have looked after her two-masted refit. Based on a draught at the National Maritime Museum, Greenwich, England.

have been similar in design. A further six sloops with four guns and four swivels, and of a slightly larger tonnage, were built between 1700 and 1705.

The next step in schooner development is slightly hazy. The fore-and-aft-rigged Royal Navy schooner in W Burgis' etching of Boston, dated 1725, is still unknown and it can only be assumed to be the *Jamaica*-class sloop *Ferret* of 1711, re-rigged with two masts.

Ferret was launched on 20 April 1711 at Deptford and, according to a design by Surveyor Allin, was of 113 tons, had a compliment of 100 and carried 10 x 3-pdrs and 4 swivels.

Length at the Range of the Deck	64ft 6in
Length of Keel for Tonnage	50ft 0in
Breadth	20ft 8in
Depth	9ft 1in

When looking at the surviving draught of the sloop *Swift* conclusions can be drawn more easily. Marked only as 'Sloop, Copy sent to Woolwich, 12th June 1721', her dimensions were:

Length at the Range of the Deck	60ft 0in
Breadth	19ft 2in
Depth	8ft 3in
Draught of Water Abaft	7ft 6in
Abaft	6ft 9in
Tunns	90 ½

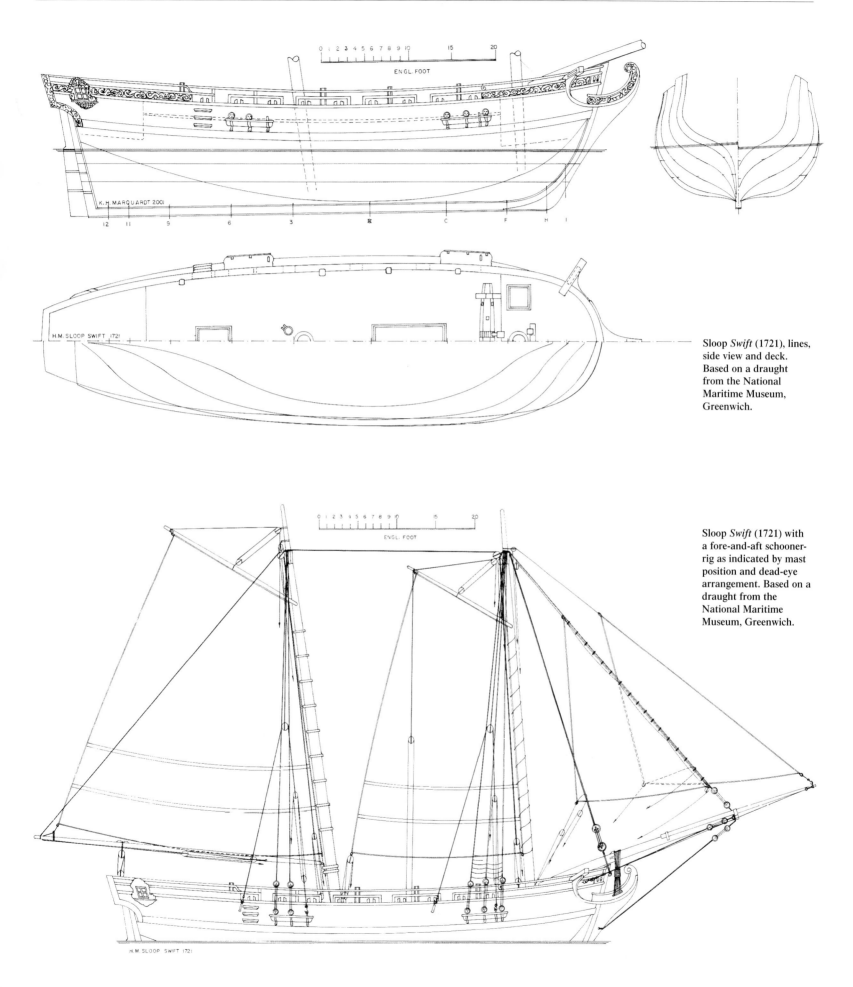

Sloop *Swift* (1721), lines, side view and deck. Based on a draught from the National Maritime Museum, Greenwich.

Sloop *Swift* (1721) with a fore-and-aft schooner-rig as indicated by mast position and dead-eye arrangement. Based on a draught from the National Maritime Museum, Greenwich.

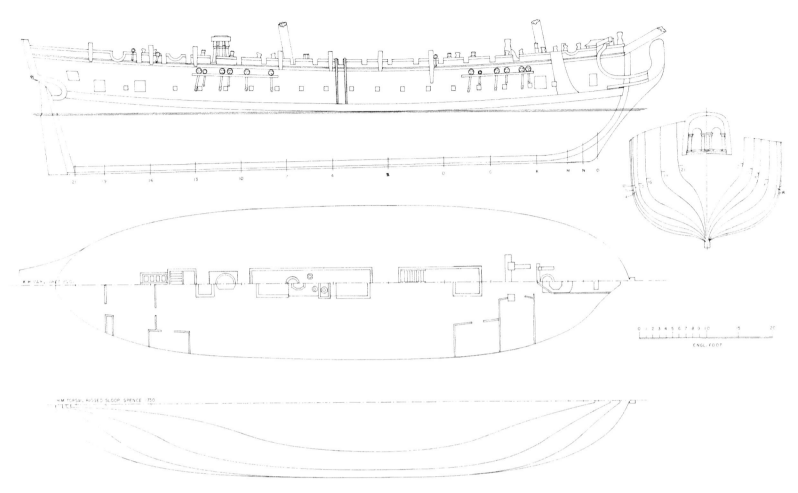

HMS *Spence* (1730), based on a draught in the National Maritime Museum in Greenwich.

It is interesting to compare these dimensions with the proportions specified for a schooner approximately 100 years later (1829)[27]. *Swift's* mainmast position is about the same as that of a common schooner and the rake slightly less. Her foremast setting was about 1½ feet further forward than the later schooner's and had slightly less rake. The mast setting alone would suggest a schooner, rather than a snow, as which she is classified in the *Sailing Navy List*[28]. This is obvious by the very limited number of dead eyes – three and an eye bolt for the tackle at the foremast and two and an eye bolt for the tackle at the mainmast. With no dead eye or eye bolt for backstays provided, the masts were pole-masts, which excluded the snow rig entirely. Her deck was stepped, with forecastle and poop rising by 2½ feet, and while having an open rail, that rail was laid out for four guns with another four swivel posts fitted to each side. She could also be propelled with 18 sweeps. A scroll decorated the head, with an ornate quarter badge and a carved rim to the stern. The uppermost plank at front and rear was painted with intertwined leaves. *Swift* was launched on 19 August 1721 and sold out of service in 1741.

The large sloop *Spence*, of 206 ⁵³⁄₆₄ tons, was launched on 24 June 1730 at Deptford Dockyard and sold in 1749. Built with a pinque stern like *Royal Transport*, she was the shorter vessel by 3 feet. What makes her stand out to be a contender as a schooner are her strongly raking masts and their positioning, which was not unlike other schooners.

The draught 'Shark Sloop built at Portsmouth', plan no. 3654 and marked in the *Sailing Navy List* as ketch-rigged

(main and mizzen mast), provides us with a main- and foremast positioned and raked like a schooner. The sloop was launched at Portsmouth Dockyard on 7 September 1732 and sold out of service in 1755. A vessel of 201 ¹³⁄₆₄ tons, her upper deck, with seven gun ports, had breaks for forecastle and poop deck. It is unfortunate that positive rig identification cannot be made because of the missing dead eyes and channels, but the masts make her a probable schooner.

St. Ann was only a small vessel of 36 tons and as the draught stated 'a Portuguese Scooner that arri'd w'th a Packet from Lisbon in July 1736 and was taken of at Portsmouth in August following'. She may have been a Portuguese Navy advice boat, but with no armament, gun or swivel indicated the probability of her being a yacht is even greater. She had a decorated quarter badge and two windows to each side with two further windows to stern. The deck had a break for the cabin at the rear quarter and on the draught a stern lantern and a probable lion figurehead are indicated. Her dimensions were:

Length of the Keel for Tunnage	46ft 9in
Breadth Extreme	12ft 1½in
Depth at O from up'r Edge of o. Keel to gunwale	8ft 0in
No of Tuns	36 ²¹⁄₆₄
Draught of Water Afore	4ft 4in
Abaft	5ft 2in

The draught of *St. Ann* is interesting as the dimensions are given for spars and sails; they are the first clear indication of

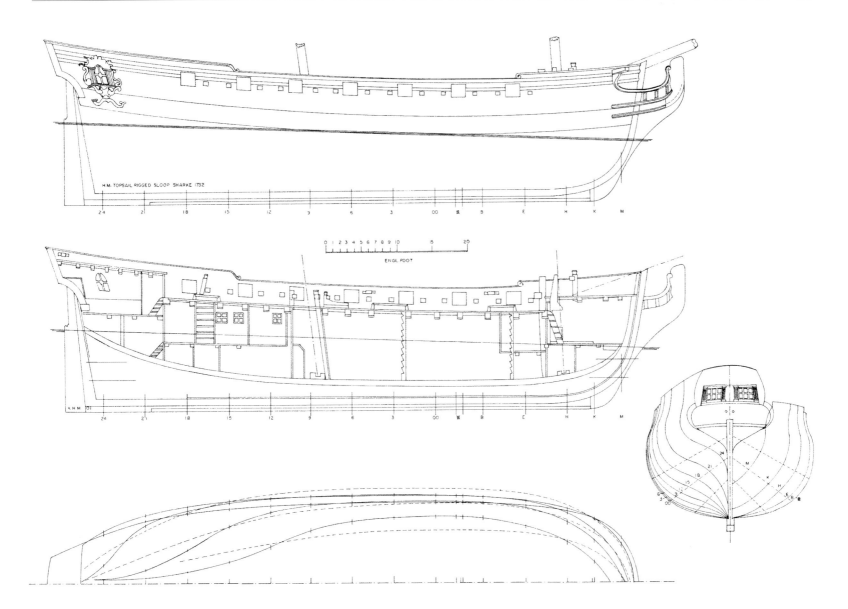

a topsail schooner. Surviving draughts of the 1830s to 1840s do show vessels that could be schooners, but they only provide mast position and rake with the right number of dead eyes and it remains guesswork whether they were in fact brigantines or topsail schooners. *St. Ann*'s dimensions, written down in 1736, are clear proof that she was a topsail schooner:

Main Mast: From the Deck to the Hounds	44ft 5in
Pole Head	5ft 9in
Whole Length	56ft 2in
Gaff	10ft 4in
Fore Mast: From the Deck to Hounds	41ft 10in
Pole Head	6ft 5in
Whole Length	54ft 10in
Gaff	10ft 11in
Bowsprit: Before the Stem	15ft 8in
Whole Length	20ft 9in
Flying Jibboom	13ft 0in
Boom	30ft 8in
Spread yard	29ft 10in
Fore Tops'l yard	26ft 4in
Topg'lt yard or Pidgeon, each	13ft 0in

The sail sizes were measured in running sailcloth lengths:

Main Sail	120 yd 38in
Fore Sail	116 yd 31in
Jib	54 yd 52in
Square Sail	125 yd 3in
Tops'l	56 yd 7in
Topg'lt or Pidgeon	14 yd 12in

The sail sizes reveal that the pole-masts used on *St. Ann* were similar to those on *Royal Transport* and those shown on Burgis' 'A View of Boston', which indicates a preference for this type of mast on schooners between 1695 and 1735.

Emphasis on recorded naval schooner construction shifted in the following decades to North America, where small, armed craft were needed during the Seven Year War (French/Indian War) of 1756–1763. Several schooners were built on the Great Lakes, but besides names and general information nothing is known of them. Three were built in 1755 at Oswego on Lake Ontario: *Lively,* also known as *Farquer,* was taken by the French one year later and retaken in 1759 at Niagara; *Vigilant* and *George* were also taken in

HMS *Sharke* (1832), based on a draught from the National Maritime Museum, Greenwich.

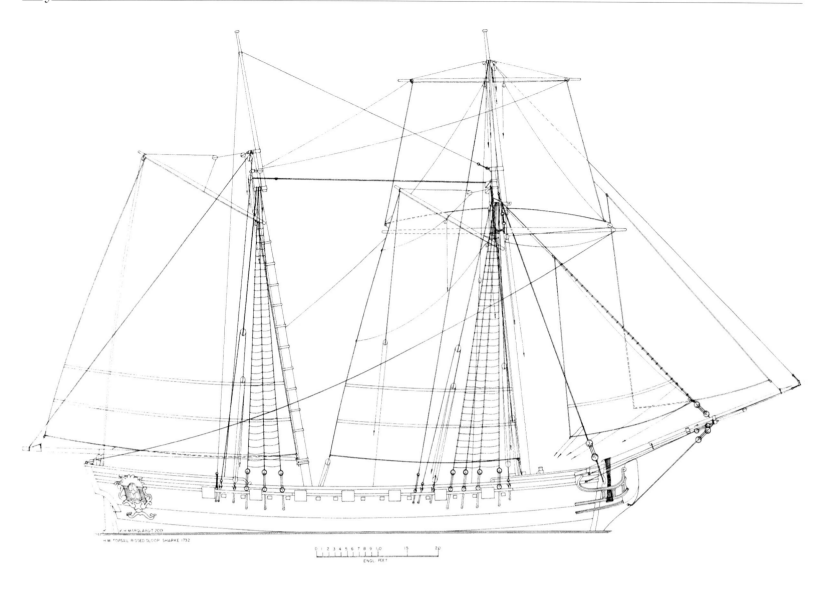

HMS *Sharke* (1832):
rigged as a topsail
schooner; based on the
draught seen on page 31.

1756 by the French. Over the following ten years three armed schooners were built at Oswego: *Murray*, in 1759, *Mercury* of six guns, in 1763 and *Brunswick*, in 1765. In 1760 at Lake Champlain British troops took a French-built schooner of eight guns. Schooner construction was also active on the Upper Lakes during that period. *Victory, Huron* and *Michigan* were built at Navy Island in 1763, while the armed schooners *Boston* and *Gladwin* were launched in 1764. Dimensions and other data of these vessels remain unknown. H I Chapelle mentions the schooner *Carleston*, which was rebuilt at St. Johns on Lake Champlain in 1776, and for which a simple draught survives.

Dimensions:

Length on the range of the deck	59ft 2in
Length of the keel for tonnage	46ft 10in
Breadth extreme	20ft 0in
Depth in hold	6ft 6½in
Burthen in tons	98 $^{50}\!/_{94}$

On 25 November 1757 Commodore Moore RN, then Commander-in-Chief of the North American Station, purchased a 130-ton, Virginia-built schooner *Barbadoes*. The term 'Virginia-built', first mentioned here, was used for a type of schooner built on the shores of Chesapeake Bay. Charles G Davis writes about these particular vessels:

'The boats of these waters are peculiar. The Swedes who settled in this region were shipbuilders and farmers and they modified their national types of schooners to suit the shallow water conditions of this new country. The world-famous Baltimore Clippers are said to have originated at St. Michaels, in Talbot County.' [29]

Another small 67 $^{7}\!/_{94}$-ton schooner, *Sally,* which was built in Marblehead, Massachusetts in 1754, was purchased on 7 August 1763 in Newfoundland and taken into His Majesty's Service as *Grenville*. The known dimensions and other data are:

Length over Deck	54ft 11in
Length of keel	43ft ⅜in
Extreme Breadth	17ft 2½in
Depth in Hold	7ft 4in

She carried 12 guns of unknown caliber and had a crew of 20. Purchased for survey service, her claim to maritime fame was her first master: James Cook sailed in her for five years

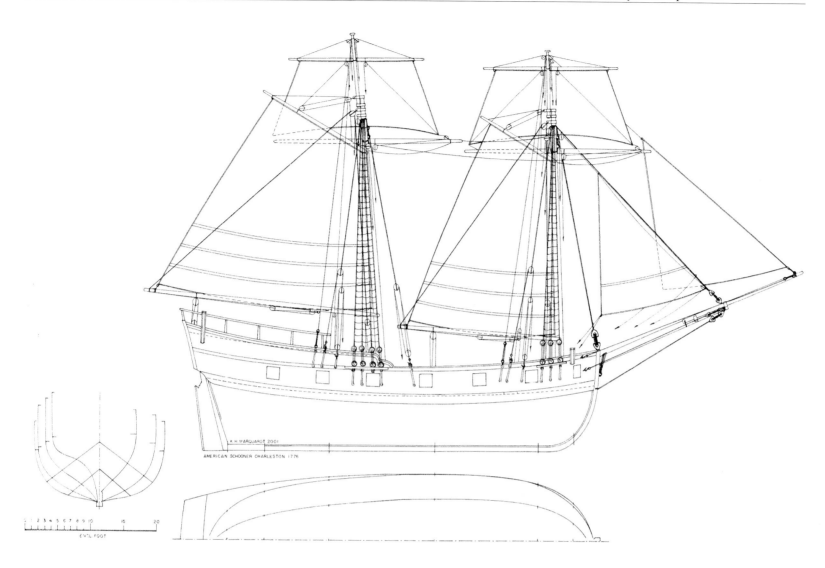

AMERICAN SCHOONER CHARLESTON 1776

American schooner
Carleston (1776) from
Lake Champlain.

through every nook and cranny of the Labrador and Newfoundland coastlines to chart that hostile environment, crossing the stormy North Atlantic every winter to prepare his charts in England. In 1768 he handed *Grenville* over to the vessel's mate Mr Lane, who became her second master. She was finally broken up in 1775.

In 1764 Commodore Palliser, at that time Commander-in-Chief of the North America Station and mentor of James Cook, purchased the 99 ⁵⁷⁄₉₀-ton schooner *Egmont*. The year 1764 is also prominent in the history of the schooner as the date that schooners were, supposedly, introduced into Europe from America. This idea was triggered by the Admiralty's advice to the Navy Board of 7 January 1764 to purchase six sloops or schooners for the North America Station so that they could be more efficient in their fight against smugglers:

'... and to cause the said Vessels to be registered on the List of the Royal Navy by the following names Vizt

Chaleur

Gaspee

Magdalen

Hope

St. John

St. Lawrence

and their Complements to be established at thirty men each...'.[30]

Chaleur, as the first name listed, is frequently seen as the first schooner in the Royal Navy, just because the term 'schooner' had graduated into the official Navy List. As we have discovered, however, *Chaleur* is only one name in a long list of schooner-rigged vessels in the Royal Navy, beginning with the William III yacht *Royal Transport* of 1695. The purchase order of those six vessels requested sloops or schooners, and four schooners and two sloops were bought. The first two names *Chaleur* and *Gaspee* were allocated as sloops, with the former not actually becoming a schooner until 1768. After two years of service on the Bahamas Station, *Chaleur* was recalled and reached Halifax on 18 June 1768. There the master's log stated on 1 July: 'Carpenter empd. Converting the Sloop into a Schooner pr order of Commodore Hood'[31]. In Halifax she underwent a hull survey and it became obvious that major repair to her bottom was needed, which could not be done at the local shipyard. She was therefore patched up and sheathed to sail for England, arriving at Plymouth on 9 September where the Lords of the Admiralty ordered His Majesty's Schooner *Chaleur* to be repaired at Woolwich. After inspecting the damage the yard officers recommended selling the vessel instead of spending money on repair and the schooner was paid off on 19 November 1768. The so-called 'first schooner' in the Royal Navy was only rigged as such in her last four months of active duty and the well-known schooner draught No. 4518, Box 64 'Chaleur taken off at Woolwich November 1768' was actually produced at the end of her working life.

Surviving Admiralty draughts offer a relatively detailed picture of many of the later schooners. Not only do we know the shape of Marblehead schooners, but also of Virginia-built schooners from the shipyards around Chesapeake Bay, and we can compare these draughts with European developments of the same period. A few of these early draughts, such as *Chaleur*, *Marblehead* and *Berbice*, indicate American designs, while *Sultana* and *Halifax* are obviously

European. *Sultana's* dimensions as of June 1768 at Deptford Yard when she was taken off:

Length on the Range of Deck	50ft 6in
Length on the Keel for Tonnage	38ft 5⅛in
Breadth moulded	6ft ¾in
Depth in Hold	8ft 4in
Burthen in Tons	52 ⁶⁸⁄₉₄
Armament	8 swivels
Crew	24 men

Built at Boston, Massachusetts, by Benjamin Hallowell and purchased by the Royal Navy in 1768 for £292 9s 0d, *Sultana* served on the North America Station until 1773, when she returned to England and was paid off. In an auc-

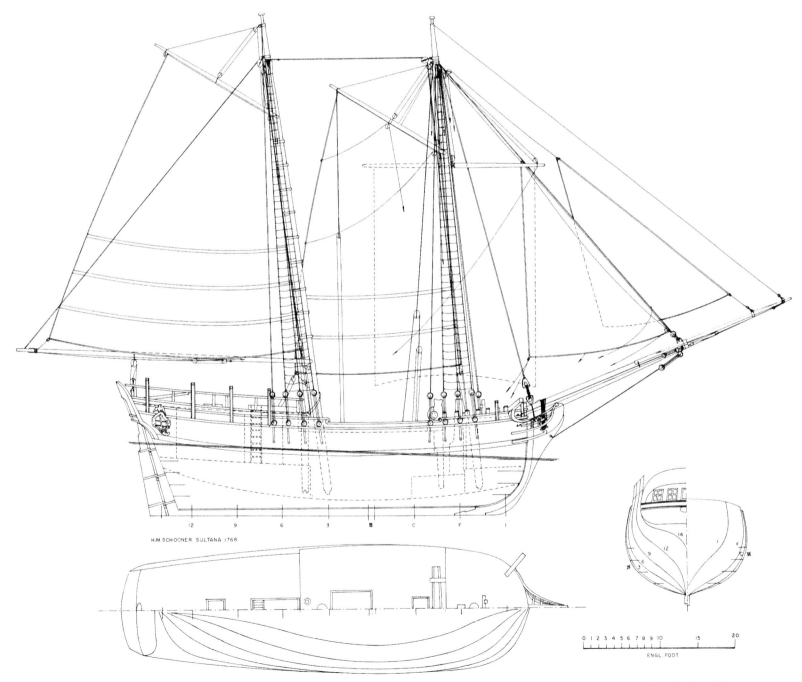

H.M.SCHOONER SULTANA 1768

HMS *Sultana* (1768) based on an Admiralty draught. The rig is reconstructed from mast and spar dimensions taken after the vessel was bought into the Royal Navy.

SWEDISH TOPSAIL RIGGED YACHT 1768

tion on 11 August 1773 in Portsmouth she was sold to John Hook Jr for £85.

European development during that time is highlighted in Chapman's work where we see schooner-rigged yachts or, as Chapman described them in his index, 'Pleasure Vessels for Sailing'. They had a deadrise comparable to *St. Ann*, but their dimensions were larger. The yacht draught on plate XLIII/2 was probably rigged as a topsail schooner, while XLIV/4 had three dead-eye pairs and could only have been fore-and-aft rigged.

Dimensions XLIII/2:
Length between pp.	71ft 11in
Breadth moulded	18ft 7in
Draught of Water	6ft 11in
Oars	6 pairs

Dimensions XLIV/4:
Length between pp.	62ft 8in
Breadth moulded	16ft 8in
Draught of Water	5ft 4in
Oars	6 pairs

In 1777–8, Fredrik H af Chapman built a 110 foot-long and 22 feet 3 inches-wide schooner-yacht for his King, Gustaf III of Sweden. Although she was designed for heavy armour the King requested that only swivels and saluting guns be installed. Named *Amphion* after Zeus's son, the bearer and spreader of culture, she made her maiden voyage in the summer of 1778 and from the outset did not fulfill sailing expectations. Even after her rig was altered from schooner to brigantine she remained a poor sailer. *Amphion* served during the 1788–1790 war between Sweden and Russia as the King's headquarters. She took part in the battles of Fredrikhamn and Viborg, and both battles of Svensksund, and just evaded capture at Viborg by Russian ships. The King's court had to abandon ship and she was very nearly lost but her captain, Lieutenant Eschelson, finally managed her escape under heavy enemy fire. *Amphion* had a long life in the Swedish Navy and served between 1850 and 1858 as flagship of the

Swedish yacht in Chapman's *Architectura Navalis Mercatoria* (1768) plate XLIII/2, fitted with a double-topsail schooner rig.

Swedish Fleet, was then until 1885 used as an accommodation-ship, at which date and after a service of 107 years she was finally broken up. Her great cabin and stern are preserved at the Sjöhistoriska Museum in Stockholm. Chapman designed and built a further two schooners, *Jehu* and *Fröja*, for the Inshore Fleet[32].

As previously discussed, Continental schooner construction is also documented during the 1760s in France, where, in 1767 at Rochefort, the famous shipbuilder Chevillard the Younger built the *Afrique* of eight 4-pdr carriage guns. The Navy List of 1780 named another three schooners at Rochefort, *Avant-Garde, Ambulante* and *Artésienne,* but no further information is given[33]. In 1769 in Brest Ollivier built an unnamed fore-and-aft schooner for which E Pâris[34] provided dimensions:

Length over Deck	15.727m
Width to Length Ratio	1:4.7
Extreme Breadth	3.333m
Armament	6 x 4-pdr carriage guns

Another unnamed topsail schooner of 21 metres, mentioned by E Paris, had a width to length ratio of 1:3.76, and Pierre Ozanne's engravings from a time before the French Revolution show several French schooners. Danish schooner-rigged vessels are known since 1769, when F M Krabbe at Frederiksvaern in Norway designed skerry boats (see Chapter 3) and soon after this date the master shipwright Gerber constructed a schooner for the Danish fleet.

Architectura Navalis Mercatoria, as the name suggests, is a work concerned with merchant ships and does not include warship design, although it does list privateers, the vessels of war that were armed and equipped by merchants during hostilities and commissioned by the Admiralty to harm enemy merchant shipping. That a large number of such vessels, thirteen all together, are found in this work is understandable in a century of hostility between Sweden and Russia. Two of them are schooners, designed to outrun and overpower merchant ships but not strong enough to withstand a fight with a similarly sized man-of-war. Chapman wrote in his 'Treatise On Shipbuilding':

Swedish yacht in Chapman's work of 1768, plate XLIV/4. This vessel was probably rigged as a fore-and-aft schooner.

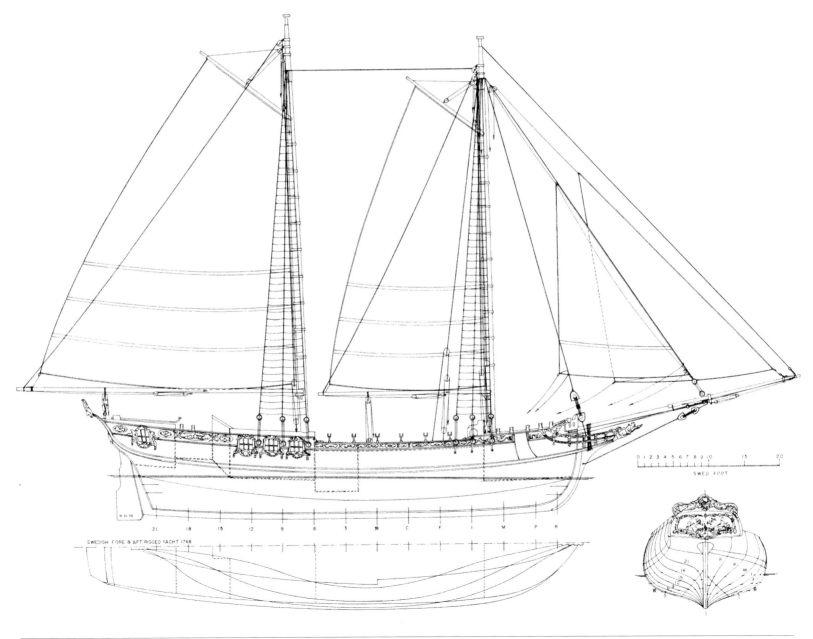

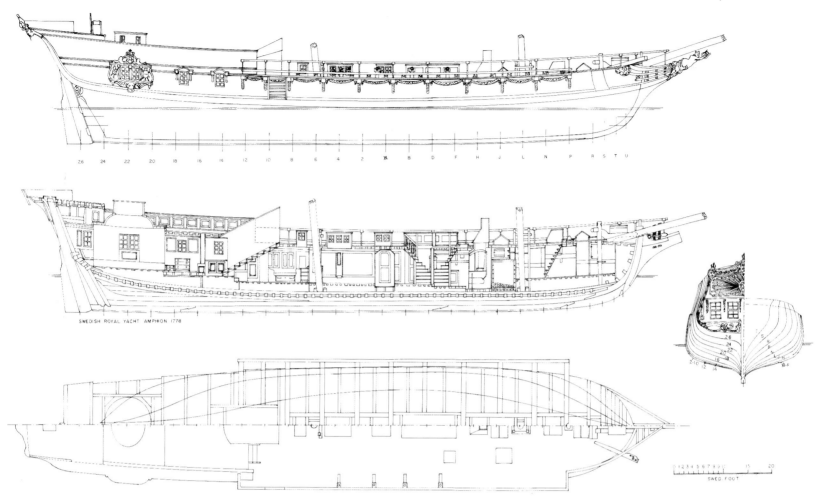

Swedish Royal yacht *Amphion* (1778), reconstructed from contemporary and modern model plans at the Krigsarkivet, Stockholm.

'As to the scantling of the timber for the construction of Privateers, the object of these ships being only to serve in war, it is not necessary to build them of greater strength, than the probable period of their being wanted requires; on which account, the least scantling possible is given them, with a view to economy in expense.'

The use of schooner-rigged privateers probably goes back further than this period, while many more crossed the high seas in the ensuing decades of conflict, but Chapman's draughts are the first known purpose-designed schooners of that kind.

Dimensions of the larger vessel, listed as XL/11:

Length between the pp. of Stem and Sternpost	93ft 9in
Breadth moulded	23ft 9in
Draught of Water abaft	9ft 9in
Crew including Officers	100
Months Provision	2
Months Water	1
Pairs of Oars	10
Carriage guns on forecastle	2 x 6 pdr
Swivel guns	32 x 3 pdr

The vessel's armament was mounted according to new inventions credited to Chapman, which later found universal acceptance. The carriage guns were on pivoting skids

A French 12-gun schooner at anchor by Pierre Ozanne, dated no later than 1788. The vessel still carries the ensign of the Bourbons.

Swedish privateer (1768)
on plate XL/11 by
Chapman, double
topsail schooner-rigged
with a new flushdeck
arrangement.

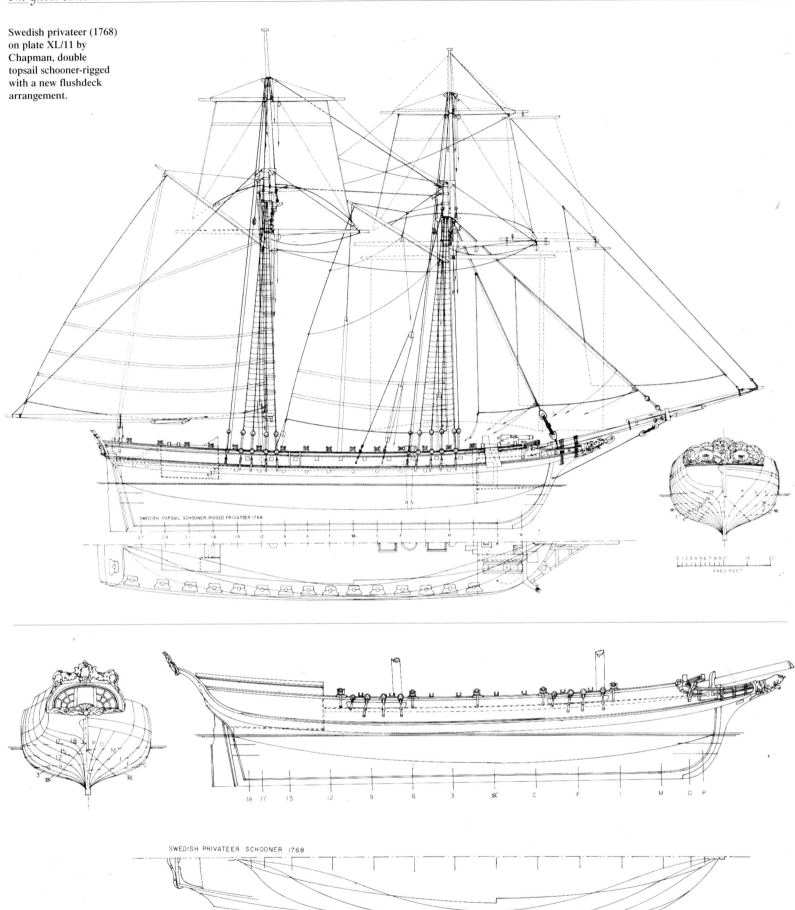

SWEDISH TOPSAIL SCHOONER-RIGGED PRIVATEER 1768

SWEDISH PRIVATEER SCHOONER 1768

Swedish privateer (1768)
on plate XL/12 by
Chapman.

0 1 2 3 4 5 6 7 8 9 10   15   20
SWEDISH FOOT

A modern ½-inch scale model of HM armed schooner *Berbice*. Built by and courtesy of Dieter Marung, Bautzen, Germany, from plans by the author.

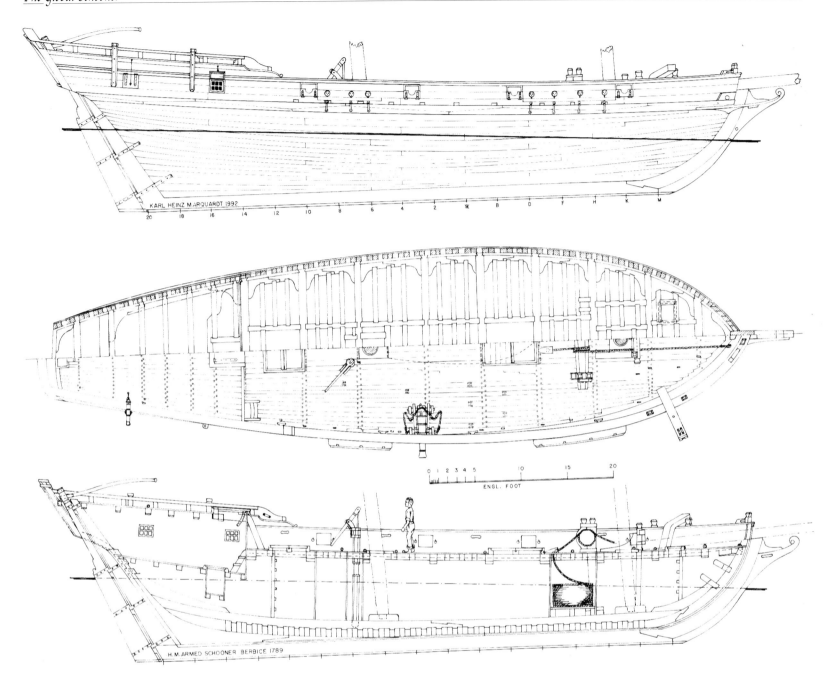

HM armed schooner *Berbice* (1789), after an Admiralty draught at the National Maritime Museum, Greenwich: side view, deck and longitudinal view.

and the 3-pdr swivels (howitzers) set into solid timber forks (see Chapter 3). The flushdeck arrangement was also unusual on this schooner: the forecastle is only a small step to mount the pivoting guns and the trunk cabin is just a square superstructure of four feet in height in front of the helm.

Dimensions provided for the slightly smaller No. XL/12:

Length between the pp. of Stem and Sternpost	70ft 0in
Breadth moulded	18ft 6in
Draught of Water abaft	7ft 6in
Crew including Officers	50
Months Provision	2
Months Water	1
Pair of Oars	8
Carriage guns on Deck	2 x 4 pdr
Swivel guns	10 x 3 pdr

Both schooners had a very steep deadrise similar to those on the later Baltimore Clippers. They are possibly forerunners of those fast vessels from the shores of Chesapeake Bay, built by Swedish shipbuilders, or their descendants, who settled there. Their design was not taken from the lines of a French lugger as some historians believe; the American vessels were more austere, had more sternpost draught and rake and were inspired by the Bermudan way of stepping masts. By taking the best of both Swedish and American design the Virginia-built schooner was created, a vessel with a reputation for superior speed, which made its mark as a privateer during the American Revolution. Unfortunately, there are no surviving shipwright's draughts of the early days of that so important era in schooner development, which is a result of the American habit of building ships according to models and not draughts as Lauchlan McKay explains in *The Practical Shipbuilder:*

'As vessels are almost universally built from models in the United States, and as it is much the most accurate and preferable method, I shall commence by showing that mode of construction'. [35]

He then goes on to discuss the reasons behind this slightly archaic practice:

'The ship-builder has labored, in the larger portion of our country, under the necessity of working by guess. The publications of other countries have been large and expensive, full of intricacy, scientific rather than practical, and consequently of little use to the uneducated mechanic.'

Information on American vessels that are important to the history of schooner development comes from draughts of those that later served in the Royal Navy, the oldest surviving draught being 'His Majesty's Arm'd Schooner *Berbice*'. This one-sheet draught is dated '5th August 1789' and registered under No. 4525, Box 64 I. It contains a sheer plan, bodylines, deck plan as well as a line and stern drawing.

Dimensions of *Berbice*:

Length on the Range of the Deck	72ft 9in
Length of the Keel for Tonnage	54ft 0in
Breadth Extreme to the 2-inch plank	20ft 6in
Burden in Tons	100

She had a width to length ratio of 1:3.55 and her sternpost draught exceeded the stem's by three feet. The sternpost's rake was extreme and the wing-transom's width was, at 46 per cent of the extreme breadth, actually below average.

The late Howard I Chapelle[36], the eminent marine historian, saw the vessel as one of these glorified privateers of the American Revolution, purchased in 1780 and taken into the Royal Navy as a tender in Antigua 'in the West Indies. According to Chapelle she was surveyed and condemned on 12 September 1788; however, this story does not coincide with the date on the draught and information received from G Slatter of the National Maritime Museum in Greenwich, which considers the vessel as being captured from the Americans and bought by the Royal Navy in 1789. The draught date of 5 August 1789 therefore probably reflects the vessel's appearance at the time of acquisition. The

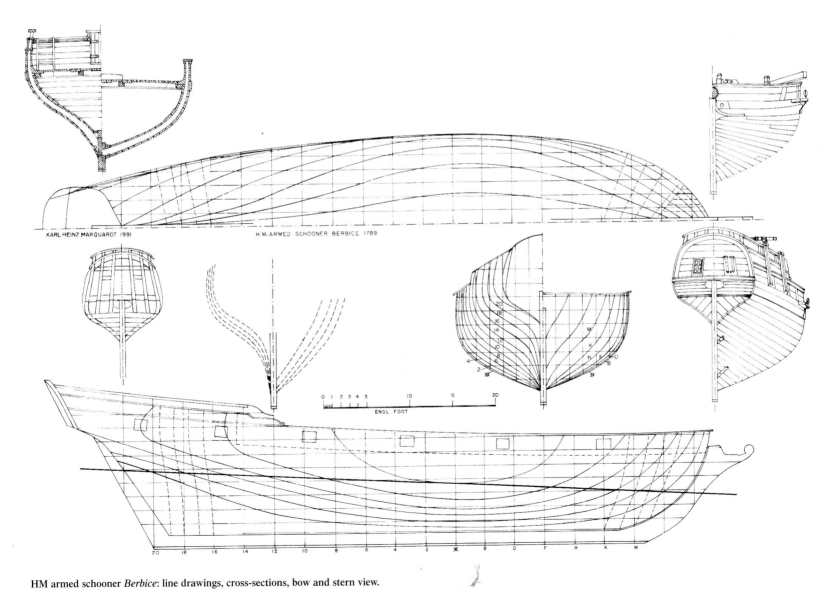

KARL HEINZ MARQUARDT 1991   H.M. ARMED SCHOONER BERBICE 1789

ENGL. FOOT

HM armed schooner *Berbice*: line drawings, cross-sections, bow and stern view.

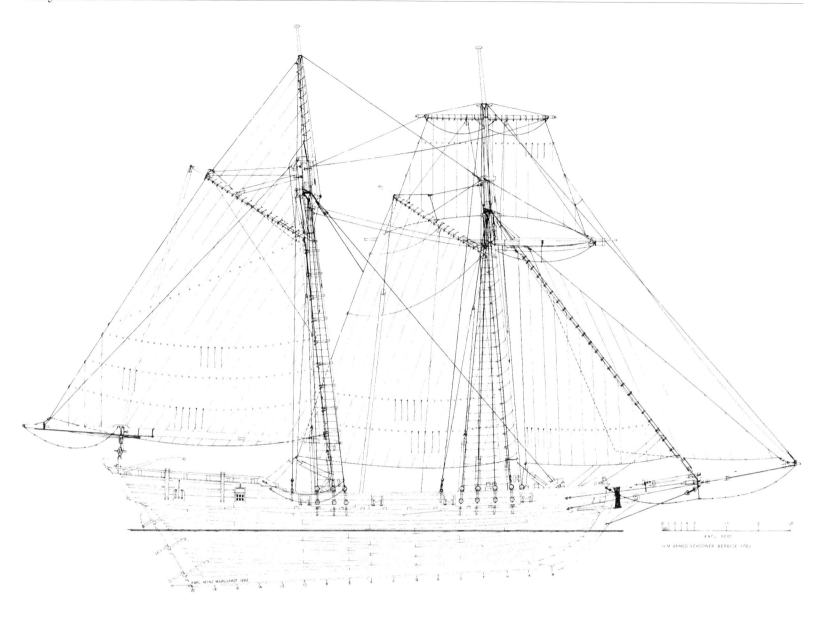

**HM armed schooner
Berbice: complete
rigging plan.**

Berbice was first listed in the Royal Navy in 1793, slightly
misspelled as *Birbice*, with Lt T Oliver in command. After
serving all her time on the West Indies Station, the schooner
was driven ashore during a storm and lost on the Island of
Dominica on 3 November 1796.

She therefore did not come into the hands of the Royal
Navy during the Revolutionary war, but in 1789 at a time of
peace and as George Washington was being inaugurated as
the first President of the United States. With the reference
'Arm'd Schooner' on the draught and the conjecture that this
vessel was presumably captured from the Americans, one
can only state that American naval forces did not exist
between the end of the Revolution and 1791 (the last
American Navy vessels were sold in 1785). The only infer-
ence can be that this heavily armed and fast-running vessel
was built for some kind of illicit trade either during or after
the Revolution. It would not have been the first time that
'privateering' continued after the end of war – piracy is
known throughout the ages.

The formidable armament on *Berbice*, as presented on H
I Chapelle's drawing from 1959, consisted of two 12-pdr
carronades, six 4-pdr carriage guns and eight swivel guns

(2-pdr?). Even when considering that four of the swivels did
not appear on the original draught it still remains a very
heavy armament for a peace-time 'merchant vessel' and
underlines the assumption that the vessel was built for more
dangerous endeavours than legitimate trade. Since the Royal
Navy probably had the draught taken soon after the
schooner's acquisition (to be forwarded to the Admiralty) it
would have represented the vessel as purchased and not as
modified for service in the Royal Navy. The draught does
not hint at any modification of the vessel after purchase, as
many such draughts do. With the Baltimore ships register
only starting in 1789, some uncertainty remains about her
place of build and the launching date, and therefore the vessel's history before purchase can only be a matter of specu-
lation.

Berbice still had a risen quarterdeck as had earlier, and
even some later, American schooners. H I Chapelle mentions that this practice ended around the early 1790s and
schooner development in America was soon inspired by the
flushdecked pilot-boats of US ports such as Norfolk,
Savannah, Charleston; notably, the famous Baltimore
Clippers were generally of the flushdeck type. Not known as

such during the Revolutionary war, when the Chesapeake Bay-built schooners were classified as Virginia-built, the name Baltimore Clipper only became synonymous with all the fast American schooners during the early nineteenth century. With ship registration in Baltimore not known before 1789, Chapelle pointed to the positive effect the French Revolution had on shipbuilding around the Bay. From 62 registrations in 1789, the registration in 1797 showed 281, an increase of 452 per cent. It is unfortunate that besides the *Berbice* draught not much is known of these vessels.

Two further Virginia-built schooner draughts dated just after that period are found in D Steel's *The Elements And Practice Of Naval Architecture 1805*. One, entitled 'A Virginia Built Boat fitted for a Privateer', is a schooner of 158 ^{11}/$_{94}$ tons, while the other of 133 ^{9}/$_{94}$ tons is classed as 'A fast Sailing Schooner'. Both schooners were flush-decked with an extreme sternpost rake and had a steep deadrise. Chapelle dates their build as between 1780 and 1795.

Another of the few remaining early draughts is that of the French Republican schooner *Coureuse*, taken off at Plymouth dockyard in June 1795. The schooner must have been a very fast sailer: after a chase lasting 19 hours she was captured on 27 February 1795 off the coast of France by the 40-gun frigate HMS *Pomone*, a former French prize praised by Fincham as one 'of the finest frigates that had yet been in the possession of the English'. *Coureuse* was then about ten years old, having been built in New York probably for the French Navy. Being refitted at Plymouth, she served in the Royal Navy as dispatch vessel on the Mediterranean Station. She was paid off in September 1796 and subsequently sold.

Dimensions of *Coureuse*:

Length over the Range of Deck	55ft 10in
Breadth moulded	15ft 9in
Breadth extreme	16ft 0in
Depth in Hold	6ft 5in
Draught at Sternpost	8ft 0in
Tonnage	55 ^{35}/$_{94}$ tons
Armament	8 x 2-pdr swivels
Crew including Officers	23

HM armed schooner *Berbice*: masts and spars.

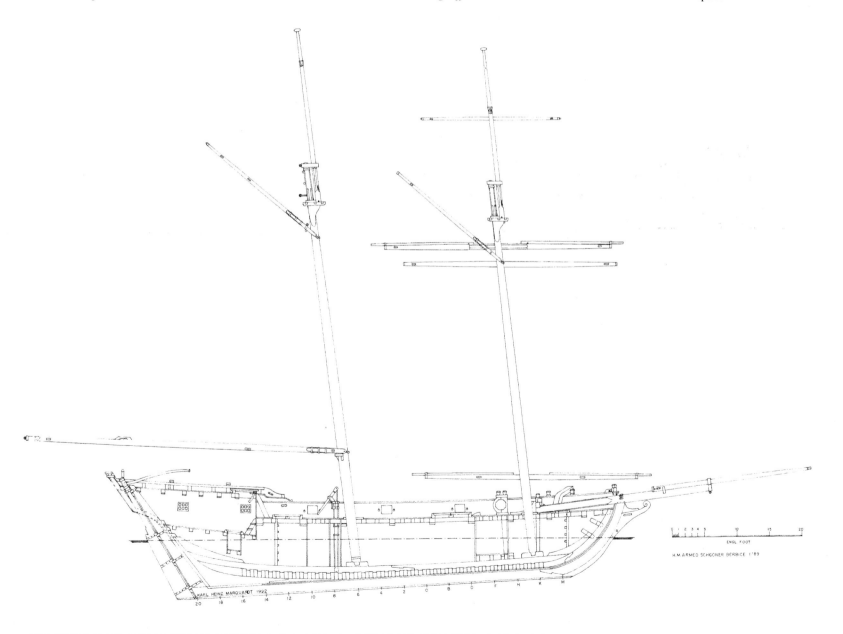

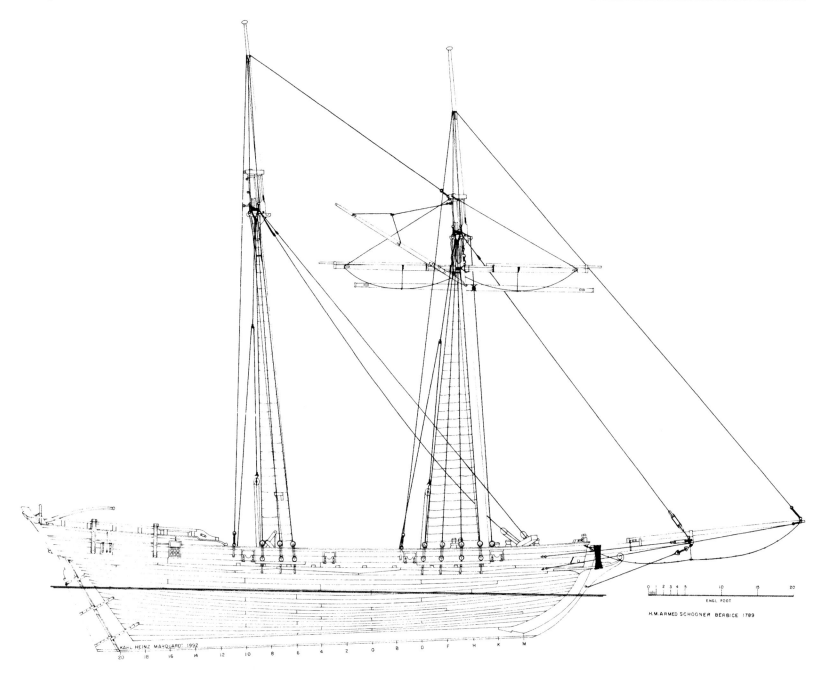

HM armed schooner
Berbice: standing
rigging.

French interest in Baltimore Clippers is very well documented in M Marestier's book *Memoire Sur Les Bateaux A
Vapeur Des Etat-Unis D'amerique*, published in Paris in
1824. Marestier, a French Navy engineer spying in America,
included the descriptions and dimensions of 18 schooner-
rigged vessels in his book on early American steam ships.
His work also provided line drawings of five Baltimore clipper schooners, two pilot boats, a Revenue cutter and included five further sail plans of these vessels. Since these were
not navy vessels they will be considered more closely in the
appropriate chapters. The Appendix 'The American
Schooners' of his description of the new American steam-
boats begins with:

'The schooners of the United States are so often praised in
the French Navy that I have accordingly procured plans of
some of them. I present, in two plates, the plans of eight vessels of this type, which are published in order that the lines

generally used in them can be made known, but in order to
judge better, in a general way, the proportions usually followed by the Americans, I not only report on the principal
dimensions of the eight shown in the plans, but also those of
ten others of various sizes.' [37]

The largest schooner in his listing, a privateer of 16 guns,
was named *Mammouth*, a very appropriate name since she
was, by 1812, the largest schooner built in the United States.
With a length of 114 feet $^{11}/_{16}$ inch, and a beam of 28 feet 8$^{13}/_{16}$
inches, she had an aft draught of 16 feet $^{3}/_{32}$ inch. While sailing as a privateer she was renamed *Southern Independence*
and rigged as a brig. As Marestier says, 'There have been
larger schooners constructed since, but usually they are soon
rigged as brigs'. At the opposite spectrum of his report was
the description of a Virginia pilot boat of 57 feet 2$^{7}/_{8}$ inches
in length and 18 feet 2$^{15}/_{32}$ inches in width.

The lines of another small pilot-boat of 46$^{11}/_{64}$ tons, *Swift*,

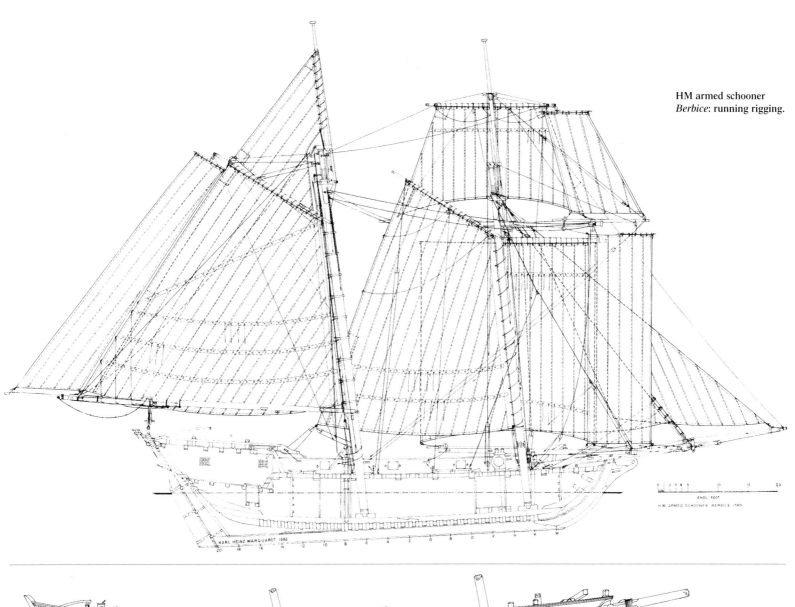

HM armed schooner
Berbice: running rigging.

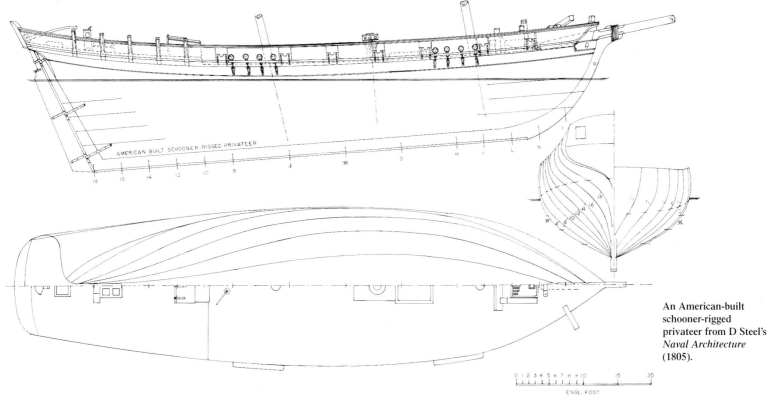

An American-built
schooner-rigged
privateer from D Steel's
Naval Architecture
(1805).

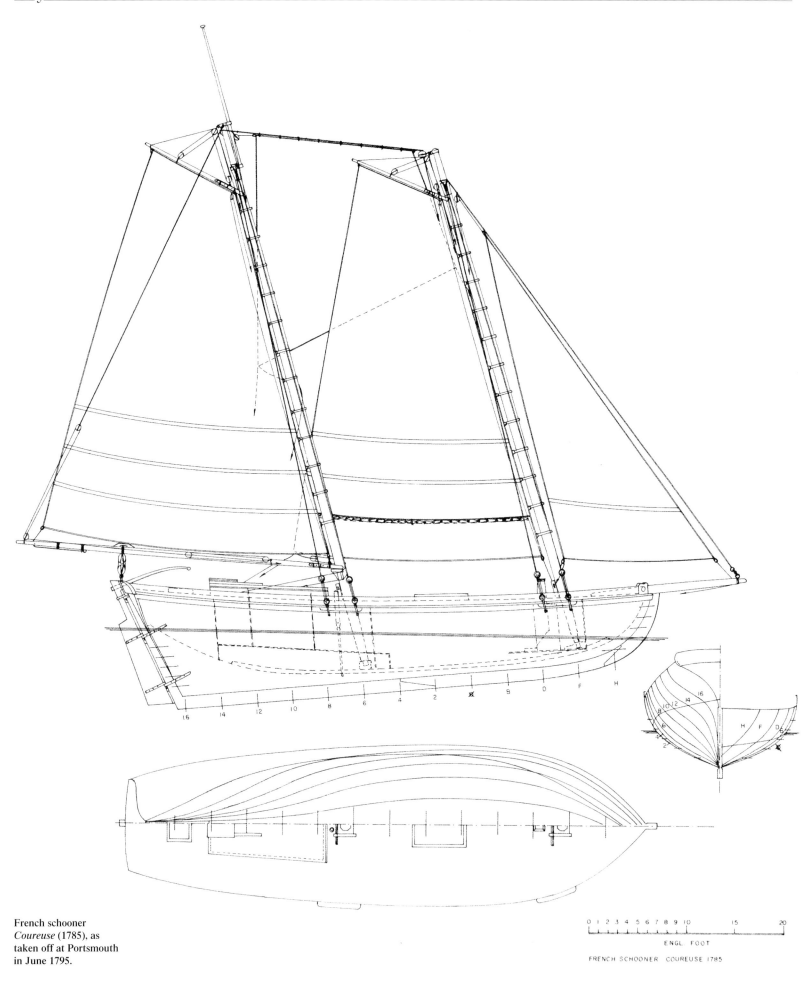

French schooner
Coureuse (1785), as
taken off at Portsmouth
in June 1795.

0 1 2 3 4 5 6 7 8 9 10 15 20
ENGL. FOOT

FRENCH SCHOONER COUREUSE 1785

influenced the construction of several Royal Navy schooners. Sailed in 1794 by Captain G Oakes from Norfolk, Virginia, to Cork in Ireland she remained in British service and was used by the commanding officer of Portsmouth dockyard, where her lines were taken off on 12 March 1803. These lines were then duplicated in a draught of slightly larger advice boats to be sent by the Navy Board to its Bermuda agent for the building of 12 such schooners in Bermuda. The Bermudan shipbuilders were displeased with the original draught and revised it, so that the final outcome was completely different to the ships that the Admiralty had ordered. It became the *Ballahoo* class of 17 Bermuda-built six-gun schooners, with the draught also being copied for the *Cuckoo* class of 12 two-gun schooners built in 1805 in Britain. The extreme lines, low-lying flushdeck and strongly raking masts of the pilot-boat model thrived as the dominant type of privateer schooner in these tumultuous times soon after American Independence. They grew from the diminutive 40 tons of the original pilot boats to more than 200 tons and became formidable fighting machines during the Napoleonic War. Mainly built in the United States, and a mainstay of their fighting capability in their 1812 war against Britain, pilot-boat-model schooners were also used in increasing numbers in the navies of the main combatants. Again, the lines of these vessels are mainly preserved in the Admiralty Collection of the British National Maritime Museum.

An interesting draught from just before the turn of the century is the French schooner tender *Ant*. This schooner, probably built in France, was taken by the Royal Navy in June 1797 and employed as an armed tender until 1815. Her stem was that of a sloop, while the sternpost had a rake close to that of American pilot boats. Her cabin roof rose by approximately one foot above deck. The sheer line was interrupted with a small wash-strake on fore deck and double high planking aft of the mainmast. Above that and forward to aft of the foremast ran an open rail.

Dimensions of *Ant*:

Length in the Range of Deck	62ft 3in
The Keel for Tonnage	44ft 2¾in
Extreme Breadth	18ft 10¼in
Moulded	18ft 6¼in
Depth	8ft 7in
Burthen in Tons	86 ³⁷⁄₉₄

E Pâris [38] preserved the lines of three other French schooners of that period. A small note on the drawing '*Echelle du módele*' – 0m 0.34 – and a simple indication of the deck's line with a small quarterdeck step indicate that these lines were taken off a half-model. The famous French shipwright M Olivier is supposed to have built *L'Agile*, *La Biche* and *La Decouverte*, all of which had a length over deck of approximately 82 feet and a width of 21 feet 6 inches, with a ton-

Lines of the *Ballahoo* or *Fish* class schooners of 1803.

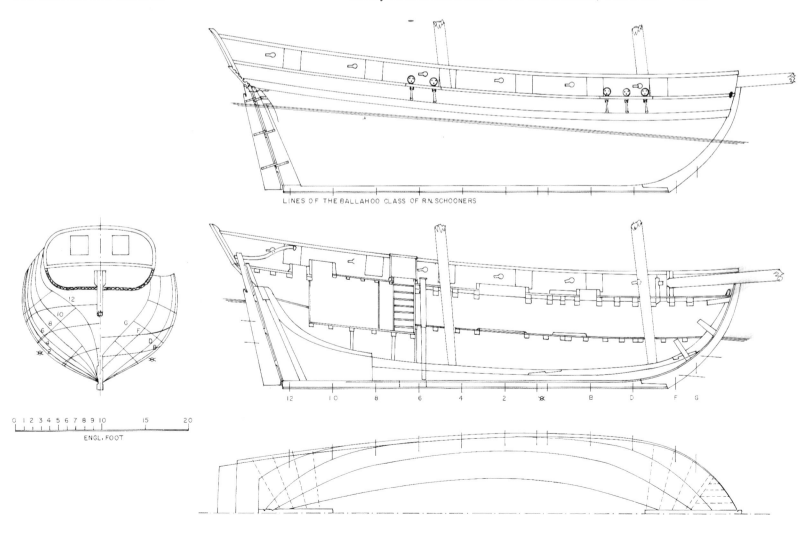

LINES OF THE BALLAHOO CLASS OF R.N. SCHOONERS

0 1 2 3 4 5 6 7 8 9 10   15   20
ENGL. FOOT

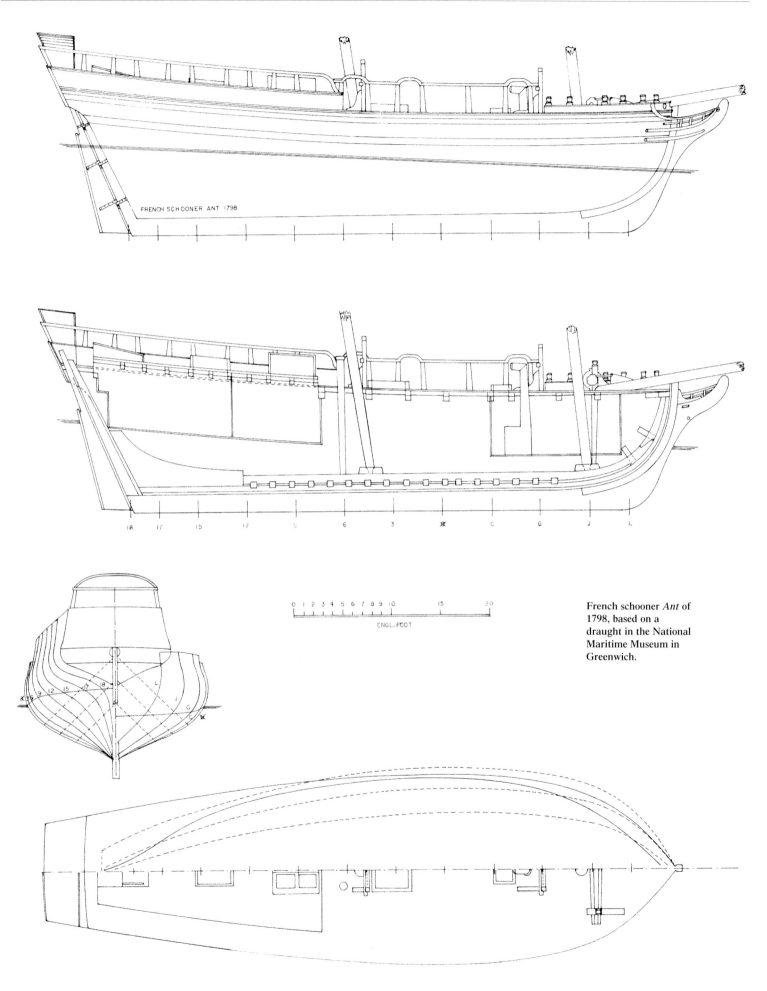

FRENCH SCHOONER ANT 1798

ENGL. FOOT

French schooner *Ant* of 1798, based on a draught in the National Maritime Museum in Greenwich.

French 12-gun schooner *La Favorite* in a watercolour by A Roux (1808). *(Courtesy of Peter Tamm Collection Hamburg)*

nage in the range of 170 tons, but little evidence survives about these schooners.

Dimensions of a similarly sized French schooner *Decouverte*:

Length in the Range of Deck	81ft 6in
Length of keel for tonnage	70ft 4in
Breadth	21ft
Depth	7ft 4in
Burthen of tons	164 ⁵⁶⁄₉₄
Armament	8 x 12-pdr carronades

Decouverte was captured by the Royal Navy on 30 November 1803 at Santa Domingo and served at the West Indies Station until sold in either 1808 or 1816. The French schooners must have been fast sailers but were regarded as too narrow in their beam for necessary stability. They were of an experimental nature and are considered by some to be copies of American schooners purchased after the Revolutionary war, although this theory is only based on the incorporation of an extreme sternpost rake of approximately 20 degrees (which is also evident in the *Ant*) and their peculiar mast positioning. These masts were of unequal rake, with the schooner-mast only leaning aft by about five degrees, while the mainmast's rake equalled that of the sternpost.

H I Chapelle mentions such a mast constellation as a Ballahou rig, which is also known as a Bermuda schooner rig, which was popular with smaller pilot boats after about 1806. With no mention of that definition in period literature, Fincham remarked that the Schooner of Ballahoe, 'has pole-masts and short gaffs, and a fore staysail brought to the end of the bumpkin'. More than half a century later Admiral W H Smyth gives another description of a Ballahou:

'BALLAHOU. A sharp-floored fast-sailing schooner, with taunt fore-and-aft sails, and no topsails, common in Bermuda and the West Indies. The foremast of the ballahou rakes forward, the mainmast aft.' [39]

His description of the foremast raking forward has nothing in common with either Chapelle's or Fincham's Ballahou rig and how the one description could be used for two very different rigs cannot be ascertained. While pilot-boat pictures from 1815 and 1825 identify with the French draught and show a slightly aft-leaning foremast, the reported forward-raking foremast belonged to the Periagua or Perry-Auger rig, a schooner rig without bowsprit, used during that time along the American East coast for lighters and ferry boats. The young US Navy had fourteen gunboats rigged in that fashion (see Chapter 3).

With mast and sternpost rakes of the *L'Agile* draught borrowed from Bermudan designs, the other parts are dissimilar to known American features. These French schooners were double ended, with a much more rounded sheer sweep than the very straight-looking American clippers. A quarterdeck wash-strake masked the pointed stern by extending into a small pinque stern. Aft of the mainmast the deck was stepped by one foot, marking a quarterdeck as on *Ant*'s draught. The schooners were probably of an experimental design, similar to the four British experimental schooners *Eling, Redbridge, Netley* and *Milbrook* of 1797.

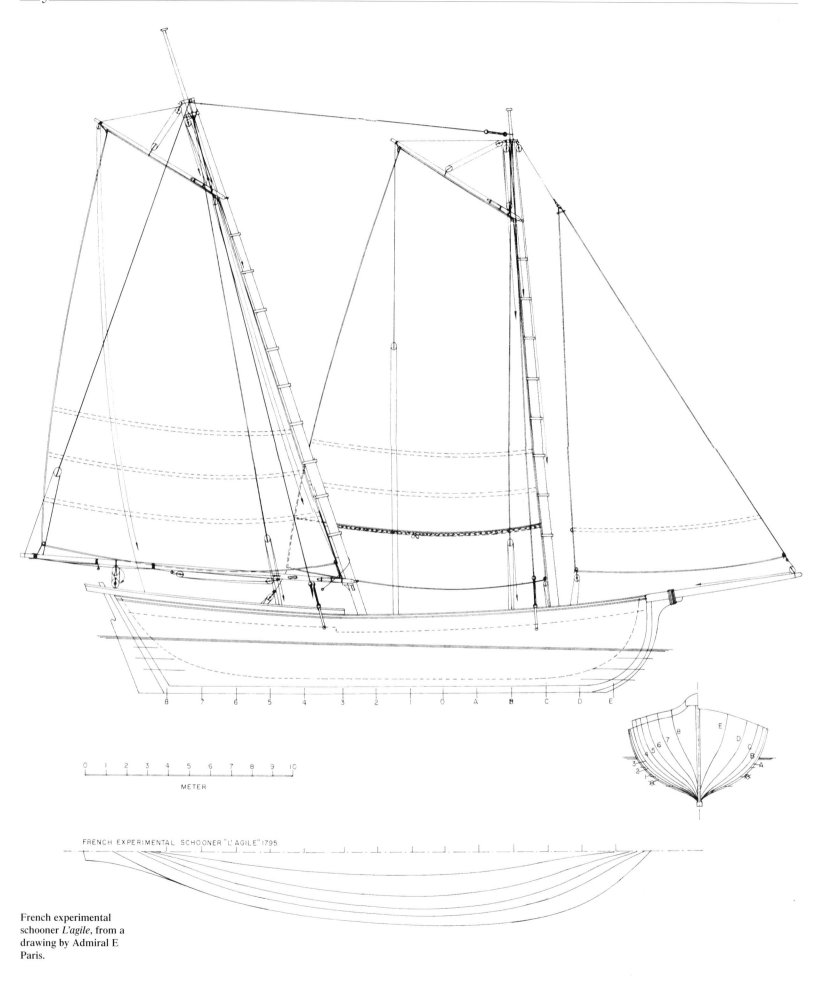

METER

FRENCH EXPERIMENTAL SCHOONER "L'AGILE" 1795

French experimental
schooner *L'agile*, from a
drawing by Admiral E
Paris.

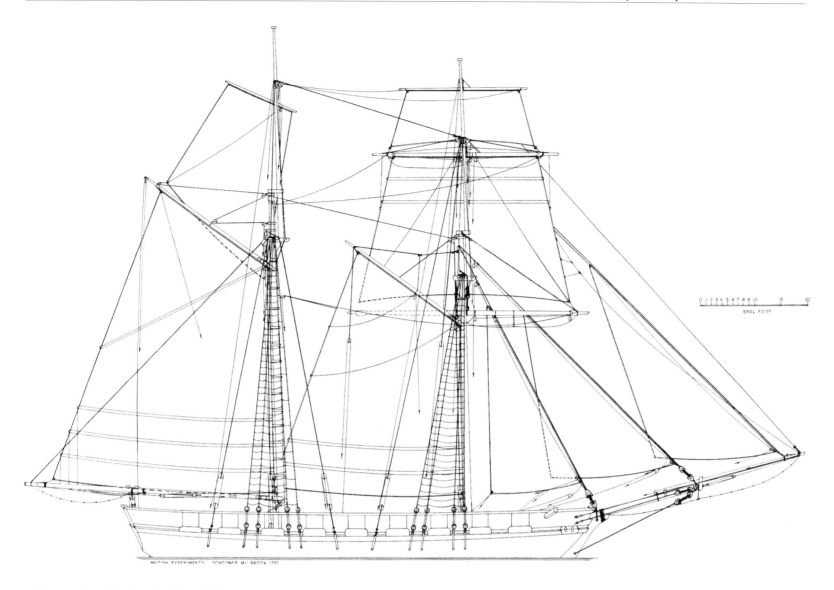

BRITISH EXPERIMENTAL SCHOONER MILBROOK 1797

It may be said that the Royal Navy was not building schooners in England at a rate comparable to the newly created United States. With all the prizes, enough building capacity in Bermuda and purchases from the US the need did not arise. Just before the new outbreak of hostilities between England and France *The State and Condition of the Navy on the 1st December 1792* [40] listed only three armed schooners, but such summaries cannot be relied on for accuracy with regard to small craft. The pool of smaller craft in navies has always increased through purchase as soon as war resumes. Almost a century after Peregrine Osborne's unorthodox inception of the schooner a similar major break with convention came with the experimental craft previously mentioned.

Sir Samuel Bentham, a shipwright by profession, learned his trade at the dockyards of Woolwich and Chatham and studied at the Naval College at Portsmouth, obtaining further knowledge in naval architecture by visiting foreign countries. Recruited into Russian service by Prince Potemkin, he made his name by building *Vermiculars*, a sizeable linked river craft propelled with up to 100 oars, initiated the non-recoil shell-firing gun and was instrumental in fitting those to vessels of the Russian Black Sea Fleet. In 1788 he attacked a much larger Turkish fleet in the Asow Sea with a

flotilla of explosive-shell-firing small gunboats and had a resounding victory. This was one of the first applications of explosive shells and incendiary carcasses in sea battle. Promoted to Brigadier General he left Russia and re-entered British service in 1795, soon to become Inspector General of Naval works and a Commissioner of the Navy. His brilliant mind and knowledge of ship construction in other parts of Europe quickly recognised shortcomings in British dockyard procedures. Use of machinery for repetitive and heavy work was virtually unknown on British shipbuilding sites and one of his early recommendations was the introduction of steam engines in naval dockyards. By March 1797 the first engine was in operation at Portsmouth dockyard, driving the pumps and a sawmill. It was against prejudice from all sides, Admiralty as well as workers, that he succeeded not only in establishing steam-powered pumps and sawmills, but also metal-mills. His introduction of steam power and machinery in British dockyards marked a new era in shipbuilding. Having overcome prejudice against steam-driven machinery, much opposition had to be faced before the execution of his other improvements, the building of basins, deep docks and jetties, but his perseverance paid off. Previously nearly all ships had to be fitted out afloat in the harbour, with all materials shipped to them. This caused

General Bentham's experimental schooner *Milbrook* (1797). The rigging is reconstructed.

delays and led to much embezzlement. As John Fincham, a near contemporary master shipbuilder, notes:

'It is intended to notice only a very few of the improvements which general sir Samuel Bentham introduced into the service. But amongst these may be mentioned the construction of caissons, or floating dams; and the first caisson that it was proposed to build in England was that at the entrance of the great basin in Portsmouth dockyard, in the year 1798, and which was completed in June, 1801. Caissons had been used for some years in foreign dockyards; but they were of a different construction, and were sunk by being charged with ballast.' [41]

Bentham's caisson was formed like the hull of a vessel, with keel and stems fitting into a groove in the masonry of the piers. It was fitted with pumps and a penstock, and by sinking the caisson into place the penstock was raised and water entered the hull. To lift, the penstock was closed by low water and the remaining water pumped out. Produced under considerable opposition, a great number of sceptical observers from all branches of the service witnessed the installation and the result spoke for itself. This caisson was in constant use for the next 50 years and was only replaced by a similar caisson with minor design improvements. Fincham remarked on its success: 'This fact supplies a proof of the unreasonableness with which opposition to inventions is often urged'.

Beside his own inventions of machinery and tools, Bentham was also instrumental in setting up Isambard Kingdom Brunel's block-making machinery and reformed British shipbuilding industry during his time in office. As a learned shipwright his inventiveness was also applied to the creation of small warships and he designed the oddest sailing ships afloat, the double-ended *Dart* and *Arrow*, two 18-gun ship sloops with sliding keels and other new implements. Hobbs' small dockyard at Redbridge was not only the place of their construction but also the birth place of a further four schooners, built to Bentham's rather original thoughts, which included structural bulkheads, peculiar, unconventional under-water lines, a different rudder shape with geared steering, an iron windlass and ballast below the keel. As with his other work, these designs were ahead of their time and led the way for future ship construction. Fincham, who dedicated a number of pages of his work to Bentham, wrote:

'The decks were without sheer, and the beams were secured to the side by a thick water-way and binding strake, which were scored down on the beams, and bolted through the side; the whole acting in combination, similar to a plan practised by the French. But their transverse strength depended chiefly on the athwartship bulk-heads, and the braces which connected the two sides. The frames of these ships were farther apart than usual, and of small scantling; whilst the outside plank of the bottom was thicker, and more so at the keel, and opposite to the main deck. The planking was chiefly of oak, except at the lower part, where it was of beech or elm; and there was but little inside planking. The vessels were built

without knees, carlings, or ledges; and it was considered that by this mode of building, a saving would be effected of one-third of the materials, whilst a further great advantage would be gained by the use of smaller timber; such timber, being of young growth, might be obtained from trees which were felled to thin the plantations for the benefit of the trees which were to grow to maturity, would become seasoned in a shorter period, and be rendered therefore cheaper, and also more durable.' [42]

Fincham mentions further that these vessels had copper-lined water tanks, where the water was still as sweet two years later as it was on the day it was stored. Carronades on the non-recoil principle were used as the armament on the vessels, a design soon adopted on other ships. As Fincham states, 'by 1804 carronades were ordered to be fitted in all his Majesty's ships, on the non-recoil principle, under the immediate directions of brigadier-general Bentham'. Not unlike the first schooner's influence on the rigging of eighteenth-century ships, Bentham's unconventional vessels comprised many new ideas, stirring the minds of future shipbuilders. An accolade by Fincham said it all:

'In the construction of these vessels considerable genius and originality of conception were displayed, and there were in their peculiarities some points of decided merit. They were good sea-boats, and sailed remarkable well; and the last of these vessels which he built, the *Netley*, is said to have shown great superiority, especially in working to windward in blowing weather.' [43]

Dimensions of *Milbrook* and *Netley*, two of these remarkable schooners (for *Eling* and *Redbrige* see Chapter 3):

Milbrook (built by Hobbs at Redbridge in 1797 and wrecked on the Burlings on 26 March 1808)

Length on deck	82ft 6in
Length of the keel	67ft 6in
Breadth extreme	21ft 6in
Depth in hold	9ft 8in
Tonnage	125 tons
Men	50
Armament	16 x 18-pdr carronades

Netley (built by Hobbs at Redbridge in 1797, captured by French ships in the West Indies on 17 December 1806, retaken on 10 July 1808 and wrecked)

Length on deck	86ft 6in
Length of the keel	71ft 0in
Breadth extreme	21ft 8in
Depth in hold	11ft 2in
Tonnage	176 tons
Men	50
Armament	16 x 24-pdr carronades

Little is known about schooners on the North Sea's southern continental fringe during most of the eighteenth century. In 1943 W V Cannenburg described a Dutch armed schooner model and remarked:

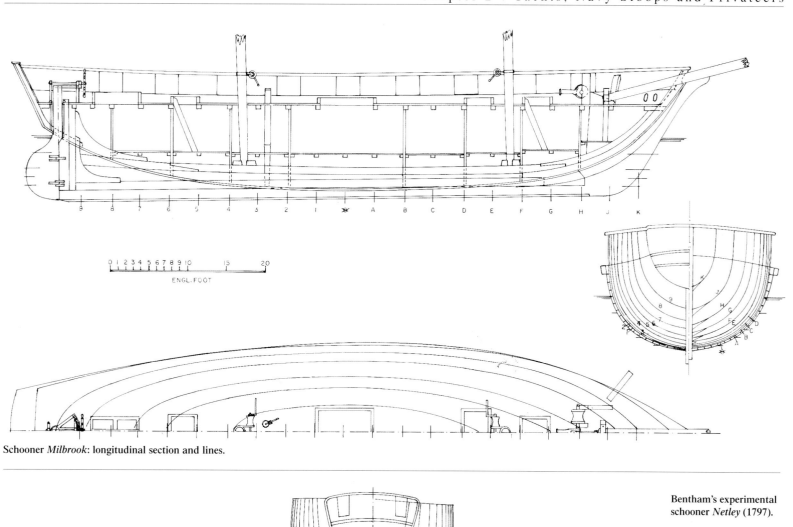

Schooner *Milbrook*: longitudinal section and lines.

Bentham's experimental schooner *Netley* (1797).

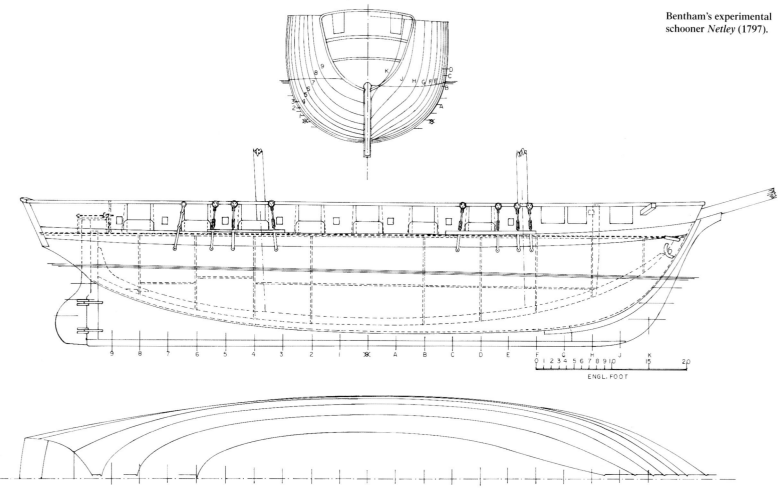

'These fast running vessels were in this country built not before the transition from the 18th to the 19th century by following the Americans, of which we even took the name "Schooner".' [44]

He put the building of such armed schooners into the outgoing years of the eighteenth century and also stated that they varied in size between 30 and 400 tons and carried from 6 to 22 guns. By contrast, in 1789 Gerrit Groenewegen provides us with a topsail-schooner-rigged '*Kanonneer boot zeylende by de wind*' [45]. Further draughts of Dutch gunboats from around 1800 will be considered in the following chapter.

Scandinavian schooner construction during the tumultuous times at the beginning of the new century was still very much in the tradition of F H af Chapman. A good example of a vessel of that time is the Danish packet schooner *Ornen* of 142 ⁶⁰⁄₉₄ tons. The Norwegian gunboat *Axel Thorsen* from 1810 is another worthy example and will be discussed in following chapters. In 1813 Admiral Puke acquired the American fast-sailing merchant schooner *Experiment*, which came into Karlskrona with Russian goods aboard and was part of the Swedish Navy until 1859. This vessel inspired a design change in the Swedish Navy, and from her lines the armed schooners *Puke*, *L'Agile*, *Falk* and *Activ* were built. These schooners carried two 4-pdr carriage guns and six 12-pdr carronades.

American schooner *Experiment* (1812), bought into the Swedish Navy.

Dimensions of *Experiment*:
Length over Deck	71ft 6in
Breadth extreme	23ft 1in
Depth	8ft 10½in

These turbulent years saw enormous improvements in schooner development and beside the two-masted rig a three-masted version emerged, commonly known as tern schooner. Early three-masted schooners appear in naval reports of the 1790s and after 1806 became a fairly common sight with pilot-boat schooners. The French *Pandour* was listed in 1796, again in 1796 a three-masted British schooner was reported to be cruising in the Caribbean Sea and in 1800 another tern schooner was recorded chasing the American schooner *Experiment*. The first known draught of such a vessel goes back to that of the American-built *Revenge*, built in Baltimore in 1805. She was purchased in 1806 by the Royal Navy and named *Flying Fish*.

David Lyon[46] wrote that ex-*Revenge* was acquired in 1805 and became the pattern for the British *Shamrock* class of armed schooners, launched in Bermuda in 1808–09. H I Chapelle's[47] explanation about this particular vessel is more detailed. The Baltimore ships register tells us that *Revenge* was launched in early 1805 and built by William Flannigan for J B Salenave. Her last owner N W Easton of Baltimore, according to an Admiralty order of 12 November 1806, sold her in the West Indies to the Royal Navy, as she was 'uncom-

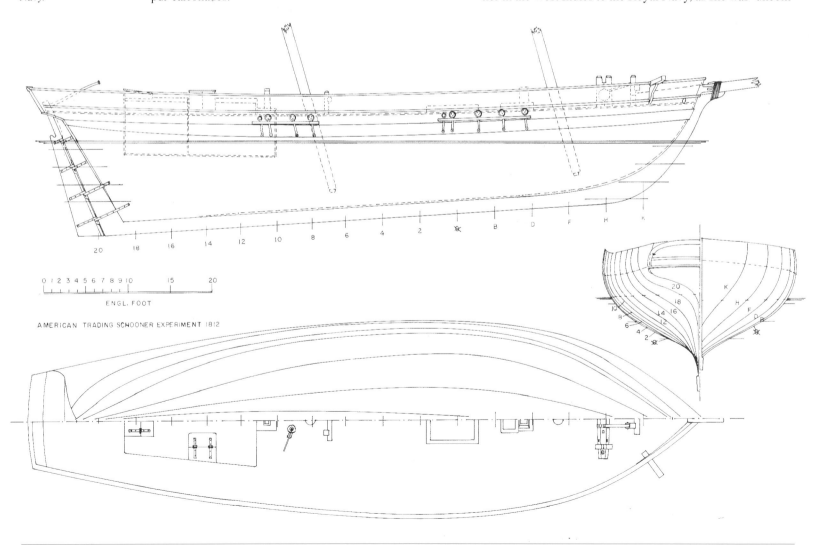

ENGL. FOOT

AMERICAN TRADING SCHOONER EXPERIMENT 1812

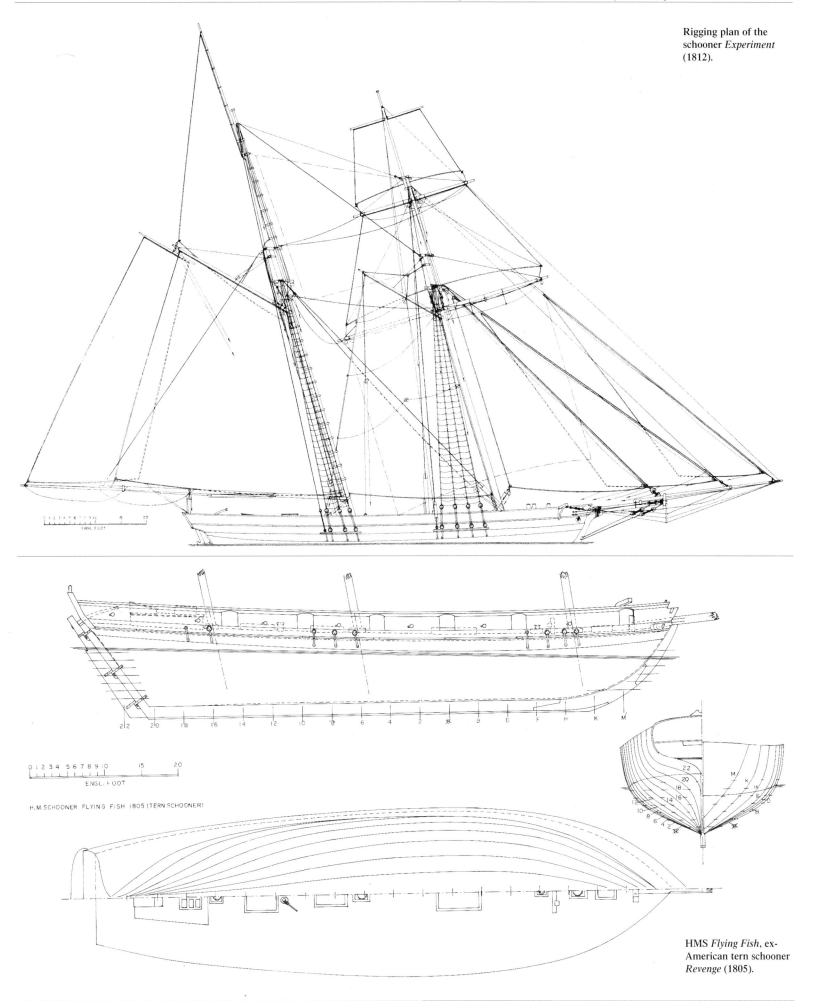

Rigging plan of the schooner *Experiment* (1812).

H.M.SCHOONER FLYING FISH 1805 (TERN SCHOONER)

HMS *Flying Fish*, ex-American tern schooner *Revenge* (1805).

Rigging plan of *Flying Fish*.

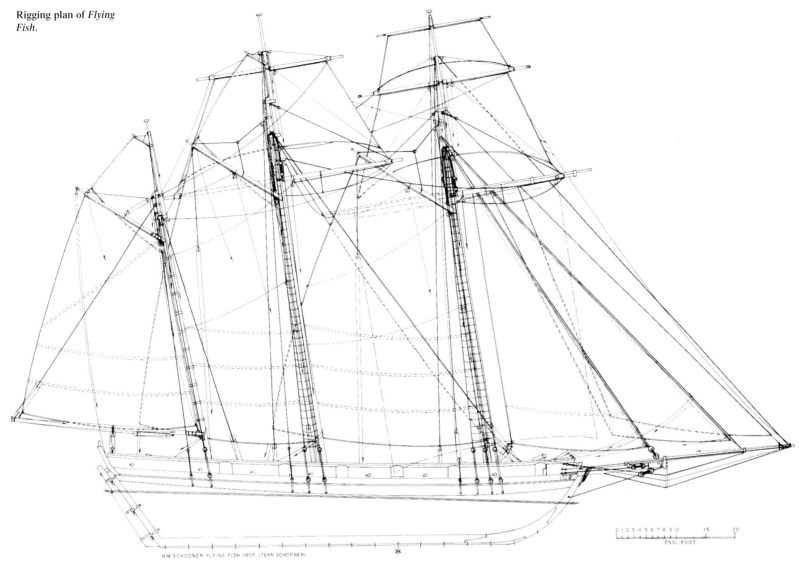

H.M. SCHOONER FLYING FISH 1805 (TERN SCHOONER)

Two French topsail schooners from an Antoine Roux sketchbook of 1813.
(*Courtesy of Peabody Museum, Salem, Massachusetts*)

monly well built' and a 'remarkably fast sailer'. Little is known of her sailing history, only that she was grounded and bilged on a reef off San Domingo on 15 December 1808. Her registered dimensions were 59 feet 6 inches on the keel, 21 feet 3 inches breadth, 8 feet depth and 106 $^{45}/_5$ tons according to the carpenter's measurement. The dimensions on her draught made at Portsmouth in September 1806 are slightly different. This small example makes us aware that dimensions of a vessel taken at different ports will seldom be the same.

Length between perpendiculars	78ft 8in
Length of keel for tonnage	60ft 8in
Breadth moulded	21ft 3¼in
Breadth extreme	21ft 7in
Depth in hold	7ft 10in
Burthen in tons	150 $^{32}/_{94}$
Crew	about 50
Armament	10 x 9-pdr carriage guns or 12-pdr carronades

The *Shamrock* class of tern schooners, which resulted from the lines of *Flying Fish*, ex-*Revenge*, were of similar dimensions to the above and carried two 6-pdr carriage guns and six 12-pdr carronades. The class consisted of *Shamrock,* wrecked on 25 February 1811 on Cape Saint Mary, *Thistle,* wrecked on 6 March 1811 near New York, *Bramble,* sold 1815, *Holly,* wrecked off San Sebastian 29 January 1814, *Juniper,* sold 1814, and *Misteltoe,* sold in 1816. *Flying Fish* was a popular name during that period, with at least a dozen vessels in the Royal Navy alone. One of the vessels of the same name can be traced as the French privateer *Poisson Volante,* a 12-gun vessel of 130 ⁷/₉₄ tons, which was captured on 30 June 1803 off San Domingo by HMS *Vanguard* and, together with another French schooner *La Supérieure,* was taken into British service as *Flying Fish.*

Sir Robert Seppings, one of the great British shipbuilding innovators, became involved in schooner design in 1829 when he produced a three-masted schooner, the *Seagull.* Being a peacetime vessel she was not strongly armed, only carrying two 6-pdr brass carriage guns and four 12-pdr carronades. Launched on 28 November 1831 she was a large vessel of 279 ⁷/₉₄ tons, and from 1834 until 1852 was used as a packet before being broken up.

Schooner rigs were applied to many types of hull during those eventful years at the turn of the century, even on cutters. Cutter-schooner sounds like a contradiction in terms, but experience showed that a single-masted cutter rig, like a single-masted sloop rig, became unwieldy beyond a certain size. Large cutters were therefore often re-rigged as schooners in England, or as brigs in France. Their clinker-built, wide-bodied hull, with a near horizontal bowsprit

beside an unadorned stem and the distinctive cutter masts – even with a schooner rig – meant that such vessels were still cutters. In his 1780 watercolour 'A Topsail Schooner' Edward Gwyn showed a large clinker-built cutter, carrying 16 guns, and fitted with a figurehead and cutter masts stepped with cutter-style deeply roached topsails.

Armed British cutter-schooner from 1780 reconstructed from a watercolour by E Gwyn. The rig is typical for that hybrid type, but the hull is that of a sloop with a quarterdeck and a figurehead.

HMS *Seagull* (1829), based on an Admiralty draught at the National Maritime Museum in Greenwich.

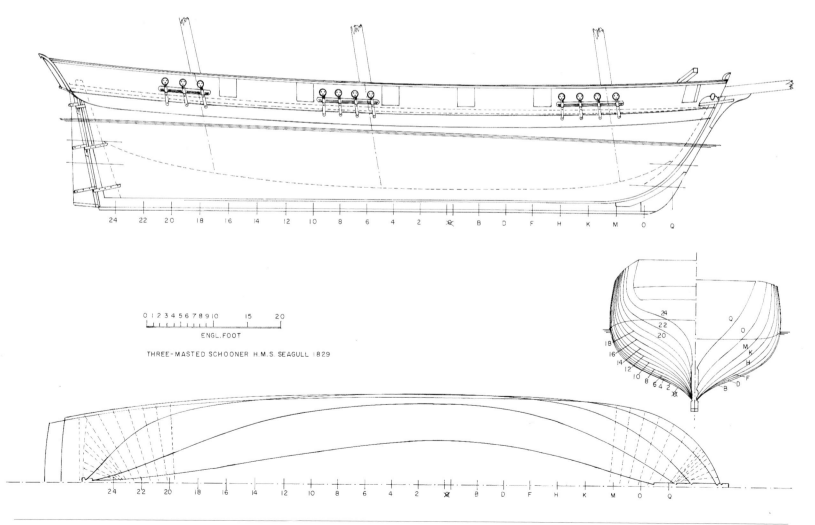

0 1 2 3 4 5 6 7 8 9 10   15   20
ENGL. FOOT

THREE-MASTED SCHOONER H.M.S. SEAGULL 1829

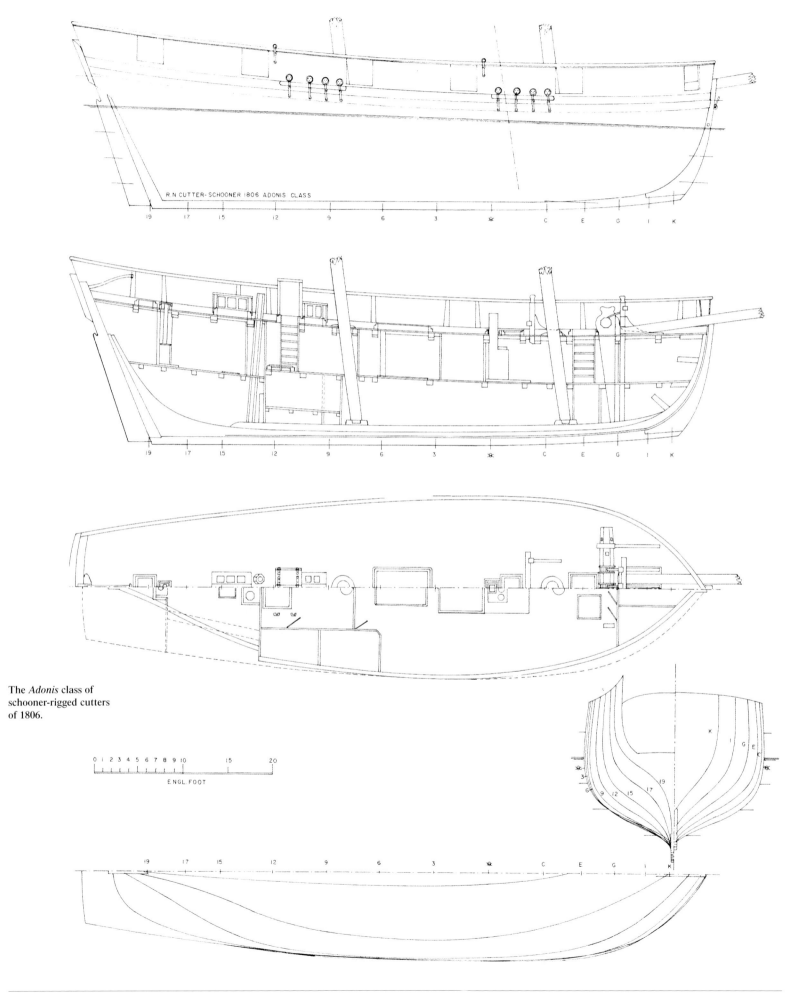

R.N.CUTTER-SCHOONER 1806 ADONIS CLASS

The *Adonis* class of
schooner-rigged cutters
of 1806.

0 1 2 3 4 5 6 7 8 9 10   15   20
ENGL.FOOT

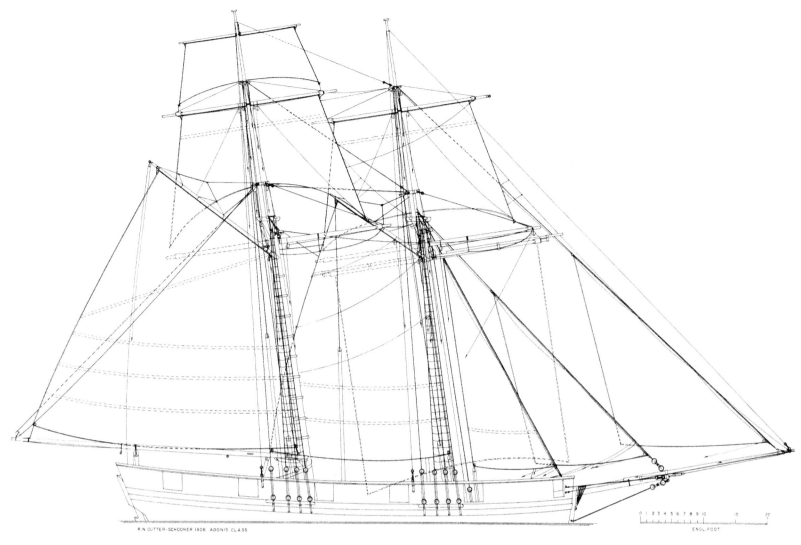

R.N. CUTTER-SCHOONER 1806 ADONIS CLASS

ENGL. FOOT

Probable rig of the *Adonis* class of cutter-schooners.

D R MacGregor [48] described the British schooner *Helena* of 225 tons, built 1778, as an example of these large cutter-schooners. In David Lyon's *Sailing Navy List, Helena* is mentioned as a brig sloop. She was taken by the French early in her career, retaken in 1779 and after sailing from England on 7 October 1798 foundered in the North Sea. With French preference for rigging larger cutters as brigs, both accounts would be based on fact. With a cutter's hull and the bowsprit mounted at starboard side of the stem's head, she had masts fitted with topgallant masts and integrated topmasts, which are cutter masts. An 1801 watercolour by A Roux of a large, unidentified British clinker-built cutter-schooner, carrying 12 guns and 8 swivels, provides a good example of such a vessel.

It was originally planned that the British *Adonis* class of 10-gun cutters should have cutter rigs, but instead the ships received schooner rigs. That class of twelve vessels was built in Bermuda from 1806 and their recorded tonnage was 142 ¹⁸⁄₉₄ tons.

In 1809 Sir Henry Peake designed a further three large cutters, *Pigmy, Algerine* and *Pioneer*. They were built in 1810 by King at Upnor and rigged as schooners. *Pigmy* was sold in 1823, *Algerine* was wrecked on Gallipagos Rocks at the north side of Little Bahama Bank on 20 May 1813, and *Pioneer* went to the Coast Guard in 1824 and was sold in 1849.

Dimensions:

Length over Deck	82ft 6in
Length of Keel	70ft 6in
Breadth extreme	22ft 8in
Depth in Hold	10ft 6in
Burthen in tons	192 ⁶²⁄₉₄
Crew	60
Armament	10 x 18-pdr carronades

The 1809 *Decoy*-class vessels were cutters of 200 ⁸⁄₉₄ tons. It is not known if the three vessels of that type were also schooner rigged, as they were large enough for a two-masted rig.

Another example of a schooner-rigged cutter can be seen in *Bramble*. Launched in 1822 at Plymouth Dockyard, she served in 1842 as a survey vessel and was given to the New South Wales Government in 1853. In colonial service she was re-rigged as cutter. Armed with ten guns, her main dimensions were:

Length over Deck	70ft 9in
Length of Keel	52ft 4in
Breadth extreme	24ft 2½in
Depth in Hold	11ft 0in
Burthen in tons	161

Clincher-built British cutter-schooner from an A Roux sketchbook of 1801.
(*Courtesy of the Peabody Museum Salem, Massachusetts*)

Crew	50
Armament	2 x 6-pdr carriage guns
	8 x 2-pdr carronades

The slightly smaller *Nightingale* was launched at Plymouth in 1825 as a 6-gun cutter tender. Of 122 tons, she was later schooner-rigged and after only four years of service wrecked on the Shingles on 17 February 1829. The *Lark* class of 1829, designed by Seppings, was another group of cutter tenders of even smaller tonnage than *Nightingale*. Consisting of *Lark, Quail, Raven, Jackdaw, Starling* and *Magpie*, they were all, at one time or another, rigged as schooners, with the exception of *Raven*, which was yawl rigged.

Dimensions of the *Lark*:

Length over the range of deck	60ft 9in
Length of keel for tonnage	49ft 5in
Breadth extreme	20ft 3in
Depth in hold	9ft 0in
Burthen in tons	107 $^{73}/_{94}$
Crew	30
Armament	2 x 6-pdr carriage (brass)
	2 x 6-pdr carronades

The *Lark* was launched on 23 June 1830 at Chatham dockyard and 1835 re-rigged as schooner. Loaned from 1849 to 1858 to the Liberian Government she was broken up in 1860.

The years leading up to 1845 are well represented in the history of schooner development by three armed schooners of approximately similar size from both sides of the Atlantic. They were, as this type of ship had been throughout the previous 150 years, workhorses of the navies. Samuel Humphreys designed the 10-gun *Boxer* class of three schooners, which was built in 1831 in the United States for the West Indian Station. The first of the 6-gun *Hornet* class of four schooner-brigantines, designed by Sir Robert Seppings, was also launched in 1831. The Royal Navy used them as packets, tenders or transports.

Dimensions and armament of the American schooner *Boxer*, which was launched on 22 November 1831 at Charlestown, Massachusetts:

Length between pp.	88ft 0in
Breadth moulded	23ft 6in
Depth in hold	10ft 6in
Burthen in tons	194
Armament	8 x 24-pdr carronades
	2 x 9-pdr carriage guns

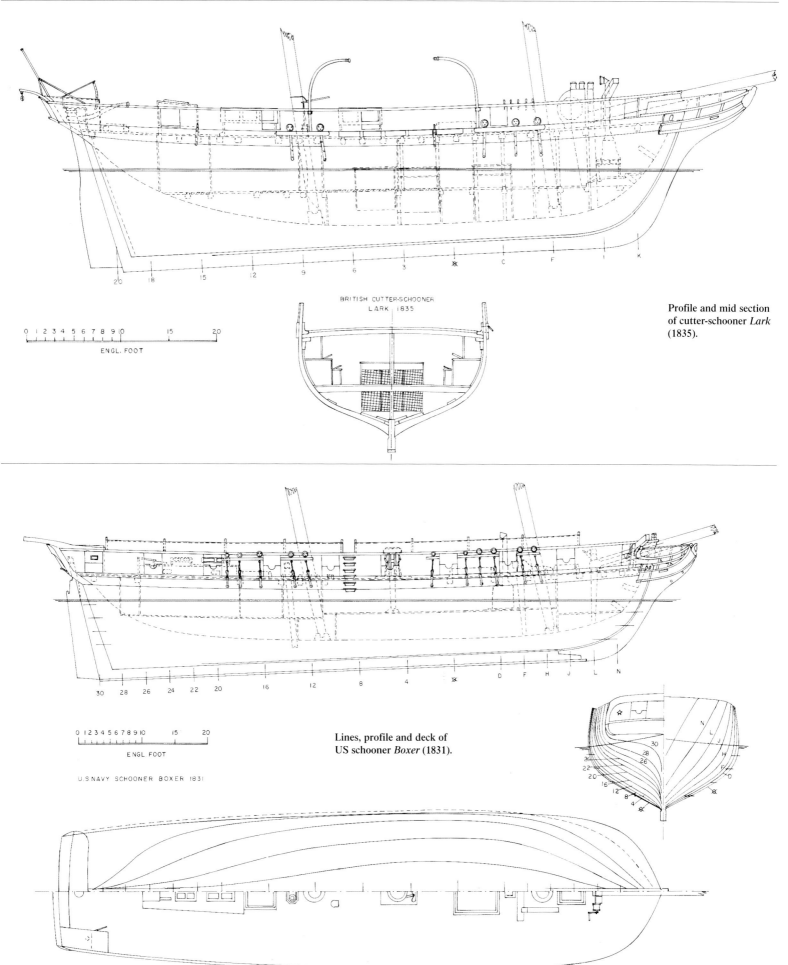

BRITISH CUTTER-SCHOONER
LARK, 1835

0 1 2 3 4 5 6 7 8 9 10   15   20
ENGL. FOOT

Profile and mid section
of cutter-schooner *Lark*
(1835).

0 1 2 3 4 5 6 7 8 9 10   15   20
ENGL FOOT

Lines, profile and deck of
US schooner *Boxer* (1831).

U.S NAVY SCHOONER BOXER 1831

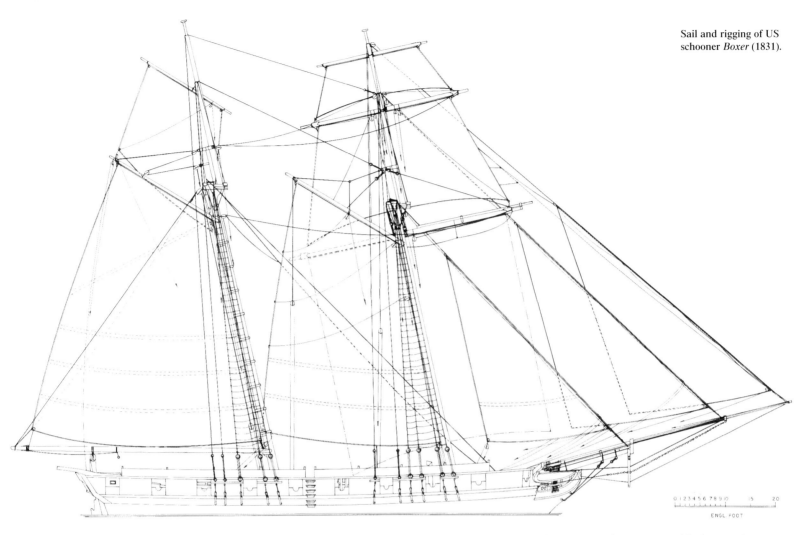

**Sail and rigging of US
schooner *Boxer* (1831).**

Masts and spars	whole length	heads or yard arms
Main mast	76ft 0in	8ft 6in
Fore mast	74ft 0in	8ft 6in
Main topmast	33ft 0in	12ft 0in pole
Fore topmast	35ft 0in	12ft 0in pole
Fore yard	58ft 0in	2ft 0in
Fore topsail yard	34ft 0in	2ft 0in
Fore topgallant yard	22ft 0in	1ft 3in
Bowsprit	29ft 0in outboard	17ft 0in
Jib boom	34ft 0in outside cap	17ft 0in
Flying jib boom	30ft 0in outside cap	13ft 0in
Fore gaff	26ft 0in	
Main gaff	24ft 0in	
Main boom	49ft 6in	
Gaff topsail yard	32ft 0in	

Dimensions and armament of the British *Hornet*, which was launched on 24 August 1831 at Chatham Dockyard:

Length over the range of deck	80ft 0in
Length of keel for tonnage	64ft 5½in
Breadth extreme	23ft 0in
Depth in hold	9ft 10in
Burthen in tons	182 89/94
Armament	2 x 6-pdr carriage guns
	4 x 12-pdr carronades

The third of the three important mid-nineteenth-century schooners, the French schooner *Le Hussard* of 1845, is slightly larger than her American and British counterparts. From Draught No. 50 in Admiral E Pâris' *Souvenirs De Marine* the following dimensions can be ascertained:

Length over deck	30m = 98ft 5⅛in
Breadth extreme	8.5m = 27ft 10½in
Depth in hold	3m = 9ft 10⅜in
Armament	2 long guns (18- or 24-pdr)
	2 carronades (18-pdr?)
	4 swivel guns (1½-pdr?)

Nothing could be found about her history. The 1845 date given by Pâris was probably her year of launching. Five years later, in the 'List of French Ships Afloat, 1st April 1850' in Fincham's *History Of Naval Architecture of 1851* there is no mention of *Le Hussard*, which means that her service life must have been very short.

With all contemporary maritime writers assigning the schooner mainly to England and America, even more than a hundred years after Peregrine Osborne's successful experiment, this rig still did not have the same impact in English naval ship-building as it did across the Atlantic. This becomes very evident when one compares, for example, the number of schooner-rigged vessels in the Royal Navy in 1805 to those of other rig designations. In a total of 949 list-

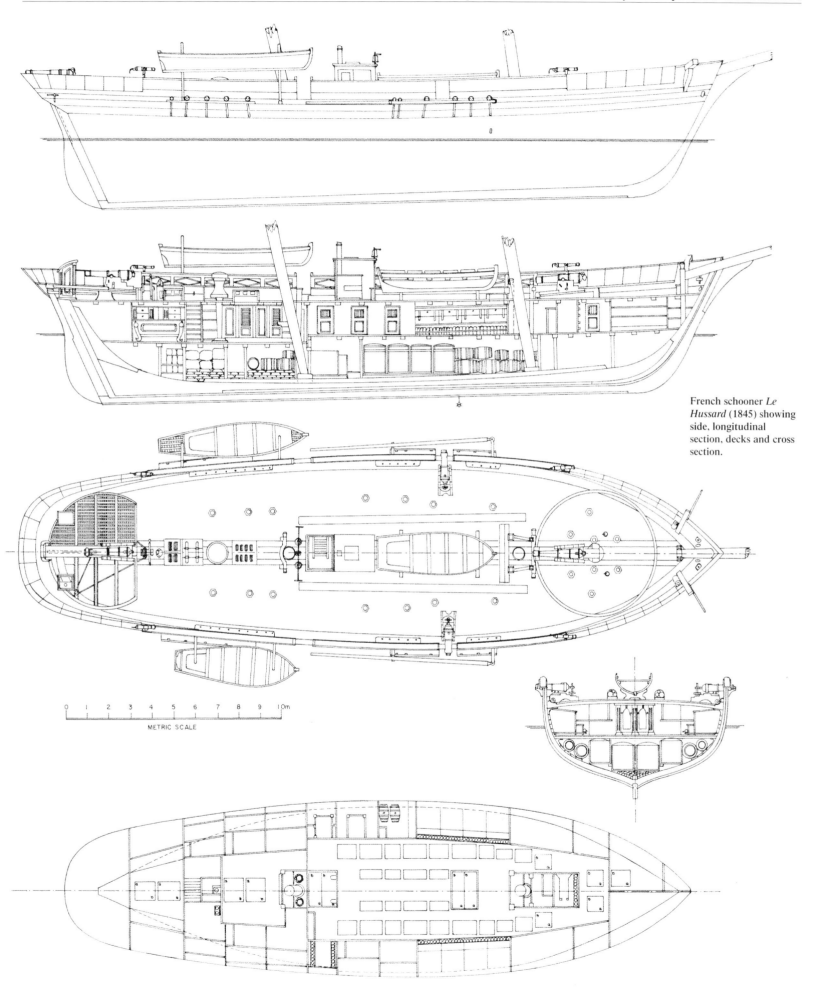

French schooner *Le Hussard* (1845) showing side, longitudinal section, decks and cross section.

0 1 2 3 4 5 6 7 8 9 10m
METRIC SCALE

Profile with sails and rigging of Royal Navy schooner *Hornet* (1831).

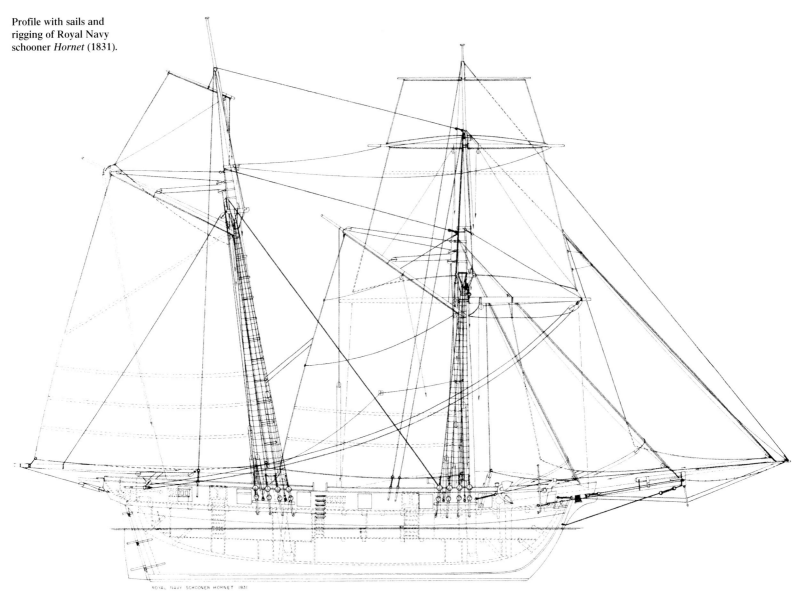

Sleipner, schooner of the Royal Swedish/Norwegian Navy (1839 to 1866) in an oil painting by an unknown artist.

ed ships there are 4 schooners, 11 armed schooners and 12 schooner-rigged gunboats but 25 cutters, 66 brigs and 125 brig-rigged gunboats[49]. The significance of schooners in the US Navy also diminished in the decades after their big struggle for independence. As H I Chapelle notes:

'The unpopularity of the schooner in the Navy remained unchanged until the end of the usefulness of the sailing man-o-war, in spite of the extraordinary popularity of the rig in the merchant marine in the same period and the record of the earlier privateers and naval schooners'.[50]

———————◆———————

Notes:

27 Fincham, J, *A Treatise on Masting Ships & Mast Making* (London, 1829, 1854) repr. Conway Maritime Press Ltd (London, 1982) p.72

28 Lyon, D, *The Sailing Navy List: All the Ships of the Royal Navy Built, Purchased and Captured – 1688–1860,* Conway Maritime Press (London, 1993) p.52

29 Davis, Ch G, *Ships of the Past*, Bonanza Books (New York, 1929) p.37

30 PRO ADM 2/433 pp.459–60

31 Hahn, H M, *The Colonial Schooner 1763–1775*, Conway Maritime Press Ltd (London, 1981) p.41

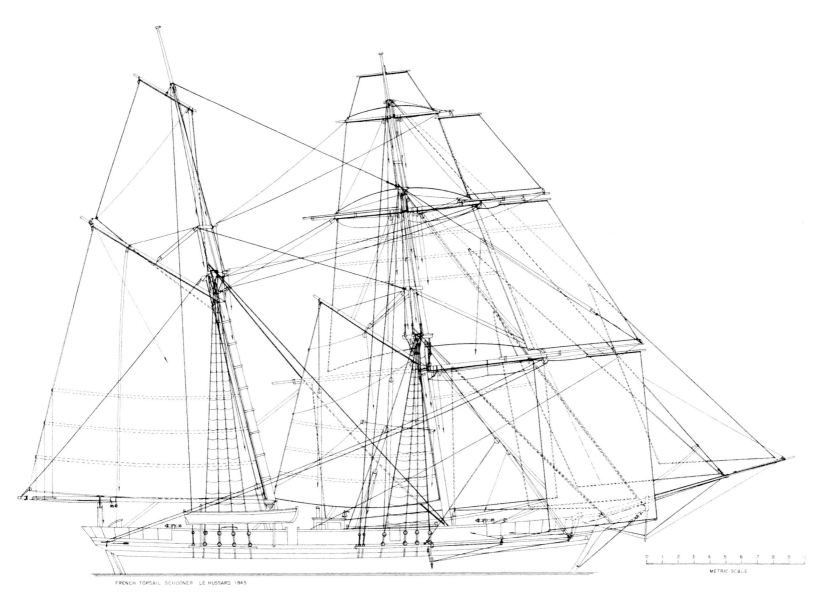

FRENCH TOPSAIL SCHOONER LE HUSSARD 1845

METRIC SCALE

[32] Harris, D G, *F. H. Chapman, The first Naval Architect and his Work,* Conway Maritime Press Ltd (London, 1989) pp.86–92, 224

[33] Boudriot, J, *The Seventy-four Gun Ship,* J Boudriot (Paris, 1987) Vol.3, pp.264–265

[34] Pâris, E, *Souveniers de Marine* (Paris, 1884), Vol.2, repr. Butzinger Verlag (Hamburg, 1972) p.112

[35] McKay, Lauchlan, *The Practical Shipbuilder,* Collin, Keese and Co (New York, 1839) repr. Macdonald and Jane's (London, 1974) pp.7, 11

[36] Chapelle, H I, *The History of American Sailing Ships,* W W Norton & Co. Inc. (New York, 1935) pp.142, 145

[37] 'The American Schooners', an extract from *Memoire sur les Bateaux a Vapeur des Etats-Unis D'Amerique* (Paris, 1824) by M Marestier, Ingenieur de la Marine Royale, Chevalier de le Legion d'Honneur. Also quoted in Chapelle, H I, *The Baltimore Clipper,* Marine Research Society (Salem, Mass., 1930) pp.112–133

[38] Pâris, E, *Souvenirs de Marine,* repr. Butzinger Verlag (Hamburg, 1972) Vol.5, p.270

[39] Smyth, W H, *Sailor's Word Book* (London, 1867), repr. Conway Maritime Press (London, 1991) p.71

[40] Archibald, E H H, *The Fighting Ships in the Royal Navy 897–1984,* Blandford Press (Poole, Dorset, 1984) p.359

[41] Fincham, J, *A History of Naval Architecture* (London, 1851) repr. Scholar Press (London, 1979) p.128

[42] Ibid., p.132

[43] Ibid., p.132

[44] Cannenburg, W V, *Bwschrijvende Catalogus der Scheepsmodellen en Scheepbouwkundige Teekeningen 1600–1900,* Nederlandsch Historisch Scheepvaart Museum (Amsterdam, 1943), p.29: '*Deze snelloopende vaartuigen werden hier the lande voor het eerst gebouwd bij den overgang van de 18e naar de 19e eeuw in vavolging van den Amerikanen, van wie wij tevens den naam "Schooner" overnamen*'.

[45] Groenewegen, G, *Verzameling van Vier en tachtig Stuks Hollandsche Schepen,* J van den Brink (Rotterdam, 1789) No.8

[46] Lyon, D, op. cit., p.282

[47] Chapelle, H I, *The Search for Speed under Sail,* Conway Maritime Press Ltd (London, 1983) p.167

[48] MacGregor, D R, *Merchant Sailing Ships 1775–1815,* Argus Books Ltd (Watford, Herts, 1980) p.85

[49] Archibald, E H H, op. cit., p.366

[50] Chapelle, H I, *The History of the American Sailing Navy,* Bonanza Books (New York, 1949) p.382

Rigging plan of *Le Hussard* (1845).

Chapter 3

—— ♦ ——

Coastguards and Gunboats

GUARDING shores against incoming illegal goods is as old as smuggling itself and coastguard services were long established by the end of the seventeenth century. William III's war with France during the last decade of that century strained the nation's coffers and custom and excise duties were vastly increased to compensate. With prohibition of certain French goods and trade restrictions on others declared, resulting shortages led to increased smuggling. A motley collection of small customs vessels, known as custom smacks, dealt with it as well as they could, but they were not efficient enough. Smuggling in tobacco, wines, brandy, silk or laces and, to a larger extent, in wool, got rapidly out of hand. Annually 120,000 packs of wool alone were brought into the country illegally. To stop this from deteriorating even further the Customs Commissioner Charles Godolphin proposed, in August 1698, to organise a better, more effective service: 'For the better guard of the coasts to prevent the running of French goods during the high duties'. Having gained full support from the Customs Board for his new scheme, he established within a year 21 custom sloops all around the coast of England and Wales[51]. This event turned a mixed group of customs vessels into a small fleet of new and well-equipped sloops and marked the beginning of the British Revenue Cutter Service. Custom vessels became known by the term 'sloop' rather than 'smack'. We do not know what kind of rig these sloops carried and it would be too easy to accept that early type designation for her rig, as has been done so often. In the early years of the eighteenth century the term 'sloop' was not restricted to one-masted vessels with a boom sail, and we only have to think of T R Blanckley's definition that sloops were 'sailed and masted as men's fancy led them', to be reminded of it. *Bonetta,* mentioned before, was one of those early sloops which were built to similar specifications as custom sloops. Guarding the coastline against insurgents during a war was not very different from taking revenue from unwilling smugglers. In light of our knowledge of rig development, to assume that sloops were either single-masted and boom-rigged or brigantine-, ketch- or snow-rigged when two-masted would be too single minded. A certain number of schooners must be considered part of any fleet of small craft after 1695.

A very well documented period of schooners fighting illegal trading, and therefore guarding the coasts of His Majesty's Colonies, occurred just after the French and Indian (the European Seven-year) war of 1755–1763. With the combatant navies busy, control over colonial merchants and ship-owners became very loose. Although settlers were already suffering from the effects of the war high taxes were imposed, which led to smuggling and tax evasion becoming endemic. The newly appointed Governor of Quebec, James Murray, reported on 27 September 1763:

'The Knowledge I have of this continent, and the Experience I have had of the many Abuses committed in the different Custom Houses in America – several of which have been reported to the Commissioners of His Majesty's Customs – have long convinced me, that smuggling was to be prevented by his Majesty's Ships of War only.

'The distribution of the Frigates appears to me admirable; but as Your Lordship desires I should offer any Hints, which I may think conducive to this Salutory End, I take the Liberty to observe, that without Cutters and stout Shallops, to cruize within the River St Lawrence from the Isle aux Coudres to the island Anticosti, it will be impossible to prevent a very great Contraband Trade from the Islands of Miquelon and St. Pierre.

'That These Islands are already filled with French Merchandise, is most certain; that Said Merchandise may be pour'd into Canada by Shallops which will hug the Shore, and take refuge in the Shallow Bays, where no Frigates, nor even Cutters dare approach them, is most Evident. It is not in the Power of Man in such an Extensive River as this, to prevent smuggling on Shore; It must, and may, be done a float by Vessels drawing as little Water, as those made use by the Smugglers; but these Vessels must be under the Direction of His Majesty's Sea Officers, and should be manned from the Crews of the King's Ships; if manned by the Inhabitants of the Province, and under the direction of any Residenter of this Country, it is easy to foresee the Consequences.

'In my former Reports I have had the Honour to make the above Observation in part, and I now beg leave to add that it will be very necessary, His Majesty's Sea Officers should be empowered to examine, when they please, all the fishing Posts in the Lower parts of this River, many of which, it is fear'd, will become Magazines of French Goods, and a Law prohibiting the Use of every French Commodity in this colony is much to be wished for.' [52]

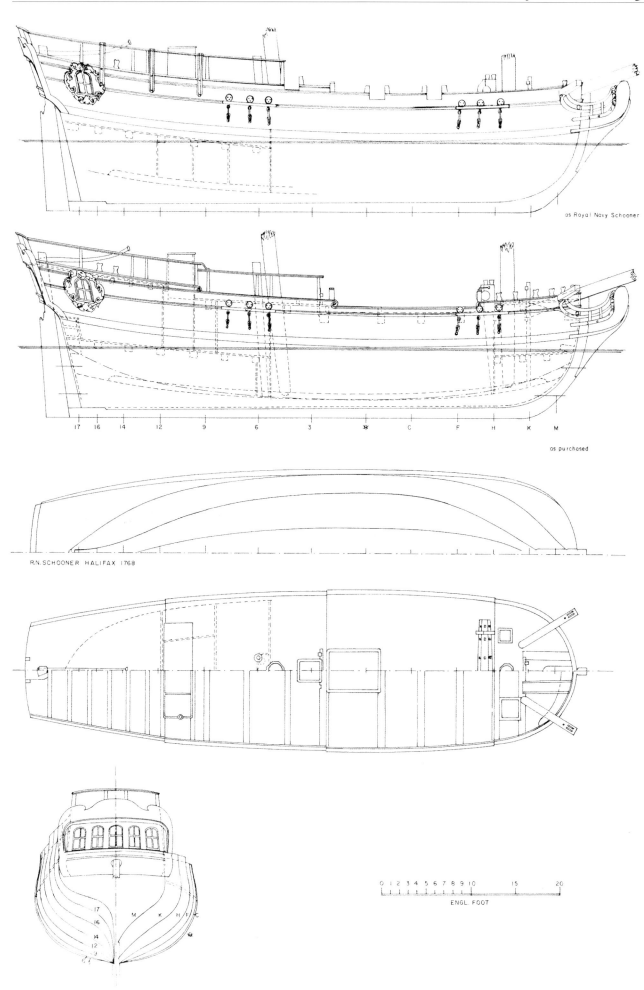

Lines, deck and profile
of Royal Navy schooner
Halifax (1768).

as Royal Navy Schooner

as purchased

R.N. SCHOONER HALIFAX 1768

0 1 2 3 4 5 6 7 8 9 10   15   20
ENGL. FOOT

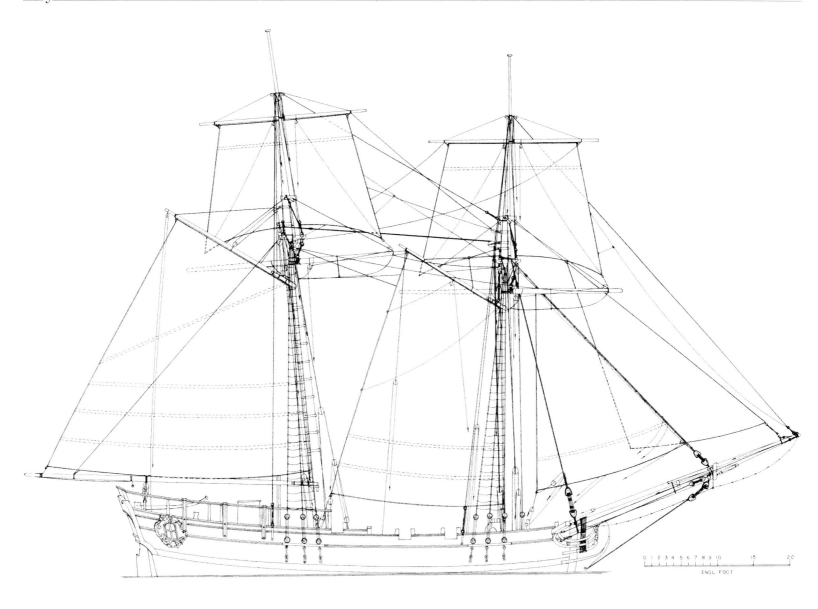

In that climate of discontent the British Parliament decided to stop the great drain on colonial revenue income by employing ships and personnel of the Royal Navy's North America Station as collectors of colonial duties. The shortage of small craft in that fleet, needed for a good control of the shallow and indented coastline, led the Admiralty to issue the well-known order of 7 January 1764:

> 'Rear Admiral Lord Colvill, Commander in Chief of His Majesty's Ships and Vessels in North America, to cause Six Marblehead Schooners or Sloops to be purchased for His Majesty.' [53]

So the schooners and sloops mentioned in chapter 2, from *Chaleur* to *St Lawrence*, were bought to join in the combat of illegal trade. The British schooner fleet grew to 24 vessels in these years of gathering tension between 1764 and 1775. One of the vessels, the schooner *Halifax* of 83 tons, was built at the end of 1765 at Boston as a packet and was bought into the Royal Navy at the request of Commodore Hood. On 15 February 1775 she hit a rock off Sheep Island near Machias and was lost.

Dimensions of *Halifax*:

Length on the range of deck	58ft 3in
Length of the keel for tonnage	46ft 10½in
Breadth extreme	18ft 3in
Depth in hold	8ft 10in
Burthen in tons	83 ⁷⁄₉₄
Crew	30
Armament	6 x 3-pdr carriage guns
	8 x swivels

For a hundred years galleys were used in Scandinavia to defend those narrow passages between the offshore islands. With the first of that Mediterranean type of vessel being built about 1665 in Gothenburg, Sweden, the last were launched in Denmark between 1764 and 1767. They were replaced in 1786 with shorter *Skærbaats* (skerry boats) as R C Anderson[54] has noted. The dimensions in his work suggest a vessel of 66 feet by 17½ feet, armed with two 18-pdr forward and six howitzers. With skerry boats only lightly armed, he was describing an early Danish gunboat. J H Röding's words in regard to skerry boats are worth mentioning here:

'A small armed vessel, of which several cover between the skerries the entrance to Stockholm.

'The skerry fleet consists of skerry boats for the defence of the skerries.' [55]

There is evidence that skerry boats made an earlier appearance than Anderson suggested. The first known draughts are from 1768 and in 1769 master shipwright F M Krabbe at the dockyard in Frederiksværn, Denmark, built two boats, *Elgen* and *Bæveren*. This type of boat, possibly with a square rig, could well have been used in this northern country as far back as the seventeenth century, but we can only go on the evidence found in the first known draughts. A list of the Danish/Norwegian Fleet from 1650–1700[56] mentioned a brigantine *Næsvis*, which was launched in 1688 in Copenhagen and condemned in 1719. She carried 4 guns of unknown calibre and her principal dimensions (50ft x 10ft x 4ft) were slightly smaller then the later skerry boats. A similar list of Swedish ships from 1688–1693 by H J Börjeson notes that in 1688 at Göteborg the *skärbâtar Portugisen*, *Falken* and *Hjorten* were in a very bad condition. The 1769 Danish skerry boats were in their layout not unlike late-seventeenth-century brigantines with Norwegian attributes. They had the same triple fore-and-aft deck division, with the

middle part open for rowing thwarts, the same number of oars and pieces of armament as J Furttenbach described for a *bergantino* in 1629[57]. *Elgen* was fore-and-aft schooner rigged and it was proposed that *Bæveren* have a Norwegian three-masted yacht rig (square-rigged *jecta* style). Their dimensions are given as:

Length between perpendiculars	54ft Norwegian
	(1ft = 313.7mm)
Breadth extreme	11ft 6in
Height in the middle	5ft
Draught at stern	3ft 3in
Draught at bow	2ft 9in
Midship height of oar above waterline	2ft 9in
Distance between oars	3ft 6in
Distance between frames	1ft 4in
Pairs of oars	10
Crew	approx. 50
Armament	2 x 2-pdr howitzer
	6 x ½-pdr swivel

Danish/Norwegian skerry boats had a small stern cabin of about six feet in length and four to five feet in height for the master, similar to cabins on vessels of the south west coast

Royal Danish/Norwegian skerry boat *Elgen* (1769): side view, deck and profile.

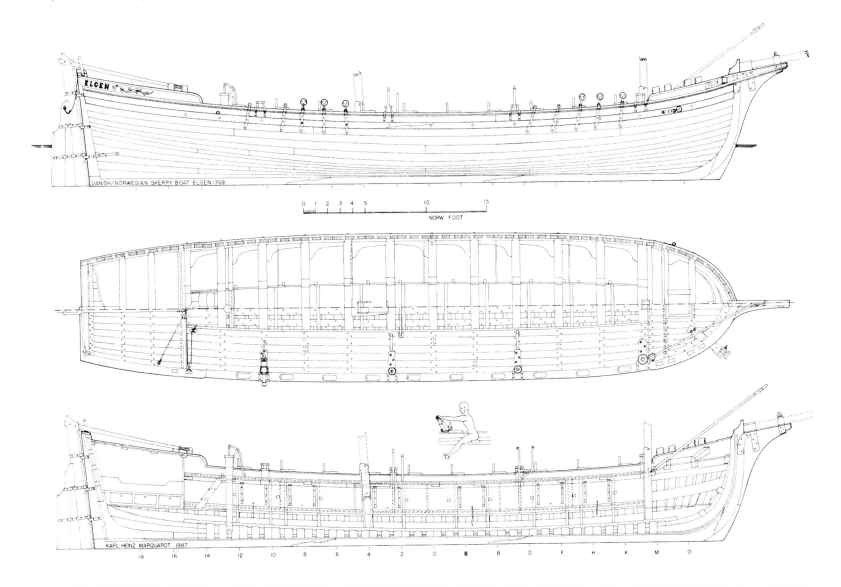

ELGEN

DANISH/NORWEGIAN SKERRY BOAT ELGEN 1769

0 1 2 3 4 5   10   15
NORW FOOT

KARL HEINZ MARQUARDT 1987

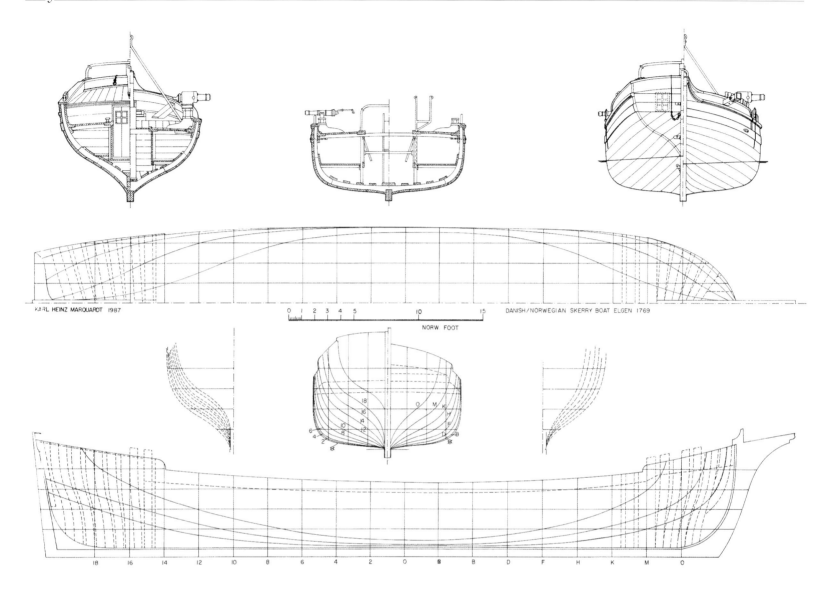

KARL HEINZ MARQUARDT 1987   0 1 2 3 4 5   10   15   DANISH/NORWEGIAN SKERRY BOAT ELGEN 1769

NORW. FOOT

Elgen: lines, cross
sections and bow and
stern view.

of Norway, the Sognefjord *Storebâten*. Whilst stern windows are not marked on the original draught, a similar cabin on these even smaller merchant boats shows them[58]. They can therefore not be ruled out and are included on the drawing. Crew sleeping quarters were beneath the side decks. They were very low rooms of not much more than two feet in height, with a length of six feet and a width of three feet. They could be entered from the open mid-ship space. The relatively flat deck beams were also used as thwarts for the oarsmen, with foot rests fitted aft of these, about one-and-a-half feet lower. The rudder tiller arrangement was not given on the draught. With the main boom only two-and-a-half to three feet above the cabin deck swinging, the tiller had to be just above deck, so the movement could either be controlled by a tackle or by using a hinged stick, as a 1880s photograph of a *storebâten* demonstrated.

Anchor size must have been according to the accepted rules about three hundredweight. Even with the vessel's draught showing catheads, no place for a capstan or a windlass can be ascertained, which suggests that the anchor's cable must have been taken in with the help of a strong tackle. Oar length (see Appendix 4, page 230) for a 30-ton vessel with the given height above water of 2 feet 9 inches

would have been 22 feet. The oars rested during sailing periods in iron forks that stood in the binding strakes.

An unusual feature on a vessel that size in the second half of the eighteenth century were masts in trunks, so called tabernacle masts. J H Röding[59] described the trunk as only being used on small and open boats (see *speeljachts*), while D Steel[60] considered their use on sloops, smacks, barges and lighters that go through bridges. Usually these masts were light enough to be lifted up by one or two men into a position for the stay tackle to become effective; however, for heavy masts a certain mechanical device was used, which could be permanently or temporarily installed. It followed the same sheer principle as for fitting masts: two spars were set abreast the mast into steps at the waterways and crossed just above the fore stay tackle where they were lashed to the fore stay; when the tackle was loosened, the stay remained in the same angled position as before and the mast could be lowered and set up completely without any complication. Not shown on the original draught, this device was added when the plans were redrawn. Pictures of mast sheer booms in action are only known since the early nineteenth century, but lever action is not just an invention of the industrial era: it is as old as man's ingenuity itself.

Elgen, skerry boat of the Royal Danish/ Norwegian Navy of 1769. Model was built in 1955 by author. (*Courtesy of the Marinemuseet Horten, Norway*)

Elgen skerry boat model: portside. (*Courtesy of the Marinemuseet Horten, Norway*)

Elgen skerry boat model: bow section. (*Photographed by the author*)

Elgen skerry boat model: deck view toward the cabin. (*Photographed by the author*)

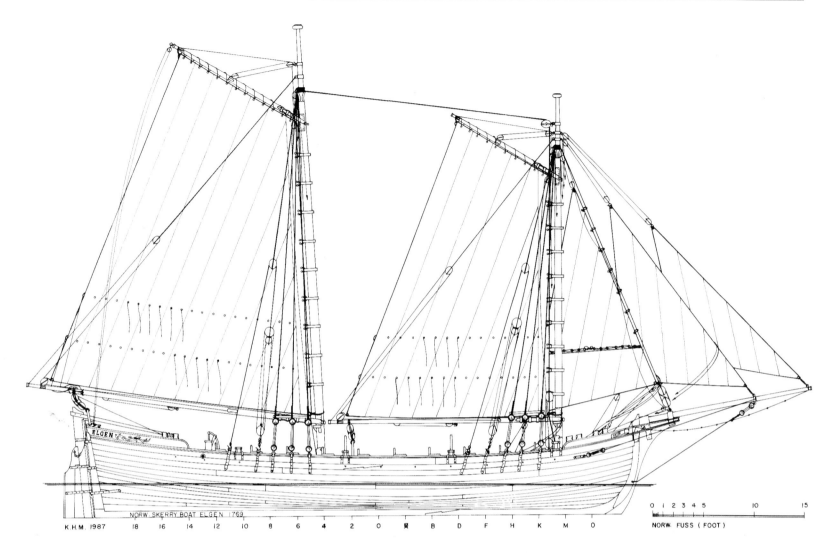

NORW. SKERRY BOAT ELGEN 1769.

K.H.M. 1987   18   16   14   12   10   8   6   4   2   0   B   D   F   H   K   M   O

0 1 2 3 4 5   10   15

NORW. FUSS (FOOT)

Elgen: complete rigging plan.

In April 1789 George Washington took his oath of office as first President of the United States and gave Alexander Hamilton, his treasury secretary, the task of creating a Revenue service. With smuggling and tax avoidance a well-established national pastime during the long years of colonial rule and the revolution, Hamilton's first and hardest job was to curb the illegal importation of goods. By presenting Congress with a bill to establish the US Revenue Cutter Service he proposed ten boats of 36–40 foot keel, each crewed with a captain, a lieutenant and six marines. The bill was passed in August 1790 and the forerunner of the current US Coast Guard swung into action. Built in different yards along the coast, the vessels ranged in size from 35–70 tons, relatively small vessels, and nine of them were schooner rigged:

Massachusetts	70 ⁴³⁄₉₄ tons; launched 23 July 1791, Newburyport
Scammel	51 ⁸⁸⁄₉₄ tons; launched 24 August 1791, Portsmouth area
Argus	35 tons; launched 1791, New London
Vigilant	48 ⁹⁄₉₄ tons; launched 1791, New York
General Greene	35 tons; launched 5 August 1791, Philadelphia
Active (sloop rigged)	Launched 12 April 1791, Baltimore
Virginia	50 tons; launched 1791, Hampton
Diligence	47 tons; commissioned June/July 1792, Washington
South Carolina	35 tons; launched 1792/1793, Charleston
Eagle	50 tons; launched early 1793, Savannah

Support by the coastal population for government intervention into their 'free trade' was low or none at all and even a judge (Thomas Bee) decided that the President's wishes were not law and therefore not binding. Another truth brought home during the next few years was that these first Revenue vessels were too small, too slow and too lightly armed to be a threat to anyone but small smuggling vessels.

Even with the fledgling United States declaring their neutrality in the new hostilities between Britain and France in 1793, France claimed certain rights under the Franco–American treaty of 1778 and waged war with privateers against British shipping leaving American ports, mainly Charleston and Philadelphia. Since these small revenue cutters were all the armed vessels that the United States possessed, they had no power to stop these flagrant breaches of US neutrality. The French privateers captured British ships even inside the three-mile zone. French revolutionists had

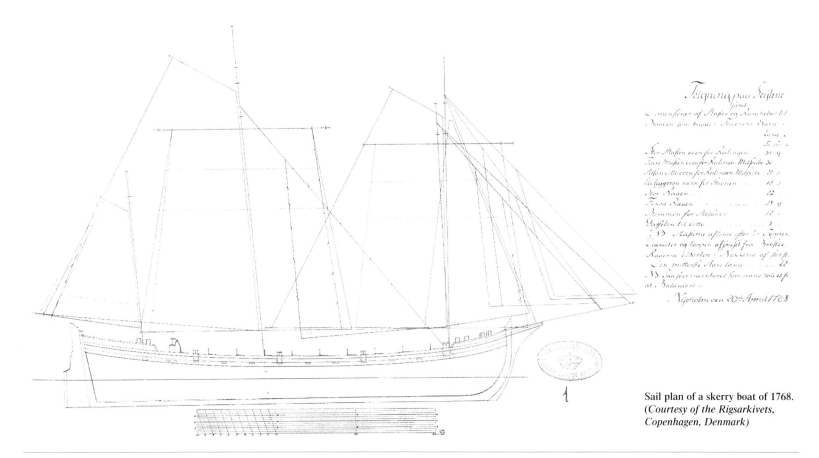

Sail plan of a skerry boat of 1768.
(*Courtesy of the Rigsarkivets,
Copenhagen, Denmark*)

Elgen: masts & spars

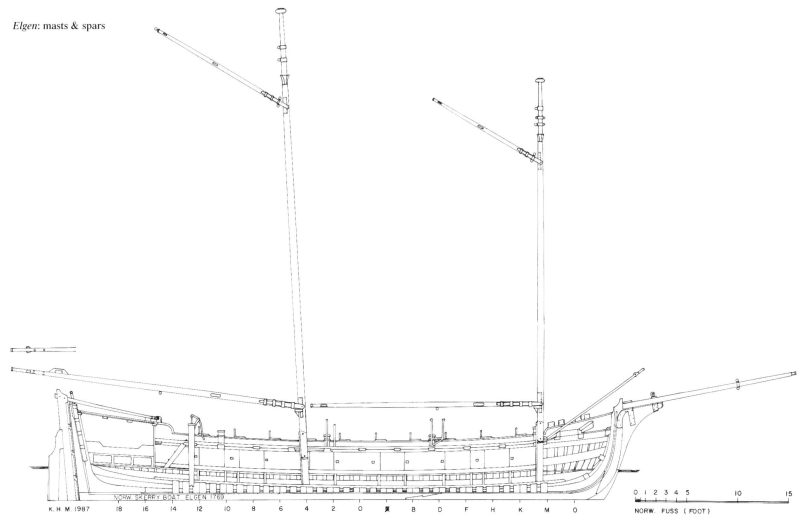

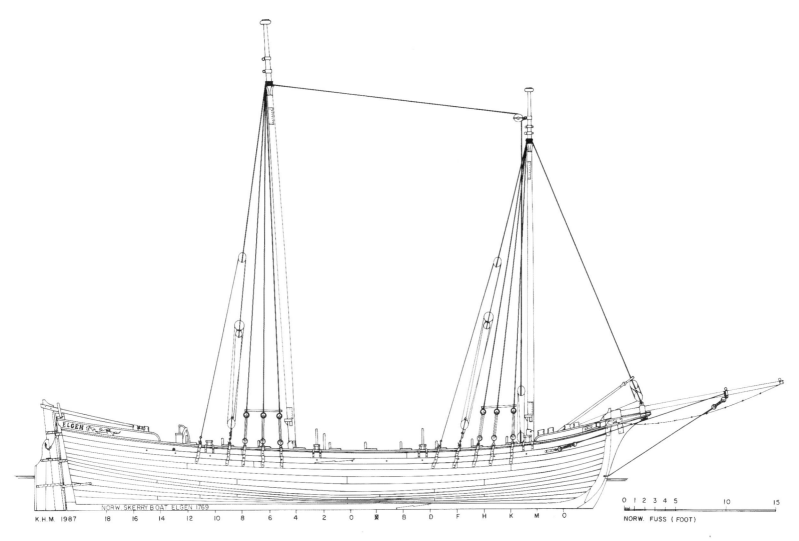

Elgen: standing rigging.

not much respect for international law and when revenue cutters tried to enforce that law, French privateers became so bold that they began to seize American ships also. Such action forced the United States into a quasi-war with France. Eight new, larger, revenue cutters were ordered and on 27 March 1794 the US Congress passed an act to build six frigates. This event is seen as the birth of the US Navy. Another act five years later placed the Revenue Cutter Service inside that newly founded naval establishment. The eight new revenue cutters were:

Virginia (2nd)	14-gun schooner of 187 tons; launched 1797, Norfolk, Virginia
General Greene (2nd)	8-gun schooner of 98 tons; launched 1797, Baltimore
Diligence (2nd)	12-gun schooner of 187 tons; launched 1797, Philadelphia
Governor Jay	12-gun schooner of 187 tons; launched 27 June 1798, New York
Pickering	14-gun brig of 187 tons; launched July 1798, Newburyport, Mass.
Eagle (2nd)	4-gun brig of 187 tons; launched 4 August 1798, Philadelphia
Scammel (2nd)	14-gun schooner of 187 tons; launched 11 August 1798, Portsmouth
Governor Gilman	14-gun schooner of 187 tons; launched August 1798, Portsmouth
South Carolina (2nd)	12-gun schooner; launched 27 November 1798, Charleston

The newly formed US Navy, totalling 45 ships together with the 8 new USRCS schooners and brigs, served in combat against the French until 1801, capturing 99 armed enemy vessels. By the end of that war the duties of revenue cutters extended beyond the scope of preventing smuggling: they surveyed the United States coastline, charted rivers and harbours, set up lighthouses, acted in the protection of public health and tried to suppress the slave trade. No draughts are known of the vessels listed above; however H I Chapelle[61] provides copies of three classes of revenue cutters designed in 1815 by William Doughty. They were of 31 3/94 tons, of 51 3/94 tons and of 79 62/94 tons and extreme examples of the pilot boat type. The smallest and the largest of these are redrawn here.

Main dimensions of the 31-ton vessel:

Length on the range of deck	48ft 6in
Breadth moulded	14ft 6in
Depth in hold	5ft 0in
Custom house tonnage	31 3/94

Elgen: sails and running
rigging.

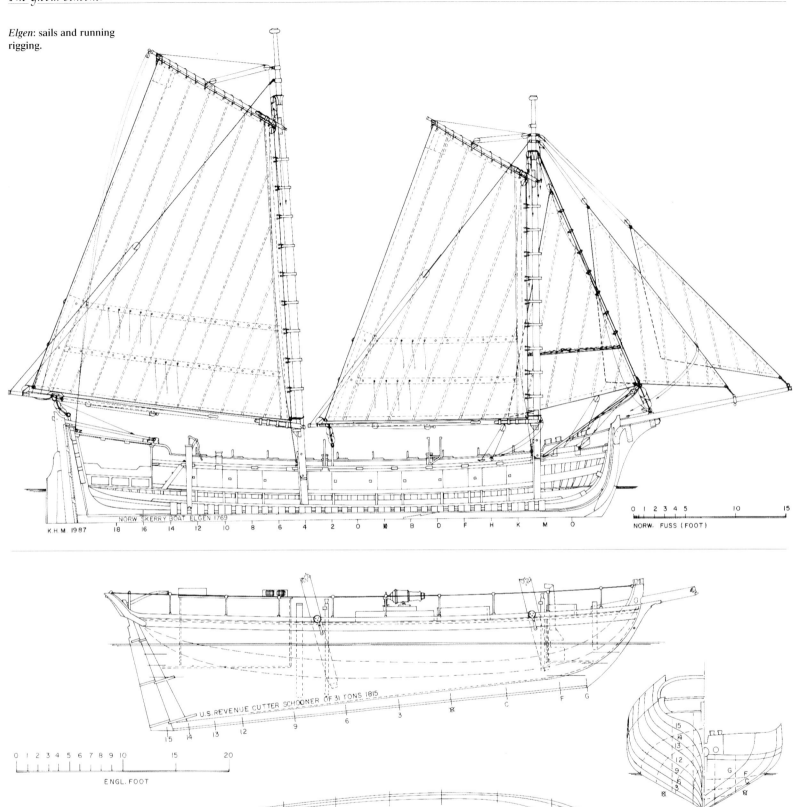

NORW SKERRY BOAT ELGEN 1769

K.H.M 1987

NORW. FUSS (FOOT)

U.S.REVENUE CUTTER SCHOONER OF 31 TONS 1815

ENGL. FOOT

An 1815 design of a United States Revenue Cutter Service schooner of 31 tons, by W Doughty: side, deck, lines and profile.

Masts and spars:

Mainmast (whole length)	48ft 6in, head 4ft 0in, diameter 12in
Main topmast (whole length)	14ft 0in
Foremast (whole length)	47ft 0in, head 4ft 0in, diameter 12½in
Fore topmast (whole length)	14ft 0in
Main boom	29ft 0in
Gaffs	10ft 0in
Bowsprit (outside)	9ft 0in
Jib boom (outside cap)	9ft 0in
Squaresail yard	29ft 0in
Flying topsail yard	15ft 0in

Masts and spars:

Mainmast (whole length)	64ft 0in, head 5ft 0in, diameter 1ft 3in
Main topmast (whole length)	18ft 0in, pole 4ft 0in
Foremast (whole length)	62ft 0in, head 5ft 0in, diameter 1ft 3in
Fore topmast (whole length)	14ft 0in, pole 4ft 0in
Main boom	42ft 0in
Gaffs	15ft 0in
Bowsprit (outside)	12ft 0in
Jib boom (outside cap)	12ft 0in
Squaresail yard	40ft 0in
Flying topsail yard	24ft 0in

Dimensions of USR Cutter *Surprise* of 80 tons designed by W Doughty:

Length on the range of deck	69ft 6in
Breadth moulded	19ft 0in
Depth in hold	6ft 9in
Custom house tonnage	79 $^{62}\!/_{94}$

USRC *Surprise* was built and completely fitted out in just nine days in 1815 and sent from New York to Charleston to serve. Proving too deep for that coastline, she saw service from 1817 onwards at Norfolk station. Two other schooners of the same class, USRCs *Dallas* and *Crawford*, were built in 1821 for Savannah station, with *Dallas* being lost on 19 February 1822.

USRC schooner: rigging and sail plan.

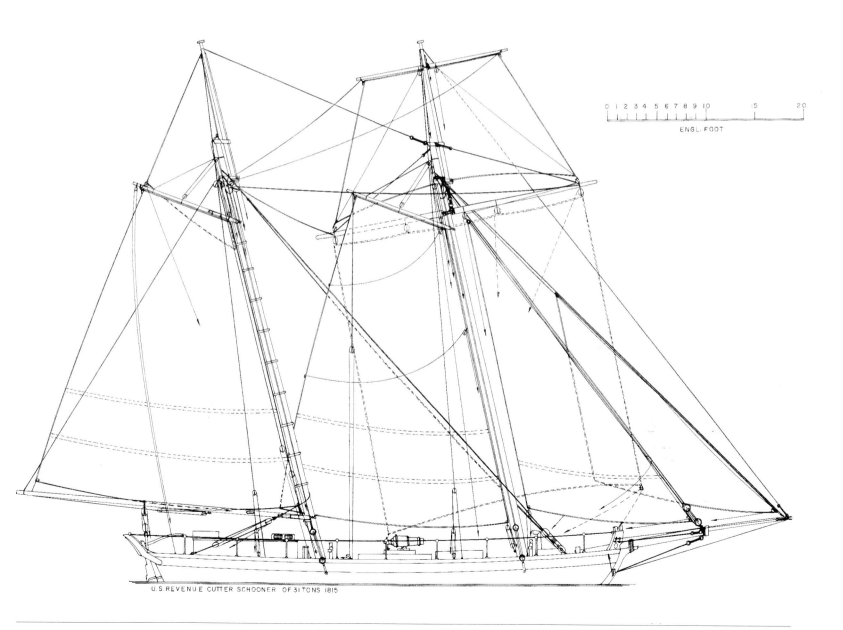

0 1 2 3 4 5 6 7 8 9 10   15   20
ENGL. FOOT

U.S. REVENUE CUTTER SCHOONER OF 31 TONS 1815

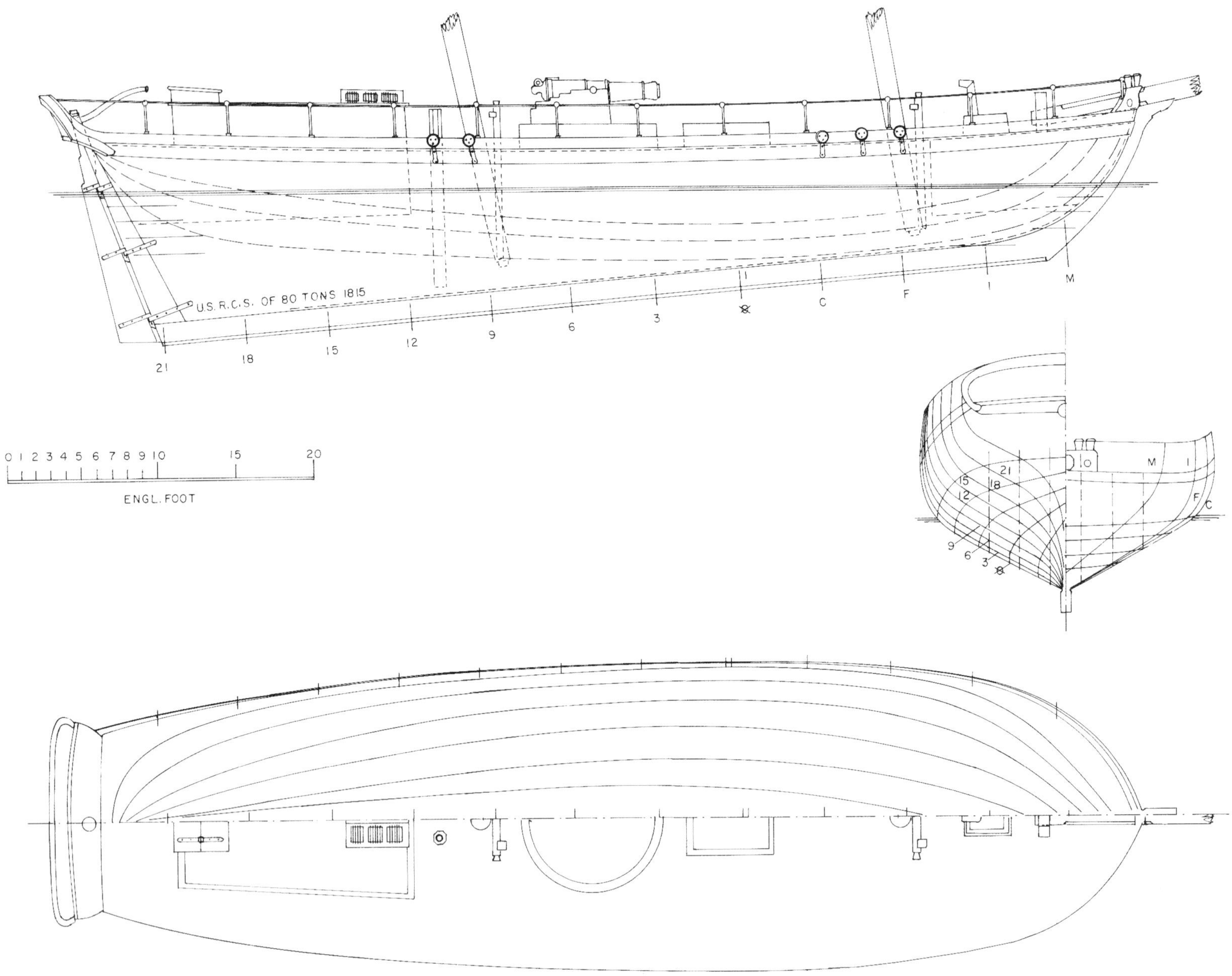
U.S.R.C.S. OF 80 TONS 1815
21
18
15
12
9
6
3
C
F
I
M
0 1 2 3 4 5 6 7 8 9 10 15 20
ENGL. FOOT

An 1815 design of USRC schooner *Surprise* of 80 tons by William Doughty.

M Marestier provides draught and dimensions of another revenue cutter, which is similar to the 51-ton, Doughty-designed vessel. It forms No. 18 of his collection of US schooners[62]:

Dimensions of No. 18 in metric and imperial measurements:

Length	16.60m or 54ft 5 7/6in
Beam	5.16m or 16ft 11 1/8in
Depth at bow	1.63m or 5ft 4 5/32in
Depth at midsection	1.83m or 6ft 1/32in
Depth at stern	3.05m or 10ft 1/16in
Overhang of bow	2.90m or 9ft 6 1/8in
Distance midsection is forward of centre	3.12m or 10ft 2 13/16in
Rake of sternpost	1.07m or 3ft 6 1/8in
Spacing of frames	nearly 0.38m or 1ft 3in
Length of mainmast	17.40m or 57ft 1in
Length of foremast	16.80m or 55ft 1 9/32in
Length of bowsprit	3.40m or 11ft 1 13/16in
Length of topmasts	4.90m or 16ft 7/8in
Length of main boom	10.40m or 34ft 1 3/8in
Length of gaffs	4.00m or 13ft 1 7/16in
Length of lower yard	10.40m or 34 ft 1 3/8in
Length of topsail yard	5.20m or 17ft 11/16in
Length of jib boom beyond bowsprit	3.00m or 9ft 10 1/16in
Diameter of mainmast	0.34m or 1ft 1 3/8in
Diameter of foremast	0.36m or 1ft 2 5/32in
Heads of lower masts	1.39m or 4ft 6 11/16in

When considering the pilot boat type, it is essential to take note of L McKay's draught Plate 2 of such a vessel, which he explains here:

> 'Plate 2, comprises the sheer draft body and half-breadth plans of a Pilot Boat, which would no doubt make an excellent sailer. The Stem is much plumber than has usually been fashionable, but nevertheless it is the prevailing fashion of

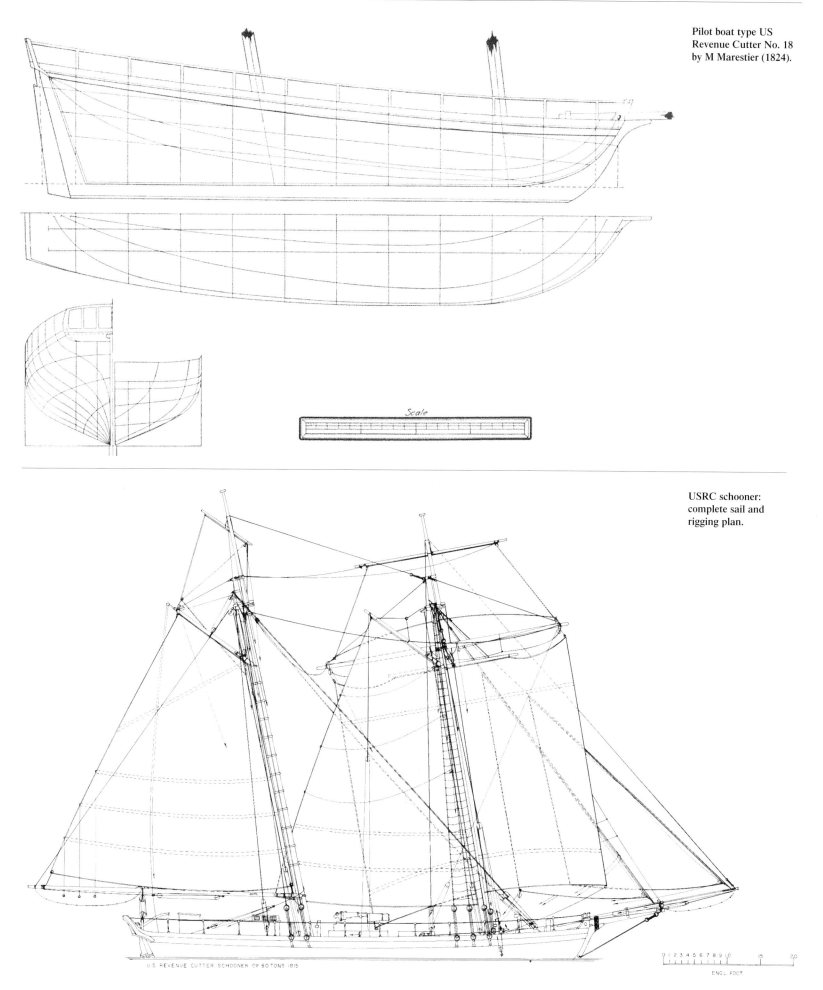

Pilot boat type US
Revenue Cutter No. 18
by M Marestier (1824).

Scale

USRC schooner:
complete sail and
rigging plan.

U.S. REVENUE CUTTER SCHOONER OF 80 TONS 1815

0 1 2 3 4 5 6 7 8 9 10   15   20
ENGL. FOOT

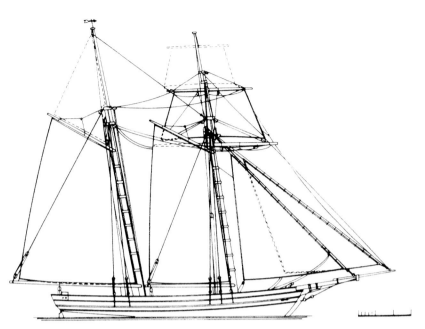

Sail plan of a topsail schooner by Marestier.

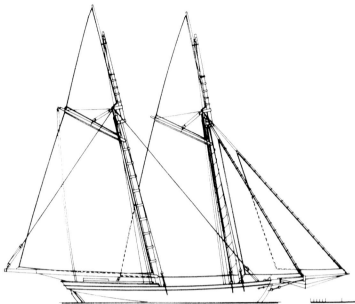

Sail plan of a fore-and-aft-rigged schooner by Marestier.

the South. The Mobile and Mississippi boats are all built on this plan, or at least all the new ones, and all who have seen them at sea will readily acknowledge their superiority over any boats either in the old or new world.'[63]

Dimensions of McKay's Pilot boat:

Length between pp.	59ft 0in
Breadth moulded	18ft 2in
Depth moulded a'ships	8ft 0in

Another type of coast-guarding vessel, the sailing gunboat, was born out of sheer necessity to defend river estuaries or small sea-lanes in that gigantic struggle at the turn of the nineteenth century. Rowing gunboats were already known in greater numbers during the Seven-Year War and the American War of Independence, and the development of the sailing gunboat began some years later.

The L McKay draught of a Pilot boat marked as Plate 2.

'Gun-Boat, (chaloupe cannonière, Fr.) a boat fitted to carry one or more cannon in the bow, so as to cannonade an enemy while she is end on, or advancing towards him; they are prin-

cipally useful in fine weather, smooth water, and shallow ground, to cover the landing of troops'[64].

During the French Revolutionary War of 1793–1801 small merchant craft of every kind – hoys, barges, luggers etc – were converted to carry one or two large 18- or 24-pdr guns, but only the specially designed gunboats carried either a brig or schooner rig. Firing over bow or stern, they were effective small platforms of long-range artillery that could fight off larger ships while being only minimal targets themselves.

The Gerrit Groenewegen[65] etching of a '*Kanoneer boot zeylende by de wind*' gives an early artist's impression of these gunboats. The double topsail schooner-rigged gunboat that it portrays is not unlike the draught of a Dutch schooner-rigged gunboat of 1803. Appearing in Groenewegen's published work in 1789 it pre-dates the French/English hostilities. Another early gunboat, the Danish *Steece*, was part of the captured Danish fleet after the bombardment of Copenhagen in 1807. Beside nearly all their large ships, the Danish fleet also lost 6 brigs and 25 gunboats. This captured fleet was transferred to England during a time of autumn

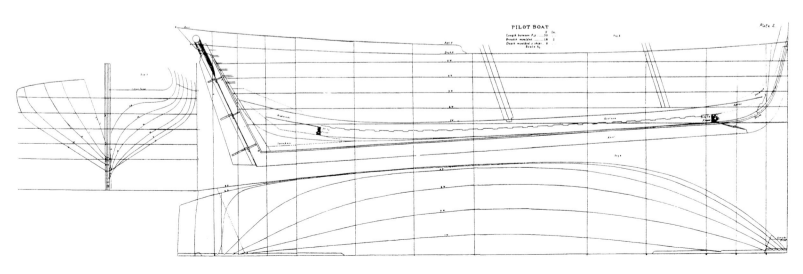

gales and many of the gunboats were lost. *Steece* survived and was taken off on 18 March 1808 in Chatham. By comparing the draught of *Steece* with the skerry boat draught from 1768 a certain similarity can be found. She was 97 tons and four feet longer than the skerry boat mentioned by R C Anderson, named a gun brig in Lyon's work, and could not have been rigged as brig. She had only two chain plates for dead eyes and one for a mast-tackle, which pointed very much to a simple fore-and-aft rig. From her draught layout one cannot conclude that she was a gunboat with large guns fitted fore and aft; it is more likely that she had a large gun on a turntable between the masts. Named a 'Danish Gunboat' on the draught, she was propelled with 30 oars, had a small stern cabin half above deck and a minimal depth in hold, all facts which point less to a gunboat that to a coast-guard vessel similar to *Elgen*.

Röding's work makes it apparent that the term 'gunboat' was widely accepted by 1794, as he has the German word *Kanonenboot* and the French *Chaloupe kanonniere* in his vocabulary. D Lyon[66] lists more than 80 gunboats as part of the Royal Navy in these last years of the eighteenth century, several of them captured French vessels. Although none of those on Lyon's list is classified as being schooner-rigged, the Royal Navy summary of 1805, as mentioned previously,

Etching of a schooner-rigged Dutch gunboat from 1789 by Gerrit Groenewegen.

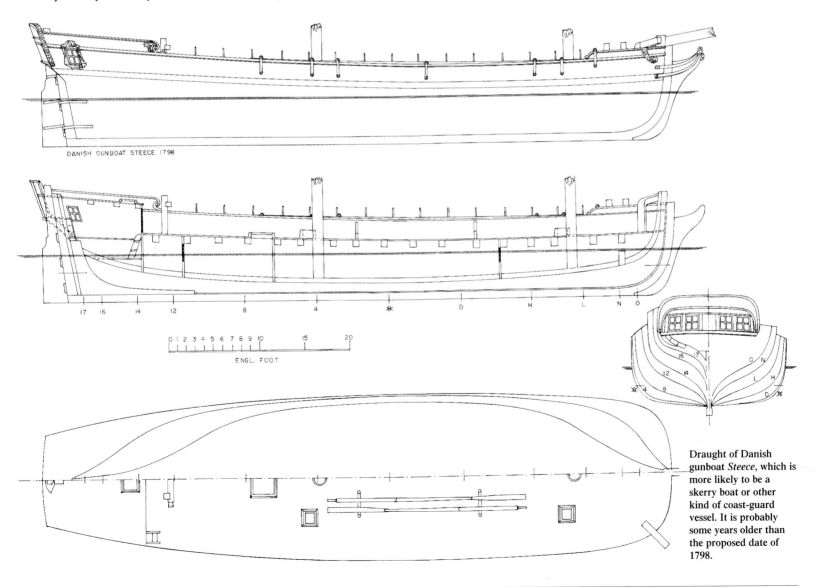

DANISH GUNBOAT STEECE 1798

0 1 2 3 4 5 6 7 8 9 10   15   20
ENGL. FOOT

Draught of Danish gunboat *Steece*, which is more likely to be a skerry boat or other kind of coast-guard vessel. It is probably some years older than the proposed date of 1798.

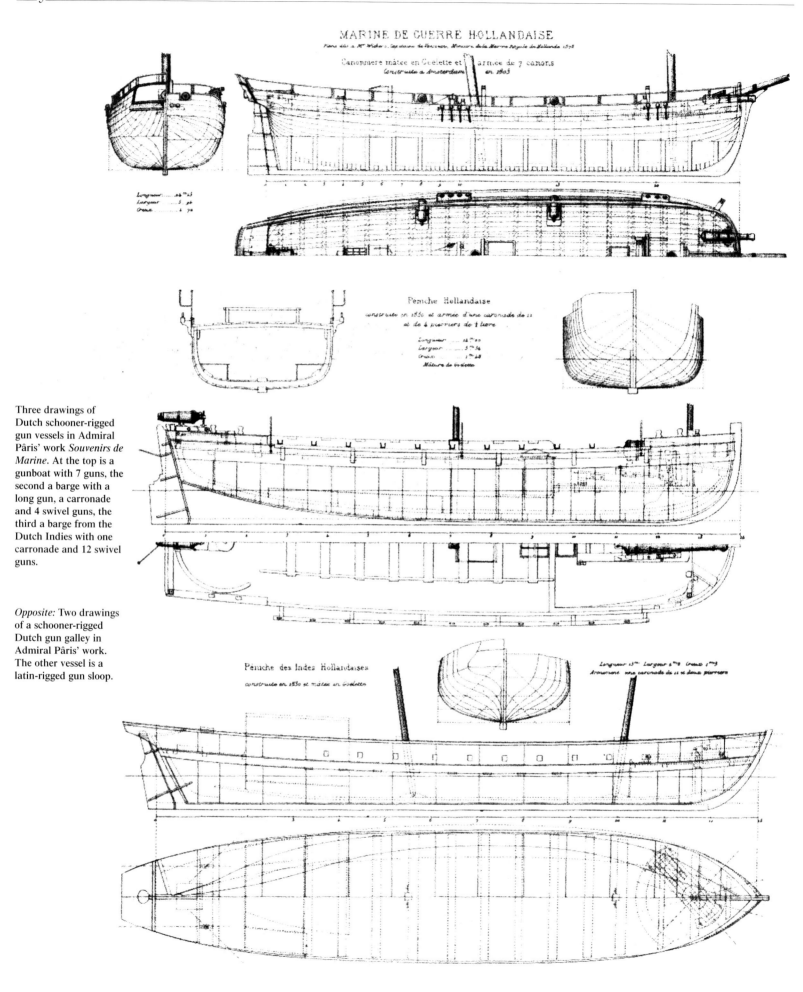

MARINE DE GUERRE HOLLANDAISE

Canonnière mâtée en Goelette et armée de 7 canons

Péniche Hollandaise

Three drawings of Dutch schooner-rigged gun vessels in Admiral Pâris' work *Souvenirs de Marine.* At the top is a gunboat with 7 guns, the second a barge with a long gun, a carronade and 4 swivel guns, the third a barge from the Dutch Indies with one carronade and 12 swivel guns.

Opposite: Two drawings of a schooner-rigged Dutch gun galley in Admiral Pâris' work. The other vessel is a latin-rigged gun sloop.

Péniche des Indes Hollandaises

MARINE HOLLANDAISE 1800

CANONNIERE-GALERE

Plans dus à Mᵉ Wichers, Capᵉ de Vaisseau, Ministre de la Marine

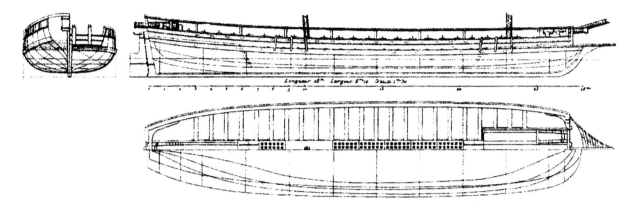

CHALOUPE CANONNIERE

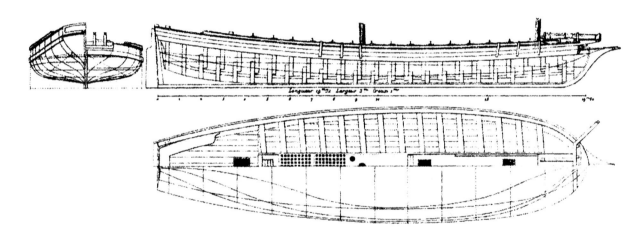

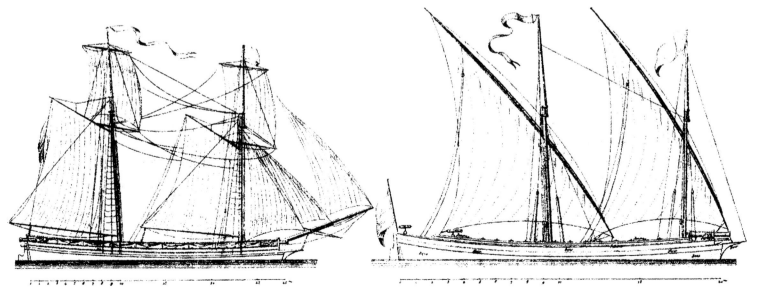

Voilure de la Canonnière-Galere.   Voilure de la Chaloupe Canonniere.

listed 12 schooner-rigged gunboats. Except for these, of which a few came probably from the *Conquest* class of 1794, and two experimental British schooners *Eling* and *Redbridge,* knowledge of schooner-rigged gunboats comes from the Netherlands, Denmark, Norway, Sweden and the United States.

Admiral Pâris[67] drew several Dutch gunboats, some marked as schooner-rigged. One of these is the type sketched by Groenewegen, with two probably 18-pdr carriage guns forward and one at the stern. Four probably 12-pdr French-type *obusiers* were placed fore and aft of the mainmast toward the sides. The gunboat was built in 1803 at Amsterdam:

Length	24.23m or 79ft 6in
Breadth	5.94m or 19ft 6in
Depth	2.72m or 8ft 11in

Pâris also introduces a Dutch craft in the shape of a longboat

with an oversized deck, armed with a long, 18-pdr gun forward, a 12-pdr carronade over the stern and four swivels. Built in 1830 and fitted to use 20 oars, the vessel was designated '*Mâture de Goëllete*' or 'schooner-masted':

Length	14.00m or 45ft 11in
Breadth	3.34m or 10ft 11 1/2in
Depth	1.48m or 4ft 10in

Even smaller than this vessel was an 18-oared craft of the Dutch Indies built in 1830. Marked as schooner-rigged, the masting is stepped *Periagua* style, or as Admiral W H Smyth termed it in 1867, in *Ballahou* fashion. As Admiral Smyth states this was common in the Bermudas and West Indies. The vessel was armed with one 12-pdr carronade and two swivels.

Her dimensions:

Length	13.00m or 42ft 8in

Drawing of *Redbridge* (1796) as designed by General Bentham.

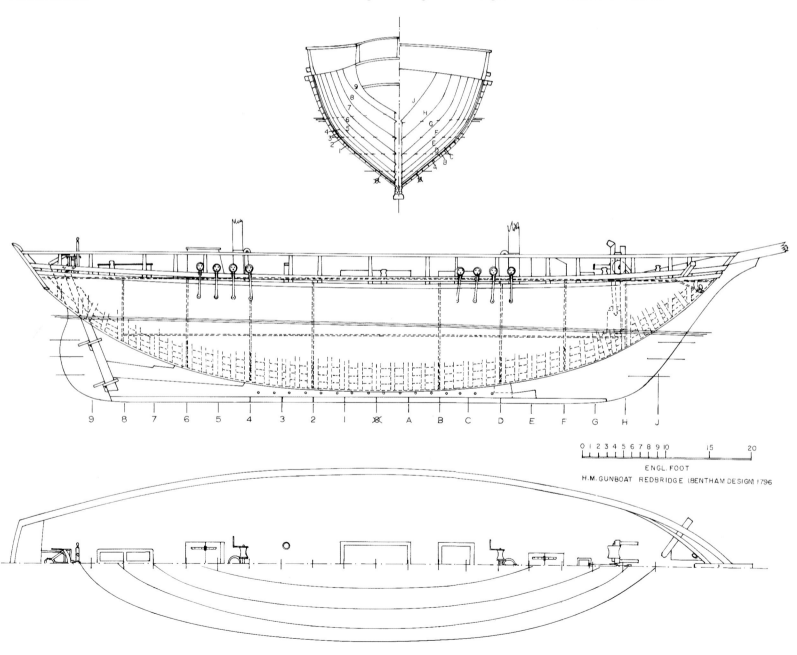

Model of *Axel Thorsen*, Royal Norwegian gunboat of 1810, built by the author in 1956. *(Courtesy of the Marinemuseet Horten, Norway)*

Breadth	2.80m or 9ft 2in
Depth	1.30m or 4ft 3½in

A 46-oared, Dutch-built galley from 1800 is another schooner-rigged craft found in Pâris' work[68]. This very unusual-looking craft symbolised the search for an ideal gun platform in these early gunboat years. It also underlines the point that schooners were designated by their rigging and not by hull shape or size. The galley's armament consisted of three long, probably 24-pdr guns on the usual galley sledge carriages, two of them forward and one at the stern.

Dimensions given are:

Length	28.00m or 91ft 10⅜in
Breadth	6.10m or 20ft 0in
Depth	1.50m or 4ft 11in

General Bentham's 1796 designs of *Eling* and *Redbridge* are considered schooner-rigged gunboats. They were the two smaller of the four Bentham experimental schooners (see Chapter 2). Armed with 12 x 12-pdr carronades and two bow-chaser, 12-pdr carriage guns, the six carronades each side were formidable broadsides. From the original draught it cannot be ascertained how the main aspect of a gunboat, the forward carriage guns, were deployed.

Dimensions of the *Eling* class:

Length on deck	80ft 6in
Length of the keel	64ft 6in
Breadth extreme	21ft 6in

Depth in hold	11ft 3in
Draught afore	11ft 0in
Tonnage	158
Crew	50

The vessels were built in 1796 by Hobbs at Redbridge under the direct supervision of General Bentham. *Eling* was broken up in 1814 and the French took *Redbridge* off Toulon on 4 August 1803; she remained in French service until 1814.

More conventional in design was the *Conquest* class of 12 gunboats. Most were schooner-rigged initially, with some later being re-rigged as brigs. Designed by Henslow in 1794, and of 146⁴¹⁄₉₄ tons, several of these shallow-depth vessels were fitted with Lt Schank's new invention, the 'sliding keels' or dagger boards. Their armament consisted of two 24-pdr long guns as bow chasers, two 18-pdr carronades as stern guns and ten 18-pdr carronades in their broadsides. These vessels had a crew of 50.

Dimensions:

Length over the range of deck	75ft
Length of keel for tonnage	62ft 3⅛in
Breadth extreme	21ft
Depth in hold	7ft

Other gunboats of this class were:

Aimwell and *Pelter*, launched on 12 May 1794 by Perry at Blackwall. The first was broken up in 1811, while the second was brig-rigged after 1798 and sold in 1802.

Drawing of the
Conquest class of British
gunboats of 1794.

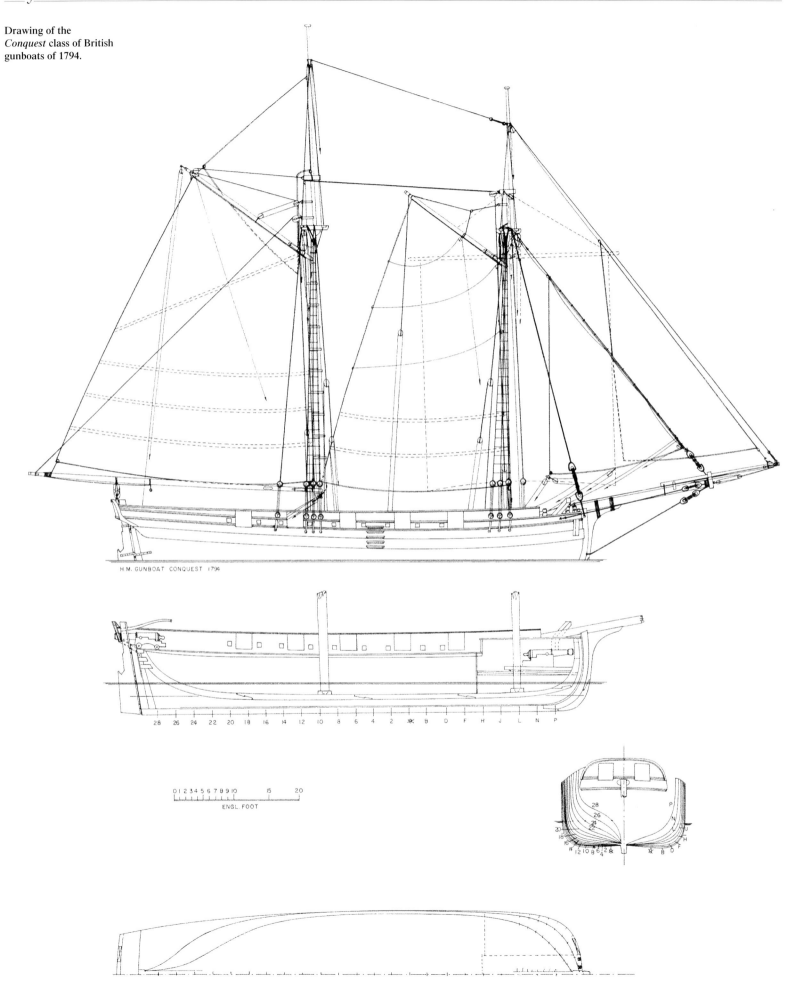

H.M. GUNBOAT CONQUEST 1799

Model of *Axel Thorsen*
(1810): bow section deck
view.
(Courtesy of the
Marinemuseet Horten,
Norway)

Model of *Axel Thorsen*
(1810): stern section.
(Courtesy of the
Marinemuseet Horten,
Norway)

Sail plan of a Norwegian
gun schooner of 1822.
(*Courtesy of the
Krigsarkivets Stockholm,
Sweden*)

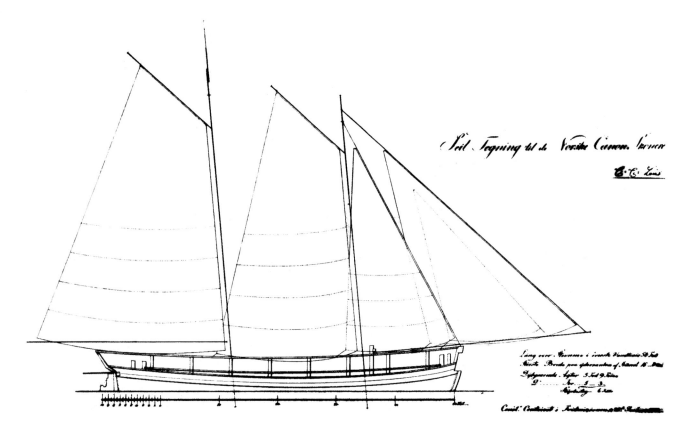

Swedish gunboat
draught of 1822.
(*Courtesy of the
Krigsarkivets Stockholm,
Sweden*)

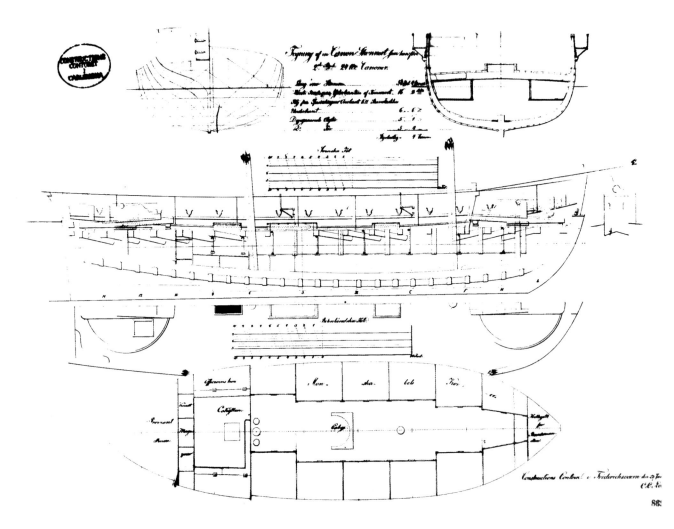

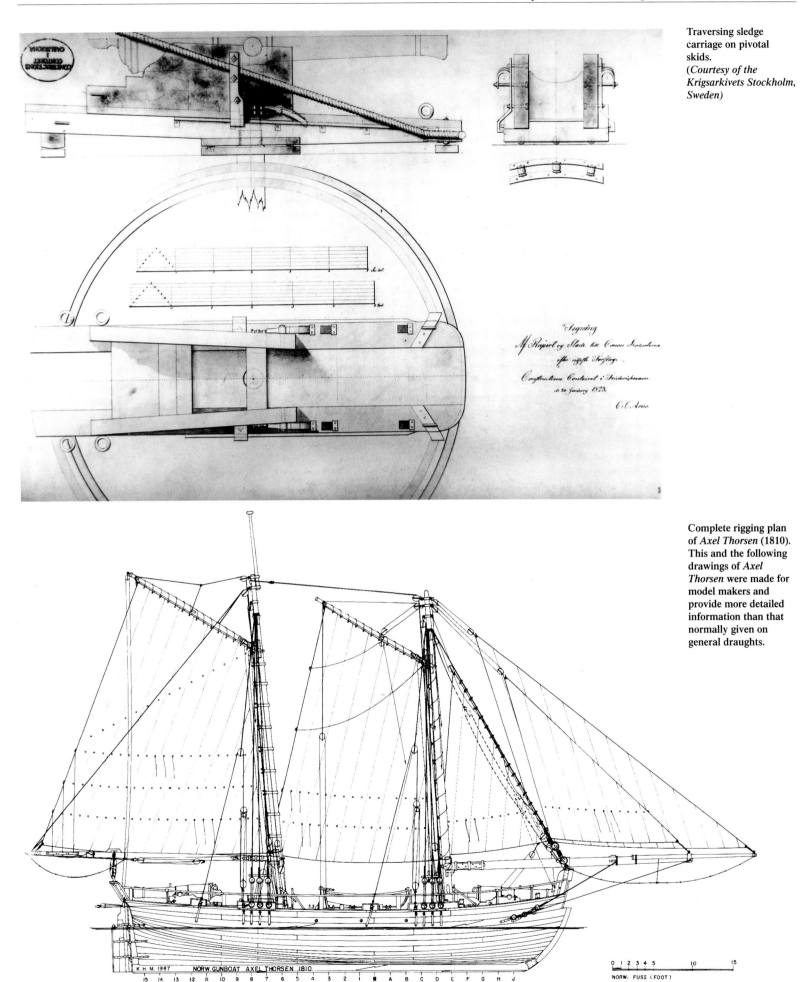

Traversing sledge carriage on pivotal skids.
(*Courtesy of the Krigsarkivets Stockholm, Sweden*)

Complete rigging plan of *Axel Thorsen* (1810). This and the following drawings of *Axel Thorsen* were made for model makers and provide more detailed information than that normally given on general draughts.

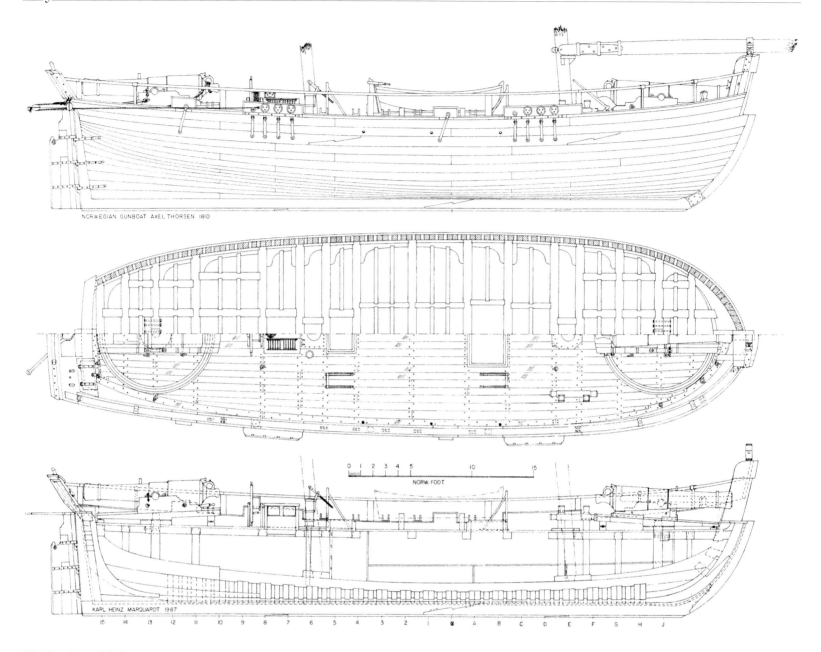

NORWEGIAN GUNBOAT AXEL THORSEN 1810

KARL HEINZ MARQUARDT 1987

0 1 2 3 4 5   10   15
NORW. FOOT

Side elevation and deck and beam profile plan of *Axel Thorsen*, gunboat of the Royal Danish/Norwegian Navy (1810). Body lines, cross-sections and stern views are on page 96.

Borer and *Plumper*, launched on 17 May 1794 and 17 April 1795 respectively by Randall at Rotherhithe. *Borer* was fitted with sliding keels in 1796 and scuttled in 1808 as a breakwater. *Plumper* was re-rigged as a brig in 1798 and sold in 1802.

Attack, launched 29 August 1794 by Wilson at Frindsbury. Sliding keels were fitted in 1796 and she was sold in 1802.

Conquest was also built in Frindsbury but by Brindley. She was launched in July 1794, fitted with sliding keels in 1796 and sold in 1817.

Fearless, built by Cleverley at Gravesend, was launched in June 1794 and wrecked in February 1804 in Cawsand Bay.

Force, launched in 1794 by Pitcher at Northfleet, was fitted with sliding keels and brig-rigged in 1796 and sold in 1802.

Swinger was launched by Hill at Limehouse on 31 May 1794 and was sold in 1802.

Teaser was launched by Dudman at Deptford on 26 May 1794. She was altered in 1798 (re-rigged or sliding keel?) and sold in 1802.

Tickler, launched 28 May 1794 by Wells at Deptford, received a brig rig in 1798 and was sold in 1802.

To prevent the Danish fleet from eventually joining Napoleon's side, a strong British Navy contingent and 17,000 soldiers under Lord Gambier sailed to Denmark in late summer 1807 to offer British protection. With his fleet anchoring in the Sund, an ultimatum was issued to the Danish ruler to accept protection and hand over the whole Danish Navy for the duration of the war to the Royal Navy or be considered a hostile country. With this strong ultimatum being rejected, British troops encircled Copenhagen and bombarded the city. Large-scale destruction and uncontrollable fires forced a Danish surrender on 7 September 1807 and all warships near Copenhagen were taken and brought to England. Ninety-two transport ships carried the booty found in the Danish supply arsenals. However badly defeated, Denmark could not be neutralized. Without many large ships

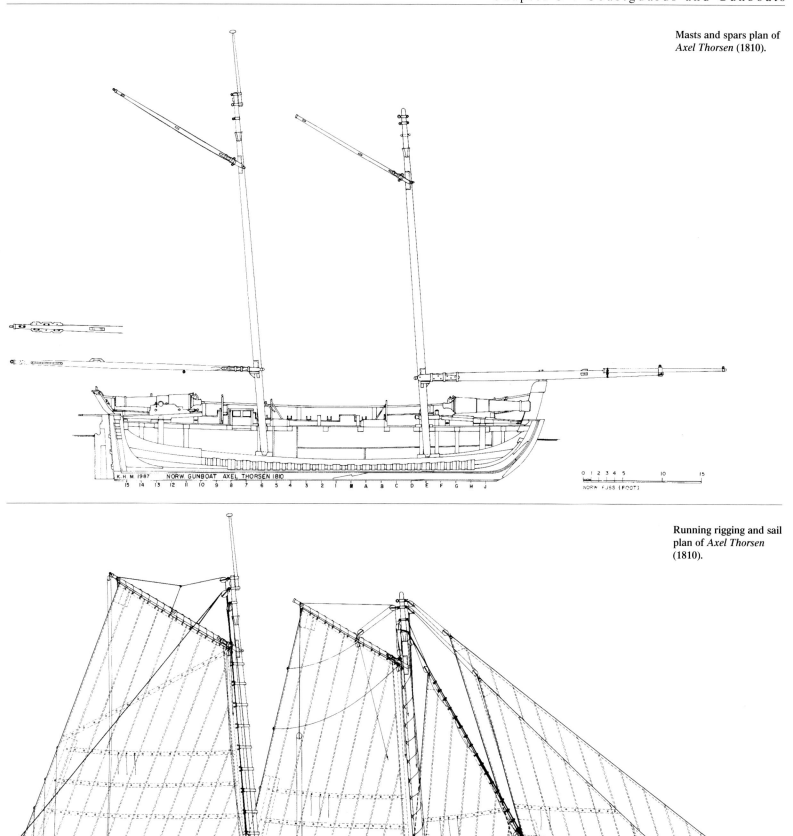

Masts and spars plan of
Axel Thorsen (1810).

Running rigging and sail
plan of *Axel Thorsen*
(1810).

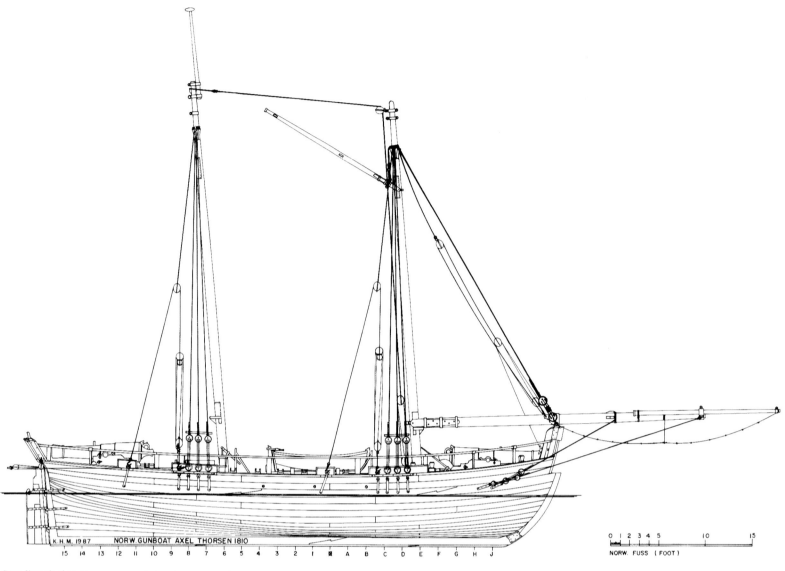

K.H.M. 1987   NORW. GUNBOAT AXEL THORSEN 1810

15 14 13 12 11 10 9 8 7 6 5 4 3 2 1 A B C D E F G H J

0 1 2 3 4 5   10   15

NORW. FUSS (FOOT)

Standing rigging on
Axel Thorsen (1810).

left in the Danish fleet, the kingdom's shipyards produced a multitude of gunboats and privateers. Falconer mentioned in 1815 that by 1813 the Danish Navy consisted only of a small contingent of larger ships but retained 120 gunboats. They virtually stopped all unwelcome traffic through the Danish sea-lanes into the Baltic Sea. The long coastlines of Norway however, then part of Denmark, remained completely defenceless. Norwegian citizens contributed in a large way to protect themselves by organizing their own coastal-defence force, which by the end of that war had grown to 122 maritime units. By 1814 the age-old close tie with Norway was cut as a result of Denmark being on the losing side of the war. Norway was consequently ruled in personal-union with Sweden and their coastal-defence force became part of the Swedish Navy.

The larger of the Norwegian coastal-defence vessels were schooner-rigged gunboats, similar to the *Axel Thorsen*. The *Axel Thorsen* was launched on 28 April 1810 at Trondheim and, until 1815, belonged to the coastal-defence flotilla there. In the ensuing four years she sailed in the cold and inhospitable Finmark for fishery protection. During the cholera epidemic of 1831–2 the vessel cruised the coast in an increased surveillance effort. Paid off in 1839, she was sold and used as a merchant vessel. A further 25 years as a

commercial carrier would not have harmed her structural stability. She was, as a veteran of 54 years, sturdy enough to be chosen in 1864 as the expedition vessel for the Swedish Spitzbergen expedition of Baron Nils Adolf Erik Nordenskjöld. Sailing for a further eight years in the arctic she was lost at sea after 62 years of active service, 29 of them as warship.

As a gunboat she was of 71 tons, rigged in fore-and-aft schooner-mode and armed with two 24-pdr sledge-mounted guns on pivoting skids. Her 12 oars were actually not enough to be a powerful propellant, and were instead used more as a device for position correction while firing. The height of the 23-feet-long oar handle at a standing man's chest suggests that rowing was undertaken in standing position.

Dimensions of *Axel Thorsen*:

Length between pp.	56ft 2in Norwegian measure
Breadth extreme	16ft 7in
Depth in hold	6ft 0in

A contemporary description of a gunboat of similar size, the *Balder*, was given by her captain in his diary, from which the former director of the Norwegian Marinemuseet, the late Captain T K Olafsen, translated a section:

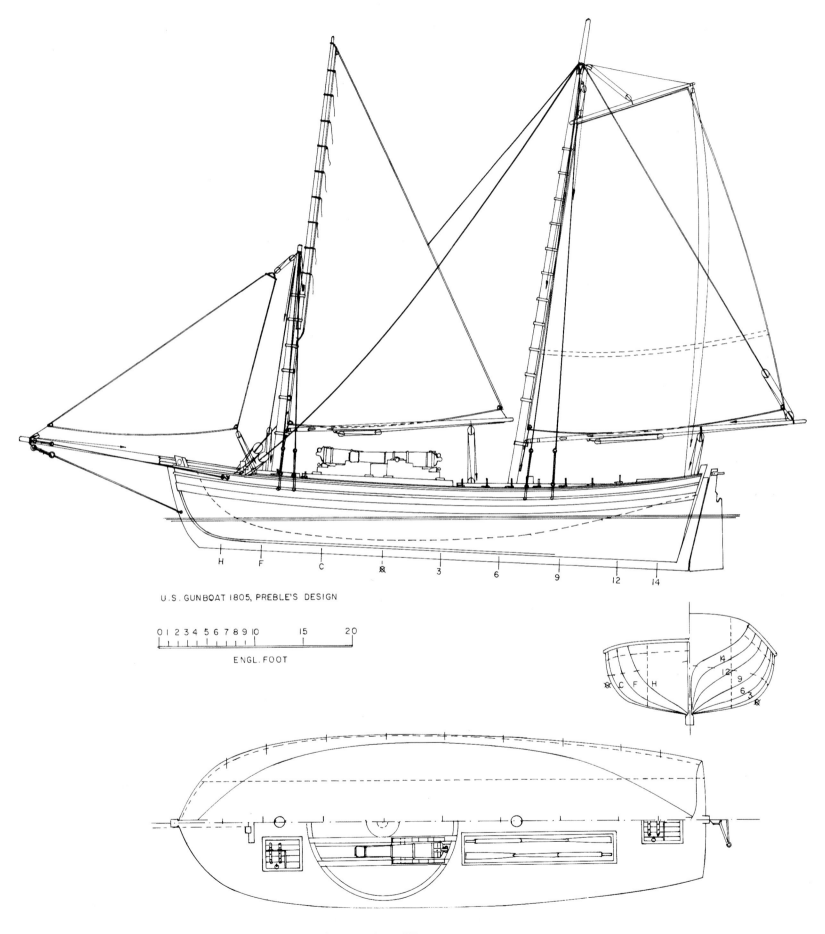

U.S. GUNBOAT 1805, PREBLE'S DESIGN

0 1 2 3 4 5 6 7 8 9 10   15   20

ENGL. FOOT

The design of American gunboat *Preble*, with sliding-gunter-rigged foremast (about 1805).

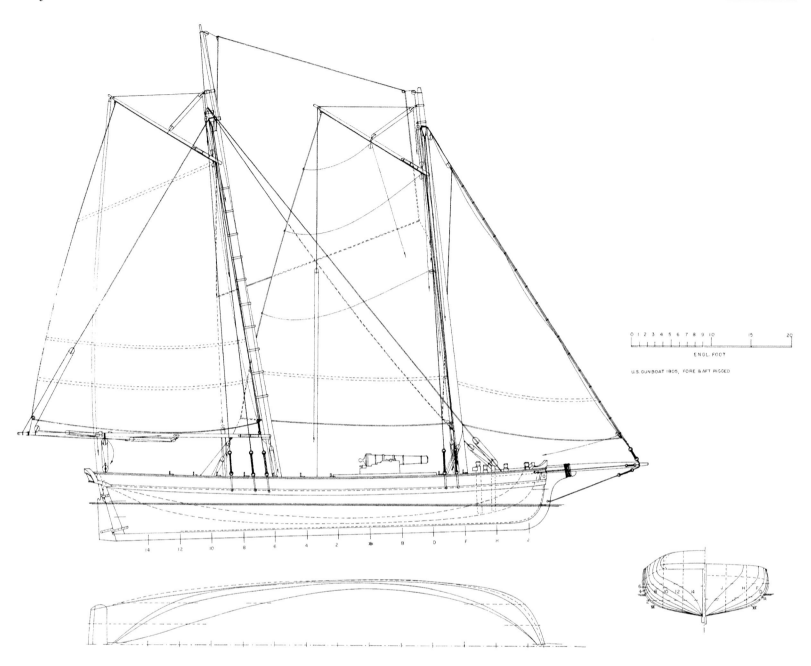

0 1 2 3 4 5 6 7 8 9 10   15   20
ENGL. FOOT

U.S. GUNBOAT 1805, FORE & AFT RIGGED

American fore-and-aft schooner-rigged gunboat from 1805.

'BALDER was 17.60m (51ft Norwegian) long, 5.20m (16ft 6½in) wide and 1.50m (4ft 8½in) deep. With a displacement of 71 tons she was armed with two 24-pounder, facing forward and aft, and two four-pdr howitzers each side. The large guns were mounted to traversing skids, which could be swung to each side on a semicircle. The masts could be lowered and the vessel could be moved with 30 oars. The crew consisted of 45 officers and men and five soldiers.

'Below deck was the storeroom, accessible through a hatch in the cabin wall. The cabin could be exited through the crew quarters and then over a stairway up to the deck. In the center of the crew quarters stood a large oven. The crew slept in three stages (3 watches) and there was no standing height in these quarters. The guns could not be used while the mats were lowered.' [69]

Two-masted gunboats appeared on the other side of the Atlantic around the turn of the century. One, designed by J Humphreys in 1799, was named a galley, not because of her

hull shape but her two-masted Latin rig. Authority was given for 10 gunboats to be built with an 18- or 24-pdr gun in the bow and 4 howitzers or swivels on stocks. This marked the beginning of gunboat construction in the US Navy. When the quasi-war with France came to an end in 1801 the building programme of the new navy ended and construction sites were neglected or sold off. By the end of that year, trouble with the Bay of Tripoli, who ordered attacks on American merchant ships, forced the US government to rethink their policy. A naval force was sent into the Mediterranean and the apparent lack of small craft for an efficient blockade of Tripoli led, as Commander Preble took charge in 1803, to the building and buying of gunboats. Rig experimentation went from single Latin through two-masted Latin to a type of schooner rig with the foremast sliding-gunter rigged. That type of rig was soon replaced on the eleventh and twelfth gunboats with a fore-and-aft schooner rig.

When New York State placed an order of gunboats in 1806, the draught forwarded by a young shipbuilder,

Christian Bergh's periagua-rigged US Navy gunboats of 1806.

PERIAGUA-RIGGED U.S. GUNBOAT 1805

0 1 2 3 4 5 6 7 8 9 10   15   20
ENGL. FOOT

Body lines, cross
sections, inside the stern,
bow and stern view of
Axel Thorsen (1810).

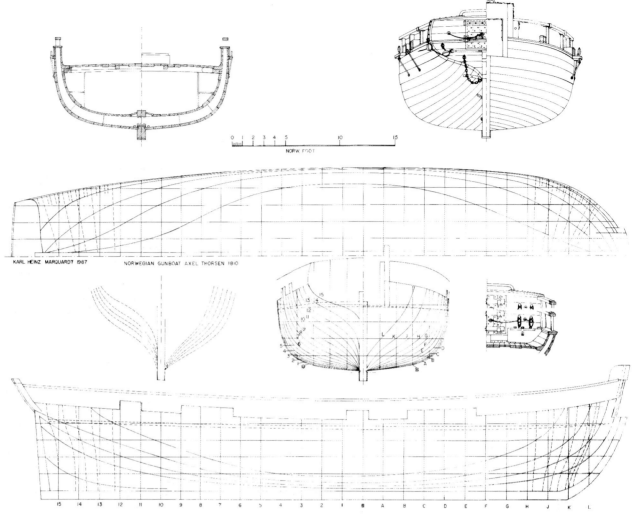

KARL HEINZ MARQUARDT 1987   NORWEGIAN GUNBOAT AXEL THORSEN 1810

Christian Bergh, broke entirely with convention. His design
aimed to be a fast sailer, and instead of the rigs used previously on gunboats he introduced the handy rig of New York
ferryboats and lighters, popularly known as *perry auger*.
That *periagua* rig had its origins in the primitive rig of
South-American and Gulf-of-Mexico pirogues. It was a two-
masted fore-and-aft rig without a bowsprit, so that the foremast stood on the keel footing and leaned forward, while the
mainmast raked aft at a similar angle. The foresail was
loose-footed while a boom spread the mainsail. A large flying staysail could be set between the two mastheads. The
dimensions of these gunboats, listed as numbers 50–57 and
99–104 in the US Navy, were 47 feet 4 inches on the keel,
18 feet moulded beam and 5 feet 6 inches depth in the hold.
Each was armed with one 34- or 32-pdr long gun on a pivot
and two 12-pdr carronades, although the carronades were
not fitted to the later series, which had trunk cabins.

In the 1820s, the midship-based, pivoting, large-calibre
long gun, first found only on gunboats, became the main
weapon to fight piracy and a number of US schooners were
fitted with them alongside their broadside carronades.

———— ◆ ————

Notes:

[51] Smith, G, *King's Cutters, The Revenue Service and the War against Smuggling*, Conway Maritime Press (London, 1993) p.21

[52] PRO ADM 1/4126

[53] PRO ADM 2/433 pp.459–460

[54] Anderson, R C, *Oared Fighting Ships*, Percival Marshall (London, 1962) p.99

[55] Röding, J H, *Allgemeines Wörterbuch der Marine* (Hamburg, 1794), repr. Uitgeverij Graphic Publisher (Amsterdam, 1969) Vol III Index, Schwedisch–Deutscher, p.82: 'Skjärbat, Ein kleines bewafnetes Fahrzeug, dergleichen verschiedene in den Scheeren vor Stockholm die Einfahrt decken. Skärgardsflotta, Die Scheerenflotte welche aus Scheerenböten besteht zur Vertheidigung der Scheeren.'

[56] Holck, P, *Lists of Men-of-War 1650–1700*, part III, Danish–Norwegian Ships, S.N.R. Occasional publications No.5 (Greenwich, 1936)

[57] Furttenbach, J, *Architectura Navalis* (Frankfurt, 1629), repr. Schiffbautechnische Gesellschaft e.V (Hamburg, 1968) p.80

[58] Færöyvik, B & O, *Inshore Craft of Norway*, Conway Maritime Press (London, 1979) pp.52–3

[59] Röding, J H, *Allgemeines Wörterbuch der Marine* (Hamburg, 1794), repr. Uitgeverij Graphic Publisher (Amsterdam, 1969) Vol.1 p.892

[60] Steel, D, *Elements of Mastmaking, Sailmaking and Rigging*, from the 1794 Edition, E W Sweetman (New York, 1932) p.193

[61] Chapelle, H I, *History of American Sailing Ships*, Bonanza Books (New York, 1935) p.193

[62] Marestier, M, *Memoire sur les bateaux a vapeur des Estats-Unis d'Amerique* (Paris, 1824)

[63] McKay, L, *The Practical Ship-Builder* (New York, 1839), repr. Macdonald & Janes (London, 1974) p.26

[64] Falconer, W A, *A New Universal Dictionary of the Marine, improved and enlarged by William Burney Ll.D* (London, 1815) repr. MacDonald and Jane's (London, 1974) p.176

[65] Groenewegen, G, *Verzameling van Vier en tachtig Stuks Hollandsche Schepen*, J van den Brink (Rotterdam, 1789) No.8

[66] Lyon, D, *The Sailing Navy List, 1688–1860*, Conway Maritime Press (London, 1993) pp.256–260

[67] Pâris, E, *Souvenirs de Marine*, Vol.1 (Paris, 1882), repr. Karl Butziger Verlag (Hamburg, 1972) p.42

[68] Ibid., p.37

[69] Private correspondence between author and T K Olafsen (1955)

Chapter 4

♦

Merchantmen and Slavers

WE know of trading schooners from early American newsletters. Research by the late William A Baker[70] tells of Boston port records in May 1716 mentioning the new type-name 'scooner' and in August of the same year the Gloucester town records spoke of the loss of a new fishing scooner. The Boston Newsletter of 4–11 February 1717 reported the Schooner *Anne's* first departure for South Carolina[71] (see Chapter 1). However, there is no documentation on the shape of that early schooner-rigged mercantile craft except for vague artistic impressions of early schooners, as in Burgis' 'A View of Boston' from 1725 or Ashley Bowen's primitive sketches from 1746–60. Their hulls could not have differed from those of other rigs but without reliable pictures any reconstruction would merely be conjecture. From the 1760s onward better documentation shows vessels with a square- or pinque-stern without stem adornments, like those in sketches by Pierre Ozanne (1737–1813), naval engineer and captain in the French Navy.

It is from Frederik H af Chapman that we learn schooner hulls could be shaped like any other ship or vessel. He included a wide range of merchantmen types in his excellent drawings[72] including a 159-ton, schooner-rigged bark (XXVII/4), a 115-ton frigate (VII/9) and the slightly smaller packet boats (XLI/2 and XLII/4). The first actual drawings of schooner-rigged merchant vessels date from the 1760s and are Admiralty draughts of American craft and the Swedish draughts discussed in chapter three. The bark drawn by Chapman comprised a full-bodied hull, with flush-decking and rough-tree rails. Her bow was without a head and adornments. The frigate hull showed a short quarterdeck and a slightly risen forecastle, with a rough-tree rail securing the main deck area. This vessel carried a figurehead, and also had a decorated quarter badge and stern. The larger of the two schooner-rigged packets (73½ft between perpendiculars) is drawn with a siren as figurehead, only a slight step to the quarterdeck, a quarter badge and stern decoration, an open rail and an armament of eight howitzers.

The 1765 watercolours of the Salem schooner *Baltick*, which are by an unknown artist, are the earliest good pictures of a Marblehead-type trading schooner. The only question arising from these impressions of the vessel is with regard to her set of flags. She flies the red ensign, which in itself says nothing about her duties, but the additional jack and pennant indicate government service, as a number of different sources agree: a pennant is used to denote, 'All Her Majesty's Ships and Vessels in Commission' (J W Norie & J S Hobbs, 1848); 'It denotes that a vessel is in commission or actual service' (W A Falconer, 1815); 'It is the badge of a ship-of-war' (Admiral W H Smyth, 1867). The jack carried on top of the bowsprit, a union flag, also makes her a Royal Navy vessel since merchant vessels had the union flag with a red border around. With no martial implements visible one wonders what duties this vessel fulfilled – perhaps she was a revenue vessel or a transport. She is also shown with a large main stay-sail, which flew probably on a temporary stay-sail stay and not on a permanent main stay.

A watercolour by William Ward gives another excellent picture of a similar craft, in this case the Salem, Massachusetts, schooner *Fame* of 1795. A topsail schooner with cutter-masts, with a deeply roached fore topsail and overly large fore topgallant, she also hoisted a main topgallant gaff sail and stun'sl's on her schooner-mast.

The draught of the Danish packet schooner *Ornen* dated 1807, the time of her capture after the surrender of Copenhagen, indicates a Scandinavian style similar to the gunboats and the later Baltic Sea schooners. She had a

A small British, pinque stern, topsail schooner drying her sails. Etching by Pierre Ozanne from about 1780.

Gouillette les Voiles au Sec

1er Cah

N° 9

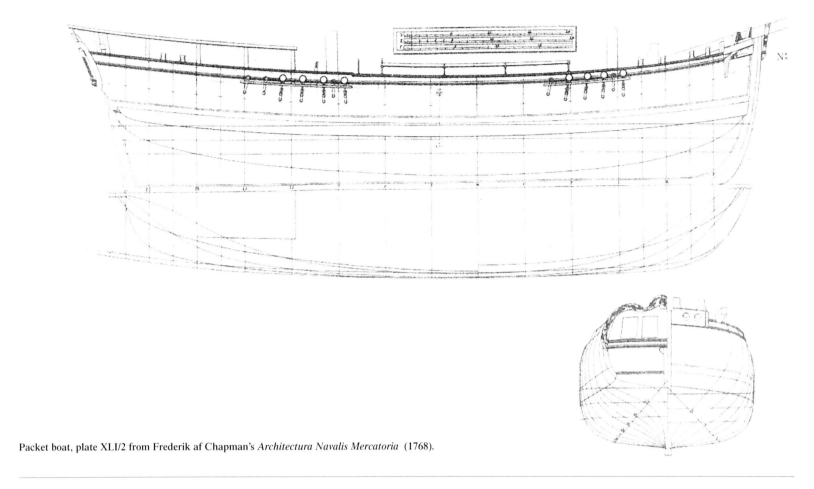

Packet boat, plate XLI/2 from Frederik af Chapman's *Architectura Navalis Mercatoria* (1768).

Schooner-rigged bark by Chapman (1768).

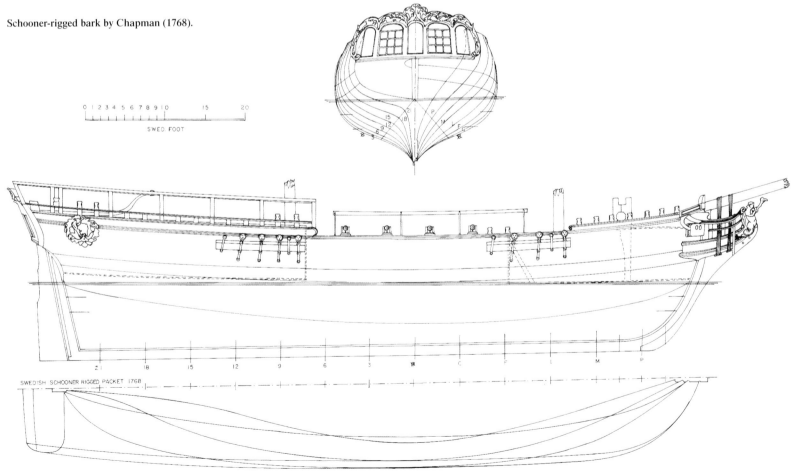

SWEDISH SCHOONER RIGGED PACKET 1768

slightly risen quarterdeck, her sheer had five half-round open gun ports and was topped with an open handrail.

Röding's maritime work from 1794 provides information on a Portuguese vessel that is completely different to these North European merchant schooners. Röding described *Lancha do Alto*, figure 270 in volume IV, as 'a small vessel used in Portugal'. She was double-ended and carried only two polemasts and a short bowsprit with jib boom but neither main nor schooner-mast boom; her sails were loose footed.

Small fishing vessels with their rig deriving, like the *speeljachts*, from the early Dutch *torentuig* could have been built with a flat, pinque or round stern, but could also been double-ended like the American Chebacco Boat and Block Island Boat. Some carried gaffs, others a rig known as bermudian, which had a direct link to the Dutch origin (see Chapter 1, How it began).

Only two of the surviving four Admiralty schooner draughts of that period could possibly provide an idea of American merchant or fishery schooners. Draught 4520/64 depicts a 'Marblehead schooner built at New York in July

1767', while the other draught is of *Chaleur*, which was only rigged as schooner during the last four months of her naval life. An older model of the Marblehead-type schooner[73] exists at the Smithsonian Institute in Washington DC, where it is listed as a fishing schooner known as a 'heel tapper'. This model is in its lines and general appearance very like the draught of 1767, although the gun ports are not shown. The other two surviving Admiralty draughts of American vessels *Sultana* and *Halifax* can be compared with Chapman's schooner-rigged packet (XLII/4) and their lay out and sheer plans were certainly European-inspired.

An early nineteenth-century draught of an English-designed merchant schooner has the distinction of being the oldest known draught of an Australian-built vessel. 'Schooner For Port Jackson' of 1802/03 is a draught with an interesting story. Captain Arthur Phillip, Commander of the First Fleet, set foot on Australian soil on 26 January 1788 with 736 convicts, 206 marines and an assortment of officials, servants and children in his care and founded the penal colony of New South Wales. A penal colony relied on there being minimal chance for convicts to escape, which meant

The American schooner *Baltick* of 1765 by an unknown artist. (*Courtesy of Peabody Museum, Salem, Massachusetts*)

American schooner *Fame* (1795) of Salem, Massachusetts, shown in a watercolour by William Ward (1800). (*Courtesy of Peabody Museum, Salem, Massachusetts*)

that private building of ships or any kind of vessel was strictly forbidden. However, eight months after founding the colony Philip, now Governor, sent a despatch to London regarding the difficulties of keeping in regular contact with the penal outpost, Norfolk Island, without extra craft. He stressed the need for two vessels of 30 to 40 tons, which should be sent out in frame, and a few shipwrights to build them. The Governor repeated his plea in August 1790 when he specifically asked for two small schooners and a barge for river transport. These two letters caused the Admiralty to act and on 14 February 1792 a schooner of 41 tons in frame arrived in Sydney aboard the *Pitt*. After being put together she was named *Francis* and taken into service on 24 July 1793. Indispensable in transporting coal from Newcastle, grain from the farm settlements on the Hawkesbury River and for maintaining the link to Norfolk Island, *Francis* was the first Australian schooner and the motherland's answer to Governor Philip's first request. After serving the colony for more than a decade she stranded on a beach near Newcastle harbour on 21 March 1805.

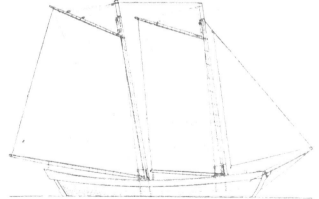

Eighteenth-century American Pinky (Chebacco Boat).

Although they had sent one vessel, the Admiralty did not meet all the Governor's needs. Understandably, providing vessels for a little penal colony on the other side of the world would not have been high on the Admiralty's agenda, particularly in light of the Government-imposed restrictions, and

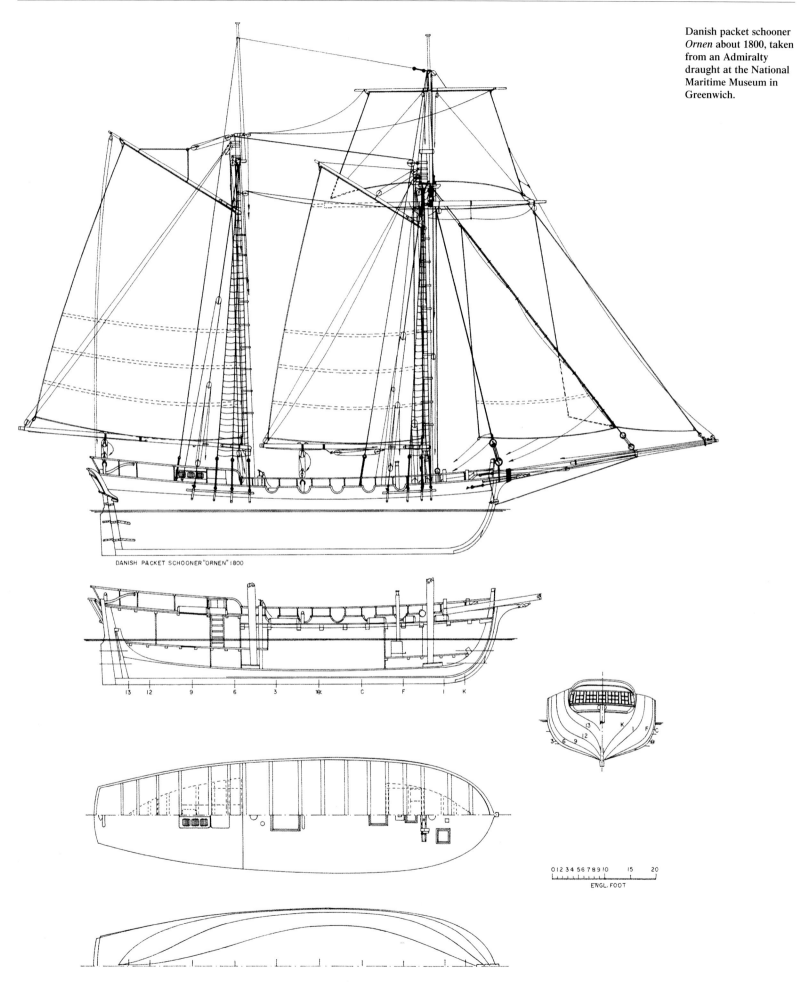

DANISH PACKET SCHOONER "ORNEN" 1800

Danish packet schooner *Ornen* about 1800, taken from an Admiralty draught at the National Maritime Museum in Greenwich.

0 1 2 3 4 5 6 7 8 9 10   15   20
ENGL. FOOT

Portuguese small vessel
Lancha do Alto **from the**
Tejo estuary, about 1790.
(J H Röding, *Wörter*
Buch Der Marine **[1794]**
plate XXXVIII).

to produce the drawings of two vessels, which were exactly those specified so many years before by Governor Arthur Phillip. One was a sailing vessels of 60 tons and the other a flat-bottomed, swim-headed barge. The sailing vessel draught showed an alternate mast set up, as one-masted sloop and as schooner. With the draughts prepared in 1802, last-minute corrections in mast positioning and some construction lines were made in January 1803 and a note on the draughts advised that: 'A Copy of this was sent to Chatham 22th January 1803 to be forwarded to the *Calcutta* bound to Port Jackson'.

HMS *Calcutta* sailed on 24 April 1803 together with the store ship *Ocean* to establish another penal colony at the newly discovered Port Phillip Bay. In a letter to the Governor of New South Wales (dated November 1803, shortly after arrival at Port Phillip Bay), *Calcutta*'s Captain Woodriff also stated that he had 'furniture for a schooner and a sailing barge to be built at Port Jackson', a fact also confirmed in a Governor's despatch to London in which Governor King wrote:

events in revolutionary France gave them more serious concerns. Put on ice for the duration of the conflict in France, the colony's need for further transport vessels was considered again when peace returned for a short while. In the knowledge that there was already a certain shipbuilding capacity in Sydney, the Admiralty ordered the Navy Board

'I have received the plans of two vessels, also masts and other spars which Captain Woodriff informs me together with the copper work is designed for those vessels; one of which will be begun as soon as possible after *Calcutta*'s departure, as that ship has taken away every carpenter we have to repair her defects.' [74]

'A schooner with a View of New York' (about 1780) by Dominic Serres from his *Liber Nauticus* (1805).

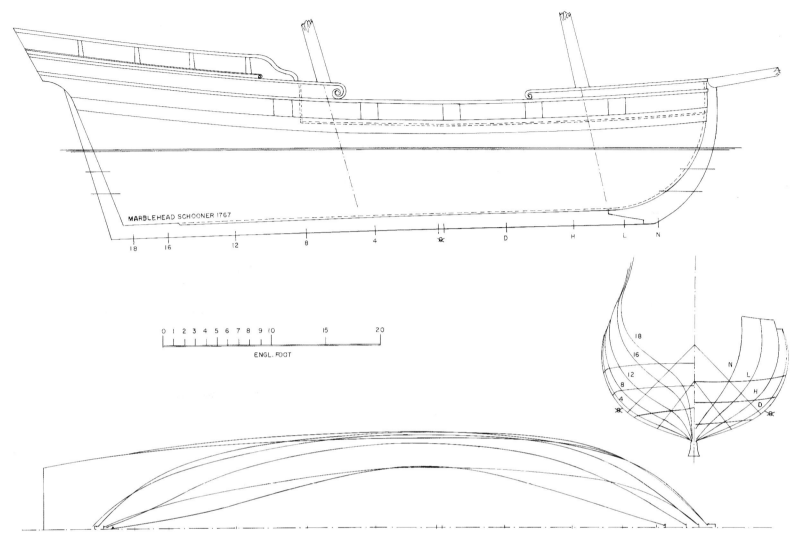

MARBLEHEAD SCHOONER 1767

ENGL. FOOT

It cannot be ascertained from available historic sources whether a government vessel was actually built according to the 'Schooner For Port Jackson' draught, but the keel of a private schooner of similar dimensions and tonnage was laid in Sydney in 1805 and launched in March 1807 for the Sydney merchant Thomas Reiby. The *Mercury*, as she was named, was the only schooner of that size dimensions constructed at that time. Reiby was an influential former ship's officer and trader and it is highly possible that he bought the draught, furniture, copper and masts etc, from a Governor who had no need for these particular items. *Mercury* made several voyages, traded with Fiji and other places in the South Sea until she was wrecked on 2 March 1813 at Shoal Haven[75]. No contemporary illustration of that vessel exists but one can assume that the 'Schooner for Port Jackson' and *Mercury* are identical. The schooner's significance to early Australian trading is recognised today with the author's drawing of the vessel on the Australian 20 Dollar note.

Dimensions of the 'Schooner For Port Jackson 1802/03' as given on the draught:

Length on the range of the Deck	53ft
of the keel for Tonnage	42ft 2in
Breadth Extreme	17ft 6in
Depth in Hold	8ft
Burthen in Tons	60 $^{13}\!/_{94}$

The two-sheet draught is now in the care of the National Maritime Museum at Greenwich (Nos 4533 and 4534, Box 64). The draught consists of a sheer plan with superimposed longitudinal view, line drawings, a deck plan and frame disposition. The sheer plan shows two rigging propositions (schooner and sloop) and ticked lines mark late corrections to masts, bowsprit and a few waterlines. The vessel represents a small merchant craft for the transportation of goods and is not dissimilar from those in North European and American waters. The only real difference is the stern.

Marblehead schooner, developed from an Admiralty draught at the National Maritime Museum in Greenwich.

Miniature model in a bottle of *Earl Of Egmont* (1767) a Marblehead schooner. *(Model by and photo courtesy of Mr Bernd Braatz, Berlin)*

Usually designed with an overhanging stern and counter, the stern on this early Australian schooner is that of a boat, more at home with Baltic galeasses, yacht-schooners or English shallops. Why that type of stern construction was chosen for the colonial schooner remains a mystery. The Navy Board probably expected only a limited shipbuilding practice in the young colony and therefore kept the vessel's structure as simple as possible.

Those unpretentious schooner-rigged vessels earned a good reputation for trading from or to small ports. Their extreme manoeuvrability together with their need for fewer deckhands than equally sized single-masted vessels made them the ideal cargo carrier, and after the first full century of development the schooner sailed on all seven seas. The years after the Napoleonic wars added even more dimensions to their already colourful trading palette.

Fast-running schooners built in America, Britain or North Germany transported fresh and dried fruit from the Mediterranean to Northern European harbours. Malaga, Messina and Mentone were the main trading ports for fresh fruit, whilst the port of Triest dealt mostly in currants and

'Homecoming', an oil painting by the author of the schooner *Mercury* entering Sydney Cove, Port Jackson, New South Wales.

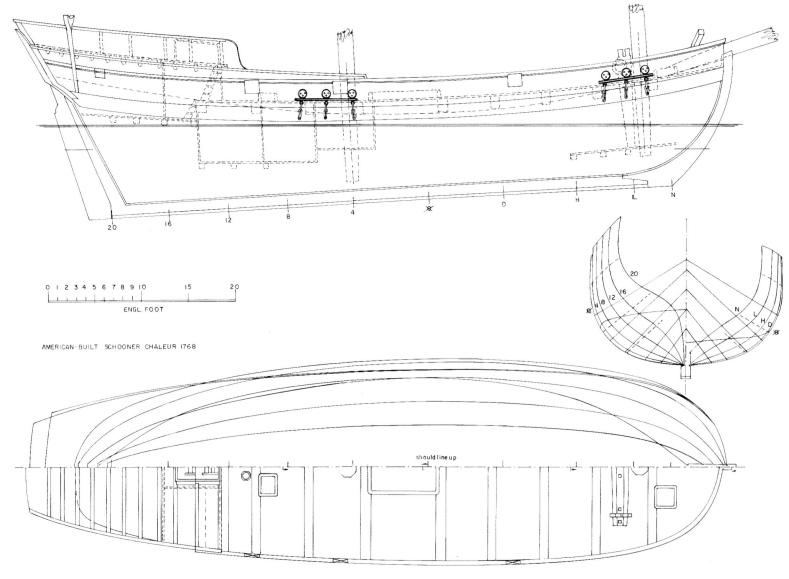

0 1 2 3 4 5 6 7 8 9 10   15   20

ENGL. FOOT

AMERICAN-BUILT SCHOONER CHALEUR 1768

should line up

Schooner *Chaleur*, developed from an Admiralty draught.

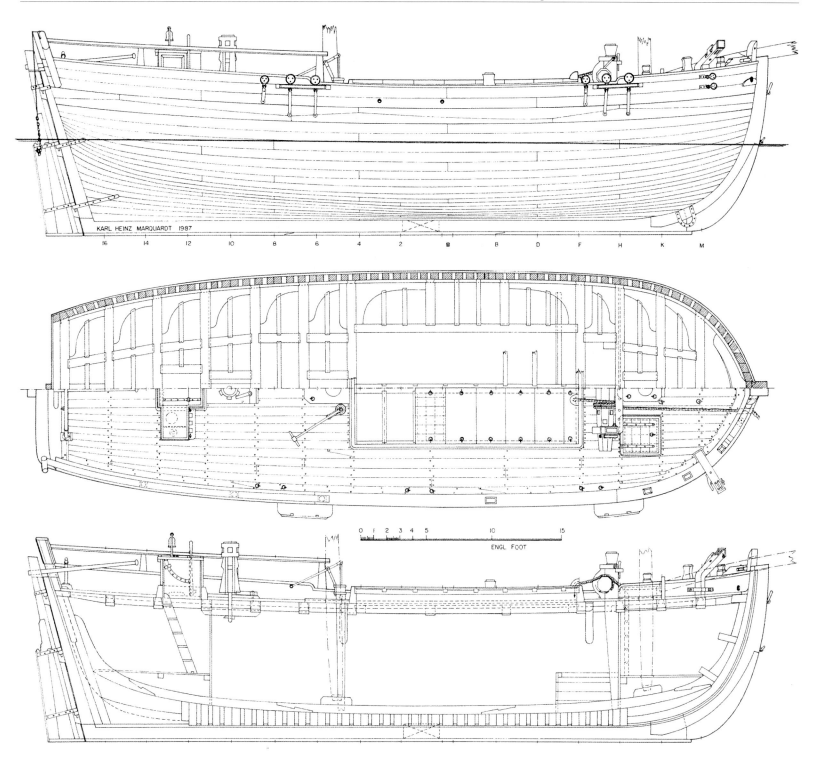

KARL HEINZ MARQUARDT 1987

16 14 12 10 8 6 4 2 ⊠ B D F H K M

0 1 2 3 4 5   10   15

ENGL FOOT

sultanas, etc. As there was a risk of damage if too large a quantity of fruit was packed into one vessel, the fresh fruit trade usually employed vessels smaller than 150 tons. Known as fruit clippers or *fruchtjagers* by the public these fast vessels were mainly schooners from England, Bremen and the lower Weser River. Bremen schooners were known for their speed and were employed not only by the merchants of that city but also those of Hamburg and other Nordic states. In their usual route they sailed west with salt to Newfoundland, where they took on a load of dry cod – the common lent fare of Southern Europe's catholic population – and, completing the circuit, brought back fresh fruit to England and the continental North Sea ports. Some of those

fast British schooners, such as *Time* and *Hellas*, later ventured into the Far Eastern opium trade. H Szymanski[76] mentioned 16 *fruchtjager* sailing from Bremen in 1841 and 24 leaving Blankenese (Hamburg) in 1846. Another German maritime writer, O Höver[77], spoke of a model of the schooner *Delphin* of 1839 as being the typical fruit clipper of the Lower Weser. Based on the Baltimore Clipper model, it is not known if the schooner was bought in America or built on the Lower Weser from an American pattern. She was registered in Bremen from 1839 to 1842 as topsail schooner and later as schooner-brig (brigantine); her flag number was 144, she had 85 lasts, she was captained by B Spille and owned by J A Graesers Handlung, Bremen.

'Schooner For Port Jackson' (1802/03): sheer plan, deck arrangements and longitudinal view. Based on a draught at the National Maritime Museum, Greenwich

Model of *Mercury* ex
'Schooner For Port
Jackson':
½-inch scale,
starboard side view
with frames visible.
*(Model and photograph
by the author)*

At the other end of the schooner scale was the full-bodied koff. Originating from the Netherlands, she was soon as popular in German North Sea ports, especially along the Friesian coast where banks of sand and mud fell dry during the outgoing tide, known as the Wattenmeer. Not all of these vessels had a schooner rig, the more typical rig being one-and-a-half masted. In 1850 889 koffs were registered in the Netherlands with 297 alone at the East Friesian inland port of Papenburg, and many of these were known as schooner koffs, with their size ranging from 25 to 300 tons. The great number of koffs in all ports between Amsterdam and Hamburg suggests that these were viewed as the ideal merchant craft for most of the traded goods and the conditions of the North Sea's southern coast. Although they were not always the fastest vessels, they were reliable. Round-built fore and aft, they were roomy and had a flat bottom to stand

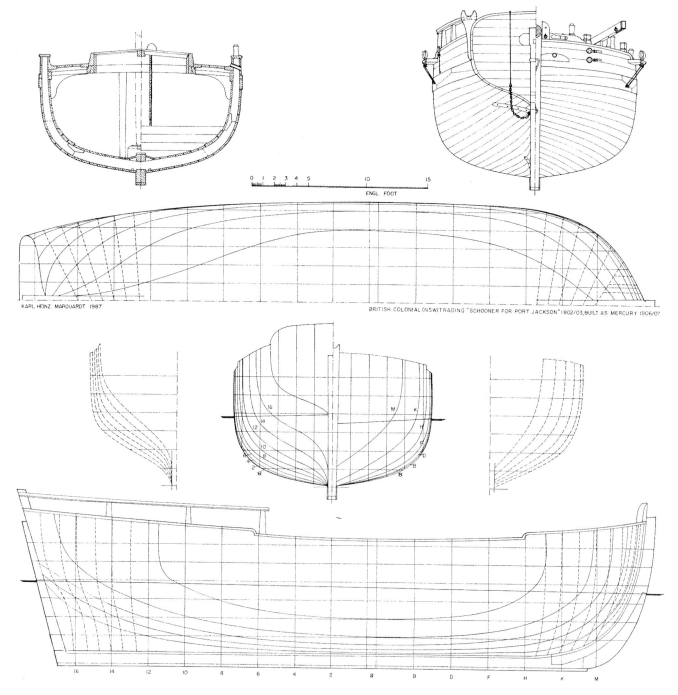

'Schooner For Port
Jackson' (1802/03): line
drawings, bow and stern
view, main frame fore
and aft cross sections.

Mercury ex 'Schooner For Port Jackson': portside with planked bottom.
(Model and photograph by the author)

Mercury ex 'Schooner For Port Jackson': starboard stern three-quarter view.
(Model and photograph by the author)

Complete rigging plan of 'Schooner For Port Jackson' (1802–03).

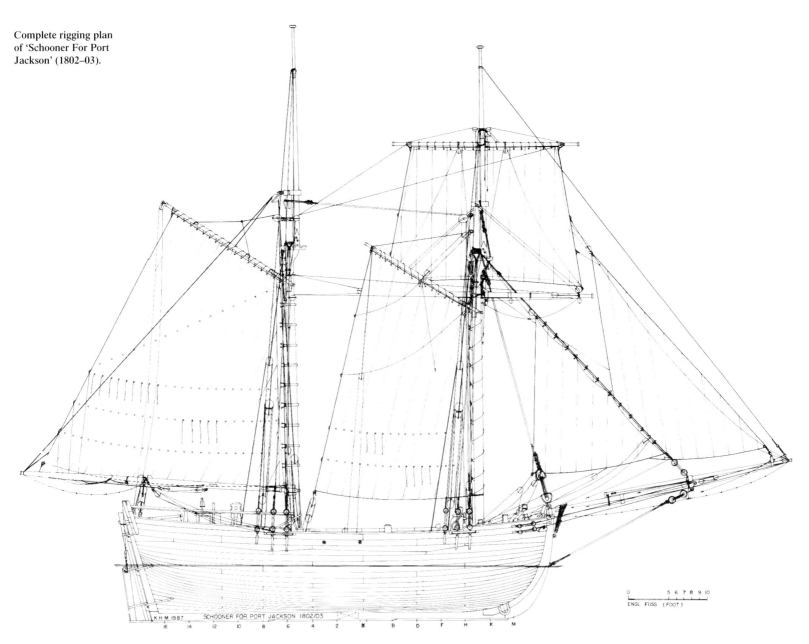

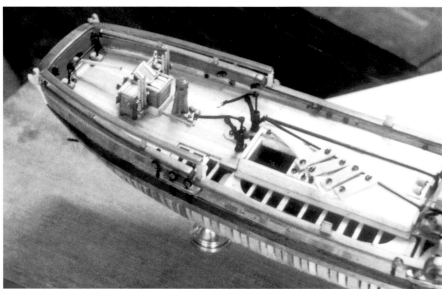

Mercury ex 'Schooner For Port Jackson': starboard deck details without masts and rigging.
(Model and photograph by the author)

upright on the mudflats when the tide went out. Their sailing abilities were not very laudable as an old Friesian proverb makes clear: '*Kuffen un Smakken sünd Waterbakken, Prunkers op the Ree un Dwarsdriwers op Sea*' (Koffs and Smacks are water troughs, show-offs in the roadstead but obstructionists at sea). An 1840 draught and model of the 96-ton schooner koff *Concordia* can be found at the Maritiem Museum 'Prins Hendrik' in Rotterdam. *Concordia* was built at Pekla and had a length of 101 Groningen feet. E Pâris provides another draught of a 250-ton schooner built in 1841[78], which includes a very detailed rigging plan and a sail plan marked with dotted lines.

H Menzel[79], a historian on German coastal craft and author of two books, built an excellent model of an 1840 Dutch schooner koff of 100 lasts by following a draught held at the Nederlands Scheepvaartmuseum in Amsterdam and a sail plan of another Rotterdam-built vessel of the same year.

Soon after the guns fell silent and peace returned to Europe and the New World, attention turned to the abolition

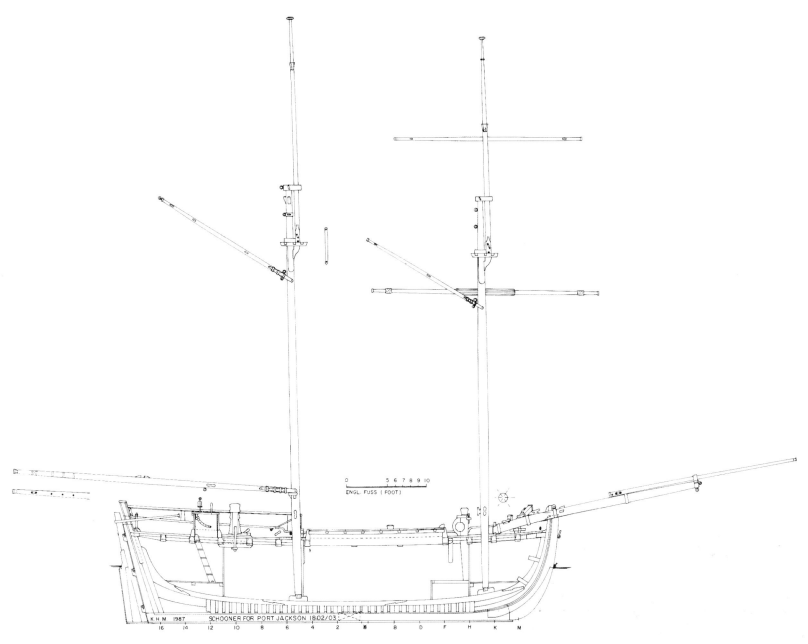

ENGL. FUSS (FOOT)

K H M 1987   SCHOONER FOR PORT JACKSON 1802/03

of the slave trade. England had already freed all her slaves in the colonies before the end of the Napoleonic Wars and other nations joined in treaties to suppress the trade completely. The transportation of slaves from Africa to America had no official backing anymore and became illegal. The mode of transport changed from larger, roomier ships to faster, smaller craft to avoid that ever-increasing net of naval surveillance. In 1820 the US Congress passed an act that made slave-trading an act of piracy, therefore a capital crime punishable by death, but with a good profit to be made there was always an adventurous or criminal element in the community to defy the law. How profitable this trade with human life was can be shown in the example of the American slaver *Henriquetta*, which made six trips to the African coast before being captured by the British frigate *Sybille* and turned into the successful slaver-chaser *Black Joke*. During those six trips she landed 3,040 slaves in Brazil and made $400,000 for her owners in less then three years. Considering this in twenty-first-century terms, it was a multi-million-dollar profit. Decreasing in numbers, slave

trading went on until the American Civil War, but the blockade of the African coast and other stringent measures dealt its commercial death-knell in the years between 1845 and 1850. Initially the vessels favoured for the illegal trade were the many lightly built and obsolete brig- or schooner-rigged privateers of the last war, mostly Baltimore Clippers. In later years the shipyards along Chesapeake Bay specialised in lightly built, unpretentious, fast schooners for slavers and Baltimore Clipper became synonymous with this cruel business. Their length was usually in the range of 80–100 feet and they over-rigged for speed. Like wartime privateers, slave-carrying vessels had a built-in obsolescence, cheaply constructed without any expensive decoration, and most of them would not have been built to a draught but to a half-model. They only had to last for a number of voyages across the Atlantic before they were discarded. Some of the vessels were taken into naval service after capture and these provide us with the few draughts that remain. The Baltimore-built, 172-ton schooner *Dos Amigos* was captured off the coast of Africa in 1831 and purchased by the Royal Navy as *Fair*

Longitudinal plan, with all masts and spars, of 'Schooner For Port Jackson' (1802/03).

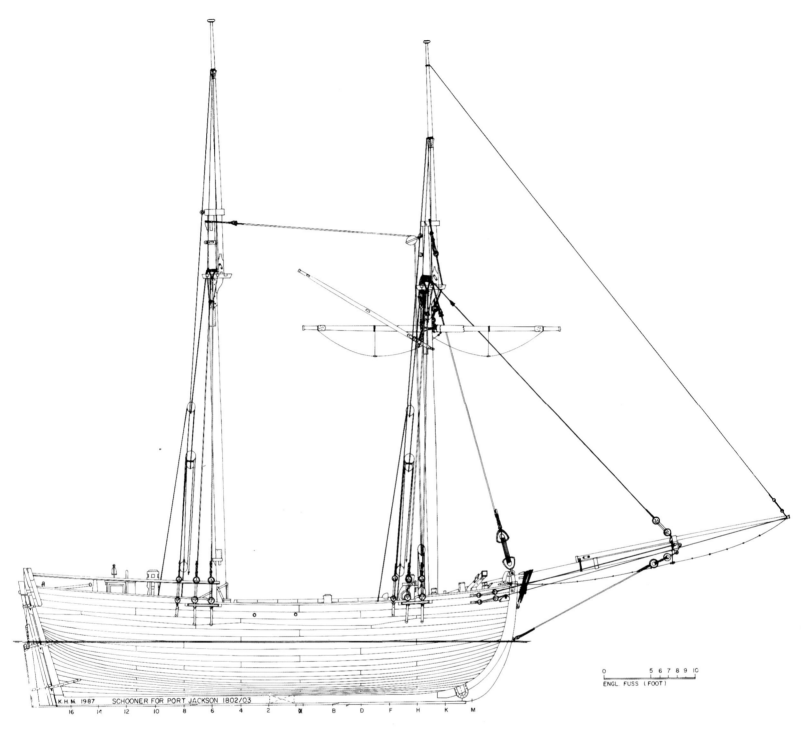

K.H.M. 1987   SCHOONER FOR PORT JACKSON 1802/03

ENGL. FUSS (FOOT)

Standing rigging on 'Schooner For Port Jackson' (1802/03).

Rosamond. Her dimensions as taken off in Portsmouth 10 October 1832 were:

Length on the range of the Deck	83ft 0in
Length on the keel	61ft 1½in
Length for tonnage	74ft 11¼in
Breadth over gunwales	23ft 2¼in
Breadth moulded	22ft 8¼in
Breadth for tonnage	23ft ¼in
Depth in Hold	10ft 4½in
Burthen in tons	172 ²⁷⁄₉₄

The *Dos Amigos* drawing shows the one 32-pdr carronade on its mid-ships pivot mount, which was so typical on slavers.

From a listing in David Lyons' *Sailing Navy List* (p.293) we learn that, as *Fair Rosamond*, the vessel had a crew of 40 men and carried an 18-pdr carronade and a bored-up 18-pdr carriage gun. She was broken up in 1845.

As we have discovered, schooner rigs were useful in nearly every aspect of naval warfare as well as in maritime trade. One cannot follow in depth every line of service or trade for which the schooner was used, nor can every hull type with a schooner rig be registered. A good example is the Danish schooner-yacht, a merchant vessel with a full bow and flat, large stern, like the 'Schooner For Port Jackson' but with finer underwater lines. Evidence of pre-1850 use of the schooner rig on this particular hull is lacking here. For similar reasons locally important trading or fishing vessels from

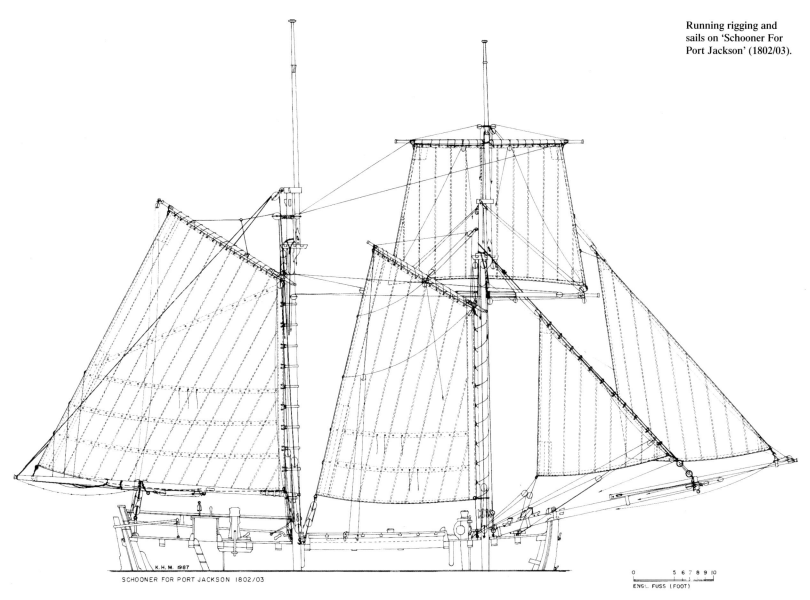

SCHOONER FOR PORT JACKSON 1802/03

0 5 6 7 8 9 10
ENGL. FUSS (FOOT)

K.H.M. 1987

around the world will remain unnoticed. The field of global use of the schooner grew so large that not every detail can be reported in one book. However, their employment in the sealing and whaling trade was big enough not to be disregarded. It is known that in 1818 the *Elizabeth and Henry*, a 92-ton schooner built with convict labour in Port Maquarie, Hobart, sailed with a sealing gang to Maquarie Island. Other sealing schooners working during the first half of the nineteenth century in that lucrative trade in the Southern Ocean included *Sally, Governor Brisbane* and *Caroline*. Whalers in the waters near Tasmania included the schooners *Australian*, built in Hobart in 1825, *Elizabeth and Mary* of 92 tons and the first vessel built in Van Diemens Land, the 40-ton schooner *Henrietta*, launched in 1812. Sealing and whaling turned the convict settlement Hobart, in the first half-century of its existence, into a very prosperous town.[80]

Another two outstanding aspects of schooner use must not go without notice: exploring and mapping our globe. Not all vessels involved were naval ships like the 1829-built cutter-schooners *Lark* and *Starling* of 107 tons (Africa), or the cutter *Bramble* of 161 tons. Known from a sail plan to have been schooner-rigged when she entered the service in 1842, *Bramble* saw much service in the East Indies and in Chinese

Model of the Bremen *fruchtjager* (fruit clipper) *Delphin* of 1839. (*Courtesy of Focke Museum, Bremen*)

A Dutch schooner *koff*
of 250 tons (1841) from
E Pâris, *Souvenirs de
Marine*, Vol. 1/45.

MARINE HOLLANDAISE

Plan d'un Kof de 250 tonneaux 1841

Dessin du a Mr Wickers, Capitaine de Vaisseau, Ministre de la marine 1878

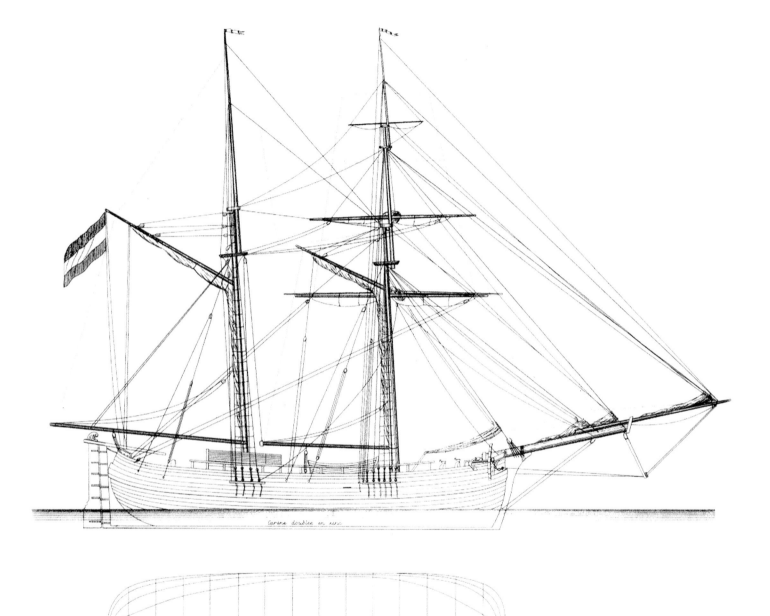

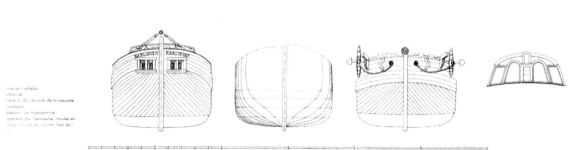

Model of a Dutch schooner *koff* of 100 lasts (1840): portside view.
(Model by and photograph courtesy of Mr Horst Menzel, Hamburg)

Model of a Dutch schooner *koff* of 100 lasts (1840): portside deck view.
(Photograph courtesy of Mr Horst Menzel, Hamburg)

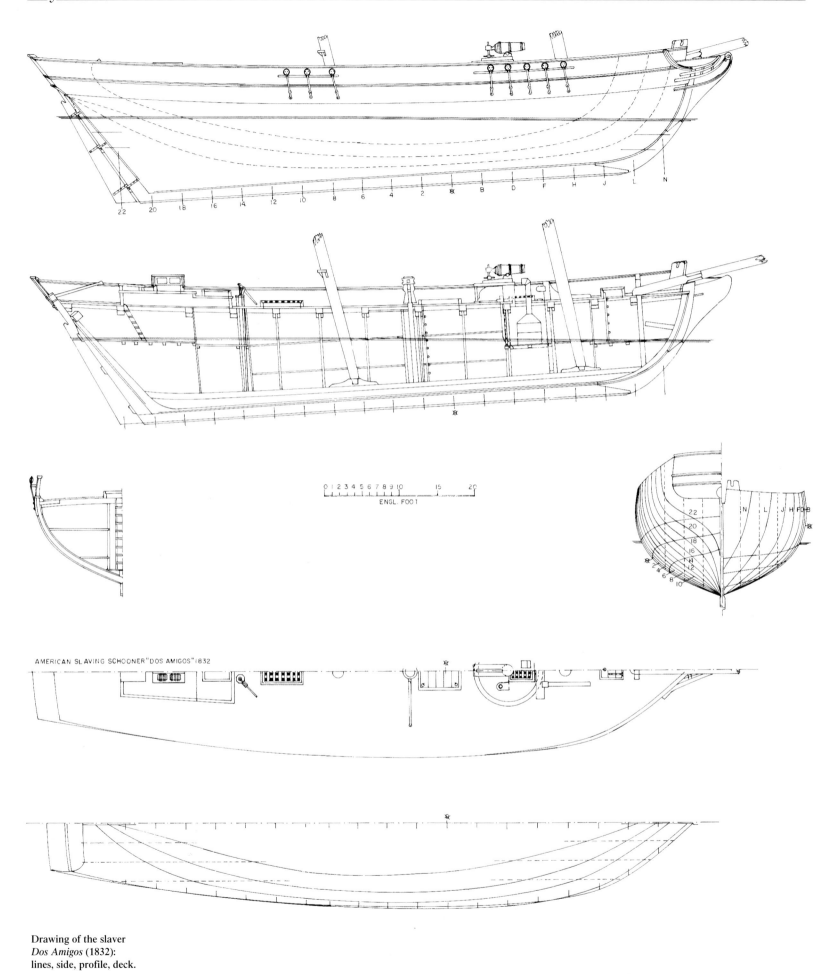

AMERICAN SLAVING SCHOONER "DOS AMIGOS" 1832

0 1 2 3 4 5 6 7 8 9 10   15   20
ENGL. FOOT

Drawing of the slaver
Dos Amigos (1832):
lines, side, profile, deck.

AMERICAN SLAVER "DOS AMIGOS" 1832

waters. As a tender to HMS *Fly* and HMS *Rattlesnake* she was active between 1842 and 1850 surveying the Great Barrier Reef, the Torres Strait and the coast of New Guinea. In the 1850s she was handed to the New South Wales Government as a tender, whereby, as an early photo from 1859 indicates, her rig reverted to a single-masted cutter. Sold in December 1876 to be used as a lightship, she was broken up in Sydney in 1885. The earliest known schooner in survey service was the small 67-ton Marblehead schooner *Sally,* which was purchased by the Royal Navy in 1763 and named *Grenville* (see Chapter 2). She was James Cook's first independent command and for five years he surveyed in her the stormy coasts of Labrador and Newfoundland.

It was during the famous *Beagle*'s first survey voyage to the south coast of South America that Captain Phillip Parker King bought, in Rio, the captured slaver-schooner *Bella Josephine* of 95 tons to speed up his survey assignment. Captain King renamed her *Adelaide* and she remained in the Royal Navy as tender at Rio Station. During that period *Beagle* rescued the crew of another schooner, the British sealer *Prince Of Saxe Coburg,* at the western entrance to the Magellan strait. On *Beagle*'s second survey voyage to these inhospitable lands Captain Robert FitzRoy hired two small schooners of 9 and 15 tons, the *Paz* and *Liebre,* for coastal

survey around Bahia Blanca. Some months later in March 1833 he tried to emulate Phillip King by purchasing, in Port Luis on the Falkland Islands, the 170-ton sealing schooner *Unicorn,* renaming her *Adventure* after *Beagle*'s store ship of the first voyage. But unlike King's purchase, the Admiralty did not sanction his transaction and after accomplishing some survey work at the Falkland Islands and various other places *Adventure* had to be disposed of in Valparaiso in August 1834. She had a fore-and-aft rig when purchased and in January 1834 was changed to topsail schooner. FitzRoy also hired another small schooner, the *Constitucion,* to search for the first two vessels, which had left on their survey assignment eight months before and from which no word had been heard. During that part of the famous 'Darwin' voyage, Robert FitzRoy therefore had the use of four schooners. Another schooner crossed *Beagle*'s path during her third voyage, the Australian survey. A land-exploring party under Lieutenant George Grey had been taken aboard *Beagle* for an expedition into Northwestern Australia, and in Cape Town this group hired the schooner *Lynher* to sail directly to the north-west Cape. Seven months later *Beagle,* searching for the party which was by then overdue, found *Lynher* short of food in Hanover Bay and came across the ill and famished Grey expedition several days later.[81]

Rigging of the slaver *Dos Amigos*, based on a draught at the National Maritime Museum, Greenwich.

'The Schooner *Enterprise* 1841 (Built in Hobart Town 1831)', a watercolour by George McCrea. (*Courtesy of the State Library of Victoria*)

Schooners had their well-earned place in the fifth continent's early history: the very first seagoing vessel assembled there was the *Francis,* and the *Henrietta,* a schooner of 40 tons, was the first vessel built in Tasmania in 1812; the explorer Captain Mathew Flinders was captured by the French and imprisoned on Mauritius while sailing to England in a small schooner of 29 tons, the *Cumberland*; and Australia's second largest city was 'founded' by a schooner. As a whole fleet of convicts (the First Fleet) had laid Sydney's foundations, so 47 years later Melbourne was founded when a small, unpretentious-looking Tasmanian trading schooner, the *Enterprize,* brought a handful of free settlers to the banks of the Yarra River. The pressure of overcrowded prisons in England had led to the foundation of a convict settlement on the shore of one of the most beautiful natural harbours at the other end of the world, and it was again the pressure of overcrowding that led people to sail across the treacherous Bass Strait to find land for a new settlement, only this time it was another type of overcrowding. The landowners on the Island of Van Diemens Land, today's Tasmania, grew so prosperous that the herds of sheep were running out of space. Founded just three decades before on the River Derwent, after a failed settlement attempt inside Port Phillip Bay, the small township of Hobart developed quickly into a busy harbour. The island turned into a thriving farming community, which only a decade after settlement began exporting grain, potatoes and hides to Sydney; its main harbours, Hobart and later Launceston, were soon recognized by international whalers and sealers as ideal places for purchasing fresh vegetables, meat and livestock. Industry in other ship goods, repair or building of vessels also began to flourish. It became the hub of South Pacific whaling and sealing. This early pioneer atmosphere gave rise to a small full-bodied trading schooner of 55 tons, the *Enterprize.* She was registered on 7 July at the Port of Hobart Town under No.4/1830 as being built by the shipwrights William Venan and William Harvey.

Dimensions of *Enterprize*:

Length over the Range of Deck	50ft 8in
Breadth extreme	16ft 5in
Depth in Hold	8ft 3in

Schooner-rigged, she carried a standing bowsprit, had a flat stern, was cravel-built with no galleries and a scroll adorned the stem. Her first master was John Aldridge. After her first years of trading in agricultural goods, she was sold in Sydney and carried coal between the New South Wales towns of Newcastle and Sydney. In 1835, when landowners on Tasmania's north shore looked towards the mainland for new pastures, the Launceston hotel owner John Pascoe Fawkner bought the newly available *Enterprize* for £430. Describing her as a safe and sound vessel with one bow a foot wider than the other, fully built and a slow sailer, Fawkner brought her to Launceston.

There he and his settlement party, comprising a Captain John Lancey, a blacksmith James Gilbert, his wife Maggy and a farmhand Charles Wyse, boarded the vessel. Another party who could not charter their own vessel joined them: the landowner George Evans, his servant Evan Evans and two carpenters Robert Hay Marr and William Jackson. Together with the ship's crew of two deckhands and the master, Captain Peter Hunter, the full complement of people aboard came to twelve. Beside the necessary tools to start life in the wilderness and food supplies to survive for the first few months, the vessel had seeds, fruit trees, livestock (two horses, one pig, three dogs and a cat) and other farming goods aboard. Setting sail on 1 August 1835, progress was slow because of bad weather and Fawkner left the vessel at George Town to attend to his business. Their first destination was Western Port Bay where they looked for fresh water and good fertile land. Unsuccessful for a whole week, they decided on 16 August to abandon search and sail into Port Phillip Bay. After another four days of searching the bay, a larger freshwater river was found and the *Enterprize* was towed up river until, on 29 August, rapids barred further advance. There they also found fertile soil and started to build a hut. With this simple act a rapidly growing village was founded. When Governor Bourke visited the still illegal town a little over a year later, it already had a population of more than 500 and in the nearby hills over 100,000 sheep grazed. He gave the settlement his seal of approval and named the town after the British Prime Minister, Lord Melbourne.

Enterprize remained in the hands of Fawkner as the settlement's supply ship. She visited Melbourne for several years and was last mentioned in the Sydney Morning Herald of 29 July 1847 as being stranded on 5 July 1847 at the bar in the Richmond River and completely wrecked by the pounding waves with the loss of two lives[82].

The idea of an *Enterprize* rebirth took shape when a handful of history-minded Melbourne citizens founded the Enterprize Committee early in 1990 with the aim of recreating that important schooner. The author, as the marine historian of that group, created from pictures, dimensions and general contemporary nautical knowledge a set of reconstruction drawings of the schooner to produce a historically

A beginning has been made. Keel, stem and sternpost are set and first frame mouldings can be seen. The old No. 4 Storage shed on the Yarra, a remnant of the disappearing old harbour facilities, became for six years the shipwright's workshop.

The unofficial 'launch' of the vessel on 30 August 1996. The hull is picked up by a 50-ton crane and put into her natural element.

Deck details of the
Enterprize replica.

The launch of the
Enterprize on 30 August
1997 at Williamstown, a
western suburb of the
City of Melbourne.

The schooner *Enterprize* pictured sailing into Port Philip Bay, and on
a commemorative Australian $1.00 postage stamp.

The schooner's designer (author) and shipwright Eric Erikson aboard *Enterprize* after being put to water at the Melbourne Maritime Museum, about 100 metres away from the original landing site.

accurate vessel. A marine architect amended the draughts according to modern specifications for a passenger sailing vessel to get Marine Board approval. On 29 August 1991 these early efforts culminated in a ceremonial keel-laying by the Governor of Victoria, the Hon Dr D McCaughey. After a further five years the finished hull was unofficially launched on 30 August 1996 from her historic construction site (only a hundred metres from the original landing place). The Enterprize Committee dissolved through luck of funds and the rights were transferred to a newly formed Enterprize Trust.

The hull was towed across Hobson's Bay to a new construction side at Williamstown, where the new main sponsor, Mr Harry Tyrrel, made it possible to complete the fitting of masts and rigging without delay. Then on 30 August 1997, 162 years after the *Enterprize* landing on the Yarra, Mrs

Australian trading schooner *Enterprize* (1830): sheer plan, deck view and profile, cross-sections and body lines. Model plan prepared from the initial replica draughts for *Model Shipwright*.

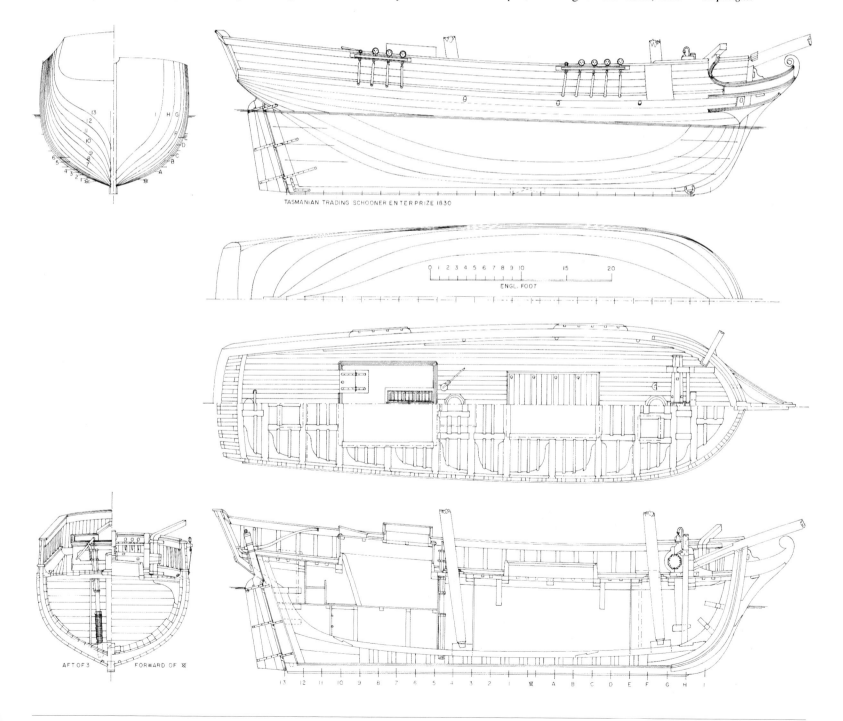

TASMANIAN TRADING SCHOONER ENTERPRIZE 1830

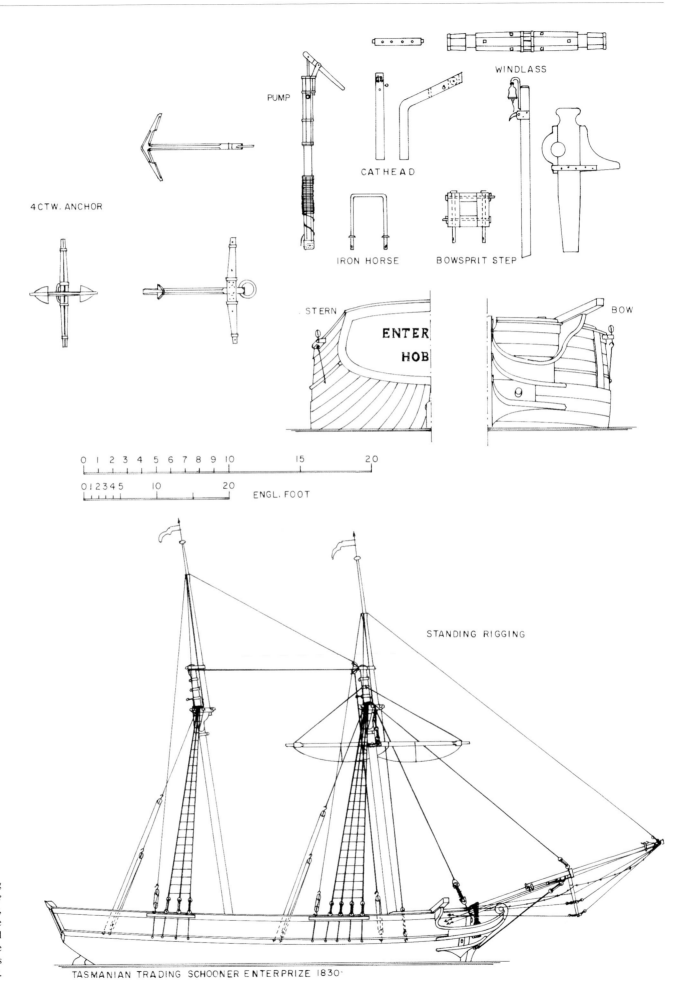

4 CTW. ANCHOR

PUMP

CATHEAD

WINDLASS

IRON HORSE

BOWSPRIT STEP

STERN

ENTER
HOB

BOW

0 1 2 3 4 5 6 7 8 9 10   15   20

0 1 2 3 4 5   10   20   ENGL. FOOT

STANDING RIGGING

Australian trading schooner *Enterprize* (1830): standing rigging, bow and stern, and some deck furniture. Model plan prepared from the initial replica draughts for *Model Shipwright*.

TASMANIAN TRADING SCHOONER ENTERPRIZE 1830·

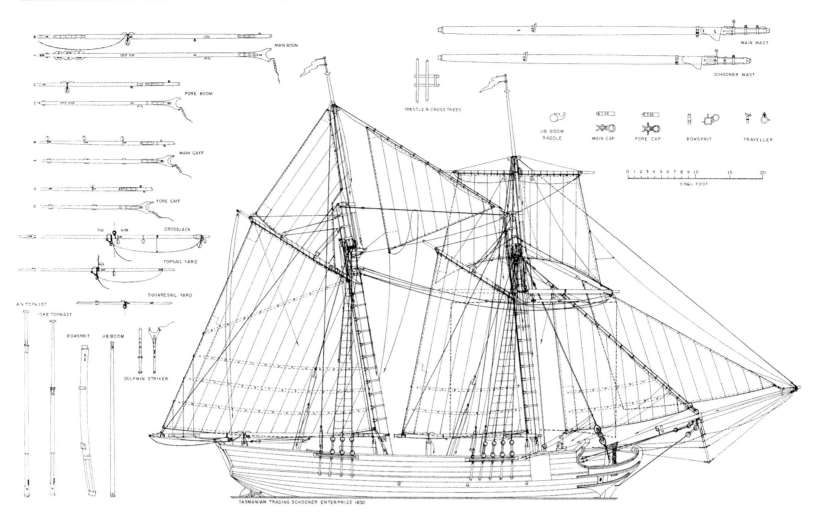

MAIN BOOM

FORE BOOM

MAIN GAFF

FORE GAFF

CROSSJACK

TOPSAIL YARD

SQUARESAIL YARD

MAIN TOPMAST

FORE TOPMAST

BOWSPRIT   JIB-BOOM

DOLPHIN STRIKER

TRESTLE & CROSS TREES

JIB BOOM SADDLE   MAIN CAP   FORE CAP   BOWSPRIT   TRAVELLER

MAIN MAST

SCHOONER MAST

0 1 2 3 4 5 6 7 8 9 10   15   20
ENGL. FOOT

TASMANIAN TRADING SCHOONER ENTERPRIZE 1830

Felicity Kenneth, the wife of the Premier Minister of Victoria, officially launched her in the presence of the Governor of Victoria, the Lord Mayor of Melbourne and the Deacon of the Anglican Church. The dream of Hedley Elliot, the initiator, and the original Enterprize Committee, came to fruition. Even with the sailing replica subject to modern specifications and not a historian's perfect dream, it brought a forgotten but historically important vessel back into the limelight of a bustling modern metropolis.

After sea trials she became a major feature on Port Phillip Bay and for a few hours returned many Melbournians to the founding days of yesteryear. *Enterprize* took part in the tall-ships race from Sydney to Hobart and sailed a few times across the 'roaring forties', recreating that historic voyage from Launceston to Port Phillip Bay. Being forgotten by so many for so long, *Enterprize* is now a household name. As a result of this exercise in rescuing a little, but significant, vessel from oblivion, 30 August is officially recognised as Melbourne Foundation Day: even small schooners can make big waves.

The story of the commercial schooner has so many facets that it cannot be discussed in full within one chapter. Much, therefore, remains unsaid and some readers may look in vain for certain aspects of vessels of which not enough detail can be found. With this small trader of the southern seas our kaleidoscope of schooner use, shape or form will come to a close, but we will have a last look at a few special vessels and early steamships that carried the rig.

Other craft

The advantages of the Peruvian balsa raft's sliding keel were known in Europe since Joris van Spilbergen sketched such a raft on to the pages of his journal in 1615. It was approximately 175 years later in 1774, in Boston, that Master's Mate John Schank, posted to the North America Station, re-invented the principle in a more formal way when he fitted a boat for Lord Percy with a sliding keel, claiming that it could be worked without a rudder. A single, long, sliding keel proved to be unpractical for larger boats and having meanwhile risen to the rank of Captain in the Royal Navy, Schank fitted, in 1789 at Deptford, three sliding keels to another boat and proposed to the Admiralty the building of a cutter with such keels. The 65-foot *Trial* cutter, built at Plymouth in 1790, proved to be a great success as a low-draught vessel and saw service on inshore patrols along the French coast. More vessels were built according to that principle with one outstanding example. The brig *Lady Nelson,* a 52-foot, 60-ton vessel built for inshore exploration with three sliding keels and nicknamed 'His Majesty's Tinderbox', was launched at Deptford on 13 January 1800. After being fitted out she sailed for Australia and became the first vessel to navigate the Bass Strait in a west–east direction, thereby discovering Port Phillip Bay. She worked for more than 20 years on the Australian coast, set up a small colony on Van Diemens Land and, to honour the inventor of her sliding keels, named a Mornington Peninsula promontory, south-east of Melbourne,

Australian trading schooner *Enterprize* (1830): complete sails and rigging, mast and spar details. Model plan prepared from initial replica design for *Model Shipwright*.

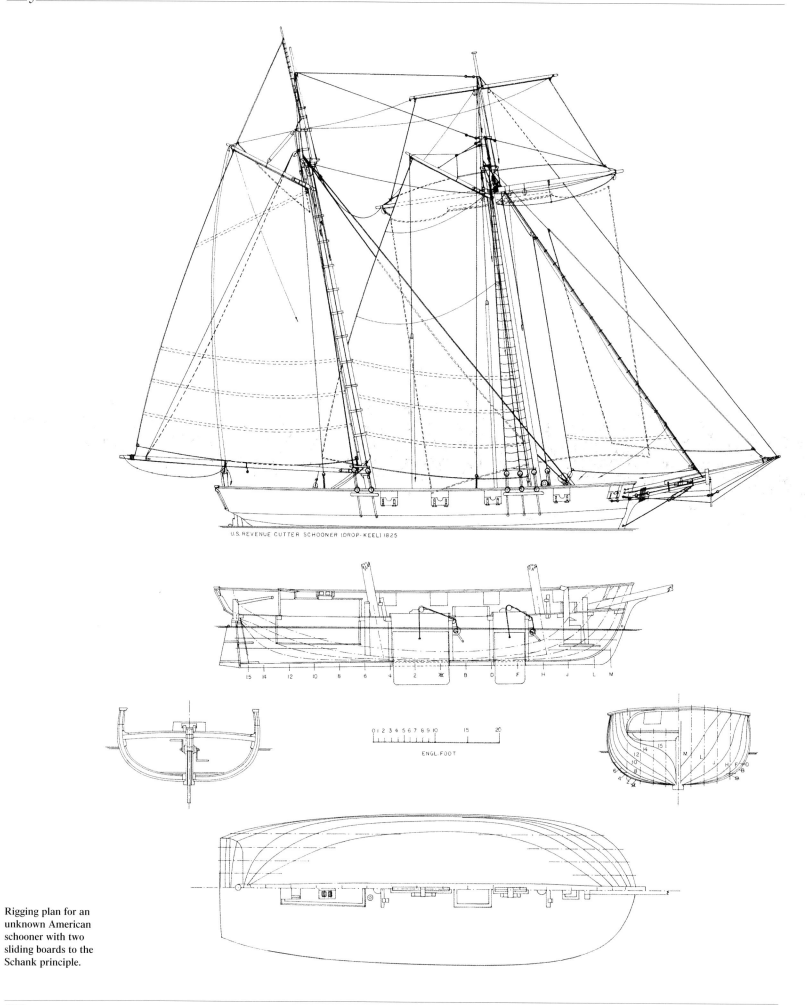

U.S. REVENUE CUTTER SCHOONER (DROP-KEEL) 1825

ENGL. FOOT

Rigging plan for an unknown American schooner with two sliding boards to the Schank principle.

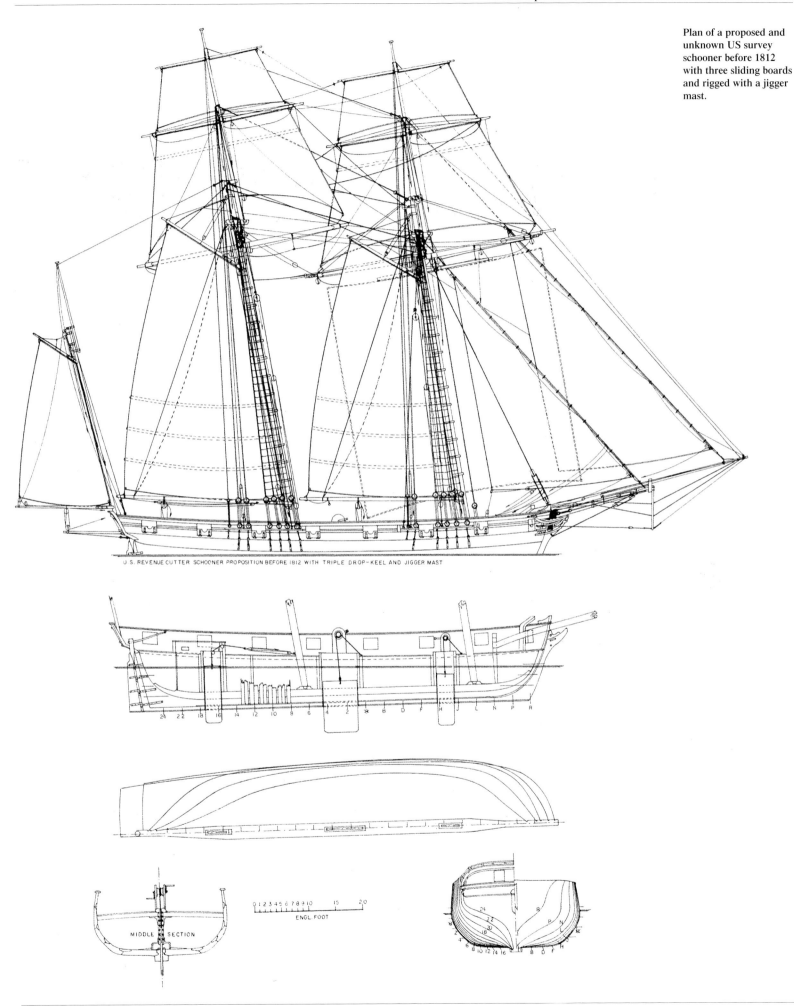

U.S. REVENUE CUTTER SCHOONER PROPOSITION BEFORE 1812 WITH TRIPLE DROP-KEEL AND JIGGER MAST

MIDDLE SECTION

ENGL. FOOT

Plan of a proposed and unknown US survey schooner before 1812 with three sliding boards and rigged with a jigger mast.

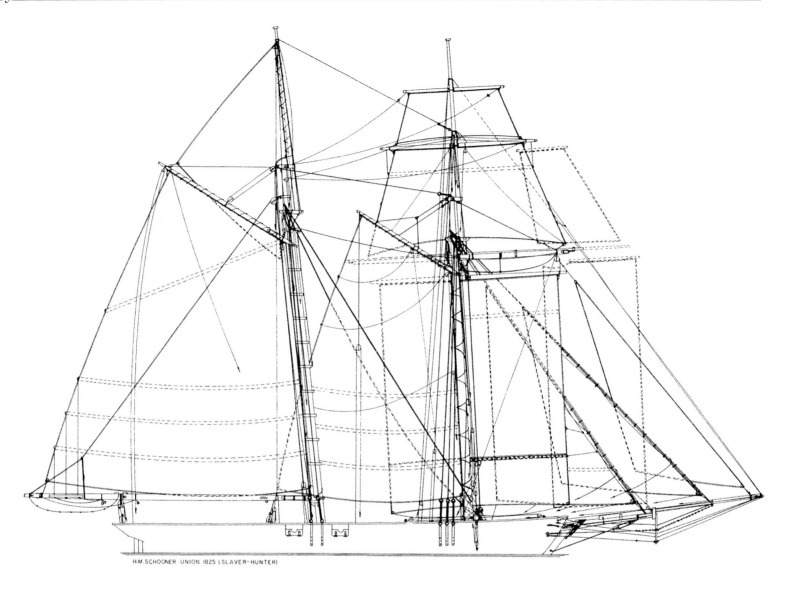

H.M. SCHOONER UNION 1825 (SLAVER-HUNTER)

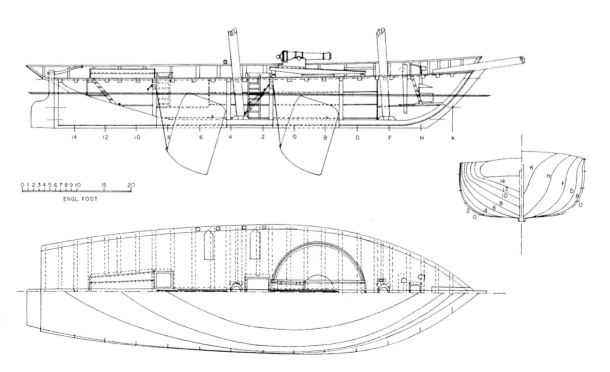

0 1 2 3 4 5 6 7 8 9 10   15   20
ENGL. FOOT

Plan of HM Schooner
Union (1823), based on
Admiralty draughts at
the National Maritime
Museum, Greenwich.

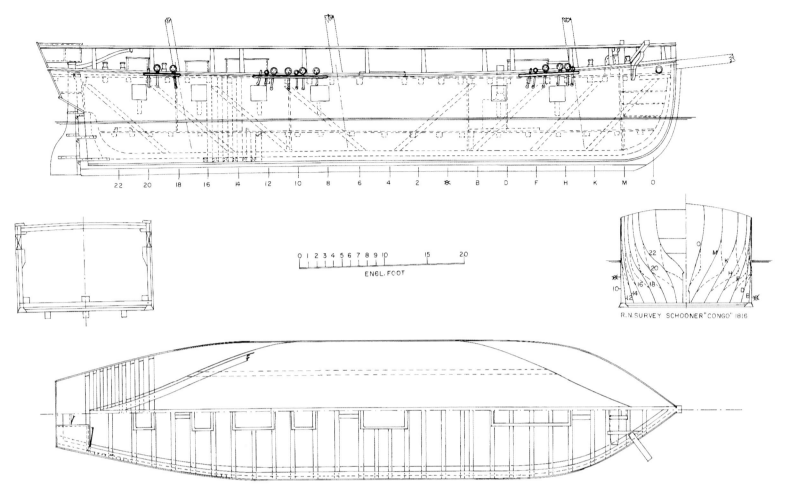

ENGL. FOOT

R.N. SURVEY SCHOONER "CONGO" 1816

Cape Schank. Her tragic end came in February 1825 when natives stormed her off Baba Island, north-east of Timor where she was driven ashore. A sliding keel schooner *Peggy* from about the same period has been preserved at the Castletown Maritime Museum, Isle of Man, while an undated American draught of a schooner with sliding keels according to Captain Schank's invention is preserved. This draught was proposed as a vessel for survey and defence of the coasts of Florida and Mexico and prepared by James Hutton of Philadelphia before 1812. Her dimensions were:

Length between perpendiculars	74ft 0in
Length on keel	57ft 10in
Moulded beam	24ft 0in
Depth in hold	6ft 6in
Armament	14 x 12-pdr carronades
	or 14 x 6-pdr carriage guns

In 1825 the famous American master shipwright William Daughty designed a class of revenue cutters with two drop-keels for being stationed in shoal waters. They were schooner-rigged vessels of 60 feet in length between perpendiculars and named *Pulaski* and *Louisiana*. The latter was stationed at New Orleans and captured the Colombian privateer schooner *Bolivia*, before being sold out of service in 1830. *Pulaski* served at the Key West Station until 1833. A further development of Captain Schank's sliding board idea was the pivoting centreboard. It's invention is considered to be that of a British naval officer named Shuldham in

1809, but an American patent was granted in 1811 at Washington to Joshua Jacobs and Henry Swain of New Jersey. As H I Chapelle notes:

> 'The introduction of the centerboard had a great effect upon the American commercial sailing vessels. Beginning with small craft – sloops and schooners – centerboards were gradually applied to vessels of greater size.' [83]

There are two known draughts of centreboard schooners, from 1823 and 1833. The earlier is of HM schooner *Union*. Built in 1821 at Kingston, Jamaica, as *City Of Kingston*, a merchant vessel of 84 tons, she was purchased into the Navy in 1823. The draught was probably established in 1823 after acquisition and has the fitting of a large pivot gun and of two small carronades each side, marked fore and aft of the mainmast. The vessel had two centreboards and remained in Royal Navy service until she was wrecked on a reef in the West Indies on 17 May 1828. Her dimensions, not marked on the draught, were approximately:

Length between pp	80ft 2in
Breadth moulded	23ft 8in
Depth in hold	6ft
Draught at rear	6ft 6in

Santiago is the second centreboard schooner of which a draught survives. Built by W H Webb at New York in 1833 for a New Orleans owner and the Cuban trade, she was, as

HM survey schooner *Congo* (1816): sheer plan, deck and cross section, based on draughts at the National Maritime Museum, Greenwich.

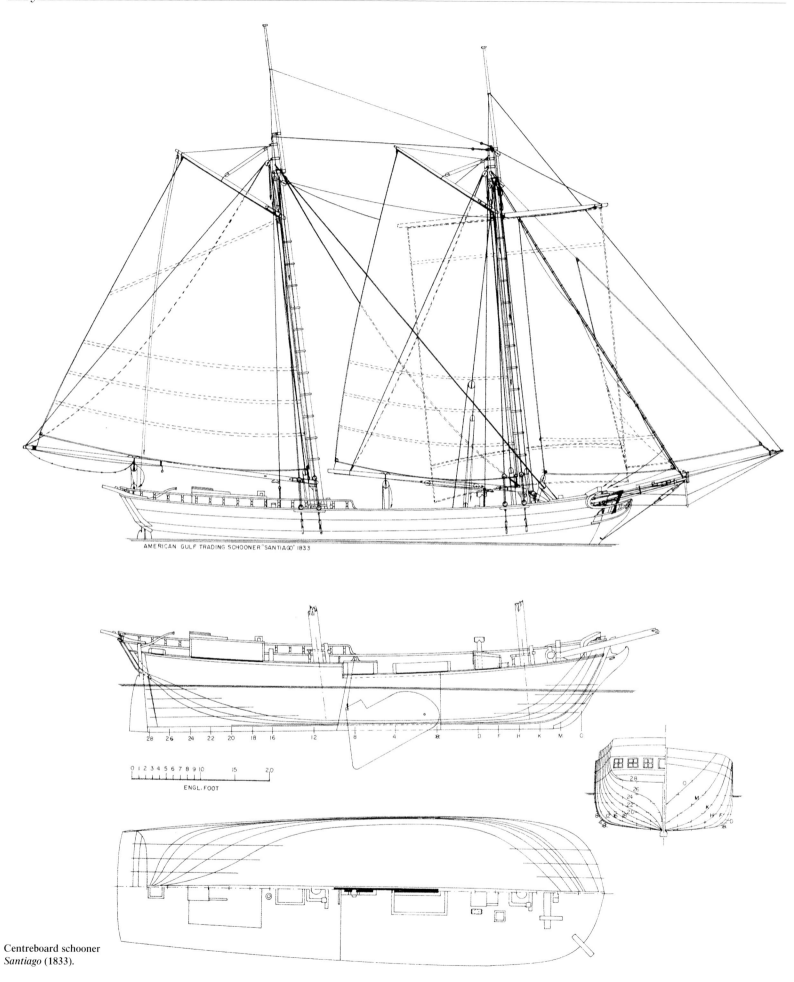

AMERICAN GULF TRADING SCHOONER "SANTIAGO" 1833

Centreboard schooner
Santiago (1833).

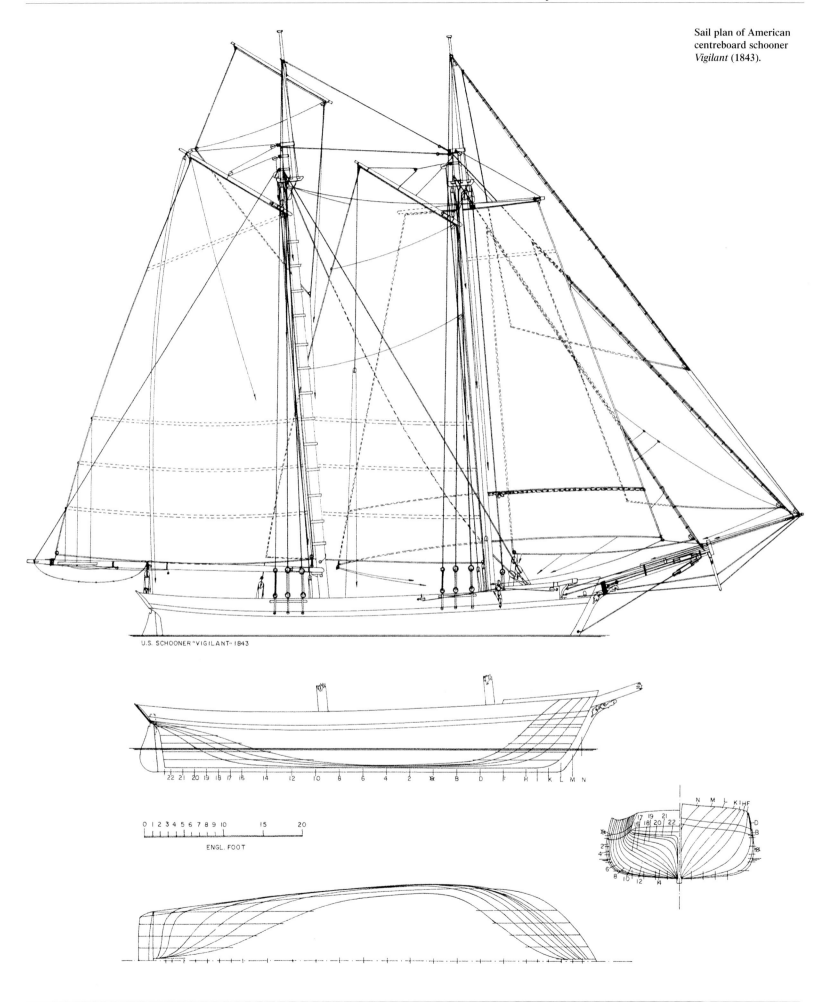

U.S. SCHOONER "VIGILANT" 1843

0 1 2 3 4 5 6 7 8 9 10   15   20

ENGL. FOOT

was *Union,* a fore-and-aft rigged schooner. In 1843 Webb built another even smaller centreboard schooner, the *Vigilant* for the US Government Shoal Water Service in the Gulf. He writes:

> 'Draft of water with 6 tons of ballast and everything on board ready for sea-voyage from New York to New Orleans, was 3 feet. Keel 6 inches below timbers. She was lost soon after arrival in a severe hurricane.' [84]

Dimensions of *Santiago* and *Vigilant*:

	Santiago	*Vigilant*
Length on Deck	67ft 3in	56ft 0in
Beam moulded	20ft 4in	8ft 5in
Depth in Hold	6ft 1in	4ft 8in
Tonnage	72 $^{55}/_{95}$	50

In the rigging of early steamships the schooner fore-and-aft and topsail rigs were predominant. With the very first steamship for the Royal Navy, *Congo* designed by Seppings, ending in failure, most of the following generations of paddle steamers were also handsome schooners. After the end of the Napoleonic Wars, an expedition was planned in 1815 to explore the River Congo and, on the suggestion of J Rennie a famous civil engineer, a steamship was built and aptly named *Congo.* Launched on 11 November 1816 at Deptford she was fitted with a Boulton & Watt 20- NHP beam engine. The 30 tons weight of the engine made her overweight, and with a draught of 8 feet 6 inches the paddles could not work properly and the vessel became very cranky. After a second dissatisfying trial her engine was removed and she became a survey schooner.

Dimensions of *Congo*:

Length	70ft
Breadth	16ft
Depth	8ft 0in
Burthen	82 $^{57}/_{94}$ tons
Armament	1 x 12-pdr carronade, 12 swivels

In 1821 the British Post Office ordered the mail packets *Lightning* and *Meteor* to be built and they began a reliable service between England and Ireland. *Lightning* was a fore-and-aft schooner that came to fame when King George IV embarked in her for Dublin on 12 August 1821. This being the first Royal steamship voyage, she was renamed *Royal Sovereign King George IV,* later shortened to *Royal Sovereign* and in 1837, when taken into the Royal Navy, she was renamed again as *Monkey.* Another *Lightning* was built in 1823 and rigged as a topsail schooner, serving as a survey ship with the Baltic Fleet until at least 1854.

Only a few years later in 1826 Captain F Hastings RN persuaded the Greeks to buy three steam warships in their fight for independence. Of these, the *Karteria* became a legend. Armed with four 68-pdr carronades, she captured or destroyed, in one year alone, 27 Turkish vessels. Her size of 400 tons made her a formidable warship. Her rig was that of a four-masted, fore-and-aft schooner. Her exploits convinced the Royal Navy of the value of steam fighting ships.

The list of famous steamships under schooner rig is long but only a few more shall be considered, since this book is mainly aimed toward the pure sailing ship. A small paddle steamer was built in 1829 by Caleb Smith of Liverpool to serve as a ferry on the river Mersey. Being later on the Belfast–Dublin–London service, she was bought in 1837 by the newly formed Peninsular Steam Navigation Company. Her name was *William Fawcett* and she is now seen as the first ship of the famous P & O Line. With a length of only 87 feet she could accommodate 12 passengers; she was rigged as topsail schooner.

Sirius, the first ship to cross the Atlantic under continuous steam power, in 18 days and 10 hours, was also a two-masted topsail schooner. Of 703 tons she had a length of 208 feet; her engines had 320 NHP and were of the side-lever type. She left Cork Harbour on 4 April 1838 and when she arrived in New York her average speed had been 6.7 knots. Another first Atlantic crossing by a screw-propelled iron vessel bettered that time by 3 days and 13 hours: the famous *Great Britain* set this new record in 1845 with an average speed of 9.3 knots. The *Great Britain,* the largest schooner in the epoch under consideration, was built at Bristol between 1839 and 1843 to plans by I K Brunel and was rigged as a six-masted schooner with the mainmast topsail rigged.

Principal dimensions of *Great Britain*:

Length between pp	322ft
Breadth extreme	50ft 6in
Depth in hold	32ft 6in
Draught	16ft
Gross tonnage	2936 tons
Passenger capacity	360

Notes:

[70] Baker, W A, 'Fishing Under Sail in the North Atlantic' in B W Labaree's *The Atlantic world of Robert G. Albion,* Wesleyan University Press (Middletown, Connecticut, 1975) p.59

[71] Edson, Jr M A, 'The Schooner Rig, A Hypothesis', *The American Neptune* Vol.XXV, No.2 (1965) p.82

[72] Chapman, F H af, *Architectura Navalis Mercatoria* (Stockholm, 1768, repr. Rostock, 1962)

[73] Davis, Ch G, *Ships of the Past,* Bonanza Books (New York, 1929) p.24

[74] Government of Australia, *Historical Records of Australia 1788–1805,* National Library Canberra, ACT

[75] Evans, V, *Early Shipbuilding in Australia,* unpublished MS. (Sydney, 1953)

[76] Szymanski, H, *Die Segelschiffe der deutschen Kleinschiffahrt* (Lübeck, 1929) p.19

[77] Höver, O, *Von der Galiot zum Fünfmaster,* Angelsachsen Verlag (Bremen, 1934), repr. Norderstedt (1975), p.119.

[78] Pâris, E, *Souvenirs de Marine,* Vol.1 (Paris, 1882), repr. Karl Butziger Verlag (Hamburg, 1972) p.45

[79] Menzel, H, *Smakken, Kuffen, Galioten,* Schriften des Deutschen Schiffahrtsmuseums, (Bremerhaven, 1997)

[80] Lawson, W, *Blue Gum Clippers and Whale ships of Tasmania,* D & L Book Distributors (Launceston, Tasmania, 1949)

[81] Marquardt, K H, *HMS Beagle, Survey Ship extraordinary,* Conway Maritime Press (London, 1997)

[82] Bateson, Ch, *Australian Shipwrecks 1622–1850,* AH & AW Reed (Sydney, 1972) p.208

[83] Chapelle, H I, *The Search for Speed under Sail 1700–1855,* Conway Maritime Press Ltd (London, 1993) p.279

[84] Webb, Wm H, Plans of Wooden Vessels from the year 1840 to the year 1869 in *Nautical Research Journal,* Vol.34, No.2 (1989)

Chapter 5

◆

Construction and Fitting

GUIDELINES governing the construction of ships during the eighteenth and early nineteenth century will be explored within this chapter. Considering the worldwide acceptance of the schooner, the guidelines come from several Continental sources as well as English references. The guidelines, prepared for and by shipwrights, were only references to average data, and therefore the model maker should not take them as absolutes. This is underlined by words of Frederic H af Chapman:

> 'The art of proportioning the pieces, which enter into the construction of a ship, depends altogether on practice. A ship that is to be laden with iron, with salt, or other wares of a considerable specific gravity, likely to strain the ship at sea, or the working of which may tend to loosen the parts of the ship, ought to be more solidly put together, than a ship whose cargo is to be light merchandise, as fir, timber, planks &c. The difference of the wood also renders necessary a difference in the scantling, in order to obtain the same solidity.
>
> 'The solidity of a ship does not depend solely on the strength of the Scantling of the wood; great care ought to be taken also to work it properly, as well the timbers for frames as the planking; to unite well all the parts of the edifice, and to establish properly each piece in its respective place.
>
> 'As to the scantling of the timber for the construction of privateers, the object of these ships being only to serve in war, it is not necessary to build them of greater strength, than the probable period of their being wanted requires; on which account, the least scantling possible is given them, with a view to economy in expense.' [85]

Guided by these words of a great shipwright, the following description begins in the traditional way, with the ship's keel.

Keel

Authors of the past related keel proportions to those of larger ships. Thus Duhamel, Röding, Korth and Bobrik agreed that the height of a keel should be calculated by taking an eighth length of keel (in = ft), therefore height = $\frac{1}{96}$ times length. Width was given as 10 lines 8 points for every inch, or approximately $\frac{9}{10}$ of an inch (1in = 12 lines, 1 line = 12 points). Af Chapman noted in his list of ship timbers for

merchantmen and privateers only the width of keel, ranging by merchantmen lengths between perpendiculars of 110ft and 50ft from $\frac{1}{98}$ to $\frac{1}{90}$ and by privateers of similar lengths from $\frac{1}{112}$ to $\frac{1}{103}$[86].

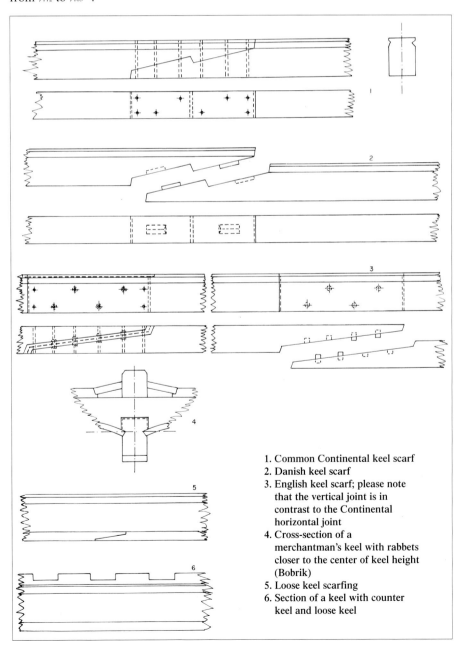

1. Common Continental keel scarf
2. Danish keel scarf
3. English keel scarf; please note that the vertical joint is in contrast to the Continental horizontal joint
4. Cross-section of a merchantman's keel with rabbets closer to the center of keel height (Bobrik)
5. Loose keel scarfing
6. Section of a keel with counter keel and loose keel

Elsewhere he explained that a keel's height should be one-and-a-half times its width. Estimates published in 1835 by G D Klawitter[87] were very close to these. He referred to larger ships having a height of one-seventh or one-eighth length of keel (in = ft), and indicated a sliding scale by stating a quarter or a fifth ($\frac{1}{48}$ or $\frac{1}{60}$ x length of keel) for smaller vessels. The width of keel assumed with $\frac{5}{9}$ times height, he explained additionally that the square of height should have been twice the square of width.

Regarding a keel's reduction of width toward stem and sternpost Frederic af Chapman remarked in passing that the fore end was $\frac{11}{12}$ and the aft end $\frac{5}{6}$ the width at the middle. The height of a keel's rabbet was equal to garboard-strake thickness, with the rabbet's top edge supposedly a third or half the plank's thickness away from the keel's top. The depth of a rabbet was a third of its height. Duhamel and Röding[88] referred to three-quarters of its height and Bobrik[89] suggested that rabbets on merchantmen were at half keel height.

The length of a keel determined whether it was constructed from one or two pieces; if two, the joining of the two keel pieces was done by scarfing. A scarf was 'the type of joint formed by notching or cutting the ends of two pieces so they interlock and can be bolted to form one continuous piece'[90]. Duhamel and Röding spoke of the length of scarf as four times the keel's thickness, whereby thickness can probably be interpreted as height, while Klawitter pointed to a scarf length as being six to eight times the keel's width. Large English ships had a minimum scarf length of five feet. Klawitter, a continental shipwright, explained three types of scarfs. One he regarded as commonly used, the second one as English and the third as Danish. In contrast to the first and third, an English keel scarf was not fitted horizontally but vertically. Bobrik and Rees[91] confirmed this in their writings and one has only to inspect English draughts to see that these vertical scarfs occur time and again. In respect to this it must be noted that only keels were joined vertically, keelson scarfs had a horizontal cut.

Danish scarfs were customary on the continent, and had a hook of $1\frac{1}{2}$ to $2\frac{1}{2}$ inches. They differed only slightly in the additional use of two prismatic tenons for greater stability. At a distance of one-eighth of the scarf's length away from its ends, the tenons were three-quarters of the keel's width as length, one-third of it as width and one tenth as height. An English scarf, as already mentioned, ran vertically through the keel without a scarf hook, yet a number (four or more) of cylindrical tenons were driven tightly into $1\frac{1}{2}$-inch deep, drilled holes. Before joining the bevelled keel piece parts together, a tarred flannel cloth was laid in between. Called a water-cloth, it prevented moisture penetration into the keel's fibre via the scarf. Furthermore a $\frac{3}{4}$- to 1-inch thick piece of timber recessed with tenons into the top of the scarf, again with an intermediate layer of tarred flannel. One bolt, preferably of copper, per foot length of scarf was considered appropriate for the connection. Half of these were driven in from the top and the other half from the bottom, with the opposite ends riveted. The English method saw these bolt holes drilled through the somewhat larger cylinder tenons. In addition, two further bolts were driven through the ends of the vertical scarfs.

Extra attention during keel construction had to be given so that none of the scarfs were placed near a mast position. Steinhaus, a naval architect from the mid-nineteenth century, is very particular on that point:

'Keel scarfs must be kept as far as possible from the masts and arranged of not less than ten feet distance away from these; otherwise mast pressure, enlarged by the setting of shrouds, could easily open them up, enough to allow water to penetrate the ship, thereby developing one of the worst types of leakage. Not so much in size, but because of difficulties by caulking.' [92]

Oak, red beech and elm were named by the various sources as keel material. Oak dominated earlier lists of ship timbers, including those by Duhamel and Chapman. Klawitter also mentioned oak but, because the timber easily split, expressed his preference for red beech over oak. The reason given was that when scraping rocky grounds, oak keels tended to break but those made from beech rarely leaked. Bobrik suggested elm, an opinion shared by A Rees, who named it as material for English ships.

The loose or false keel

In his eighteenth-century work on shipbuilding Duhamel du Monceau described the necessity of a loose keel: 'A piece, called a false or loose keel, will be laid beneath a damaged keel and helps largely to reduce a ship's drift.' This remark was annotated by the German translator of his work, Captain C G D Müller: 'Because of the last mentioned advantage are loose keels also very often fitted under brand new ships'[93].

Falconer wrote about the false keel in another context:

'When these [keel] pieces can not be procured large enough to afford a sufficient depth to the keel, there is a strong thick piece of timber bolted to the bottom thereof, called the false keel, which is also very useful in preserving the lower-side of the main keel.' [94]

Klawitter described the loose keel in similar fashion and mentioned short bolts, as well as iron or copper nails as fasteners. He spoke also about the added advantage of lessening drift and that, for this reason alone, full-bodied ships especially should be fitted with false keels. Their scarf-length was seen as a quarter of a keel scarf-length.

Counter keel

A counter or upper keel was mainly used in French and Scandinavian shipbuilding, while English and Dutch shipwrights did without it and placed frames directly on to the keel. A counter keel was a three- to five-inch strong plank with frame positioning steps cut into it, with its ends flanked by deadwood.

Deadwood

The tapered, connecting timbers between counter keel and apron at the fore and inner post at the rear were called deadwood. Their length reached in constructions without counter keel from the apron or the inner post, to a frame of approximately similar character in fore and rear quarters: the balance timber. While full-bodied merchantmen did not usually need more than one, sharp-lined vessels had a number of deadwood timbers set on top of each other. Röding reported that they were two-thirds the keel's width, their height being dependent on the fullness of the respective cant-timbers, which suggests that these are Continental guidelines. Falconer, who described English construction methods, mentioned a height of two-thirds the keel's and a width of not more than the keel itself.

The stem

Made from one or two pieces of curved oak, its foot butted either directly against the forefoot of the keel or to an extra, slightly angled forefoot piece (the German *unterlauf*, the French *brion* or the Danish *onderlöb*). The forefoot piece was mainly used in France and Denmark. In nearly all shipbuilding regions stem scarfs were similar to keel scarfs, but in England they could be compared with the keelsons. Duhamel mentioned the length of a scarf as four times keel thickness, while Klawitter quoted four to five times stem width.

Stem width and depth by Duhamel were equal to keel width and depth. Müller's annotation spoke of deviations in regard to English shipbuilding, including the keel's forefoot, where the stem was slightly bigger, and small vessels that had a slightly larger stem's head, while a forward tapering at each side reduced thickness by an eighth. Chapman considered equal dimensions for the lower stem and the keel's forefoot. At wales height the stem had maximum keel width and widened further at the stem's head by a sixth.

Descriptions about stem overhang are numerous and range from 1/15 to 1/8 the length of the ship, depending as much on the type and size of a ship as on the flair of the shipbuilder. Ways of joining stem and keel were also as numerous as the major shipbuilders. Only the English and Danish methods will be explained here, with the latter being very similar in many countries on the Continent.

English shipwrights fitted the stem over a length of several feet on to an accordingly recessed keel. That method was known as boxing, whereby the scarf of both components was worked like a vertical keel scarf. Röding described it as:

> 'Both butting ends are cut away to half thickness, so that these perpendicular cuts constitute a scarf, which is bolted with strong bolts. Beneath the scarf and stem is then the forefoot bolted. One find such connections especially on English ships.' [95]

The part Röding named as forefoot beneath the scarf is better known in English shipbuilding as gripe and is the lower part of a stem. If a head was formed a cutwater joined to its upper edge, while on vessels without a head the gripe's upper edge was set into the stem. To strengthen the connection of the keel/stem scarf, horseshoe-shaped gunmetal plates (horseshoe plates) covered that joint and bolted through keel, stem and gripe.

An apron was a curved piece fitted to the stem's inside face and further, as an extension of the keelson, a second

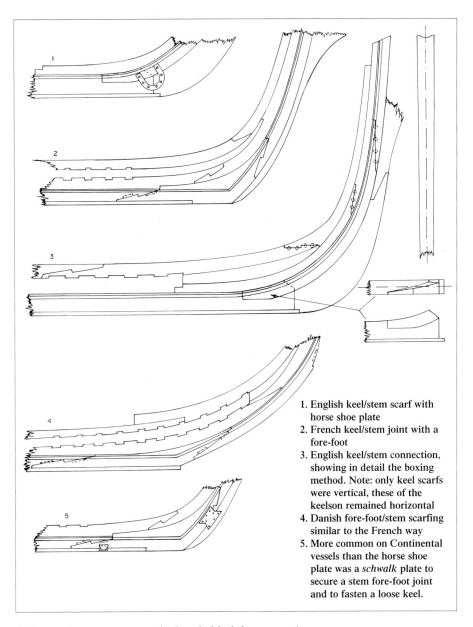

1. English keel/stem scarf with horse shoe plate
2. French keel/stem joint with a fore-foot
3. English keel/stem connection, showing in detail the boxing method. Note: only keel scarfs were vertical, these of the keelson remained horizontal
4. Danish fore-foot/stem scarfing similar to the French way
5. More common on Continental vessels than the horse shoe plate was a *schwalk* plate to secure a stem fore-foot joint and to fasten a loose keel.

timber – the stemson – reached up behind the apron. Apron width corresponded with the stem and its depth was two-thirds stem, according to Duhamel. It was fastened to the stem with strong nails, driven in two-thirds of the stem's depth.

As already indicated the Danish connection was achieved by means of a forefoot. A knee of keel thickness formed with its lower leg the foremost keel extension, while the upper leg joined the stem's lower end. Scarfs connected both ends to either keel or stem. If the stem extended by gripe and cutwater to form a head, the gripe would be placed in front of the forefoot and the cutwater at the fore face of the stem. Apron and stemson were fitted as before. Gunmetal, or schwalk, plates in the shape of a double swallowtail often replaced the horseshoe plates. Smaller plates of that type were also used for lateral fastening of a loose keel.

Rabbets of stem and keel were equal in their dimensions. All contemporary authors agreed that perpendicular markings in feet were carved in large Roman numbers into the stem to make the fore ship's draught visible. These numbers were laid out with white paint.

The Sternpost

Composed of three parts on larger ships the sternpost comprised the actual sternpost, the false post and the inner post, with the inner post next to the deadwood knee. A smaller craft's sternpost was usually not constructed from three parts. If the actual sternpost was wide enough, either false post or inner post were missing, sometimes both. The sternpost itself was straight and its lower part, the heel, fitted in tenons into the rear of the keel. In one of Müller's annotations to Duhamel du Monceau's work he remarked also on additional iron bands:

'Besides tenons [...] one also finds similar reinforcements to those on the forefoot, with iron loops passing around the sternpost and underneath the keel. Simple angle irons are on each side, of which the upper arm is nailed against the side of the sternpost and the lower one against the side of the keel.' [96]

1. Side view of a sternpost connection with a straight wing-transom
2. Rear view of the same
3. Wing-transom (upper most) and Transoms
4. Sternpost / sternson connection of a smaller vessel without an inner-post
5. Sternpost secured with a schwalk
6. Sternpost secured with a metal band led around the rear of the post and below the keel
7. Sternpost secured with an angled band

Proportional dimensions of thickness and width from the same work speak of sternpost thickness as equal to the width of the keel. The post's width at the heel should be 5 lines (5/12), more for every inch of keel height. The width towards the upper end should be gradually reduced by a third. Af Chapman saw thickness of the post below the wing-transom as equal to the greatest width of the keel, while its thickness at the heel was equal to the width of the keel at sternpost position.

These factors were still valid by the middle of the nineteenth century. Steinhaus remarked that the lower width was a little more than the keel height and the upper width was square with its thickness. Bobrik mentioned the sternpost's construction in tenons and stated that by measuring athwart ship it had the same thickness as the keel, but when measuring along the longitudinal axis it tapered from bottom to top.

The sternpost angle led to differing interpretations by contemporary writers. Some recommended a nearly perpendicular post, whereas drawings attached to these works indicate an angle of up to 6 degrees. Most of Chapman's drawings show a post declination between 8 and 15 degrees and A Rees' between 2 and 10 degrees, while Duhamel spoke of one-fifth of the stem's overhang, which corresponds closely with Klawitter's projection of 80 years later. According to Klawitter, by 1835 a sternpost sat almost at right angles on top of the keel. Schooners varied in their sternpost angle between about 6 to 18 degrees.

Sternpost rabbets were placed between 1 and 1½ inches away from the front edge. Similar to the stem, carved draught marks in feet made it possible to read the after draught.

Forward of the sternpost stood the inner post which was either butted against the keel or inserted into it with a tenon and nailed to the sternpost. Duhamel du Monceau only provides proportional dimensions of the inner post: thickness was equal to the sternpost, while the lower width was half of the sternpost and the upper width half of that again. The loose or outer post has seldom been used in the construction of smaller ships and needs no further consideration.

A sternpost knee, also known as sternson, was a strong piece of timber, with its upright arm connected to the inner post, whilst the horizontal arm rested with or without scarf on top of deadwood or butted against the keelson. Proportional dimensions come again from Duhamel du Monceau who tells us that the width of this knee was equal to the width of the pieces to which it was connected. Its neck must at least have been similar in width to the sternpost. The prongs tapered toward their ends as far as the timber allowed.

The wing-transom

The rearmost horizontally placed cross-beam, the wing transom was half embedded into the head of the sternpost and furnished with a certain convexity toward the top and the rear. It connected sternpost and fashion-pieces and was bolted to both. The wing-transom's length determined the appearance of the ship's rear quarter and thus varied accordingly. Duhamel specified that thickness and width of wing-transoms for small ships came to 8 lines (⅔in) for each foot in length. Klawitter mentioned two-thirds to three-quarters of the ship's width as wing-transom length and a thickness of 1 inch for every 1½ feet in length, correlating with Duhamel's information from nearly a century earlier. Röding spoke of a similar width to the keel but slightly more in height. A rabbet on the outside of the beam contained the buttock plank ends.

Transoms

Fitted below the wing-transom and parallel to it, the uppermost or deck-transom formed the last deck-beam. According to a vessel's size one or more transoms would be placed between the deck-transom and the lowest, usually very sharply angled, transom. Each was set against the sternpost and connected to the fashion-timbers by being combed in and bolted, or joined with tenons in the English way.

A wing-transom divided the stern, as it was colloquially known, into two parts, the lower half known in nautical terminology as buttocks or tuck while the upper half remained the stern. A hollow part, known as the counter, above the wing-transom allowed the stern to stand out further than the tuck. The part below the wing-transom was known as the square or round tuck, terminology that is still in use today. Transom thickness was given as two-thirds keel width and its width was a third more than its thickness. Rearward transom convexity was half that of a wing-transom.

Counter-timbers

Whereas the timbers considered so far were below the wing-transom, the following are those above. They are known by a variety of names, including stern-timbers. Counter-timbers were knee-timbers, butted with their lower ends against the upper side of the wing-transom. In Danish shipbuilding those were set into the wing-transom at a depth of 1 to 1½ inches. The top ends of the timber reached up to the rail. Klawitter described both counter-timber legs as being at an angle of 130 to 160 degrees to each other, while the longer leg was at an angle of 50 to 60 degrees to the horizon. The depth of the concave lower counter, according to general consent, should be kept to a minimum, in order to reduce fragility of the keel caused by the stern's overhang. Depth therefore should not have measured more than ¼ inch for every foot of the ship's length (¹⁄₄₈). The section immediately above the lower counter up to the window balustrade was usually known as the upper counter. Duhamel noted that the size of the overhang was an average of a half to two-thirds of the lower counter. Shorter counter-knees (counter-timbers) that reached the window ledges often supported the long counter-timbers (stern-timbers), which stood between windows. The outermost support timbers were the fashion-futtocks, which due to their shape influenced the stern's appearance.

A number of horizontal beams were added and joined with the vertical beams. The lowest, the counter-beam, controlled the upper boundary of the lower counter, with the second being used as a window balustrade. Both were on the outside covered with shaped timber strips (counter-ledges). Another beam above the windows provided the upper ledge,

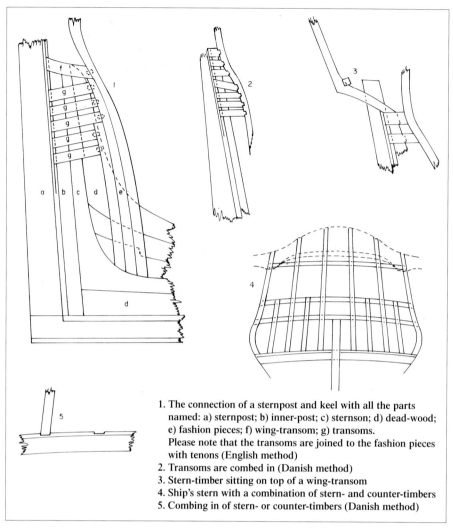

1. The connection of a sternpost and keel with all the parts named: a) sternpost; b) inner-post; c) sternson; d) dead-wood; e) fashion pieces; f) wing-transom; g) transoms. Please note that the transoms are joined to the fashion pieces with tenons (English method)
2. Transoms are combed in (Danish method)
3. Stern-timber sitting on top of a wing-transom
4. Ship's stern with a combination of stern- and counter-timbers
5. Combing in of stern- or counter-timbers (Danish method)

while the taffrail as the uppermost horizontal timber was at the top.

Proportional counter-timber dimensions are not easy to find, but from Duhamel du Monceau's *Alphabetic Tables Of Construction Parts For Men Of War*[97] it can be concluded that thickness at their lower ends was half of the wing-transom's thickness and they tapered towards the top by about one fifth. At both points the width of these uprights was approximately one tenth more than the corresponding thickness. Horizontal beams were of similar dimensions.

Frames

Frames are a vessel's ribs, sitting across and on top of the keel. They were usually made from six to ten pieces of curved timber and determined a vessel's contour. Depending on the method of construction the floor-timber was the first piece immediately above the keel or counter keel, joined then by futtocks and above them by top-timbers. Larger ships had several futtocks and men of war had 's'-shaped top-timbers intended to take in the upper part and thereby making boarding more difficult. All frames were set up in pairs.

In eighteenth-century England all frame pieces were joined together with chocks, while those on the continent were butt-joined to each other. Duhamel explained that in

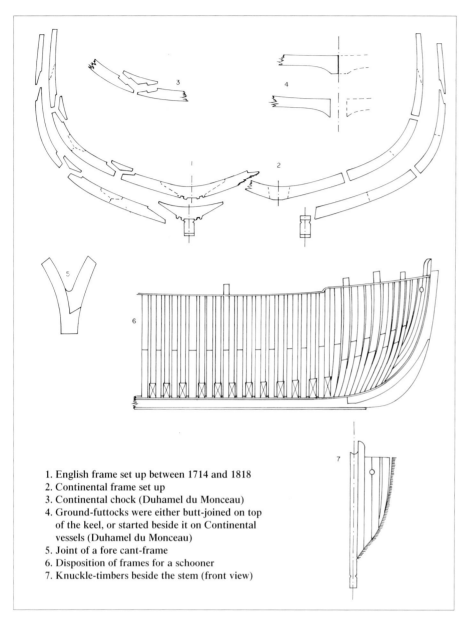

1. English frame set up between 1714 and 1818
2. Continental frame set up
3. Continental chock (Duhamel du Monceau)
4. Ground-futtocks were either butt-joined on top of the keel, or started beside it on Continental vessels (Duhamel du Monceau)
5. Joint of a fore cant-frame
6. Disposition of frames for a schooner
7. Knuckle-timbers beside the stem (front view)

pointed to short round dowels of 3 inches diameter, set 1 inch deep into the frames, through which the bolt holes were drilled and the bolts driven. Bobrik stated something similar and one illustration by H Paasch[99] made square joint-dowels visible on the frame inside. Those, as well as the round dowels, are questionable for the eighteenth century and seem more appropriate in the following century.

All authors, from Duhamel de Monceau in 1752 to Bobrik in 1848, agreed that the use of chocks in the connection of frame pieces was limited in continental shipbuilding practice to parts that had ends of insufficient thickness. Chocks in English shipbuilding were part of normal frame construction during the period 1714–1818, at which date Sir Robert Seppings introduced the butt-and-dowel connection. Seppings' change in frame construction came from the realisation that chocks added nothing to a hull's strength but considerably increased the incidence of rot. While drying out, both chock and frame timbers shrank and collected dirt in the emerging cavities, thereby assisting fungus growth. Klawitter explained further that joints between frame parts had to be worked very accurately and tarred paper should be laid in between.

As Duhamel states the thickness of a frame should be one quarter of a ship's extreme breadth in feet (for example, 12 feet would be $\frac{1}{48}$), with top-timbers reduced at the top by an eighth. Between every set of frames remained a gap of 6 to 10 inches, which was filled with salt for timber preservation, although Klawitter noted that this gap increased to 1 or 1½ feet in smaller vessels.

A description of a frame would be incomplete without mentioning limber holes. Holes of approximately 2 inches square were cut at both sides of the keel into the bottom of the floor-timbers to have any water inside the ship running towards the pumps. As Röding explains English men-of-war had a chain lying throughout, which was pulled at intervals fore and aft to clear the free flow of bilge water and keep these holes free of dirt. Klawitter noted that this chain was commonly used and not restricted to English warships.

To determine all construction pieces of a frame we need to understand the various names by which they were known.

The floor-timber

This was the lowest construction piece in a frame. The longest and least curved of these was the mid-ships floor-timber. Placed to both sides of it were floor-timbers of the flat, followed by rising floor-timbers and the acute angled crotches.

the course of this the ground futtocks extended against the floor-timber; hence the ground futtock lay with half its length beside the floor-timber and was connected to this with strong nails or bolts. The second futtock joined above the floor-timber, its lower half again connected to the ground, or first futtock. The top-timber butted against the ground futtock and was attached to the top half of the second futtock, while the shorter top-timber was scarfed, rather than butted, to the top of the second futtock.

Steinhaus noted that frames should be kept apart from each other by at least 1 to 2 inches to ensure good airing and A Rees also covered that point in detail:

'Sometimes the frames are fayed close together, or separated for air; those that are separated have dry pieces of oak fayed between them in wake of the bolts; these should all be split out before the planking is brought on, that a free passage may be given for the circulation of air.' [98]

Spacers referred to here as 'dry pieces of oak' were only temporary means for building a frame. Steinhaus additionally

The first or ground futtock

Ground futtocks were known as futtocks of the flat, while those on rising floor-timbers and crotches were designated accordingly, as futtocks of the crotches, etc.

Futtocks

Further futtocks were the 2nd futtocks, 3rd futtocks etc, and added to them were descriptions of their position in the ship's structure. The long upper ones were the top-timbers, with the shorter ones, joined by a scarf, known as short top-timbers.

Frame

The main frame was also called mid-ships frame. Although Duhamel states that it was important that the main frame sat in the correct position above the keel, the location was very badly defined. It could have been $\frac{1}{19}$, $\frac{1}{28}$ or $\frac{1}{48}$ of the ship's length in front of the centre or, as Müller mentioned in one of his footnotes, 'French shipbuilders saw fit to use $\frac{1}{38}$ for frigates and $\frac{1}{50}$ for ships of the line'. Chapman proposed that the position for sharply built ships was approximately $\frac{1}{20}$ forward of centre but for full-bodied vessels it was $\frac{1}{12}$ or $\frac{1}{13}$. Rees indicated the greatest width of a vessel as $\frac{5}{12}$ of perpendicular length from the bow, coinciding with Chapman's formula for full-bodied ships. Except for minor deviations, this information held true for English shipbuilding draughts around 1800.

A balance frame was a frame of similar shape at a distance fore or aft of the main frame in symmetrically built ships. The fore ship, or loof, timber stood approximately at the main tack's clamp location, but as Müller stated in 1791, 'English and Dutch shipbuilders do not know these two frames and even the newest French ship-builders do not care about them any more.' [100]

In order to locate the loof timber position, by following Duhamel's notes, one took $\frac{1}{36}$ of the ship's length behind the centre as position for the mainmast and from there one half of the main yard's length forward, or simply a quarter of the ship's length from the bow. The after balance timber then stood at three-quarters of that length.

The foremost frame of a ship, the fore cant-frame, sat $\frac{1}{36}$ of the ship's length away from the stem's rabbet and often carried the cat-head. Knight-heads were the knuckle timbers directly at each side of the stem. They were followed by hawse timbers, into which hawse holes were drilled. Between the hawse timbers and the fore cant-frame further filling timbers were placed. Knuckle timbers were marginally wider than frames and sat close together. They stood on the fore cant-frame and were held together on the inside by breast-hooks.

Cant-frames

This name was given to all the frames in the more rounded fore-and-aft sections of a ship's body. While a position at right angle to the keel required too much chamfer with associated loss of stability for these frames, they were generally fitted at right angles to the outside planking. Fitted aft of the after cant-frame were fashion-pieces, which formed the last frame of a ship and, as mentioned already, were connected by counter timbers to the wing- and other transoms. The term fashion-piece is sometimes only seen as the part below the wing-transom, whilst the section above was the fashion-futtock. In a square tuck construction fashion-pieces were almost level with the sternpost with a wedge-shaped piece forming the lower end (the lowest transom). In a round tuck the position of the fashion pieces depended on the sharpness of the underwater body and could be found usually somewhat more forward.

Sheer frames were all frames marked on a shipwright's draught. The hidden frames between these were known as filling timbers.

Keelson

Being placed above the floor-timbers, the keelson was recessed by 1½ to 2 inches to provide better frame support. Every second bolt of the keel–frame connection also extended through the keelson and provided a strong bond with the keel. A keelson consisted of several pieces of timber scarfed together like a keel, except in English construction where in contrast to the keel's vertical scarf the keelson's was horizontal. Röding spoke of timber chocks, which filled the spaces between keel, keelson and frames.

Keelson length was measured from the stemson's lower end to the sternson knee, or as Duhamel explained, from the inner side of the fore-foot to about two-thirds the length of the hindmost crotches. With a width equal to the keel, the part at the mainmast was kept a few inches wider. The keelson was only half to two-thirds the height of the keel. When comparing construction methods, the French total thickness of keel, counter keel and keelson was similar to a combined thickness of keel and keelson in the English method. Klawitter's keelson dimensions were 20 to 50 per cent more than the corresponding dimensions of the keel.

Falconer states that the scarfs of the keelson were not placed near a mast and were cut in such a way that the connecting bolt could go through the keelson, the scarf and the top of the frame at once.

The stemson and the sternson knee

These are curved timber extensions of the keelson over the crotches, which connect forward to the apron and aft to the inner sternpost. The upper end of the sternson knee reaches right up to the deck's hook.

Outside Planking

The planks were named, in order from the keel upwards, garboard-strake, bottom planks, planks of the floor-head, wales, topside planks and the gunwale. Sitting in the keel's rabbet, the garboard-strake was the lowest plank and, depending on the type of construction and the use of the vessel, it could have been of various thicknesses. Duhamel saw the garboard-strake as half as thick as the plank below the wales, but Müller turned this rule completely upside down in a footnote. He remarked that shipbuilders in northern nations, especially such with shallow anchorage, made garboard-strakes and bottom planks stronger than the planks between the floor-head planks and wales. The bottom planks were equal in strength to garboard-strakes and laid adjacent to them. The planks of the floor-head were in the hull's lower curvature. Depending on the ship's size four to six were fitted. Klawitter notes that:

> 'In earlier times one used to make these planks of the floor-head as strong as the wales, because especially to flat bottomed ships they provided considerable strength if their bilge struck the ground.' [101]

He explained further that in 1835 sharper built ships had their strongest plank below the wales, with the garboard-strake being the thinnest. When considering Klawitter's

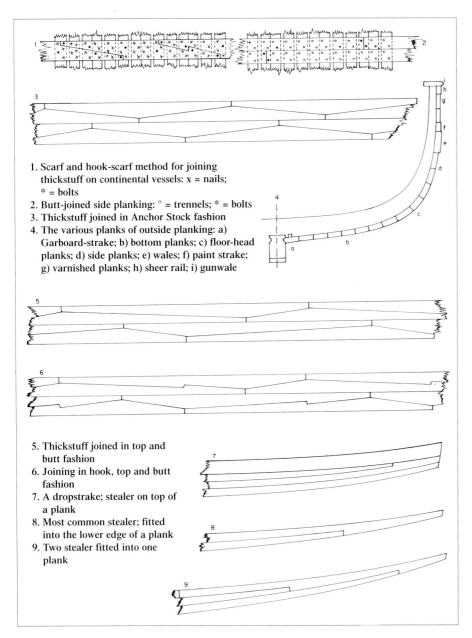

1. Scarf and hook-scarf method for joining thickstuff on continental vessels: x = nails; * = bolts
2. Butt-joined side planking: ° = trennels; * = bolts
3. Thickstuff joined in Anchor Stock fashion
4. The various planks of outside planking: a) Garboard-strake; b) bottom planks; c) floor-head planks; d) side planks; e) wales; f) paint strake; g) varnished planks; h) sheer rail; i) gunwale
5. Thickstuff joined in top and butt fashion
6. Joining in hook, top and butt fashion
7. A dropstrake; stealer on top of a plank
8. Most common stealer; fitted into the lower edge of a plank
9. Two stealer fitted into one plank

explanations of contemporary authors. Width and length were treated in a fairly similar way as Duhamel du Monceau expressed: 'A plank will generally be taken as long and as wide as the timber provides'. Successive writers, including Bobrik, used the same phrase. However, some dimensions can be obtained from tables created by Duhamel, Klawitter, Steinhaus and Rees. Duhamel's information is for a vessel of 96 feet in length and 24 feet in breadth and, although this information is not given in the other tables, the dimensions suggest vessels of a similar size:

Outside planking	Width	Thickness
Bottom planks from keel to orlop	11in	2⅓in
next below the wales	–	4¾in
those following reduce to the height of the orlop (medium width)	12in	–
the topside planks from the wale to the gunwale	11in	4in
in between the fifth wale and the gunwale	10½in	2in
		(Duhamel)
Planks above the wales	10 in	2½–3in
Planks below the wales	9–10in	2½–3in
		(Klawitter)
Floor-head planks	8–9in	3–4in
		(Steinhaus)
Planks above the wales should not be wider than	9in	(Rees)

Regarding the length of outside planks Bobrik and Rees shared the opinion that English men-of-war used English oak for planks in lengths of about 24 feet from below the wales to the unloaded waterline. For the planks below, East county oak was favoured as it was better and could be obtained in lengths of 30 to 50 feet. For the four to six bottom planks nearest to the keel elm or beech were preferred, probably for a similar reason as their preference as keel material. Thickness of all planks at the bow and around the channels was similar to that of the wales.

The planks discussed so far were mainly set blunt against each other (butt-on-butt joint) and offset above each other, which meant that garboard-strake joints should neither be placed near a keel scarf nor below a pump. As a rule, three planks were laid between two joints on the same frame. The joints of two adjacent planks were at least six feet apart, which in itself requires a minimum plank length of 24 feet. However, one can have three layers of planks in between two following vertical joints on the same frame and still have a bad shift as Bobrik instructs us in his 1848 work. He was of the opinion that joints should rather not form an orderly pattern, because opening up of one could lead to a chain reaction:

'It is therefore prudent that one vertical joint between all others will have a double distance for the shift (12 ft). The uninterrupted perpendicular sequence of vertical joints is then avoided and the planks will be twenty-four ft long. Men of war, especially in the English fleet followed exactly this particular rule.'

information one has to know that he died in 1837 at the young age of 32. His *Vorlegeblätter Für Schiffbauer, Für Die Königlichen Schiffbau-Schulen Entworfen* (Information sheets for shipwrights, developed for the Royal Shipbuilding Colleges) were published in 1835. His tenure as master shipwright and teacher at the Royal Shipbuilding College in Stettin had only just begun when he compiled this schoolbook for shipbuilding students. The theoretical knowledge embodied in this small book was therefore only based to a lesser degree on Klawitter's own experience and would have come mainly from earlier publications.

Side planks followed above the floor-head planks. Their thickness was thought to be similar to the bottom planks, up to a height of 4 feet below the loaded water-line and increasing from there to the wales until the uppermost plank (the thickstuff) was ½ to 1 inch less than the wale.

All these contrasting pieces of information are best understood if one recalls the remarks made by F H af Chapman regarding the art of shipbuilding. Planking depended on a vessel's purpose, which explains the differing

Mid-nineteenth-century data by Steinhaus spoke of a 5-feet distance between joints and at least 4 feet if one row of planks parted them. According to his words a plank's length should never be less than 30 feet.

Thickstuff

The planks directly below the wales and down to the unloaded water-line were fitted top and butt fashion, especially in men-of-war and larger merchantmen. In this method the widest part of a plank was directly below the above plank's joint and was reduced to half that width at the ends. The greatest width was at a quarter of the plank's length.

Stealer

The number of rows of planking needed for a vessel was calculated at the length of the main frame's curved surface between wales and keel divided by a plank's width. With that length differing at stem and sternpost, not only in themselves, but also in comparison to the main frame, plank widths altered gradually towards the ends. One could not, however, taper these ends to an unlimited degree. Planks at the rabbet maintained at least half of their greatest width to enable fastening. This led, particularly on a full-bodied vessel, to a larger number of planks on the main frame than the rabbet fore or aft could accommodate – a problem solved by losing excess plank ends in the layer below or above. For that purpose one plank was notched out to half its width and butted up against the second half-width plank; these were known as stealers or lost or drop strakes.

The first stealer, or drop strake, was very often placed directly below the wales to provide a better run for the subsequent planks, thereby softening the problem of curvature on a round tuck. Sometimes, the length of a sternpost's rabbet exceeded a main frame's exterior and to assist the good run of the plank below, a widening stealer came into use. Klawitter remarked that the stealers should be kept below the waterline, or they would give a vessel a bad, patched-up appearance.

Wales

These planks stood out from all others because of their extra thickness and formed one of the mainstays of ship stability. The lowest wales were situated at her extreme breadth, with the middle dipping slightly into the load waterline. As this discussion is limited to smaller vessels, we shall only consider these, commonly known as lower or main wale.

Müller regarded the continental wales as smaller than those on English vessels and believed that the wider English wales contributed to a stronger ship, using the evidence that a smaller number of English vessels, compared to French craft, broke their backs. The width of continental wales was specified by Duhamel as equal to the keel height and Röding considered English wales as two wale strakes laid side by side, so that: 'the width is twice the size as customary for other nations'. By listing various English ships Müller established that in fact such rules were used very arbitrarily: a yacht of 1 foot 2 inches keel height had wales of 1 foot 10 inches, while a cutter with a keel of similar height only had wales of 1 foot 3 inches.

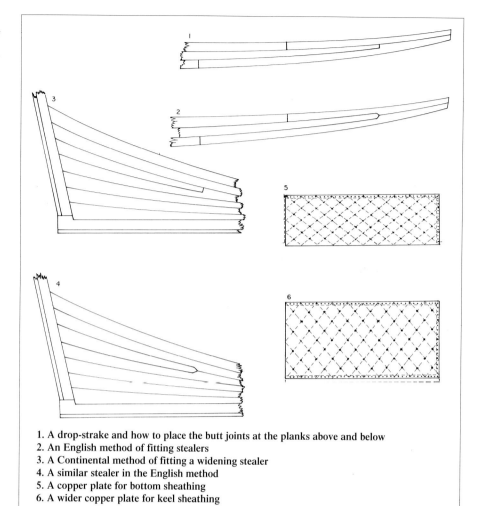

1. A drop-strake and how to place the butt joints at the planks above and below
2. An English method of fitting stealers
3. A Continental method of fitting a widening stealer
4. A similar stealer in the English method
5. A copper plate for bottom sheathing
6. A wider copper plate for keel sheathing

Encouraged by Müller's remark, a check on a larger number of contemporary schooner draughts concluded that the wales width on 80 per cent of the vessels only slightly differed from the keel height. Fifteen per cent had a width of only two-thirds to three-quarters of the keel's height, while the remaining five per cent had wales of twice the keel height. The examined draughts were of English, Continental and American origin and no special national trend could be established.

Continental wale joints were usually made with normal or hooked scarfs, contrary to English construction where mainly top and butt joints shaped the wales and the planks below (thickstuff). Certain variations were also in use including the Anchor stock fashion, a way of attachment depicted by Falconer in 1815:

'Anchor Stock, a method of working planks, whereby the butts of one plank come nearly over the middle of another plank, and the planks being broadest in the middle, and tapered to the butts, thereby appearing in shape like an anchor stock...'.[102]

A third variation to top and butt was the hook and butt method. The greatest width was again at 6 feet, but the remaining 18 feet did not taper uninterrupted. After another 6 feet, or in the counter plank 6 feet from the butt, a hook was cut in similar to a hooked scarf.

Wales were fastened to the frames with strong nails and connected with bolts to possible riders and beam knees. These bolts were driven in from the outside and clinched on the inside. On single-decked vessels the wales position was as close as possible to the deck beams, to provide greatest stability.

Varnish strakes or filling planks

In small ships these filling planks were laid directly above the wales or in between the slightly thicker paint strakes. The name derived from their protective coating: resin or spar varnish was boiled and skimmed resin from spruce or fir to which turpentine oil and sulphur were added. This mixture turned into a slightly yellow-brown transparent varnish, similar to a clear lacquer, and was used to prevent decay on planks above the wales, on masts, spars, deck timbers and furnishing.

Colour or paint strakes

Although not every vessel carried them, colour or paint strakes were directly above the wales and below the gunwale, slightly thicker than the varnish strakes. The uppermost plank below the gunwale was also known as waist rail. All planks above the wales were reduced towards the top in thickness and sometimes also in width, although the uppermost plank was never less than 2 inches thick so that oakum needed for caulking would find a secure hold. Planks above the wales were not tapered towards the ends, and remained parallel.

Gunwale or gunnel

This is the cover plank, laid flat above the tops of the futtock heads, as well as the top edge of the outer and inner planking to prevent moisture from penetrating. In thickness similar to other planks, gunwale width comprised thickness of the waist rail plus futtock head plus inner plank plus 1½ to 2 inches.

Drifts or drift pieces

These were interrupted planks that did not run continuously between bow and stern, but were only fitted to the forecastle, the quarter and the coach.

Anchor lining

These were protection boards nailed on top of the planks within the range of an anchor to shield them from damage during casting or weighing.

Fastening of planks

All planks were fitted to the frames with fasteners, or nails and spikes as they were termed in the language of the time. Nails, trennels or trunnels were made from timber and the spikes from iron, copper or alloy. The wooden nails were for use below the waterline, while metal spikes were for above water. Contemporary authors recorded that:

> 'They are large, wooden cylindrical pins, which one needed to connect the planks to the frames, especially as deep as a ship is laying in the water.' (Röding[103])

> '[They were] Used for fastening the inside and outside planks of a ship to the upright timbers.' (Falconer[104])

Both agreed that such nails should be made from good oak. Their thickness for ships up to 100 feet in length was 1 inch and for larger vessels 1½ inches. They varied in length from 1 foot to 3 feet 6 inches. Trunnels were octagonal because this shape was easier to wedge in than round rods, which also proved to be more difficult to produce. Holes for the trunnels were drilled from the inside with the trunnels being driven in from the outside.

Copper and alloy spikes fastened copper sheathing and were used as deck nails around the compass so its magnetic needle was not influenced. Iron spikes were available in sizes from less than ½ inch to 30 inches in length. They came in various shapes and with different heads to serve any imaginable fastening purpose. All planks in the upper portion of a ship's hull were fastened this way, including the deck planks. Every outside plank was locked on to each frame with two wooden nails, placed diagonally to each other. Each butt was secured with a bolt, which was made from iron and after 1783, for underwater application, from copper. Bolts were ⅝ inch in diameter for schooners and comparable vessels.

The division between wooden nails and iron spikes is easy to understand if one takes a closer look at the areas of application. Iron spikes would soon begin to rust in water, with the result that planks loosened and quickly started to rot around spikes. Similarly a wooden nail would dry out above water, drop out of its hole and loosen the planks. Hence the rule for fasteners: use timber below water and iron above.

Sheathing

For as long as ships have been built, man has known about the destructive powers of the marine worm (*Teredo navalis*) and the speed-reducing influence of marine growth like mussels, barnacles and algae. To eliminate these problems various materials have been tried with varying degrees of success. One of the oldest methods, still in use in the nineteenth century, comprised fir planks being used to lightly plank over the hull. Different forms of coating, laid under the fir planks, were tested to stop worm infestation. The Royal Navy introduced a mixture of pitch, tar and sulphur and Röding mentioned paper stuck on with tar and covered with cow hair, a description also given half a century later by Bobrik. In some cases the fir planks were covered so closely with large clout-headed filling spikes that they formed an extra skin over the planks.

Lead sheathing was another method widely in use during the seventeenth century. Fincham[105] wrote in 1851 of large-scale experimental sheathing, especially during the rule of Charles II of England (1660–1685). During the period 1670–1691 20 men-of-war were sheathed in that manner and the method was still sometimes used in the Royal Navy until about 1770. Disadvantages of lead sheathing were the extreme material weight and softness, which could not withstand, for any great length of time, the rigours of wind and weather.

Fincham also reported that the British Navy Board first

proposed copper sheathing to the Admiralty in a letter dated 18 October 1761. New research by B Lavery[106] revealed that an earlier proposal had already been made in 1708 by Charles Perry, but rejected for reasons of costing, amount of time, labour and the belief that any damage to it would be difficult to repair. Admiralty advice of 24 January 1727 speaks about the old ways of preparing ships for going to the tropics:

'To cover the bottom all over with thick brown paper, and preserving the sheathing from the worm, to fill the same with filling boards or nails, first taking care that all the iron work be examined and secured, and the seams and butts of the bottom are well shored up and caulked and payed with common tempered stuff as usual, and the bottoms all over with a good coat of soft tempered stuff, the seams and butts listed with spun hair, and that to cover the bottom with strong bag cap paper made out of old cordage, and not the sort of woollen rag, each sheet open to be about 22 inches by 18¼ inches, and each ream to weigh at least 45 pounds, scarphed with an inch over each other, and touched out at each corner, then, taking care that the sheathing board is sawed to a thickness, fayed, regularly edged, and have two rows of holes bored in each butt to prevent splitting, and well dried with fire, and paid thick with boiling tar, and that covered with hair well beat, laid very smooth, and a good quality of tar on the hair, and then fastened to the side with sheathing nails about 2-inches asunder. And when the sheathing is caulked, to have down the edges and butts as smooth as possible, and then fill it with filling heads, or nails of 1¼ inches long, or so as not to have more than – inches in the plank, the heads to be about ⅜ inch asunder, taking great care the nails and bratts are regularly drove and well soaked up that so the bottom may be as smooth as the nature of the work will admit, and then be breamed and graved.'[107]

In 1761 the first real attempt was made to tackle this dilemma. The urgency of a solution to this age-old problem is apparent in the immediate response by the Lords of the Admiralty, ordering the Navy Board only three days after its proposal to copper the bottom of the 32-gun frigate HMS *Alarm*. The ship had just returned from a tour in the West Indies with a hull badly infested with worms. Fincham reported further that, inspected after a certain period, the sheathing of HMS *Alarm* seemed to be the answer to all their predicaments. However, copper sheathing had its teething problems. It became obvious after a few years that the plates on HMS *Alarm*'s bottom were very heavily oxidised and destroyed in a large way around the iron bolts. In an experiment, the bolts were coated with a pitch-tar mixture, but this could not stop the galvanic reaction between iron and copper. In early 1783 the Lords of the Admiralty decided to discontinue copper sheathing because of the widespread damage. In consultation with shipwrights and others it was suggested that all iron bolts be replaced with mixed metal or copper bolts in the parts of the ship that were submerged, which led to alloy bolts being introduced in August 1783 and copper bolts making an appearance in the following October. These changes proved to be successful and copper sheathing was officially introduced to the ships of the Royal Navy and

soon followed in the navies of other nations. Falconer still spoke of copper sheathing as a totally new invention in his work of 1780 and referred mainly to fir planking with tar and hair. The report in his 1815 edition was predominantly directed to copper sheathing and particularly mentioned that all the ships of the Royal Navy and the East India Company were sheathed with copper. Merchantmen had, according to that report, extra thin fir planks of ⅜- to ⅞-inch thickness nailed to the bottom planking before copper plates were attached. Röding in 1794 still explained the old method, but pointed to copper plates as a new invention and the best kind of sheathing, keeping the bottom clean and oakum between the planks better in place.

The standard size of copper plates in Britain was 4 feet by 15 inches. They overlapped towards the rear and the upper edge. Steinhaus spoke of a size of 4 feet 3 inches by 15 inches (Hamburg measurement). This represents only a negligible difference between the two sizes (1217mm x 381mm [British] and 1219mm x 358mm [Hamburg]). Plates for keel sheathing were of similar length but were in Hamburg measurement 24–25 inches (573mm–597mm) wide. The considered average life span of copper sheathing was approximately three to four years.

The number of spikes needed for fastening each plate was worked out by dividing the long side into 10 sections and the short one into 4. A spike was driven into each cross point and each sector of the overlapping seam received another three, giving a total of 122 or 162 spikes for every plate.

Inner planking

Planking to the inside of upright timbers was called ceiling, foot-waling or lining. Just as for the outside planks, a ceiling had different names in accordance with its position and purpose. The one above the floor timbers was the floor ceiling, whereas the planks next to the keelson were the limberstrakes. These were loosely fitted boards, which could be removed for cleaning the limber holes. Their width was approximately six inches.

The thick-stuff was laid about the floorboards adjacent to the floor ceiling. These planks were often kept stronger than the average ceiling to add strength in case of ground contact, or when sitting dry. The strongest plank of this group should have been combed in at the height of the lower futtock chocks, as Müller mentions:

'Actually should all ceiling planks, which meet frame scarfs, be stronger than others and notched out, at least those closest to the keelson and the thick-stuff about the floor-heads. But one can find this only in large ships and even there not always. In contrast to those only nailed on, one also calls the notched out ceiling planks clamps'.[108]

The thickness of the notched-out ceiling planks should be one quarter of the keel's width, with the others being thinner. Planking directly below the thick-stuff about the floor-head as well as below the clamps was known as supporting thick-stuff. The more vertical planking between the thick-stuff about the floor-head and the clamps was the ceiling of the hold.

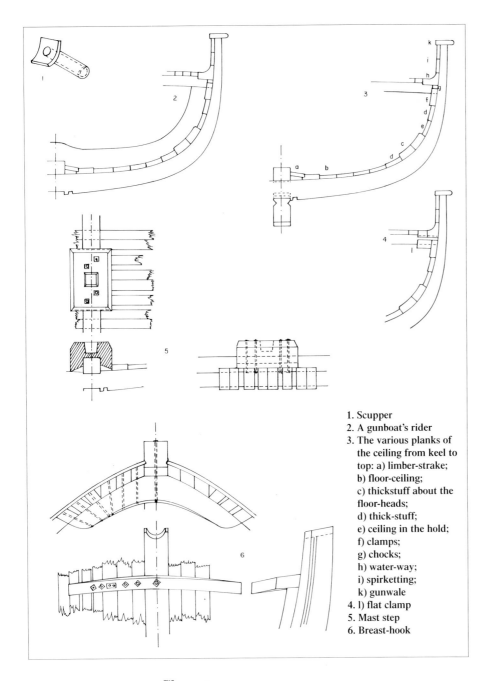

1. Scupper
2. A gunboat's rider
3. The various planks of the ceiling from keel to top: a) limber-strake; b) floor-ceiling; c) thickstuff about the floor-heads; d) thick-stuff; e) ceiling in the hold; f) clamps; g) chocks; h) water-way; i) spirketting; k) gunwale
4. l) flat clamp
5. Mast step
6. Breast-hook

Clamps

The clamps were the strong inner carrier of deck beams. Deck beams were swallow-tailed into these by half their height. Sometimes an additional flat clamp sat either above or in front of the actual clamp and beams were double-swallow-tailed. Thickness of clamps at the lower deck was considered twice that of the normal ceiling or two-thirds of the timbers against which they were sitting, which meant the thickness of an average ceiling plank was one-third of the frame's thickness. Clamps at an upper deck level had three-quarters the thickness of the lower and those at quarterdeck level again only three-quarters of the lower.

In order to allow frame timbers to be aired, Duhamel wrote that the lining was fitted half closed/ half open, which meant that there was an empty space of a plank's width after every two ceiling planks. Most northern nations did not apply that French rule and their ceilings remained uninterrupted and their seams caulked. However, frequently a few

of the planks were laid in only loosely (known as filling) and removed during harbour time to allow for ventilation. The inside planking continued above the clamps with chocks fitted in between the top-timbers and fastened to the clamps to provide good support for the chines.

Chines

Chines were not only part of the inside planking, but also the edge of the deck planking. In the building of smaller vessels chines and waterway planks were consolidated into one piece and formed the waterway. In larger ships a second and third plank were introduced along with the chines to form the group of waterway planks, which demonstrates the differences in construction techniques. Ships of medium size had only one additional plank beside the waterway. The lower side of the waterways was 1½ to 2 inches deep combed into the deck beams and half-beams, whereby half of the combing was notched out of the waterway, with the other half coming from the underlying component.

Scuppers

The rounded or square holes of scuppers led from the inner waterway groove to the outboards. The scuppers were lined with lead or copper to prevent water run-off from penetrating inner timbers and planks, thereby reducing decay. The upper edge of a waterway's groove was kept high enough above deck to allow for good caulking of the seam between it and the spirketting above.

Spirketting

Together with the thick-stuff about the floor-head and the clamps, this was one of the primary inner links of a ship's body and was for that reason not only kept thicker but sometimes also combed into the inner timbers and bolted to the external primary bracing, the wales. If a vessel was built to carry guns the spirketting beneath the lower port-sills continued in one piece and at equal width. Similarly to clamps, lengths of spirketting were connected with each other by hook-scarfs. For reasons of stability the shift of such scarfs was paramount, so a scarf would be set in between gun-ports rather than below since gun-ports already weakened the hull structure. Whilst any main connection was hook-scarfed, all other ceiling planks followed the outside planking principle. Not only were they supposed to be shifted against each other, but possibly against the outside planks as well to obtain the greatest achievable strength in construction. Planks between spirketting and gunwale were of normal size.

After analysing the outer and inner planking, a description of further inboard connections begins again at the floor:

Riders

These were single frames, set up on top of ceiling planks to strengthen a man-of-war's structure. Merchantmen had no use for riders and even men-of-war did not have them all the time, or as expressed by Falconer, 'At least till the ship was weakened by service'. Duhamel made a similar remark on the history of riders: 'Formerly they were fitted to smaller men of war not earlier than after the second or third voyage'.

Their construction was similar to frames, with floor-timbers, first and second futtocks and joints shifting in the same manner. Where keelson and thick-stuff protruded, riders were notched out to fit snugly against the ceiling. They usually reached up to the lower deck. Their floor-timbers were slightly stronger on top than those of frames and futtocks but tapered towards the head by a tenth of their thickness. Riders were normally placed near masts but could also be fitted in the middle between two gun-ports if more were needed. Nailed to the frames they were fastened with strong bolts to the ceiling, inner timbers and outside planking as well. In schooners riders were mainly needed in gunboats.

Mast steps

On smaller ships these were only large pieces of timber fastened on top of the keelson. A square hole was usually cut into the centre to receive the mast's heel.

Breast-hooks or fore-hooks

Curved timbers of differing angles, breast-hooks linked, on the inside and in a rectangular position, knight-heads, bollard-timbers, hawse-pieces and all other knuckle timbers near to the stem. Three to five hooks were placed in between keelson and lower deck, depending on a vessel's size, whereby the planks of the deck rested on the uppermost hook (deck's hook). This hook was connected directly to the knuckle timbers while the others rested on the ceiling. They were also slightly smaller than the deck's hook. According to Duhamel breast-hooks were approximately one-third thicker and twice as long as deck beam knees. A hook's inner shape was formed by timber growth, while the outside fitted snugly to the ceiling contour. Klawitter remarked that, 'The deck's hook reached to the first and foremost deck beam and was there connected with a keel scarf to the flat clamp.' [109]

In the absence of transoms in rear construction, hooks were in use there as well. As Klawitter commented: 'They are usually inside the hull in front as well as in the rear placed on top of the ceiling.'[110] Steinhaus explained this by saying:

'If a ship has no transoms, there must naturally be a corresponding number of hooks in the rear, one of which connects to the clamps and serves also as deck's hook.' [111]

The Deck

The principal parts of a deck were beams (framework) and planking.

Framework

Framework was composed of deck beams, carlings, half-beams or ledges and the knees. Deck beams made up the main components of that structure and reached from side to side. Of oak, they were set swallow-tailed into the clamps. For stability and water run-off, beams were made with a top-side curvature, the round of beam, which in a merchantman amounted to $\frac{1}{48}$ of the beam's length, but men-of-war applied a lesser round of beam, since too large a curvature would

have impeded the guns. Duhamel estimated two to three lines per foot length ($\frac{1}{72}$ to $\frac{1}{48}$) and for height and width of beams in the lower deck four lines for each foot of length ($\frac{1}{36}$).

Deck beams of the size considered here were made of one piece – only on larger ships was it necessary to produce deck beams from two or three pieces. The longest beam, the one of the main frame, was known as mid-ships beam. The number of deck beams placed in a deck's structure depended on a vessel's size. It could have been as few as 10 for a small vessel to as much as 30 for a First Rate.

Carlings were placed in a fore-and-aft direction between deck beams, giving support to the half-beams and more rigidity to a deck. Combed into the deck beams, these short timbers were 4 to 5 inches square and wider in the partner section of masts and pumps. Falconer mentioned their length as about 8 feet by 8 inches square or wider. Whilst this information referred to ships of the largest order, the former belonged to a ship of 300 tons, whose carlings had a length of approximately 5 foot. From the data provided it could be

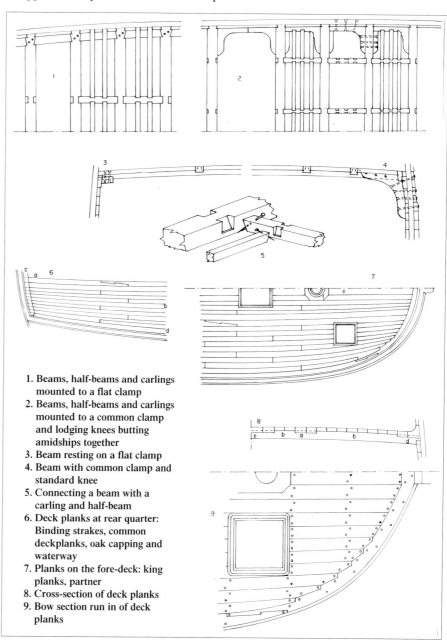

1. Beams, half-beams and carlings mounted to a flat clamp
2. Beams, half-beams and carlings mounted to a common clamp and lodging knees butting amidships together
3. Beam resting on a flat clamp
4. Beam with common clamp and standard knee
5. Connecting a beam with a carling and half-beam
6. Deck planks at rear quarter: Binding strakes, common deckplanks, oak capping and waterway
7. Planks on the fore-deck: king planks, partner
8. Cross-section of deck planks
9. Bow section run in of deck planks

concluded that a thickness/width to length ratio of carlings was 1:12.

The short beams that assisted the deck beams were known as half-beams or ledges. Klawitter notes that they were fitted parallel with them and combed into clamps and carlings and had half the height and width of deck beams. A study of a larger number of variously sized ship and vessel draughts revealed, however, they consistently had only a height and width of 0.35 to 0.4 of the deck beam's width and were mostly smaller than carlings. The same sources tell of distances of 7 inches to 1½ feet between deck and half-beams.

Deck beam knees consisted either of standard or lodging knees. In an upright position they were standard knees, bolted with their upper or horizontal arm against the side of a deck beam and with the vertical one against the nearest frame timbers. Lodging knees were placed horizontally, had again one arm bolted to a deck beam, while the other connected to several frame timbers. All lodging knees afore the

main beam fastened to the back of a deck beam, while those aft reached forward, so that the arms joined mid-ships across the frame timbers. Knee thickness was recorded as two-thirds deck beam.

Both types of knees were not always in use together and arguments arose between shipwrights about better practice, as we hear from Klawitter. Small vessels usually only had standard knees fitted near the main hatchway and sometimes all knees were replaced with flat clamps or were substituted with strong bolts, as can be noticed on the draught of a skerry-boat on page 74. An annotation by Müller to Duhamel's work clarifies this:

'Other nations used in their place spring bolts with large heads, driven from the outside through the planking and timbers, and nailed or bolted in such a manner to the beams that they could easily be covered over.' [112]

Knees in a square-tuck construction were those of transoms. They were as necessary for securing the stern structure as breast-hooks were for the bow. One arm of such a knee was bolted to the outer end of any transom and the other horizontally across several frame timbers.

Deck planking

Beside the use of normal fir planks, planking of a deck involved also stronger oak planks. These were a vessel's primary fore-and-aft deck bracing, acting in the same way as wales outboards, the inboard thick-stuff and the waterways, which formed a deck's outer boundary. The strong planks at both sides of the centre line were the partners and halfway between them and the waterways were binding strakes. All were thicker than normal planks, and were in longer scarfs rather than butt-joined; greatest attention was given to the shift between each other and against all the other thick-stuff scarfs. They were hooked and reached over two deck beams. The purpose of hooking these scarfs was to keep a deck together in its length, which was of utmost importance, if one considers that ships laboured strongly in heavy seas and could have easily sprung out on butt-joined planks. Deck stability was of no lesser significance than that of a ship's sides.

Binding strakes

These straight planks were laid over the full length of a ship parallel to both sides of the main hatchways. Their widths remained unchanged as they were not tapered toward the ends like normal planks. They were usually laid in pairs, larger ships having two pairs fitted at each side of the deck while smaller vessels only needed one pair. Wherever binding strakes rested upon deck beams they were combed in by 1½ to 2 inches and fastened with spikes long enough to penetrate the beam by three-quarters its depth. Every contemporary author had a slightly different opinion on the thickness of binding strakes: Duhamel maintained that they were one-third of a deck beam, with a width of twice that; Falconer described them as being 1 to 1½ inches thicker then other planks and being laid level with them at the upper side; Klawitter spoke of twice a normal plank's thickness.

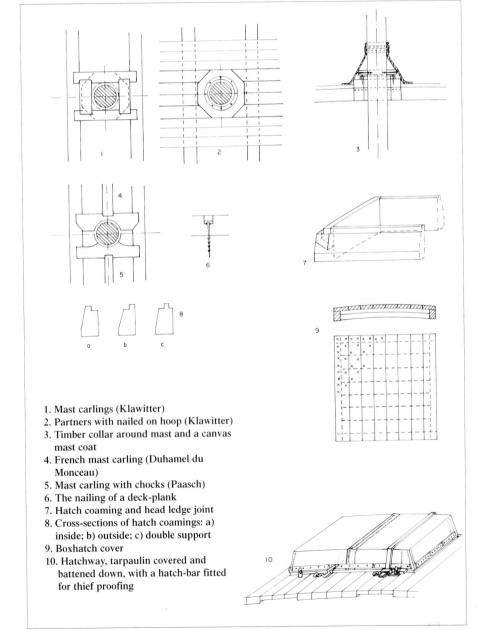

1. Mast carlings (Klawitter)
2. Partners with nailed on hoop (Klawitter)
3. Timber collar around mast and a canvas mast coat
4. French mast carling (Duhamel du Monceau)
5. Mast carling with chocks (Paasch)
6. The nailing of a deck-plank
7. Hatch coaming and head ledge joint
8. Cross-sections of hatch coamings: a) inside; b) outside; c) double support
9. Boxhatch cover
10. Hatchway, tarpaulin covered and battened down, with a hatch-bar fitted for thief proofing

Partners or King planks

These terms were given to oak planks on both sides of the centre line with holes for the masts, capstan and pumps. The housing of masts and capstans necessitated hardwood being used for these planks, which gave them a similar strength to binding strakes and waterways in their flat part. Often the holes themselves, or the timber collars around masts, were termed 'partners'. To confuse the issue, Klawitter spoke of partners as 1-foot-wide pieces of timber placed on top of carlings to form an octagon around the mast hole, thereby leaving enough room for the mast and allowing 1½ inches of play between mast and partners. This octagon should have protruded above the partner planks by half its height, pointing to a thickness of two-thirds a deck's beam.

Mast collar and mast coat

The mast collar was a two-part timber structure. Firstly a small ring was fastened around the mast hole to the partners and then a slightly broader, circular or octagonal hoop was nailed above the ring to the mast itself, acting as a cover. A tarred piece of canvas was then wrapped around the mast and over the collar for protection against water seeping through the mast opening. This became the mast coat and was in use on all weather decks. Instead of the wooden hoop or octagon, a puddening or a rope collar was sometimes nailed around the masts.

Normal deck planks

The planks were the thickness of a quarter of a deck beam and between 8 and 10 inches wide. Butted against each other they tapered toward the ends in accordance with the narrowing widths of a vessel's deck. When laying planks, it was observed that one joint stayed as far away as practicable from the next and was not placed near hatchways. A deck plank for ships up to a medium size should have consisted of not more than three lengths.

The deck's rounding inside the bow necessitated planks with end fitting cuts of more than 45 degrees to create a stepping into the waterway's inner edge. Planks with less acute an angle were only butted against the waterway, while the planks with more acute an angle were rectangular for one-third of their width and only tapered at the end. The stepping of planks, commonly done in the rounded bow section, was seldom done at the quarterdeck. When planks became too small at their ends, the stealer principle (lost strake) was applied, with only the outer deck plank or planks lost into the next. Planks in the fore deck with a head that was too pointed, as well as the very first plank beside the waterway, were sometimes also fitted as lost strakes to gain enough end width for fastening. Across the stern, planks did not butt against a waterway but rested on the deck transom and a hardwood plank covered their ends. Steinhaus gave a description of how to fasten deck planks:

'The way of fastening adds also much to the embellishment of a deck, therefore these planks are not nailed like any other but before a spike is driven in, a ¼in deep hole for its head is drilled in with a centre-bit so that the spike's head can not press into the plank and crush the timber. At such places

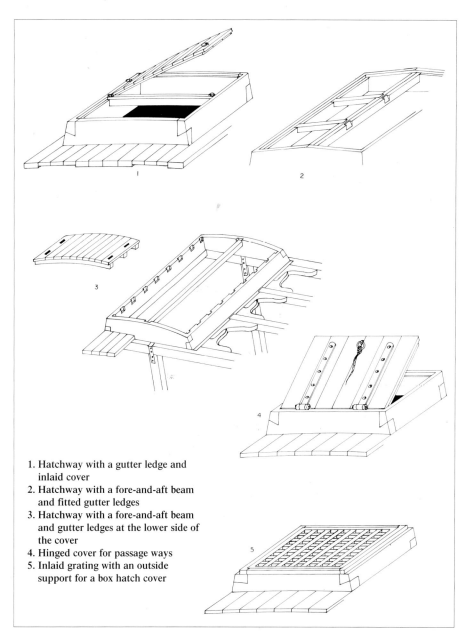

1. Hatchway with a gutter ledge and inlaid cover
2. Hatchway with a fore-and-aft beam and fitted gutter ledges
3. Hatchway with a fore-and-aft beam and gutter ledges at the lower side of the cover
4. Hinged cover for passage ways
5. Inlaid grating with an outside support for a box hatch cover

water would have the chance of easy penetration, thereby affecting the spike as well as giving rise to timber decay. The spike will then be driven in with a set-hammer and the hole closed by a fir plug, whose grain must run with the plank's grain. But before this happened, it becomes necessary to fill the hole with turpentine or varnish, otherwise the plug may easily pop out again. Through this preparation is not alone the water stopped from affecting the spikes, but one can in most places barely see where the fastening of the deck is.'[113]

Hatches or hatchways

These square deck openings, with hatch-covers or trapdoors, were necessary for loading or traffic between decks. The upright timbers surrounding a hatch opening were the hatch-head-ledges and hatch-coamings, which are often under the collective name of coaming. The ledges were placed above deck beams while those at a right angle to them and above carlings were coamings. According to Bobrik, their thickness varied according to size between 5 and 11 inches and the height was deck plank thickness plus 2–4½ inches. This height would only suffice for hatchways inside a vessel, for inlaid gratings and for those on upper deck. A merchant vessel's loading hatch ledges and coamings were usually higher, but relevant contemporary dimensions for these could not be found.

The shape of all hatch surrounds depended on the type of hatch-cover. Box hatches had their support ledges on the outside, with a higher rim on the inside keeping the lid in place and to prevent water intrusion. Hatchways with hinged lids (trapdoors) to access crew quarters, or other frequently used openings, had support ledges on the inside and a protective rim on the outside. The ledges and coamings of companionways and lights were similar to those for box hatches.

For a closer analysis of the various types of opening or hatch cover used on board, one should consider that such covers were structures to be lifted or pushed open by one man or boy, whereas the closing of loading hatchways had to be handled by two men. This means that the cover needed to be light enough for a boy to lift or push open and two men to carry. Besides weight consideration, stowage problems

1. Companionway capping
2. Inlaid cover with hollow seats (Cable outlets)
3. Companion light (Skylight)
4. Grating with a scuttle opening

would have been created on deck with overly large covers, if one or more hatchways had to be opened simultaneously. Since time immemorial seafaring people considered these problems practically, and it should therefore be considered in a modern interpretation.

Box hatches

These were one-piece hatch-covers and also the most often described in contemporary literature. The lid was nailed to a frame, embracing the upper part of head-ledges and coamings and resting on their support ledges. Since hatch cover timbers could not be of lesser strength than deck planks without weakening the deck's stability, only small openings would be covered with that type of hatch. Alone the timber weight of a 3-by-3-foot box-hatch cover amounted to 25kg. Therefore, it is easy to calculate a cover's upper size limit. Box hatches on a vessel's weather deck were only used on hatchways that were constantly closed during a sea voyage. Seaworthiness of a closed hatchway was achieved by lying a tarred tarpaulin over it and nailing long timber strips, the hatch battens, over its edges to the deck or coaming, thereby stopping sea water from entering (giving rise to the term 'batten down the hatches'). An unsecured hatch cover would have been lifted up and washed away with the first strong wave breaking over board.

Hatch covers

Covers of larger hatchways were recessed with the upper rim of the coamings on the outside. Original draughts provide a clear indication about the type of cover used and show that the broader part of the coamings, the support ledge, could be either inside or outside. Contemporary authors have commented that the width of a hatchway on larger ships was approximately one-sixth or one quarter the width of the ship, but draughts of smaller ships suggest that they had hatchways that were up to half the vessel's width. The total cover weight of such hatchways easily reached several hundredweight and had to be divided into a number of smaller covers for ease of use, with the gutter-ledges providing support. Falconer describes the role of gutter-ledges:

'Gutter-Ledge. A cross bar laid along the middle of a large hatchway in some vessels, to support the covers, and enable them the better to sustain any weighty body which may be moved or laid thereon.' [114]

For hatchways of six feet in width, the distance between gutter-ledges should not have exceeded three feet or the cover would have been too large and cumbersome. Gutter-ledges were either sitting beneath the cover edges, or have, as Röding revealed in volume II of his work (p. 176), support ledges like coamings, with a higher centre rim visible between covers.

Wider hatchways had also a fore-and-aft hatch-beam placed along the centre line, which supported the gutter-ledges and provided a means for easy handling. Similar to a box hatch, a tarpaulin was pulled over these hatch covers and battened down. Cargo hatchways were additionally fitted with two U-shaped brackets on each head ledge. Hatch bars, either timber beams or iron rods, were pushed through these U-brackets in fore-and-aft direction and secured with a lock. They provided additional stability to the hatch covers but were first and foremost a protection against cargo theft. The term 'scuttle' if it appears on a draught implies a small man-hole. Scuttles were sometimes also set into larger hatch covers to provide access without uncovering the whole hatchway.

Grating

This is a third type of cover, rarely used in merchant vessels. Fitted to the upper deck of a man-of-war, gratings were only mounted where an overcoming sea had a chance to escape, therefore the between deck had to be high enough above the waterline to justify the fitting of scuppers. Gratings were only needed for good ventilation and rarely seen on ships with only one tier of guns. They had to be covered with tarpaulins and battened down during bad weather, like any other hatchway cover. The ventilation scuttle near the stove was a typical grating-covered deck opening on merchant vessels but its coaming also had a support ledge for a box hatch to cover it during bad weather.

Companion

This was a three-feet-high timber cover over a stairway fitted on merchantmen, or other smaller vessels, on which the stairway could become awash. Bobrik describes the companion as having three walls of vertical boards with the fourth fitted with hinged doors. Whereas his description had the entrance pointing forward, Röding and others directed it to starboard. Röding also spoke of a sliding board in lieu of doors and a trapdoor instead of a concave sliding roof:

> 'Above the walls is a hinged lid or shutter which can be flapped open half or completely during good weather. Such will be closed during bad weather, also will then the lower half of the entrance serving side be closed with a sliding board, which has to be stepped over when one goes below deck. This slide prevents water from running down the stairway below deck, when a heavy sea is shipped.' [115]

This statement does not consider what would happen to the upper part of that entrance when a heavy sea swamped a ship and set the deck awash. However, it appears logical that leaving it open would have defied the intended purpose of the whole structure. Therefore that opening was probably closed with a shutter, itself hinged to the overhead lid. Bobrik spoke further of benches, often fitted to both sides of the companion, and also that a binnacle was at one end. Sometimes a cover for all stairways, the companion was mainly an attribute of the rear cabin, as contemporary authors describe: 'The stairway to the crew quarters has either a similar structure, or a trapdoor moving on hinges.' (Bobrik [116]); and 'Companion, at the after stairway leading to the cabin. The cover above the stairway to the crew quarters is named Hood' (Röding [117]).

Hinged hatch

Hinged hatches were found on the upper deck as well as below where hatch covers were needed over stairways. Box-hatches were not very suitable for such openings because stairway covers had to be pushed open with one hand, while the other hand was holding on to the steep ladder-way for safety. A loose box-hatch would not only have been unable to fulfil such a function on a rolling ship, but would have become an uncontrollable and dangerous item too. An age-old seafarer rule tells us that everything not nailed or battened down had to be tied up.

Companion light

Bobrik describes the companion light, a hatchway above the great cabin for providing daylight:

> 'While the rear cabin windows, mainly by merchantmen, are generally only opened in harbour, at sea they are closed with tight fitting port lids to protect against pounding waves from astern; a hatchway for illumination is to be found on cabin deck. It is called the companion light and covered by a box hatch with window panes fitted on the upper side and guarded against damage with wire netting.' [118]

The 'wire netting' mentioned was normally composed of two grids, each manufactured from two horizontal and several vertical iron rods, with the upper horizontal rod hinged to a fixed iron bar above the companion light or sky light's centre ridge, which enabled the grids to be lifted for cleaning. Companions and their lights were strongly connected with spikes to their coamings and those, leading to cable-tiers or cable stores, had hollow cleats covering the cable outlets. Hollow cleats were timber caps in the shape of a hollow half cone, fitted over the cable outlets to prevent the intrusion of rain and seawater. As Röding describes: 'While a cable is not in use during a voyage, these spots are like masts and pumps covered with a canvas coat.' [119]

Bits or bitts

Bits can be divided into anchor bits and mast bits. Anchor or riding bits belonged to any vessel that took her anchors in with the help of a capstan, predominantly warships. Ships equipped with a windlass had no need for riding bits, as the windlass performed their function. Riding bits were placed a short distance behind the fore mast and comprised a combination of strong timbers to belay and control the running out of cables. Assembled from two strong and square vertical posts (bit-pins) and a fitted cross-timber (crosspiece) parallel to the deck these bits stood in the hold in their own steps. Bit-pins extended about four to five feet above deck and, whenever within reach, were indented and bolted to a beam. In front of each bit-pin on deck stood strong standards, attached with bolts to the vertical pins and the deck beams below. Ringbolts were used for their sleeping arms so that cable stoppers could be applied. The aft side of the crosspiece was lined with a rounded softwood plank, fir lining or doubling of the bits to reduce cable friction. Röding hinted that some English ships had, instead of bit standards, supporters (diagonal beams) bracing the front of bit-pins to the next deck beam. Occasionally supporting knees were fitted below the cross-piece and it should also be mentioned that French ships had cross-pieces only

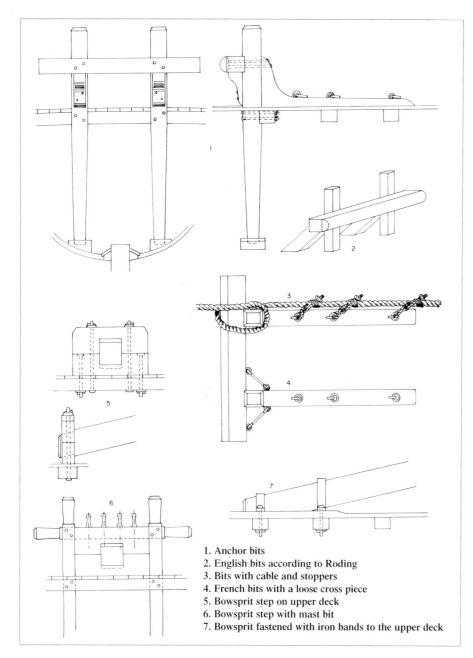

1. Anchor bits
2. English bits according to Roding
3. Bits with cable and stoppers
4. French bits with a loose cross piece
5. Bowsprit step on upper deck
6. Bowsprit step with mast bit
7. Bowsprit fastened with iron bands to the upper deck

loosely connected with hooks, merely put into place when the need arose.

Riding bit dimensions for smaller vessels are hard to find and the smallest vessel listed by Duhamel was one of 96 feet in length and 24 feet in width. Pins for that vessel were 11½ inches thick and 1 foot 1 inch wide, while the crosspiece was 11 inches thick and 1 foot wide. The fir lining was 4¼ inches thick and 6¼ inches wide. Standards equalled the pins in thickness and had at their neck a maximum width of 1 foot 3 inches. Rees[120] states that a pin's distance from the centre line was approximately 2 feet. Looking at all applicable dimensions for bits of a 176-foot ship, we learn that these differ only by three to four inches. From these two sets of dimensions one can conclude that for a vessel of only 50 feet in length, for example, they would probably be no more than 1½ to 2½ inches less than on a 96-foot vessel.

Although this way of fitting riding bits was the rule, exceptions applied to special craft, such as gunboats, where a pivoting gun carriage would render the fitting of central bits impractical. In such cases cables were belayed to bits at the sides.

Cat-heads

Generally described as short, strong beams, cat-heads protruded overboard near the bow at an angle of approximately 45 degrees (as from the centre line). Their task was to keep hanging anchors away from the vessel to prevent damage. To assist cat-heads in their task, supporters were placed beneath and against the outside planking. They were either in the shape of a knee or an extension of, usually, the second head rail. The inside part of a cat-head was fastened to the deck beams with strong bolts and iron brackets. As Duhamel describes:

'To keep the forecastle entirely clear, one makes now cat-heads out of knee-shaped timbers, whose one arm is strongly bolted inboards to spirketting and frame timbers, while the other forms the protruding piece we just talked about.'

These words are given a footnote by Müller: 'this is the normal arrangement for vessels without a separate fore-castle'.[121]

Two or three sheaves were slotted into the outer part of a cat-head and connected by a fall with the cat-block to form the cat-tackle, hooking the anchor to a-peek position. In between supporter and sheaves was a vertical hole, housing the cat-head stopper, which was secured above by a stopper knot. Leading through the anchor's ring, the cat-head stopper was run over a notch, or a sheave, at the cat-head's face. Alternatively the stopper could be led over a cleat with or without sheave at the cat-head's side. Once the anchor was secured the cat-tackle would be removed. An iron band was often forged around the fore edge to strengthen the cat-head in its slotted section.

With comparable data for small vessel cat-heads not to be found, the dimensions specified here are taken from the 'Alphabetic Dimension Tables For Men Of War' in Duhamel du Monceau's work and from Bobrik's 'Dimensions Of A Merchantman Of 330 Tons'.

Length of vessel	176ft	96ft
The cat-heads, thick	1ft 3in	10in 6 lines
wide	1ft 5in	10in 6 lines
The supporter under		
the cat-head, thick	1ft 1in 1 line	9in
Wide at a third from its neck	1ft 2in 6 lines	11in 6 lines
		(Duhamel)

Vessel tonnage	330
Cat-head, from fore to aft, or wide	11in
from above to below, or deep	10in
makes a right angle to the bow	
and rises for each foot in length	5in
outboard length (or enough, so the	
anchor is not touching the bow)	4ft 10in
inside length, from the outside of frame	4ft 9in
The cat-heads and their brackets bolted	
through the foremost deck-beam	
with bolts of a diameter	¾in

Sheaves in the outer end, in numbers   3
    in diameter   8½in
    in thickness   1⅛in
    (Bobrick)

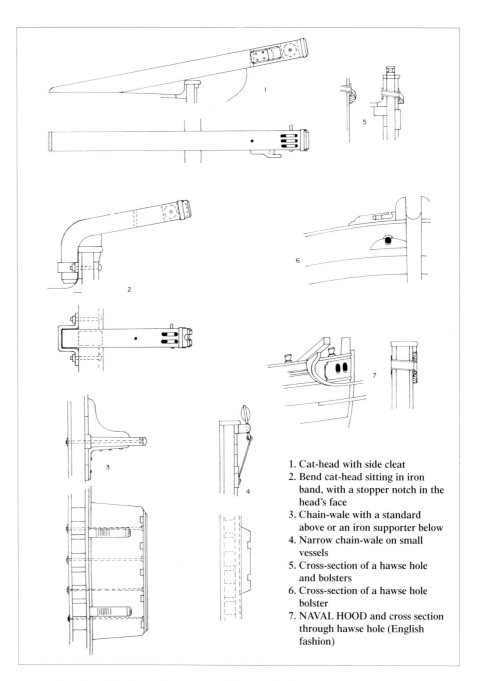

1. Cat-head with side cleat
2. Bend cat-head sitting in iron band, with a stopper notch in the head's face
3. Chain-wale with a standard above or an iron supporter below
4. Narrow chain-wale on small vessels
5. Cross-section of a hawse hole and bolsters
6. Cross-section of a hawse hole bolster
7. NAVAL HOOD and cross section through hawse hole (English fashion)

Bowsprit steps

This is the bowsprit heel's seat on deck. On smaller vessels with only one deck this sometimes consisted of a bed on which the heel could rest bolted to the deck beam, and a covering wooden cleat securely fastened to the lower bed. However, Röding explained the kind more commonly used:

'On smaller and one-decked vessels only a strong support was laid upon the deck beam who carries the bowsprit's heel and extended further over another or a pair of beams. It was then secured with one or a pair of iron brackets, tightly fitted around the heel and with their eyelets flat on deck laying, through which strong bolts are driven and secured with split-pins to plates below the beams.' [122]

Chain-wales or channels

These were thick, flat planks laid horizontally at both sides of a vessel outboards at approximately the height of the waist rail and slightly abaft the mast. Their purpose was to provide a large enough angle for the shrouds and to keep them away from the railing. Channel thickness for large ships was up to 6 inches, but for the vessels considered here it was more in the region of 2½ to 3½ inches with a taper of 7 to 10 per cent toward the outside. Channel width was about ¾ inch for every foot of a vessel's extreme breadth, depending further on mast height and the angle required for the shrouds. Therefore, width was very arbitrary.

Channel length derived from the number of shrouds, backstays and deployment of guns; hence channels on merchant vessels without armament were usually shorter than on a warship. They were fastened with long bolts to the frame timbers, whereby the bolts went through the channel's entire width and the timber thickness, to be clinched and cottered on the inside. Knees reinforced the channels, being placed either above or below the channels (sometimes both) and bolted to the timbers. Knees on the upper side were known as standards and the ones underneath as supporters. Both types could have been made from iron or timber. Knees were fitted as standard on English ships. Notches for the dead-eye chains were cut into the outer edge of the channels and then covered with a moulded ledge. The knees width was that of the channel's outer edge and its thickness 1½ to 2½ inches.

Head

Merchant vessels in the coastal trade were often built without a head, an attribute more common to vessels of war and pleasure craft. According to contemporary sources, this forward extension of a vessel's stem was supposed to fulfil three objectives:

• To have the hull cutting easier through the water.
• To strengthen bowsprit support through gammoning
• To extend lateral water pressure against the fore-ship by

enlarging the side, thus allowing the ship to sail closer to the wind and reduce drifting.

In the second half of the eighteenth century the head was already thought to be a fairly unnecessary addition to a ship's bow. Duhamel observed that the head was a very useless thing, and that if it was going to be part of the ship's design it should be as short and light as possible. Shipbuilders of his time did indeed keep the head much shorter than their predecessors, making it only as long as required for bowsprit support, the fitting of the blocks for the fore tack and the other fore sails. At this time the head was usually no more than ⅛ of a ship's length. Four decades after Duhamel's comments, Röding offers his agreement: 'The head is actually a useless burden to the fore-ship and enlarges the keel's fragility.'[123] He also named a head's length of ⅛ length of a ship as customary for that period.

Although normally made from several components, a

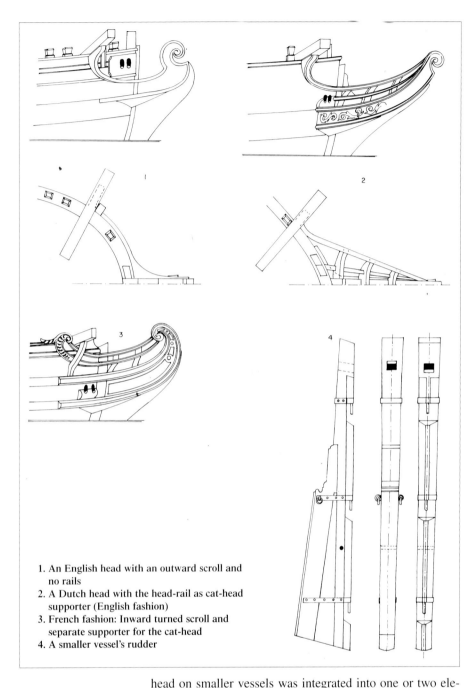

embellished with ornamental carvings or paintings, with the cheeks being usually shaped timbers. A strong, triangular filling timber was fitted in the corner between bow, stem and cheek, below the lower cheeks. That washboard or doubling of the cutwater broke the force of the sea.

Rails or head rails

These were situated above the cheeks and ran from the back of the upper cheek towards the bow near the cat-heads. On small vessels there were no more than one or two sets of rails. Similar to shaping the cutwater, the method of rail fitting was very much a local shipbuilding affair. In France the head rails finished near the cat-heads in ornamental carvings and provided extra supporters for the cat-heads, while the English method resulted in turning the upper rail into a bollard-timber (the main rail head), with the second rail becoming the cat-head supporter. Vertical head brackets were inserted to give more stability to these rails, which were only fixed at the ends. These decorated timbers joined rails and cheeks and were bolted against the cutwater standard.

Neither a floor of the head, usually a grating, nor a figurehead were much in use on small vessels. Cheeks and rails ended more often in a scroll, customarily named a scrowl. Finally in the description of the head, the holes for bobstay and gammoning should not be forgotten. The bobstay hole was situated close to the cutwater fore edge while the gammoning slot was cut into the filling piece of the cheeks.

Naval-hood

On English vessels, the hawse-holes at weather-deck level had a softwood lining (bolster) fitted for the reduction of cable wear and tear. This was called the naval hood. On French and Continental ships, plus some smaller vessels, this was usually only situated below the hawse holes.

Rudder

Also called the helm this consisted of a number of individual elements, divided here into three main groups.

Group one

Depending on its size, the rudder was built from one to three pieces, with the innermost the stock or back, and the others the after-pieces. A thin oak plank, the fish, was sometimes nailed to the back edge for protection. Rudder thickness equalled that of the sternpost, with Duhamel remarking that this was probably so in regard to its inner thickness, but that it was supposed to be swallow-tailed towards the rear. Notwithstanding this, his Dimension Tables stated the rudder thickness as that of the sternpost, without considering any widening at the rear. A century later Steinhaus also discusses rudder thickness and shape:

'The rudder, as far as it is in the water, must have parallel thickness or is slightly tapered towards the rear end. This depends however on the fullness of the underwater lines of a ship. Since until now the effect of water, namely at such depth below the surface is barely known and such unawareness will lead to mistakes in the shaping of a rudder, we will

1. An English head with an outward scroll and no rails
2. A Dutch head with the head-rail as cat-head supporter (English fashion)
3. French fashion: Inward turned scroll and separate supporter for the cat-head
4. A smaller vessel's rudder

head on smaller vessels was integrated into one or two elements (cutwater and top-timber). Cutwater thickness at the stem equalled that of the stem, but it was reduced toward the fore edge. The piece known as top-timber provided a horizontal bond of all vertical cutwater timbers, fitting on to their upper curvature. Above it sat the cutwater standard, holding cutwater and stem together. Its upward-reaching arm was sometimes shaped into a strong hook for the fore stay collar. Bolts connected the joined parts with the stem, but the elements of the head were only nailed together, which meant that accidental head damage was limited to the nailed part without affecting the stem itself. Lateral stabilisation between head and bow was achieved with the cheeks of the head. Smaller ships had one or two pairs. Placed on the wales in the bow, their tapered arms along the cutwater reached up to the figurehead. The upper cheeks ended behind the figurehead in a small scroll. The space between the figurehead and the scroll, the filling-piece of the cheeks, was sometimes from experience bring here a few improvements. It is a more often than not appearing defect on a rudder, when a ship gained some speed, that it starts to shake which gets stronger when speed increases; also that it kicks in a high running sea. Such motions are very annoying and in some cases as well very detrimental since the former can sometimes be so strong that the whole after body shakes and as a result the seams between the planks open up and leakage becomes inevitable. In such cases experience showed that a slight taper to the rear of the rudder got rid of that defect. Kicking of a rudder in a high sea is still much more dangerous. The violent throwing from one side to the other can easily break pintles and gudgeons and even the rudder itself. If a steering wheel through such extreme force suddenly turned, the man on the wheel could be thrown over it. So that nothing like this happens, such defects can be fixed from experience by making a rounded aft side of the rudder square, or if it is square to cut a hollow groove into the whole length of it.' [124]

The reaction of the sea on the rudder was important and as such was discussed by all of the maritime writers of that period. During the time of sailing shipbuilding the problems of constructing a rudder that served a ship well were only overcome by a shipwright's long experience. The examples of the Frenchman Duhamel and the German Steinhaus tell us that everyone had his own conflicting solutions. American Lauchlan McKay's has his own thoughts on the subject:

'Many practical men, both mechanics and captains, as well as merchants, object to having the lower waterlines full, on the ground that the ship will not steer well; but this I believe to be a mistake. ...Therefore I propose and recommend the straight waterline, as it must be evident to all that the water will pass by with more ease. ... The worst steering vessels are generally wide and flat, with heavy buttocks; and of all impediments to fast sailing, such a form of construction is the greatest. ... It is then very evident, that as far under water as the buttock extends, the water can have no material force on the rudder, and in many vessels the evil of hollow waterlines is prevalent in the extreme. In Eastern vessels, more especially, this fashion prevails; and in such cases it is usually said, the run is short, consequently we have to make it sharp, to make the vessel steer easy; and we, like our forefathers, conclude to make the vessel sharp from the keel one half or two thirds up the sternpost, taking it for granted, that the rudder would do little or no good from that to the surface of the water; whereas if they had filled out the run, so as to bring the lower waterlines less hollow, and eased the buttocks, the ship would steer well.' [125]

At keel level the width of the rudder equalled in inches the ship's breadth in feet, making it ¹⁄₁₂. Duhamel tells us that at water-line level the rudder was three-quarters of the lowest width at keel level (only two feet above a half) and at the head slightly more than one-third of the lowest width. Röding provided similar data but Klawitter stated:

'The width of a rudder depends on the after sharpness of a ship. Fully built ships need naturally a wider rudder than one

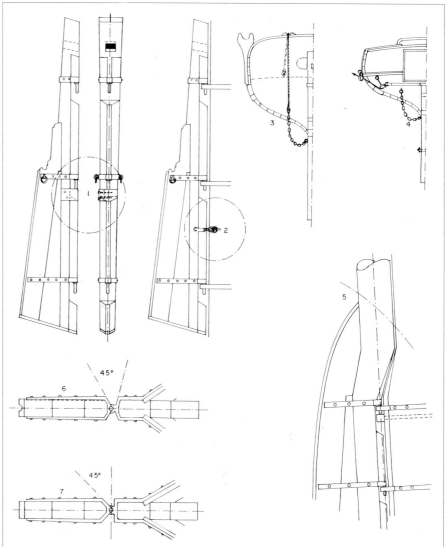

1. Wood-lock (English method)
2. Rudder strap, leathered for length of rudder's turning circle and spun over at splices and eye-bolt rings (Continental method)
3. Rudder pendant, made up from chain and rope leading over a small merchant vessel's taffrail
4. Rudder pendant from chain fitted to the transom of a small vessel of war
5. Rudder with a pintle lifting bolt around 1830. Round and forward shifted rudder stock was introduced by Gabriel Snodgrass
6. Rudder fitting from early nineteenth century onwards, with the fish being grooved
7. Rudder fitting during the eighteenth century. Please note the rectangular sternpost and the 45-degree angle on the rudder stock.

of the same size with sharper lines. An average rudder width for ships, neither sharp nor full, is that one takes ¹⁄₂in for every ft in the length of the ship.' [126]

Bobrik spoke of the lowest water-line width for men-of-war rudders as one-eighth of the extreme breadth, and one-seventh for those of merchant ships. He agreed with Duhamel that warships had a rudder three-quarters of the lowest width at water-line level, but for merchantmen he understood it to be two-thirds. Further sources vary strongly, which tells us of the problems shipwrights faced when trying to build a good rudder.

The length of a rudder was the sum of heights of the loose keel plus keel plus length of the sternpost plus 1½ to 2 feet for fitting the tiller. Müller referred to this:

'On small vessels, directly steered with a tiller on quarter-deck, it reached up to and above the quarterdeck, with others, the tiller comes into the vessel over the taffrail, therefore will be even longer.' [127]

Some writers considered that the rudder did not reach down to the loose keel, but finished a few inches above with the lower rear corner higher by about 2 inches. However, in England especially, a loose keel extension was nailed underneath to keep the rudder at full length.

The stock as the rudder's backbone was usually made from a single piece of oak, whereas, to reduce weight, softer timbers like fir were used for the after-pieces. The stock, or back, was the longest and strongest element. It took the tiller in and connected the rudder with pintles to the ship. The whole length of the side facing the sternpost was angled on both sides, usually from 42 to 45 degrees. A flat was left along the centre between these chamfers for pintle fitting, which earlier in the century was of one-fifth the stock's thickness but later was widened to a thickness of one-quar-

ter. During the first quarter of the nineteenth century the stock angle became blunter to minimise loss of strength. While the total turning degree of the rudder remained the same, the lesser degrees on the stock were taken up on the sternpost, so that in plan view it no longer looked like a rectangular wedge standing against a flat surface but like two blunt wedges pointed against each other. The stock's head was made thicker than the rest and contained a square hole to fit the tiller. Due to the stress on the head caused by tiller action, iron bands were fitted above and below the hole. Scores to fit pintles and gudgeons were also cut into the side of the stock facing the sternpost.

The first wedge-shaped, softwood plank behind the stock was the centrepiece and pointed with its tapered side upward. That and the adjacent plank were also known as after-pieces. All three were joined together with fitting bands or straps of the pintles bolted on. These after-pieces extended up to two feet above the loaded waterline, creating a step, which was the rudder's counter.

A rudder was fitted to a ship with rudder braces, consisting of pintles and gudgeons. Röding states that between four and six were needed and Steinhaus reports that they were about 4 to 4½ feet apart. A general idea about their size can be found in data collected by Bobrik on a frigate of 36 guns (1) and a merchantman of 330 tons (2):

Vessel no	(1)	(2)
Number of pintles and gudgeons (hinges) in pairs	6	5
The uppermost sternpost straps were made from iron and were long enough to embrace the sternpost head and its knee.		
The second gudgeon strap forward of the sternpost's rabbet was (long)	3ft 9in	1ft 9in
The longest, forward of the rabbet	6ft	3ft
The uppermost pintle made from iron and the straps long enough to embrace the rudder.		
All other straps long enough to be 1in away from the rudder's rear edge.		
The width of straps	4in	3in
Thickness of the bend	1⅛in	1⅛in
Diameter of pintles	3in	1⅞in
Length	1ft	9in
The lowest pintle was longer by 2in		

1. Rudder lifter according to Röding (Continental)
2. Copper sheave between pintle and gudgeon to reduce friction (English)
3. Pintles and gudgeons (English warship from 1790)
4. Helm port coat
5. Coat around the upper helm port
6. Rudder house covering an upper helm port on a French brig around 1806

All straps were fastened with half-inch spikes, spaced six inches apart, and with bolts. The hinges on copper-sheathed vessels were made from a bronze alloy, except for the uppermost, which was iron.

Nineteenth-century shipbuilding literature (Klawitter and others) mentioned a long, strong-headed bolt being driven through the entire sternpost assemblage beneath the top pintle, preventing that pintle and subsequently all others from resting directly on the gudgeon. It stopped premature wear through friction and made steering easier. The same was achieved on English ships by laying copper washers between pintles and gudgeons and nailing them to the sternpost.

Length of a hinge score was the sum of the length of a pintle plus a gudgeon's depth plus one to two inches, whereby score depth was enough for a copper sheathing not to infringe on rudder movement. To avoid strap protrusion, these were set deep enough into the chamfered stock face, with the sides also set into the rudder timbers.

It is obvious that extra precaution was taken and security of a ship's steering facility did not depend on pintles and gudgeons alone. Most common are the rudder pendants, two chains connected to ropes. They were hanging in eyebolts at both sides of the rudder's counter on the rudder's horn, also known as monkey tail. Both pendants ran either to further eyebolts in the outer reaches of the wing-transom or reached over the taffrail and fastened to bolts on deck, a method widely accepted on medium and small ships. Rudder pendants kept the rudder close to the ship if a wave unhinged it from the gudgeons. Another measure to prevent accident was a rudder strop or a wood-lock. Rudder strops were mainly used on the continent and consisted of a short rope pulled through a hole in the stock and spliced at that level to eye-bolts at both sides of the sternpost. The rope was clad in leather within reach of rudder movement to reduce wear and tear. By keeping that strop at minimum length any lifting of the rudder would be prevented. English shipbuilders preferred a wood-lock instead. Usually fitted sidewise into a score above the waterline, it completely filled the score beneath the pintle and decreased any lifting movement to a fraction. Bobrik wrote that a wood-lock was fitted at load waterline level.

A forerunner of the pintle-lifting bolt was a rudder span, or rudder lift. This was a rope that was leathered on the parts that passed the rudder, with one end fastened to an eye-bolt in the buttocks and the other leading via the helm-port on to deck where it belayed to a cleat. The span's task was to lift the rudder slightly in the gudgeons.

In the widest meaning of the word, a helm-port was a hole in the stern for the tiller to pass through on to deck. More specifically, it was also an opening in the lower counter of an overhanging stern to take in the rudder's head and the tiller. On merchant ships of less than 400 to 500 tons, where sternpost and stock often reached up to the quarter- or upper-deck, the tiller was fitted above deck. Another helm-port, therefore, had to be part of that deck. With both openings large enough to take in the entire stock and ensure its freedom of movement, and by penetrating lower counter as well as deck, a connecting aperture had to be watertight on its passage through the inside of the vessel. That strong timber structure was the rudder trunk. Every helm-port needed a rudder coat and its necessity is clearly demonstrated by Bobrik:

'To avoid an intrusion of water into a helm-port, a rudder coat, that means a tarred piece of canvas, was nailed around helm-port and rudder. In order not to interfere with rudder movement, the coat must hang downwards like a bag, sometimes even a double rudder coat was in use. Seawater renders canvas after a while inflexible, turns brittle and gets damaged by rudder motion. Consequently, waves will enter the helm-port with devastating force and cause destruction inside the stern, a vessel's weakest part, which often lead sher to founder. To prevent such a calamity, the rudder

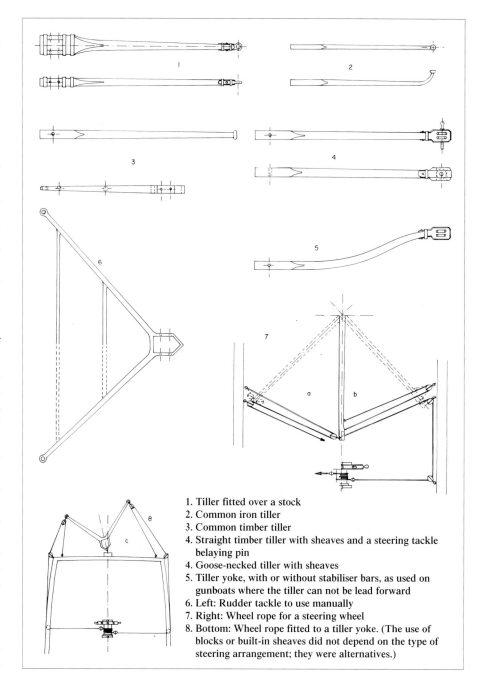

1. Tiller fitted over a stock
2. Common iron tiller
3. Common timber tiller
4. Straight timber tiller with sheaves and a steering tackle belaying pin
4. Goose-necked tiller with sheaves
5. Tiller yoke, with or without stabiliser bars, as used on gunboats where the tiller can not be lead forward
6. Left: Rudder tackle to use manually
7. Right: Wheel rope for a steering wheel
8. Bottom: Wheel rope fitted to a tiller yoke. (The use of blocks or built-in sheaves did not depend on the type of steering arrangement; they were alternatives.)

stock's upper part has been in more recent times modified to a cylindrical shape... .'[128]

Gabriel Snodgrass first introduced the cylindrical shape of the upper stock to ships of the British East India Company in 1779 and it became generally accepted in shipbuilding during the second decade of the nineteenth century. This invention brought a drastic reduction in helm-port size, thus reducing the risk of water entering, and the rudder trunk inside the cabin became a pipe that was not much bigger then the stock itself. Together with the cylindrical upper stock, a shift forward by half its diameter was initiated to make a pintle's turning point the axis of the rounded part. Bobrik gives a good description of helm-ports:

'Rudder stocks in merchantmen reach usually right up to and above the quarter-deck. To cover helm-port and rudder head,

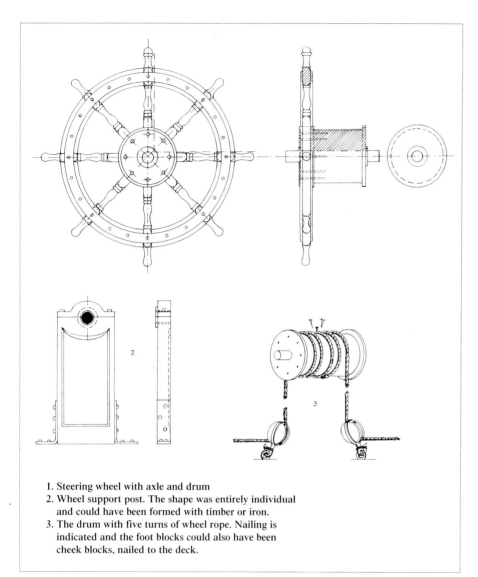

1. Steering wheel with axle and drum
2. Wheel support post. The shape was entirely individual and could have been formed with timber or iron.
3. The drum with five turns of wheel rope. Nailing is indicated and the foot blocks could also have been cheek blocks, nailed to the deck.

Only the smallest vessels and boats were steered directly by hand. In any other case a tackle was fitted to both sides of the tiller's head. One differentiated thereby between a rudder tackle, also termed a steering tackle, and a wheel rope, known also as tiller rope. The wheel rope was either fixed to the tiller's head, or at the sides, then led through blocks at the tiller's head and in the waterways towards the steering wheel, or, for vessels without a steering wheel, the steering tackle was served by hand. Röding described the latter action:

> 'On ships without a steering wheel the tiller is moved in both directions with a tackle, known as the rudder tackle. The end of its fall fastens to the side of the ship and leads around a sheave in the tiller's head, then back again to the side of the ship through a block, and from there forward of the tiller to the ship's centre, from where it will be hauled. The rudder tackle for the other side goes likewise around another sheave in the tiller's head.' [130]

Group three

A steering wheel was composed of an axle, set parallel to the keel into two supporting posts, a barrel and the actual wheel. The latter bolted to the barrel with its spokes and hub, while the axle went through its centre. The spokes reached about eight inches outside the felloes (rim) to serve as grasps, with one of them marked as mid-ship spoke. The wheel rope usually wound five turns around the barrel and, again with the helm amidships, the middle turn was nailed to the barrel and marked. The use of five turns suggests that for efficiency barrel circumference was approximately a quarter of the vessel's width (the diameter roughly $\frac{1}{12}$). Both rope ends ran vertically downward from the barrel through foot blocks toward blocks in the port and starboard waterways. The wheel, or tiller, rope was made from especially good line yarns and was not tarred, as Falconer states, 'for the purpose of traversing more readily through the blocks or pulleys'. Steering wheels can be traced to about 1703; the steering wheel visible on the St. Petersburg model of HMS *Royal Transport* from 1695 was not there before the recent restoration and so its origin is doubtful.

Further deck details will later be considered in conjunction with anchors, boats and other fittings.

a so-called rudder house stands in front of and close to the taffrail. Formed from thin planks like a companionway capping, it has on the fore side an opening for tiller movement and on the sides small cupboards for keeping paints etc.' [129]

The use of rudder houses originated before Bobrik's time, and a contemporary model of the French 24-gun brig *Le Cigne* from 1806 provides an excellent example of a similar capping. A house or a canvas coat for the upper exit of the stock was of equal importance to covering the lower helmport. Otherwise the rudder trunk would have been filled with seawater every time the deck was awash.

Group two

The tiller was a long lever, made from oak, ash or iron and used for turning the rudder. Placed either on to the stock's head, or into its square hole, the tiller was then bolted to the stock. The shape of a tiller on larger vessels was usually straight, but on smaller craft, especially when handheld, it was bent upward (goose-necked), with its end about three feet above deck to be at the correct height for the helmsman. A tiller's length was five-sixths of a vessel's extreme breadth and its thickness at the square was approximately half of the corresponding stock thickness.

Notes:
[85] Chapman as quoted in Duhamel du Monceau, H L, *Anfangsgründe der Schiffbaukunst oder Praktische Abhandlungen über den Schiffbau (1752)* translated with annotations by Christian G. D. Müller, (Berlin, 1791), repr. Horst Hamecher Kassel (1973) p.86
[86] Ibid., pp.88–9
[87] Klawitter, G D, *Vorlege-Blätter für Schiffbauer* (Berlin, 1835), repr. H Hamecher (Kassel, 1978) p.3
[88] Röding, J H, *Allgemeines Wörterbuch der Marine* Vol.1 (Hamburg, 1794, repr. Amsterdam, 1969) p.830
[89] Bobrik, E, *Handbuch der praktischen Seefahrtskunde* (Leipzig, 1848), repr. H Hamecher (Kassel, 1978) p.207
[90] Webster, N, *The Living Webster, Encyclopedic Dictionary of the English Language,* The English Language Institute of America (Chicago, 1971) p.857

[91] Rees, A, *Naval Architecture (1819–20)*, David & Charles Reprints, (London, 1970)

[92] Steinhaus, C F, *Die Schiffbaukunst in ihrem ganzen Umfang*, Hamburg (1858), repr. H Hamecher (Kassel, 1977)

[93] Duhamel du Monceau, H L, *Anfangsgründe der Schiffbaukunst oder Praktische Abhandlungen über den Schiffbau (1752)* translated with annotations by Christian G D Müller, (Berlin, 1791), repr. Horst Hamecher (Kassel, 1973) p.5: 'Wegen des zuletzt angezeigten Vortheils legt man die losen Kiele auch häufig unter ganz neue Schiffe.'

[94] Falconer, W, *An Universal Dictionary of the Marine* (London, 1780) repr. David & Charles Reprints (London, 1970) p.164

[95] Röding, J H, *Allgemeines Wörterbuch der Marine* Vol. 2 (Hamburg, 1794, repr. Amsterdam 1969) p.824: 'Beyde zusammenstossenden Enden werden auf halber Dicke eingeschnitten, so daß diese Einschnitte lothrecht eine Lasch ausmachen, welche alsdann mit starken Bolzen verbolzt wird. Unter der Lasch und dem Vorsteven wird alsdann der Unterlauf gebolzt. Solche Verbindung findet man insonderheit bey englischen Schiffen'.

[96] Duhamel du Monceau, H L, op. cit., p.8: 'Außer diesem Zapfen [...] findet man auch oft ähnliche Befestigungen, wie bey dem fore foot, durch eiserne Schleifen, die hinter dem Achtersteven um, und unter dem Kiel durchgehen. Auch wohl bloße Winkeleisen auf beyden Seiten, deren oberer Hacken gegen die Seite des Achtersteven, die untere gegen die Seiten des Kiels genagelt werden'.

[97] Ibid., pp.57–85

[98] Rees, Abraham, op. cit., p. 41

[99] Paasch, H, *Illustrated Marine Encyclopedia* (London, 1890) repr. Argus Books (London, 1977)

[100] Muller in Duhamel du Monceau, op. cit., p.221: 'Der englische und holländische Schiffbau kennen diese beyden Spanten nicht, und selbst die neuesten französischen Schiffbauer kehren sich nicht mehr daran...'

[101] Klawitter, G D, op. cit., p.14: 'Früher pflegte man diese Kimmungsplanken eben so stark zu machen, weil sie besonders den sehr flach gebauten Schiffen eine bedeutende Festigkeit gaben, wenn dieselben mit der Kimmung auf Grund kamen.'

[102] Falconer, W, *A New Universal Dictionary of the Marine, improved and enlarged by William Burney Ll.D* (London, 1815) repr. MacDonald and Jane's (London, 1974) p.17

[103] Röding, J H, op. cit., Vol.2, p.206: 'Sind große hölzerne cylinderförmige Pinnen, die man, insonderheit so tief das Schiff im Wasser gehet, dazu gebraucht, die Planken gegen die Inhölzer zu befestigen'.

[104] Falconer, W A, *A New Universal Dictionary of the Marine, improved and enlarged by William Burney Ll.D* (London, 1815), repr. MacDonald and Jane's (London, 1974) p.579

[105] Fincham, J, *A History of Naval Architecture* (London, 1851), repr. Scolar Press (London, 1979) p.94

[106] Lavery, B, *The Arming and Fitting of English Ships of War 1600–1815*, Conway Maritime Press Ltd (London, 1987) p.62

[107] PRO Adm 106/2507

[108] Duhamel du Monceau, H L, op. cit., p.26: 'Eigentlich sollten alle Weeger, welche auf die Laschungen der Innhölzer treffen, stärker als die übrigen, und eingeschnitten seyn, wenigstens die zunächst neben dem Kolschwinn und die Kimweeger. Man findet es aber nur bey schweren Schiffen, und auch da nicht allemal. Man nennt die eingeschnittenen Weeger zum Unterschiede von den bloß aufgenagelten auch Bandweeger.'

[109] Klawitter, G D, op. cit., p.17

[110] Ibid., p.8: 'Sie werden an der innern Seite des Schiffes gewöhnlich auf der Garnierung im Vorder- und Hintertheil angebracht und dienen dazu, den Steven mit den zunächst gelegenen Innhölzern zu verbinden.'

[111] Steinhaus, C F, *Die Schiffbaukunst in ihrem ganzen Umfange* Vol.2, (Hamburg, 1858), repr. H Hamecher (Kassel, 1977) p.108: 'Wenn das Schiff keine Worpen hat, so müssen natürlich auch hier die entsprechende Anzahl Bänder liegen, von denen einer die Bargweiger miteinander verbindet und so auch hier als Decksband dient'.

[112] Duhamel du Monceau, H L, op. cit., p.35: 'Andere Nationen brauchen an ihrer Stelle Federbolzen mit großen Köpfen, die von außen herein durch die Außenplanken und Innhölzer getrieben, und dergestalt an die Balken genagelt oder verbolzt werden, daß man sie leicht bekleiden kann'.

[113] Steinhaus, C F, op. cit., Vol.2, p.106: 'Auch die Art der Befestigung trägt viel zur Verschönerung des Decks bei, die Planken werden daher nicht so wie jede andere verspiekert, sondern, bevor der Spieker eingeschlagen, vermittelst eines Centrumbohrers ein ungefähr ? Zoll

tiefes Lock gebohrt, worin der Kopf kommt, damit dieser nicht die Planken berührt und das Holz zerquetscht, in welchen Stellen das Wasser alsdann Gelegenheit hat mit Leichtigkeit einzudringen und dadurch sowohl den Spieker angreift, als auch eine Fäulniß im Holze verursacht; der Spieker wird dann vermittelst eines Setzhammers eingetrieben und in dem Loche ein föhrener Pfropfen gesetzt, dessen Faden mit dem Faden der Planken laufen muß; bevor dieses aber geschieht, ist es nothwendig das Loch mit Terpentin oder Firniß auszufüllen, weil der Pfropfen sonst leicht wieder ausgestoßen werden kann. Durch diese Vorrichtung ist es nicht allein dem Wasser verhindert die Spieker anzugreifen, sondern man kann an den meisten Stellen kaum sehen wo das Deck seine Befestigung hat.'

[114] Falconer, W A, *An Universal Dictionary of the Marine* (London, 1780), repr. David & Charles Reprints (1970) p.142

[115] Röding, J H, op. cit., Vol.1, p.304: 'Auf den Schotten ist eine Klappe oder ein Dach, welches bey gutem Wetter halb oder ganz aufgeklappt werden kann. Bey schlechtem Wetter wird solches aber zugemacht, auch wird alsdann die untere Hälfte mit einem Schieber zugeschoben, über welchen man hinwegsteigen muß, wenn man unters Deck gehen will. Dieser Schieber verhindert, daß das Wasser nicht durch die Luke unters Deck laufe, wenn das Schiff Stürzseen bekömmt.'

[116] Bobrik, E, *Handbuch des praktischen Seefahrtskund* (Leipzig, 1848), repr. H Hamecher (Kassel, 1978) p.221: 'Die Lucke zum Volkslogis hat entweder eine ähnliche Einrichtung, oder eine an Scharnieren bewegliche Fallthüre oder Kappe.'

[117] Röding, J H, op. cit., Vol.1, p.804: 'Kappe der Luken. Engl: Companion, auf der Hinterluke die zur Kajüte führt. Die Kappe auf der Luke zum Volkslogis heißt Hood.'

[118] Bobrik, E, op. cit., p.221: 'Weil die hinteren Kajütsfenster, namentlich bei Kauffahrteyschiffen, nur im Hafen geöffnet bleiben, in See aber mit dichten Pforten gegen die von hinten anschlagenden Wellen verschlossen werden: so befindet sich in dem Kajütdeck eine Lucke, durch welche das Licht hineinfällt; sie heißt das einfallende Licht oder   . Scheilicht, und wird mit einer Stülpluke zugedeckt, welche mit Fensterscheiben versehen ist, die an der oberen Seite durch ein darüber gespanntes Drathnetz gegen Beschädigungen geschützt sind.'

[119] Röding, J H, op. cit., Vol.2, p.521: 'Während der Reise wenn das Tau nicht gebraucht wird, kleidet man diese Stellen, so wie die Masten und Pumpen mit einem Kragen zu.'

[120] Rees, Abraham, op. cit., p.48: 'The fore riding bitts are 1 foot 8 inches square, and placed four feet asunder or two feet on each side the middle line.'

[121] Duhamel du Monceau, H L, op. cit., p.43: 'Um die Back vorn ganz frey zu behalten, macht man jetzt die Kraanbalken aus einem Knie, dessen einer Zacken inwendig gegen die Balken und Innhölzer stark verbolzt ist, der andere bildet das hervorragende Stück, von deem wir eben geredet haben' (Duhamel). 'Dies ist die gewöhnliche Anordnung auf solchen Schiffen, die keine Back haben' (Müller).

[122] Röding, J H, op. cit., Vol.2, p.676: 'Auf kleineren und eindeckigten Fahrzeugen legt man nur eine starke Unterlage auf den Balken; der den Fuß des Bugspriets trägt, die noch über einen oder ein Paar andern Balken hinreicht. Es erhält denn seine Befestigung durch einen oder ein Paar eiserne Bügel, die über den Fuß dicht angepasst sind, und mit Augen platt auf das Deck treten, durch welche starke eiserne Bolzen getrieben werden, die unten auf Platten versplintet sind'.

[123] Ibid., p.627: 'Das Galjon ist eigentlich eine unnütze Beschwerung des Vorschiffs und befördert die Kielgebrechlichkeit'.

[124] Steinhaus, C F, op. cit., p.119: 'Das Steuer muß, soweit dieses in's Wasser taucht, eine parallele Dicke haben oder auch um ein Geringes an seinem Hintertheile verjüngt sein, welche Bestimmungen jedoch von dem Verlaufe des Schiffes an diesem Ende abhängig sind; da aber die Wirkungen des Wassers, namentlich auf einer solchen Tiefe unter der Oberfläche, bis jetzt zu wenig bekannt sind, und aus dieser Unkenntniß sich manche Fehler in der Bildung des Steuers ergeben, so wollen wir hier einige in solchen Fällen durch Erfahrung mit Vortheil angewendete Verbesserungen folgen lassen. Es ist nehmlich ein nicht selten vorkommender Uebelstand bei dem Steuer, daß es, wenn das Schiff einige Fahrt läuft, entweder ein Zittern beginnt, welches mit der Schnelligkeit desselben zunimmt, oder auch, daß es im hohem Seegange heftig schlägt; diese Bewegungen sind äußerst lästig und in manchen Fällen auch sehr schädlich, denn die erstere wird oftmals so stark, daß das ganze Hinterschiff davon erschüttert, wodurch die Nähte sich begehen müssen und, wenn dieses andauert eine Leckage die unausbleibliche Folge sein wird; in einem solchen Falle hat die Erfahrung gezeigt, daß durch eine geringe Verjüngung am Hintertheile

des Steuers diesem Uebelstande abgeholfen wurde. Das Schlagen des
Steuers ist noch viel gefährlicher und besteht hauptsächlich darin, daß
es im hohen Seegange heftig nach der einen oder der anderen Seite
geworfen wird, wodurch dann leicht die Fingerlinge und Haken, ja das
Steuer selbst zerbrechen kann; im Falle aber keines von diesem
geschieht, wird doch durch einen solchen plötzlichen Druck das
Steuerrad mit heftiger Gewalt herumgedreht, so daß der Mann, welch-
er seinen Posten dabei hat, über dasselbe hingeschleudert werden
kann; hier hat nun wieder die Erfahrung gezeigt, daß diesem
Uebelstande dadurch abgeholfen wurde, indem man das Steuer, wenn
es hinten abgerundet war, scharfkantig machte, oder auch, wenn es
platt war, eine Hohlkehle auf der ganzen Länge darin anbrachte'.*

[125] McKay, L, *The Practical Shipbuilder* (New York, 1839), repr.
MacDonald and Jane's (London, 1974) p.63

[126] Klawitter, G D, op. cit., p.23: '*Die Breite des Ruders richtet sich nach
der hinteren Schärfe des Schiffes. Völlig gebaute Schiffe bedürfen
natürlich eines breitern Ruders als scharf gebaute von derselben
Größe; eine Mittelgrüße für Schiffe, die weder sehr scharf noch sehr
stumpf sind, ist die: daß man ? Zoll für jeden Fuß der Länge des
Schiffes zur Breite des Ruders annimmt*'.

[127] Duhamel du Monceau, H L, op. cit., p.158: '*Bey kleineren Schiffen, die
auf dem halben Verdeck unmittelbar am Helmstock gesteuert werden,
reicht es ganz durch bis über das halber Verdeck. Bey andern kömmt
der Helmstock über das Heckbord in das Schiff, da wird es noch
länger.*'

[128] Bobrik, E, op. cit., p.229: '*Damit das Wasser nicht in das Hennegat
dringt, wird ein Brohk, d. h. ein getheertes Segeltuch um das Hennegat
und das Ruder gespickert; damit aber das Ruder nicht in seinen
Bewegungen durch den Brohk gehindert wird, muß dieser wie ein
Beutel lose herabhängen; zuweilen hat man einen doppelten Brohk.
Von dem Seewasser wird aber das Segeltuch bald steif, und bricht bei
den Bewegungen des Steuers. Alsdann dringen die Wellen oft mit
gefährlicher Gewalt in das Hennegat, und richten in dem Heck, als
dem schwächsten Theile des Schiffs, Verwüstungen an, die schon zum
völligen Untergange desselben geführt haben. Um diesem Uebel
abzuhelfen, giebt man in neuerer Zeit dem Ruderpfosten oben eine
cylindrische Gestalt*'.

[129] Ibid. p.231: '*Bei Kauffahrteischiffen reicht der Ruderpfosten gewöhnlich ganz durch bis über das Deck der Schanze. Zur Bedeckung des
Hennegats und des Ruderkopfs steht dann dicht am Heckbord das
sogehnannte Ruderhaus, von dünnen Brettern der Kajütkappe ähnlich
gebildet; vorne mit einer Oeffnung zum Spielraume der Ruderpinne,
an den Seiten mit kleinen Behältnissen zum Aufbewahren von
Oelfarben u. dgl.*'

[130] Röding, J H, op. cit., Vol.2, p.399: '*Auf Schiffen die kein Steuerrad
haben, wird die Ruderpinne an jeder Seite mit einer Talje bewegt,
welche die Rudertalje heit. Das Ende des Läufers derselben ist an der
Seite des Schiffes fest und fährt um eine vorne in der Ruderpinne
befindlichen Scheibe wieder nach der Seite des Schiffs durch einen
Block und von da nach der Mitte des Schiffsvor der Ruderpinne
woselbst er angeholt wird. Die Rudertalje an der andern Seite fährt
eben so um eine andere, vorn in der Ruderpinne befindliche, Scheibe.*'

Chapter 6

Masting and Rigging

AS concluded in Origin Of Schooners, two-masted fore-and-aft-rigged vessels (the mast furthest aft being the mainmast) with an additional topsail were designated topsail schooners. In her earliest concept the schooner was only fore-and-aft rigged, a fact underlined by contemporary documentation in the form of a model (*Royal Transport* of 1695) and artwork by Willem van de Velde, the Younger, before 1705 and Burgis in about 1725. Only gaff sails were hoisted to the masts and the earlier vessels had merely the main sail spread by a boom. One of the great maritime encyclopaedic minds of the eighteenth century, the German Johannes Röding, wrote that: 'The foremast has a

gaff sail set and the main mast a boom sail, of which both are of considerable height.' [131]

That notion of a schooner rig was generally observed until the middle of the eighteenth century. An exception is shown in the Burgis' etching 'A View of Boston' (1725), in which a schooner sail boom is rigged on one of the three schooners. Situated at the right middle ground of the picture, that vessel is fitted with a cutwater as well as a figurehead. She flew a jack plus a common pennant on the mainmast, establishing her as an early schooner-rigged sloop of the Royal Navy or Customs. Another sketchy drawing of a schooner sail boom is from 1747, when Ashley Bowen

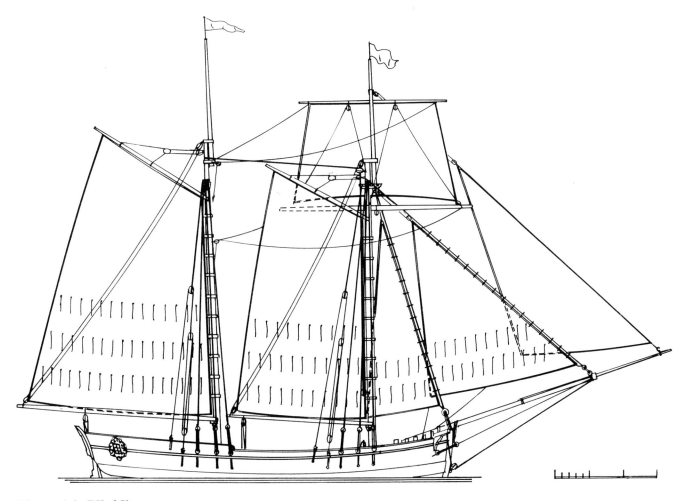

Schooner rig by F H af Chapman

immortalised the American schooner *Peter & Mary*. From then on these booms became a more frequent part of schooner rigs. There were between one and three head sails on early schooners and not every bowsprit was rigged with a jib boom.

No record, either textual or visual, can be found of the development of the topsail schooner rig between the time of Burgis' 'A View of Boston' and the drafting of the *St. Ann*. The dead eyes on the draught of the English sloop *Sharke* of 1731 strongly suggest that she had a topsail on her schooner mast, but this can only be assumed. Four dead eyes were provided for that mast but only three dead eyes for the main mast. Why would the foremost mast have one extra dead-eye pair if rigged like the main mast? Only a further strain of an additional sail justified the extra pair of shrouds. It is impossible to sustain the view taken by the American maritime historian Merritt A Edson, Jr[132] that topsail schooners existed prior to 1708. His assumption was based on a statement made in Lord Cornbury's 1708 report to the Lords of Trade and Plantations: 'There has formerly belonged to this port [New York] 32 topsail vessels, beside sloops; now we can't reckon above 28 topsail vessels and sloops'.

He considered those topsail vessels as an early form of topsail vessel. However, sloops were then only one-masted fore-and-aft-rigged vessels with a traversing gaff and a boom, as indicated in Burgis' 'A View of New York' from 1717 and 'Sloop of Boston Light' from 1720. What Lord Cornbury described as topsail vessels were the second known type of gaff-rigged craft, those with a standing gaff and without boom. Since its inception around 1625 this type of square-rigged topsail belonged to the sloop rig and was a remnant of the sprit-rigged Dutch *boeier* noted as early as 1565. There is a good example of such a vessel in 'Hoy with long-gaff sail', the 1717 work by W Sutherland[133]. Therefore, these two vessel types were not sloop and schooner, but sloop and hoy, two rigs that ultimately shaped the topsail schooner rig.

The earliest undisputed written confirmation of a topsail schooner rig is given on the draught of the Portuguese schooner *St. Ann* from 1736. According to the plan's spar and sail dimensions it is probable, but not certain, that the vessel carried not only a topsail, but also a topgallant sail. Built and rigged for speed and employed as a dispatch vessel, she carried all the known sails of the epoch to make use of even the slightest breeze. During these early years it was usually the exception, and not the rule, that was recorded, which is why the note on sail size appears on the draught.

The masts, spars and sail dimensions of the *St. Ann* provide, as an alternative to 'Topg'lt yard', the term 'Pidgeon each'. That term puzzled some modern authors, including M A Edson, Jr, who saw in it an early form of gaff-topsail and searched, without success, for a connection between the corrupted word Pidgeon and the Portuguese words *Pingente* or *Peidando*. Gaff-topsails as well as topgallant sails in schooner rigging belonged on the whole to the second half of the eighteenth century. The term 'Pidgeon' was probably used to describe additional triangular sails above the uppermost square-rigged sail. D Steel spoke of this type of sail as 'very seldom used and not usually made in general practice'[134] and called it Skyscraper. In the French nautical language several names for this particular sail can be found, including *Aile de pigeon* (Wings of a pigeon). The use of the word 'each' after 'Pidgeon' strongly indicates the use of more than one, pointing again to the skyscraper – a sail, or perhaps a pair of sails, running with their halyards over the mast truck sheaves to be hoisted to both sides of the mast. Tacks and sheets fastened to the uppermost yard. It is very probable that skyscrapers of the late eighteenth century and similar sails of the clipper era, for example the moonraker, had their origin in the Pidgeon of these small fast vessels of an earlier time.

To establish straight rules for the evolution of schooner rigging is nearly impossible. Contemporary pictorial sources portray the early eighteenth century very much as an experimental time. We can accept 1695 as the birth year of the fore-and-aft schooner rig. From the 1720s to 1735 the topsail schooner evolved and from about mid-century there is evidence of schooners with main topsails. The majority of vessels with main topsails also carried schooner sail booms. Sketches by Ashley Bowen provide some of the earliest evidence for this, beginning with *Peter & Mary* from 1747, in which the vessel carries her topsail only on the mainmast.

That sketch as well as illustrative work by P Revere (1773), E Gwyn (1780) and W Falconer (1769, 1780) point to the rigging of a spritsail yard and sail to the bowsprit of a schooner. J Baugean's etching from 1814 'An armed schooner drying her sails' shows a fully rigged spritsail topsail yard on the jib boom directly in front of the martingale, which is an obvious mistake by the artist as the sail is rendered unworkable because of the martingale stay. The armed topsail schooner portrayed by Gwyn differs in her appearance from the mainstream not so much in having topgallant sails set, but in having her topsails extremely deep roached to two-thirds of their depths, indicating the stepping of cutter masts. She has the rig of a cutter with the bowsprit mounted at the starboard side of the stem's head but otherwise has the appearance of a sloop with figurehead and raised quarterdeck and not of a cutter (cutter-built schooners were usually rigged with cutter masts). Another British armed schooner, sketched in watercolour by A Roux in 1803, gives a very good impression of those vessels. It appears that the acceptance of topgallant sails in a schooner rig became more widespread in the last quarter of the century, coinciding with the time when schooners in general were built larger. Ashley Bowen, serving as master on American colonial vessels, illustrated his journals with sketches of vessels he worked or travelled on. He indicated topgallant sails first in 1779, with illustrations by Gwyn and others appearing in and around 1780.

Even with the schooner rig being conceived in England from rigs developed by Dutch seafarers in the seventeenth century, it was only one (probably the first) two-masted fore-and-aft rig among several new developments in the eighteenth century. Later in the century it largely became an American affair, with the officially recorded number of schooner-rigged vessels in European fleets minimal by comparison. For example, between 1764 and the end of the Napoleonic wars the British Royal Navy never had more than two or three per cent of its total number of ships classified as schooners. The authors of the late eighteenth century still saw the schooner mainly as a part of the Anglo-Saxon/American maritime world, as can be seen in these comments from Röding:

> 'A two-masted rig, preferable only for long and narrow vessels. [...] By Englishmen, Americans and generally in the West Indies are schooners very often in use for the transportation of merchandise and carry 50 to 100 or more lasts. [1 Last = approx. 2 tons]'. [135]

Although there are enough draughts and other sources available to recreate a good picture of so dissimilarly shaped vessels as schooners, it is not so easy to find contemporary references to their rigging. To establish an adequately detailed description one has to rely mainly on illustrative sources and general eighteenth-century documentation on masting and rigging, which then have to be examined and cross-checked with more widely printed specifications of the nineteenth century.

Masts and Spars

Masts

Various mast types were in use and their respective rigging gives evidence to the experimental nature of schooner rigs in their early days. At the beginning plain pole masts were used, followed by ship masts with trestle and cross trees and a topmast extension with or without a long pole head for topsail-rigged vessels. Masts with an integrated topmast and a stepped light flagpole, or a topgallant mast housed in iron caps either afore or abaft the masthead were used on cutter-built schooners during the latter half of the century. These were not always of similar proportional dimensions, thus making it difficult on the whole to apply rules. By comparing a small number of eighteenth-century vessels the relative differences can be clearly seen.

All dimensions of *Royal Transport* (1695) are taken from photographs of the St. Petersburg model and related to the known hull dimensions. These of *St. Ann* (1736) and *Elgen* (1769) originate from contemporary draughts. Data for the French Schooner From Brest (1769) and the Eighteenth Century Schooner Of 21 Metres is laid down in E Pâris' work[136], while the specifications for *Sultana* come from an original draught and a Navy Board report.

Name	Length of main mast	Diameter	Rake
Royal Transport	3.40 x extr. breadth	$\frac{1}{50}$	17°
St. Ann	4.63 x "	$\frac{1}{75}$	13°
Elgen	4.00 x "	$\frac{1}{70}$	4½°
Schooner From Brest	4.55 x "	$\frac{1}{70}$	—
21m Schooner	3.00 x "	$\frac{1}{46}$	7½°
Sultana	3.40 x "	$\frac{1}{48}$	8°

In contrast, the nineteenth-century values provided by Fincham[137] (1829), Steinhaus[138] (1858) and Brady[139] (1876), are much more uniform:

Author	Length of main mast	Diameter	Rake
Fincham	2.93 x extr. breadth	$\frac{1}{40}$	15°
Steinhaus	3.10 x "	$\frac{1}{40}$	11–12°
Brady	3.47 x "	$\frac{1}{47}$	—

As far as can be ascertained from the few sources available, schooner masts in the first few decades were only pole masts without any extension, as can be seen in the model of HMS *Royal Transport*, Willem van de Velde's painting and the draught of *St. Ann*. William Burgis' etching from 1725 is not entirely explicit in this regard and the foremast could by some imagination have had a topmast stepped behind the mast. Was this a slip of the etcher's tool or was it actually there; and if it was there, what was its purpose? The stepped topmast comes to the fore in the dead-eye arrangement of HMS *Spence* (1730) and in Ashley Bowen's sketches as early as 1746. The cutter-mast with a stepped topgallant mast can be seen as a product of the last quarter of the eighteenth century.

Like all masts on smaller vessels, masts on schooners were not built but made from a single piece of timber. Proportional diameters of these masts at their heel, hounds and masthead did not deviate very much from the known estimates for larger eighteenth-century ships, and should therefore also be acceptable for the smaller vessels of that period.

Mastheads

While the Royal Navy preferred square mastheads, those on the Continent were predominantly rounded. Fincham and Steinhaus agreed that during the nineteenth century a preference for round mastheads existed everywhere. Masthead lengths on early schooners varied considerably:

Royal Transport	$\frac{1}{12}$ x length of mast
St. Ann	$\frac{1}{8}$ x mainmast, $\frac{1}{9}$ x foremast
Elgen	$\frac{1}{9}$ x mainmast, $\frac{1}{8}$ x foremast
Schooner From Brest	$\frac{1}{12}$ x mainmast, $\frac{1}{9}$–$\frac{1}{8}$ x foremast
21m Schooner	$\frac{1}{8}$ x length of mast
Sultana	$\frac{1}{8}$ x mainmast, $\frac{1}{10}$–$\frac{1}{11}$ x foremast
Royal Navy Schooners	$\frac{1}{8}$–$\frac{1}{10}$ x length of mast

In the vicinity of gaff and boom jaws masts were sheathed in copper to minimise frictional wear and tear. Steel explained that in cutters and other small craft, mast and topmast were often integrated parts, with the topmast being formed by the mast's upper third or quarter. Hounds and bolster formed then the mast's stop and the topmast's head was squared. A cutter mast's lower section of four to five feet above deck was trimmed in an octagonal shape. Above it the part up to the mast hounds or mast bibs, including the topmast section to the topmast hounds, was rounded but the head itself was squared. A mast with stepped topmast had a squared mast-

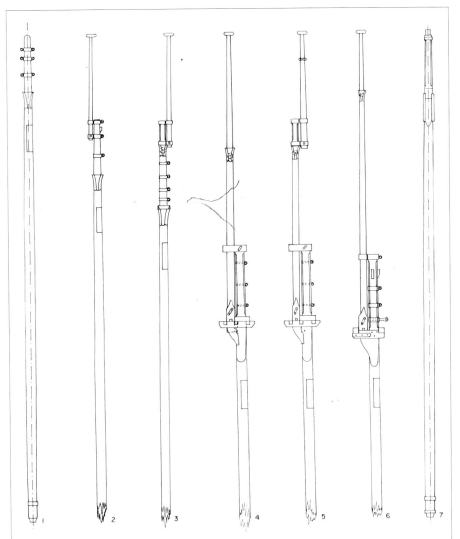

1. Pole mast with hounding, iron bands and copper cladding for the gaff
2. Same type of mast with a flagpole fitted
3. Cutter mast with a second hounding with a sheave; a topgallant mast is stepped abaft the mast
4. Mast and a topmast with a long pole-head and timber cap
5. Same mast with a topmast with normal head and an abaft stepped topgallant mast
6. Mast with a lower cap (timber), an iron cap and a short poled topmast
7. Front view of a lower mast with bibs and a normal head

hoop should be at least 14 inches above the heel and that the presence of head-weakening timber knots strongly influenced the number of head hoops. Steinhaus only referred to fitted head hoops as rigging serving parts and gave them a width of 3 to 4 inches and a thickness of ⅜ to ½ inch.

Another mast hoop, the futtock necklace, was introduced to the rigging early in the second decade of the nineteenth century. Fitted below the hounds or bibs, it first served only as an alternative point for the fastening of futtock shrouds but later also became the mast bracket for the lower yard's truss. Darcy Lever[140] remarked that Captain Tarbutt initially used this invention in 1811 on his ship, the East Indiaman *Apollo*.

Mast hounds

These were octagonal and had an upper diameter of 0.8 to 1.3 times the largest mast diameter, the lower being 0.6 to 0.75 times the largest. Topmasts had as upper 0.8 times the largest and the lower 0.6 times topmast diameter. Hounds were never larger than the cap-hole they had to be fitted through. The hound's height was ⅛ to ⅟₂₀ the mast's length. When the mast had to be prepared for cheeks, the hound section would be squared for a proper fit. Corresponding measurements were supplied by Steel. The length of hounds or cheeks was ⅞₅ times the masthead. Loose knees, known as bibs, were bolted to the fore edge of the cheeks. Made from elm, bibs were 3 to 5 inches thick, were nine-tenths of the cheek's length and three-fifths of their own length wide. A step in a bib's rear face localised its position on the cheek and four bolts connected both parts with each other.

Steinhaus and Fincham discussed the mast hounds at length. Steinhaus gave the following measurements: the length was 4 to 6 times the largest mast diameter, with the width one-and-a-third that diameter. In the upper part of the cheek the thickness equalled that of the trestletrees, but the lower end was only one third of the upper and was let into the mast by ¾ to 1 inch. Bolt diameters ranged from ¼ to ⅞ inch. Fincham provided additional information: the hound pieces, in single-tree masts, were formed with the knees in one piece. They were half as thick as the trestletrees, but never less than 3 inches. In breadth they were the same as the masthead, with an addition for the breadth of the knee formed on the fore part for supporting the trestletrees – the breadth of the knee being equal to the diameter of the topmast and possibly extended to the fore side of the fid hole. Their length was two-fifths the length of the head, without the additional length, or ⅟₁₈ the given length of the mast. Fincham also advised that cutter masts should be a length of only one-fifth of the masthead to enable a higher hoist for the gaff, and that the aft side of that part should be kept equal to the mast and rounded to avoid jamming the gaff's jaws.

Instead of iron caps and trees as supports for a lower mast's loose extension (top- or topgallant mast) a lower cap was sometimes used. That fixture should not be confused with a normal lower mast's cap. Topmast shrouds were usually led to or through the ends of crosstrees, but lower cap spreaders could be installed to fulfil that function. A more in-depth description of the lower cap can be found later. Shrouds were not rigged to masts housed in small iron caps (topgallant masts).

head, with the topmast secured within a timber cap and between trestle- and crosstrees. Masts fitted with a topgallant mast usually only used two iron caps: they were checked with a bolt through the lower cap, while a topmast between trestle- and cross-trees was secured with a fid across the trestletrees.

Three to four eyebolts for the mast's rigging blocks were driven from the back through the masthead. Of 1¼ to 1½ inches in diameter, they were clinched at the front. When these bolts were fitted iron plates were placed over the holes to stop the bolt from working loose through rigging pressure. Some ship-builders preferred to press mast hoops with eyelets over the masthead to prevent any weakening from bolt-hole drilling.

Fincham and Steinhaus both wrote about the process of making a pole mast. They agreed that at least one iron hoop should be driven on to both heel and head to forestall splitting in a one-piece mast. Fincham also noted that the heel

Trees

Contemporary sources provide specifications only for top-mast trees of larger ships, which in substance were near identical with lower mast trees of smaller vessels:

Trestletrees

Their length was 3½ inches for every yard of topmast length. Height before 1775 was $^{25}/_{26}$ inches per foot length, while post 1775 this became 1⅛ inch per foot length. Width before 1775 was three-quarters the height, while after 1775 it became two-thirds the height.

These dimensions for a ship's lower trestletrees are from an American source dated 1826[141]. The basis for measuring was the main top (half the moulded breadth in width and two-thirds the width in length). The fore top was nine-tenths of these dimensions and the mizzen top four-fifths the latter. Lengths of trestle- and crosstrees were set accordingly. Depth of trestletrees was three-fifths the mast's diameter at the partners, with the breadth being half the depth. Topmast trestletrees were in length two-fifths the lower trestletrees, in breadth and depth half the lower dimension.

Crosstrees

Their length up to 1775 was ⅞₅ topmast length and post 1775 became one-and-a-third the trestletree length. Height before 1775 was half the trestletree height and after 1775 became seven-eighths this height. Width before 1775 was equal that of the trestletree, which became one-and-a-quarter of this after 1775.

The dimensions of these as given in the American source of 1826 were: Length of the after-crosstree was three-fifths the lower crosstree, while the middle crosstree was five-sixths the after, and the foremost five-sixths the middle. Breadth was equal to the topmast trestletrees, while depth was four-fifths the breadth.

Fincham provides measurements for the crosstrees of a cutter mast: the length was one-third topmast length, the width seven-twelfths topmast diameter and the height measured five-sevenths the width, with a gradual reduction toward the ends to three-fifths of the centre's height, after being of constant height over the centre quarter. Reductions were made from the lower side and a mortise of one-sixth the cap's height was cut only into the lower cap's surface.

Fincham also gave information on general tree dimensions. The following are averaged approximations from his work:

Crosstrees: Length = ⅖ x topgallant mast length
Width = ¹/₃₂ to ¹/₃₅ x crosstree length
Height = ⁷/₁₀ to ⁹/₁₀ x crosstree width

He stated also that the foremost crosstree was one foot shorter then the hindmost.

Trestletrees: Length = ⅕ x topgallant mast length
Width = ¹/₁₆ x trestletree length
Height = 1.8 x their width

Contrary to trestletree height, which remained with only the

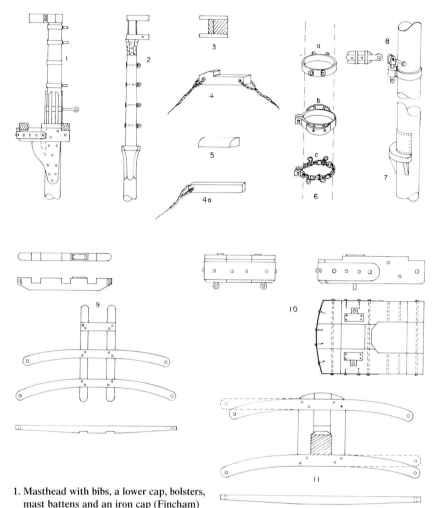

1. Masthead with bibs, a lower cap, bolsters, mast battens and an iron cap (Fincham)
2. Round masthead with hounding, bolster and iron caps for a topgallant mast
3. Bibs as seen from above
4. Topmast timber fid
4a. Iron topmast fid
5. Bolster
6. Futtock necklaces: a) Lever; b) Fincham; c) chain necklace
7. Boom jaws support and mast copper protection
8. Boom with pintle connection, about 1850
9. Trestletrees and crosstrees
10. Lower cap
11. Lower cap with cross trees. Spreaders (dashed lines) were alternately used instead during the nineteenth century.

ends chamfered, eighteenth-century crosstrees had a constant middle section of two-sevenths the length, which tapered on the lower side towards the end to half the centre height. These ends formed semicircles with holes for the shrouds 4 inches away from their outer perimeter. To join trestletrees and crosstrees, the lower side of the latter was mortised 1 inch deep at the width of the trestletrees. The remaining height of the crosstree was cut into the trestletree to achieve a flush surface when both pieces were set into each other. Crosstrees were placed in a way that the hindmost sat directly aft of the masthead, with the second at its front and the foremost 1 inch before the topmast iron plates. These were for the topmast fid to rest on and nailed abreast the topmast to both upper sides of the trestletrees.

Lower cap

Fincham described this extensively: its length measured two and three-quarter times the topmast diameter plus the masthead diameter at mast-stop level (top of hounds). Cap width was three times the topmast diameter, while height was one-fifth of that width. A lower cap enclosed the lower part of a masthead and protruded at the rear by $\frac{7}{12}$ the topmast diameter for fitting the rear spreader. As a rule the fore edge of the topmast hole was ¾ inch plus $\frac{7}{12}$ the topmast diameter away from the fore end, or was positioned in a way that a space of half the topmast diameter remained between masthead and topmast heel. The cap's fore end was rounded and a flat iron band clasped around the semicircle and extended to the fore edge of the masthead. The band, which had a width of two-thirds the cap's height – with the extended sides usually

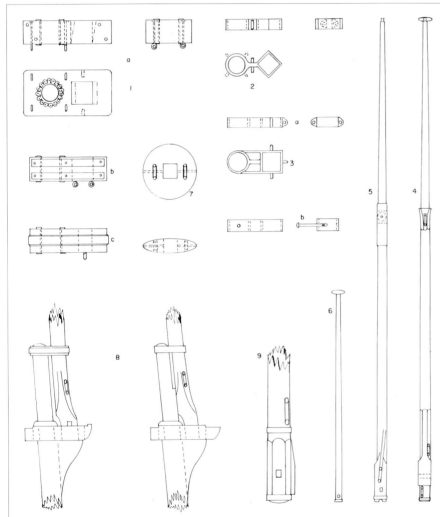

1. Mast cap: a) English before 1775, the dash-dot lines indicate alterations after 1775;
  b) Continental with iron reinforcements (Röding 1793);
  c) French about 1800, with an iron band around and slightly smaller than the English caps.
2. Iron cap for a round head: eyelets at the round part (Fincham); alternative eyelets could be placed to both sides of the connector (Fincham and Steinhaus)
3. Iron cap for a square head: a) an upper; b) a lower with a fid bolt
4. English topmast with a long pole head after 1770
5. French styled Continental topmast about 1800
6. Round topgallant mast with fid hole
7. Truck
8. Topmast heel variations according to Steinhaus, about 1850
9. Topmast heel (Fincham, English 1830)

smaller by 1½ inches – was set flush into the outside of the cap. Three bolts kept all cap segments together and a further two bolted the cap to the masthead. As lower caps were not resting on cheeks but on hounds, they continued to the upper side of the cap, with sides and rear squared and reduced to masthead thickness. From the hounds octagonal shape only the front remained in place to fix the fore and aft positions of the cap. When fitted with a lower cap, a masthead was usually rounded.

Spreader

This had a length of one-third topmast length, a width of $\frac{7}{12}$ topmast diameter and a height of $\frac{3}{5}$ its width. With the centre quarter at constant thickness, the lower sides were tapered toward the ends to $\frac{1}{3}$ that height. They narrowed in plan view slightly over these distances, the ends being $\frac{3}{5}$ the centre part, whereby that reduction at the foremost spreader was taken off the fore side and by the hindmost at the rear. With rounded ends like crosstrees they connected to the cap with two bolts. Spreaders were tenoned into the cap by one-sixth the cap height.

Bolster

Pieces of fir, these were half squared at their mast side and half-rounded on their outside. They protected the trestletrees and were fitted to the top of trestletrees between rear crosstree and the topmast iron plate, as well as to lower caps and to hounds abreast the masthead for the purpose of leading the shrouds away from the mast. Bolsters protruded by 1 inch over the outside edge of a trestletree or lower cap and were covered with tarred old canvas. Their height equalled their width.

Mast batten

Vertical battens were used to prevent masthead damage through friction by stays and shrouds. Steel gave their length as three-fifths the masthead length, while Fincham considered them only two-fifths of the same. Batten width was one-eighth or one-tenth the diameter of the masthead and their thickness half that width. Chamfered at their upper ends for easier fitting of the respective rigging, two battens were usually nailed to each side, with smaller vessels using only four battens altogether.

Mast cap

A cap fitted to the lower masthead, this guided and secured a stepped topmast. Caps were originally made from elm but were increasingly replaced by iron caps during the later part of the eighteenth century. Originally they were only for the fitting of lighter poles (flag poles etc.), but soon were used on topmasts. A timber cap's width was twice the diameter of the topmast and its depth five-sixths this diameter, while the length was this diameter plus 2 inches. The hole for the topmast was larger by approximately 1 inch than the diameter of the topmast itself (¾ inch to fit a leather sleeve and the rest for play). The fore edge of the hole was situated away from the cap's fore end by the cap's depth. A similar set up was considered for the masthead's square hole.

An iron cap was smaller in height and recorded as $\frac{7}{12}$ the topmast diameter. With its topmast guiding section tubular, the other, fitted to a rounded masthead, was made square with one corner pointing toward the topmast centre. Connecting pieces between these two sections were of similar height and had a width of half the topmast diameter. Eyelets for blocks could have been placed to the outside of the round section, to the connecting piece, or to the squared part – no fixed rule existed.

Topmast and topgallant mast

These were extensions of a lower mast. Fully rigged vessels of that period usually stepped both of these loose extensions, while smaller vessels usually only used one. Similar in shape to those mizzen top- or topgallant masts of larger ships, they could have either carried a long pole- or normal pole-head.

Construction of schooner masts varied and each mast's extension could have been stepped differently. F H af Chapman's schooner rigging plan is one of the many examples. In this the fore-topmast is set in a timber cap and trees, but on the main mast extension iron caps were used. E Gwyn's 1780 watercolour of an armed schooner shows the cutter-mast extensions stepped in iron caps, but this time as topgallant masts, placed behind integrated topmasts and shown with flying topgallant sails. Her topsails were very deeply roached for clearance of the stays.

The Chapman presentation of a schooner rig with two different masts for different rigging purposes can be better understood if we consider statements from Fincham and Steinhaus regarding the rigging of topsails on schooners. Both declared that fore topsails were rigged permanently, while those on main masts were only set flying. Such statements did not always hold true, but they let us understand that even several decades after Chapman it was still very common for topsail schooners to hoist a main topsail yard only when needed. The rig portrayed by Gwyn was underlined in a description of a schooner by Steel: '… and the topmasts fixed in iron rings, abaft the lower mast-heads.' Such fixed topmasts (topgallant masts) were rounded over their full length, unlike a stepped topmast where a squared heeling was necessary to fit neatly between the trestle- and crosstrees. The length of such heeling in England was 2π times its width, while on Continental topmasts 3½ times its width was more common. A topmast was rounded between heeling and hounds, but on English topmasts after 1770 the part between heeling and cap was left octagonal. Hounds were also octagonal shaped and the same proportional dimensions as for lower mast hounds were applied. Above the hounds the topmast extended into a rounded head or pole, topped by a truck.

Data for the conversion of a normal topmast head into a pole head was given by Steel as:

Topmast head = 3½in for every yd of topmast length
Normal pole head = topmast head + ⅕ x topmast length to the hounds
Long pole head = topmast head + ⅔ x topmast length to the hounds

For example, a topmast including masthead was 18 ft = 6 yd long. Masthead length (3½in per yd) = 21in (18ft = 216in – 21in = 195in), 195in or 16ft 3in is topmast length to the hounds. Normal pole head = ⅕ x 195 = 39 (39in + 195in = 234in), 234in or 19ft 6in is topmast length with a normal pole head. Long pole head = ⅔ x 195 = 130 (130in +195in = 325in) 325in or 27ft 1in is topmast length with a long pole head.

Changes were made to the heeling of topmasts in the nineteenth century. Steinhaus wrote about a square heeling length of 1½ times topmast diameter and above that the same octagonal length. Octagonal hounds were 1/12 times topmast length, with enough room between topmast and masthead to place the shrouds. When the topmast's heel was brought closer to the masthead, the heeling had to be offset for the space required for the shrouds. Sometimes a topmast was fitted directly in front of the masthead, which may have been good for appearance but impracticable for lowering. A construction of that kind had a step on the masthead fore side on which the topmast's counter step could rest. Instead of the (unnecessary) fid here, a wedge was pushed in between the foremost crosstree and the fore side of the heeling.

Fincham noted for such heeling a height of two-and-a-half times a topmast's diameter, with the vertical edges of the squared part chamfered by about one-fifth of its width. Topgallant masts had a squared part of three times the diameter with one-sixth width of that section chamfered, followed by an octagonal length of twice the diameter.

An iron hoop around the lower heel and a squared hole athwart ship for the fid were common to all topmasts. An upright sheave for the mast-rope was fitted diagonally about 4 inches above the squared sector. Another fore-and-aft sheave below the hounds served the topsail yard halyard. David Steel remarked that such practice may have weakened that section of a topmast.

Fids

These were loose mast-stoppers made from timber or iron, with those made of timber slightly larger. Iron fids had a length of one-and-a-half the topmast diameter, a height of one-third that diameter and a width of two-thirds the height. Timber fids had a height of half the topmast diameter.

Tabernacle masts

Masts that could be horizontally lowered to pass under bridges were not very common during the eighteenth century. Exceptions were found on the Dutch *speeljachts* of the seventeenth century and a number of smaller river craft. With not many draughts of such vessels available, the Danish/Norwegian draught of a schooner-rigged skerry boat from 1769 (see page 69) shows that this practice must have been more widespread than the lack of evidence leads us to believe. British drawings of the Commissioner Hamilton's Gunboats of 1808 and of a barge of 1815 show trunk-fitted masts, but both vessels were single masted.

Tabernacle masts were usually housed in a mast trunk and kept in position with two bolts. The upper bolt, passing through the upper part of trunk and mast above the heel, provided the hinging axis, while the lower bolt secured the mast's heel while standing. If the heel reached into the vessel's hold it was necessary to provide open mast housing, covered by a loose tabernacle plank. To lower or raise these hinged masts a stay tackle was fitted instead of the usual dead eyes or hearts, while sheer booms assisted the manouevre. Such booms were temporarily set into steps, or hinged close to the sides athwart the mast. Their upper ends crossed and were lashed to the stay above the stay tackle. These booms always maintained a correct angle for the fore stay tackle to be effective, since the fore stay alone could not have supported the lowering mast after it crossed a critical point. The same action in reverse was necessary to lift the mast out of its dead angle. Not mentioned in contemporary literature, these sheer booms were a necessity and were used for as long as people have known of lever action.

Bowsprit

Like masts, bowsprits were not always the same and variations in the making and fitting of bowsprits existed. Small vessels often carried only a bumpkin or horn bowsprit. When a bowsprit was extended by a jib boom it would have sat at starboard side, either at 45 or 90 degrees to its vertical axis, to make room for a jack staff standard knee at the bowsprit's upper side. A jib boom fitted above the bowsprit had a jack staff without standard placed in a groove at starboard on the back of a timber cap. Merchant vessels did not carry a jack and therefore the cap remained without this groove.

The heel of the bowsprit rested either in a step on deck or was bolted to the deck beams with the help of some iron brackets (see Bowsprit steps). In special circumstances jaws

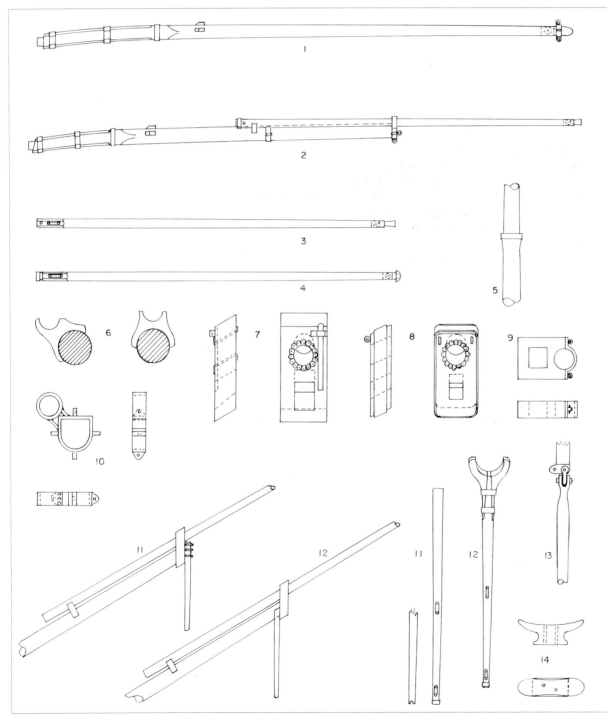

1. Spike or horn bowsprit
2. Bowsprit with a jib boom
3. Jib boom (English after 1770)
4. Jib boom (French about 1800)
5. Rigging stop worked into a bowsprit (Fincham)
6. Jib boom saddles
7. English bowsprit cap (timber) with a half round notch for a jack staff, about 1800
8. Continental bowsprit cap, smaller and with an iron band, about 1800
9. Early timber bowsprit cap with iron bracket, as for HMS *Royal Transport* (1695)
10. Iron bowsprit cap with or without the eyelets (Röding 1793)
11. Early martingale (dolphin striker), between 1785 and 1815; notched version before 1800
12. Dolphin striker with jaws, after 1815
13. Dolphin striker from about 1850
14. Belay cleat, to be nailed to masts, bowsprits etc

could be fitted and the bowsprit set like a boom against the fore mast (see drawings of *Axel Thorsen*), or it could be fastened with some iron brackets to stem and head (see drawings of *Elgen*). These are just a few possibilities; the diversity in bowsprit fitting depended entirely on the vessel's construction and purpose.

Proportional dimensions for ship-rigged bowsprits were not unlike those of fully rigged ships. The length varied between one and one-and-a-half times a ship's length, while the largest diameter was similar to a mast's, with the smallest two-thirds of that. Diameters outside the stem were fractions of the largest diameter: 1st quarter = $^{60}/_{61}$; 2nd quarter = $^{11}/_{12}$; and at the 3rd quarter = $\frac{4}{5}$. The stem was often squared with slightly chamfered edges. The bowsprit's inboard, which was usually above the stem, measured four-fifths the largest diameter. A few iron hoops strengthened that inboard section to counteract splintering. While hoops were rarely seen on eighteenth-century artists' impressions, one may notice that wooldings answered the same purpose. Wooldings were ropes wound around mast or bowsprit to prevent splintering; in case of built-masts they were used to add strength.

In his general reference to early nineteenth-century one-piece bowsprits Fincham[142] mentions one hoop at the heel and two for the head. A heel's hoop was located 2 feet 4 inches away from the inner end, while the foremost head hoop was about 4 inches aft of the cap, with the second being placed 4 inches behind the bee square. If the heeling was not strong enough, one or two additional hoops were fitted. In case of bad knotting, each timber knot was covered with an iron hoop. At the outer end a squared part of one-ninth the bowsprit's length was required for the fitting of bees. Whether bees formed an essential part of an early schooner rig could not be established. Their main function was the leading of fore topmast stays, an item on schooners usually single and set up to dead eyes or thimbles. Fincham points further to a novelty in bowsprit construction. Rather than being nailed on stop cleats for stays, stops were worked out of the full bowsprit timber, not unlike mast hounds. On small bowsprits they protruded $1\frac{1}{2}$ inches and on larger $2\frac{1}{2}$ inches over the corresponding surface. For normal stop cleats David Steel mentions[143] a length of half the bowsprit's diameter, with a width and height of one-quarter their length. Gammoning cleats were shorter by 2 inches and the other dimensions were proportional. Gwyn's watercolour of a topsail schooner (see page 57) provides another detail for the use of cleats: foot cleats were nailed to the bowsprit's upper surface – an item one only expects to find on bowsprits of a bygone era.

Horn-bowsprits on smaller vessels had an iron hoop pressed on to the outer end, with eyelets at both sides and topside. Retractable bowsprits had sheave holes cut into both ends, with the inner sheave serving the bowsprit's out-hauler.

Jib boom

Officially introduced to the Royal Navy in 1705, this innovation, like so many others, had gone through an experimental period. The 1695 model of HMS *Royal Transport* in St. Petersburg, with its original and unaltered masting and rigging, provides us with the oldest known documentation of a jib boom. It is well within the range of possibility that the

Marquis of Carmarthen in his attempt to change the known *speeljacht* rig into that of a seagoing vessel also invented the jib boom. The origin of this, the head-rigging revolutionising spar, can therefore be traced back to the Royal Navy and to a real royal ship indeed.

Royal Transport's jib boom stood at the bowsprit's starboard side. As far as photographs reveal, the heel rested in an iron band and the cap seemed to be a timber cap with an iron bracket, not unlike a cross between Dutch and English topmast caps of that time. The boom was only half the bowsprit's length and therefore shorter than known eighteenth-century dimensions, which were, within a small margin, the same as a ship's width or, as English sources stated, $^{7}/_{10}$ to $\frac{4}{5}$ the bowsprit's length. Their largest diameter, measured at the bowsprit cap or one-third from its heel, was during that period $\frac{1}{48}$ or $\frac{1}{50}$ of a jib boom's length. A gradual reduction of the remaining $\frac{2}{3}$ outside the cap was done by dividing that part into four equal sections, with the first quarter $^{40}/_{41}$, the second $^{11}/_{12}$ and the third $\frac{5}{6}$ of the largest, with the outer end $\frac{2}{3}$ of that diameter.

Originally completely rounded, English jib booms changed after 1735 to an octagonal-shaped heel of a length of $3\frac{1}{2}$ times the boom's diameter. The outer end stop of slightly reduced thickness, used for the strapping of blocks etc, was formed at a distance of one-and-a-half times diameter from the end, and was parallel until 1775 but thereafter became an inverted cone. A sheave for the traveller's outhauler was vertically inserted immediately aft of that stop, while another sheave was fitted horizontally one-and-a-half times the boom's diameter away from the heel for the jib boom's out-hauler. Between heel and sheave slot another hole was drilled for boom lashing. During the nineteenth century martingale-rigged schooners added another sheave slot for the fore topgallant stay to the one behind the stop. Continental jib booms of the earlier period usually followed the entirely rounded French design, being capped with a truck at the outer end. They usually had no stop and no sheaves inserted.

Bowsprit cap

The first known documentation of the development of the bowsprit cap can be found on the contemporary model of HMS *Royal Transport* from 1695. Evidence for the bowsprit cap can also be found in an etching of a picture by S de Passebon[144], a French captain who died in 1705. The picture depicts a French 112-gun ship with rope lashings to hold a jib boom on portside. Merchant craft later had a preference for iron caps, but there is more evidence of timber caps, especially in the rigging of naval vessels. Iron bowsprit caps were of similar dimensions to mast caps. Timber cap measurements were stated by Steel[145] as: height = 5 x the jib boom diameter; width = 2 x jib boom diameter + $\frac{1}{2}$ x jack staff diameter; thickness = $\frac{5}{6}$ x width. A cap was fitted to the end of the bowsprit with a squared hole so that its position was permanently fixed.

Saddles

Two saddles may be found on the bowsprits of schooners. One was the jib boom saddle, which was needed to keep the boom at its heel parallel to the bowsprit. It had a height of one-sixth of the bowsprit diameter and a width of half that. The jib boom saddle was placed about one-third of the boom length aft of the cap, with the sling saddle immediately in front. The spritsail yard sling saddle is considered the second saddle. Introduced in 1775, that saddle was probably used on a number of schooners, especially Royal Navy schooners, which sometimes carried spritsail yards. Only half of the jib boom saddle in height the spritsail yard sling grasped around the top half of the bowsprit.

As has been mentioned previously, specifications for eighteenth-century schooner rigging are of a very limited nature and many proportional dimensions have to be taken from descriptions of square-rigged vessels.

Martingale or dolphin striker

The martingale's history in general shipping goes back to the early 1780s and received official Royal Navy recognition in 1794. Once again, artist impressions give us early examples of their experimental use on English men-of-war and merchantmen. Among the most informative of these are watercolours by George Raper, a young sea officer in the First Fleet on her way to Australia, who depicted the ships of his fleet off Rio de Janeiro in August 1787. The newer ships are shown as being furnished with a dolphin striker, while older transport ships remained without. The ships rigged with a dolphin striker include HMS *Sirius* and HMS *Supply*, both of which could be considered older vessels as HMS *Sirius* was a former merchant ship (*Berwick*) purchased in 1871, and HMS *Supply* a former yard craft built in 1759. This suggests that they had their naval rigging renewed for their long voyage and ensuing duties as naval craft. In later watercolours of both ships Raper again showed them as rigged with dolphin strikers, each time showing the early striker with only one martingale stay visible. Steel described the fitting six years later as: '…an ash bar, fixed downwards from the fore-side of the bowsprit-cap, and by which the martingale-stay supports the jib-boom.' [146]

In the final years of the eighteenth century the martingale stay notch in the lower end of the bar was replaced with a vertical sheave. About one decade later Darcy Lever[147] spoke of two sheaves, whilst for the second decade of the nineteenth century he provides us with a picture of a double martingale. Double martingales were included on a variety of American ships during that period, ranging from schooners to full-rigged ships and it appears that double martingales were used more frequently on the other side of the Atlantic than in Europe.

The usage of martingales in schooner rigging began in the first decade of the nineteenth century. In that early period (between 1782 and 1815) the martingales were fitted to the cap front with cramps. After 1815 the martingales were provided with jaws and they moved to aft of the cap. Lever's double martingale was hinged to the cap's face. Close to mid-century the martingale moved to below the bowsprit cap where it was free to oscillate on a universal joint.

Yards

All square-sail carrying or spreading spars are referred to as yards. When looking at schooners, one will differentiate between the fore-and-aft rigged gaffs and booms and the square-rigged yards, like cross-jack yard, square-sail yard, topsail yard and topgallant yard. The club-yard (short square-sail yard), square-sail boom and spritsail yard were for a certain period also part of schooner rig development. The studdingsail yards and booms carried by so many fast sailing schooners should also be considered.

Gaffs

Early pictorial evidence of gaffs goes back to about 1628 when these were referred to as half-sprits and began to replace the cumbersome sprit of a fore-and-aft sprit rig. Gaffs in a schooner rig were used for the foremast's schooner sail and for the main sail on the mainmast. The gaff of a schooner sail was usually slightly shorter than that of the main sail. Gaff diameters varied from $\frac{1}{48}$ to $\frac{1}{52}$ times a gaff's length, with the largest diameter being about 4 feet away from the jaws. Four sectional dimensions controlled the tapering toward the outer end, those at the first quarter being $\frac{40}{41}$, at the second $\frac{11}{12}$, at the third $\frac{1}{5}$ and at the gaff's peak $\frac{5}{6}$ times the largest diameter.

Jaws were fitted at the gaff's mast-end. They enclosed half the round of mast, had a thickness of one-quarter the mast's diameter and were made from oak. The semicircle of the jaws was 1 inch larger than the mast's diameter to provide room for a leather sleeve on the inside and some clearance for movement. To assist in tilting the gaff the semicircle of jaws was set in a 40- to 45-degree angle toward the top. Each jaw tongue was scarfed to the gaff (nailed or bolted) over a length of 4 feet, with similar flats on the gaff tapered toward the mast-end to one-quarter of its largest diameter. Stability was provided by three to four iron hoops pressed on to that connection. The foremost hoop was at a distance of 11 inches from the inner end of the semicircle, with the others spaced equally. The inner halyard, the downhauler and the nock earing were served by two eyebolts driven upwards and downwards into the gaff's scarfed end. Another eyebolt extended the peak of the main gaff to hold the flag-line. According to Fincham[148] that last eyebolt became, in the nineteenth century, an iron extension with an in-built sheave bracketed to the gaff's peak. Fincham also reported the replacement of the former stop cleats with eyelets on iron hoops. Stop cleats on all yards were nailed to the fore and aft side, as a vertical placing would have interfered with and caused damage to rigging and sail. Stop cleats had a length of half the yard's diameter, with a width of one-quarter that length and a height of two-thirds the length.

In some cases a sheave was fitted vertically into the peak end for the running of peak brails. An iron ferrule was placed over the end to prevent splitting. According to Steinhaus[149] the gaff peak's length was one-seventh that of the gaff itself.

Boom

The fore-and-aft sail boom's debut came with the appearance of the *speeljacht* at the beginning of the seventeenth century. Goose-necked to a mast-bracket, its initial function was to spread a sail's foot and fasten its sheet. The length of

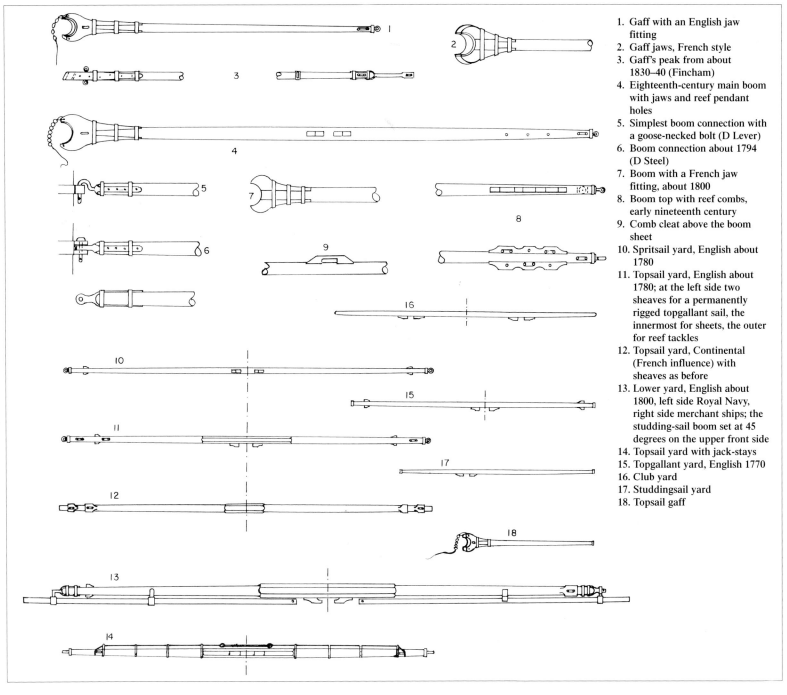

1. Gaff with an English jaw fitting
2. Gaff jaws, French style
3. Gaff's peak from about 1830–40 (Fincham)
4. Eighteenth-century main boom with jaws and reef pendant holes
5. Simplest boom connection with a goose-necked bolt (D Lever)
6. Boom connection about 1794 (D Steel)
7. Boom with a French jaw fitting, about 1800
8. Boom top with reef combs, early nineteenth century
9. Comb cleat above the boom sheet
10. Spritsail yard, English about 1780
11. Topsail yard, English about 1780; at the left side two sheaves for a permanently rigged topgallant sail, the innermost for sheets, the outer for reef tackles
12. Topsail yard, Continental (French influence) with sheaves as before
13. Lower yard, English about 1800, left side Royal Navy, right side merchant ships; the studding-sail boom set at 45 degrees on the upper front side
14. Topsail yard with jack-stays
15. Topgallant yard, English 1770
16. Club yard
17. Studdingsail yard
18. Topsail gaff

a schooner's main boom differed between 0.55 to 0.7 times the vessel's length, depending largely on the mainmast position and size of the main sail. The length of a schooner sail boom was limited, however, by the distance between main and foremast.

The largest boom diameter varied from ¹⁄₄₈ to ¹⁄₅₇ of boom length and was taken at the boom sheet's position. The reduced diameters at their respective Quarters inward were ⁴⁰⁄₄₁, ¹¹⁄₁₂ and ⅞, with the mast-end ⅔ times the largest boom diameter. The outside sheet position was at half the remaining length with a diameter of ¹¹⁄₁₂, and at peak end the diameter was ¾ of the largest.

Information covering the gaff jaws is also prevalent for the boom, except that the semicircle was right-angled and not set in an angle of 45 degrees. Steel[150] records that the eyebolt for the gaff sail's tack was driven from the top

through the boom scarf and secured below with a ring. A sheave for the sail's sheet was set vertically into the boom's outer end, where it was capped with an iron ferrule and an eyebolt was driven into its axis.

Jaws were not the only method of maintaining a turning connection with the mast. The gooseneck connection, as mentioned before, dated back to the very first known illustrations of *speeljachts* and can still clearly be recognised on Gwyn's watercolour of an armed schooner from 1780 (see page 57). Considering Gwyn's artwork and the following statement from Steel it is obvious that the gooseneck connection was widespread:

'Commonly, in the Merchant Service, an iron hoop is let on the inner end, and an iron hook or neck, driven in the middle, parallel to its axis, that hooks into an eye in a hoop, or a strap

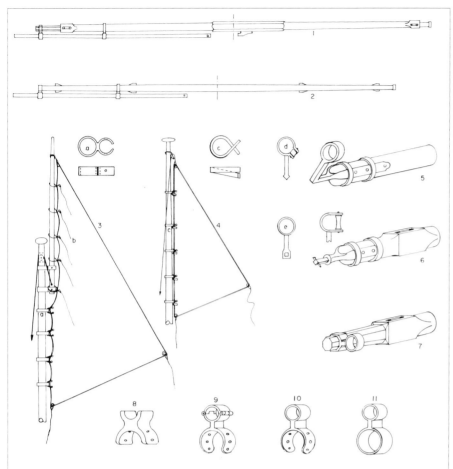

1. Left side: Continental lower yard with a studdingsail boom 90 degrees in front of the yard. Right side: English lower yard on small vessels, (without boom)
2. Square sail boom, with a studdingsail boom fitted left. The inner cleats were fitted equal to the inside width of the vessel
3. Sliding-gunter rig: a) iron double mast hoop opened up for the sail; b) reef-points at the laced section
4. Shoulder-of-mutton rig: c) timber hanks used for fastening (Röding)
5. English boom iron, squared off in 45 degrees upwards, d) with a reel after 1775 (Royal Navy)
6. English boom iron for merchant ships, e) with a reel after 1775
7. French boom iron at 90 degrees forward
8. Wooden boom saddle
9. English inner boom iron after 1775
10. English inner boom iron before 1775
11. English inner boom iron before 1745 and French still at the end of the century

round the mast, and is moused or forelocked through a hole, to prevent its lifting.' [151]

The reef comb, a type of cheek block bolted to both sides of the outer boom section is rarely mentioned in contemporary literature. While its introduction dates probably to the early years of the nineteenth century, Steel acknowledged the use of reef pendants in 1794 when he described that the outer part of a cutter's boom was pierced with up to four vertical holes for guiding the reef pendants. In 1829 Fincham referred to cheek blocks, although also only on cutters. He reports that these blocks had a thickness of half the boom's diameter and a length of three times that dimension. They were fitted alternately with holes and sheaves and placed in a direct line below the reef cringles. The rearmost hole (for the lower reef pendant stopper knot) was located at port and the rearmost sheave (to lead the pendant) on starboard side;

the second pendant was running in the opposite direction; and the third again placed like the first. The early method, having only vertical holes in the boom, did not run the reef pendants double (through the cringles) but seized them into those cringles.

Contemporary literature linked that reefing technique to cutters, as if it was only a recognised part of a cutter's rig and alien to other types of rigging. Such pointed and specific reference can lead to incorrect conclusions since a number of period illustrations also inform of its application on differently rigged vessels. Examples showing the use of reef pendants on brigs, sloops and schooners include HM brig *Lady Nelson*, American brig *Resolute*, American schooners *Midas* and *Fame*, German schooner *Vesta* and German sloop *Die Frau Marica*. This international assortment of vessels from 1795 to 1837 provides proof that reefing with reef pendants on long cutter booms was not uncommon on similarly large booms of other rigs.

The position of the boom was secured by the use of stop cleats nailed to the boom's upper side afore and aft of the boom sheet block strap, or by a comb cleat over the strap. An eyebolt went through the inner part of the boom, either from the side or from below, for hooking the sail sheet tackle, with a belay cleat for that tackle nailed nearby. A further stop cleat for the topping lift was fitted to the boom's outer stop. The jaws of gaff and boom were secured to the mast with a single parrel.

Spritsail yard

The description of square-rigged yards on schooners begins with the relatively uncommon spritsail yard. From material at hand it can be assumed that the British Royal Navy made the most use of a spritsail yard on small craft. Even in the oldest known pictorial documentation of a spritsail-yard-rigged schooner, a sketch of the Marblehead schooner *Peter & Mary* from 1747 by Bowen, the vessel is shown with a long pendant on the main mast and a jack on the bowsprit jack-staff, indicating her use in the British colonial navy. The Regulations And Instructions Relating To British Flags &C[152] state categorically that the flying of pendants on others than on vessels in HM Service was an offence punishable by law. Falconer underlines this point in his note on pendants from 1768:

'Pendent, a sort of long narrow banner, displayed from the mast-head of a ship of war, and usually terminating in two ends or points.' [153]

In 1763 six schooners were mentioned for the first time in the Royal Navy list, with a seventh added in 1767. We know now that these were not the only schooners employed by the Royal Navy at the North America Station. But it is remarkable that in his engraving 'A view of Part of the Town of Boston in New England and British Ships of War Landing their Troops 1768' Paul Revere illustrates four of these schooners, each with the bowsprit rigged as a spritsail yard. Around the same time, an illustration in Falconer's *Universal Marine Dictionary*[154] displays a schooner and a naval sloop with spritsail yards, and a pendant on the schooner verifies her naval use. A Bermuda sloop with the same yard is presented in an artwork by Dominic Serres[155], dated around 1780. Also in 1780 Gwyn illustrated a topsail schooner as an armed naval vessel, as was the yacht in Falconer's new edition from 1815[156]. All of these vessels not only had the spritsail yard and the indication of their use in the Royal Navy in common; all of the schooners in this group also rigged a schooner sail boom. An intensive study of that rigging aspect would probably unearth a great deal more relevant research material. Anyone interested in early Royal Navy schooners should certainly keep this in mind.

The English spritsail yard can only be described with relation to a ship's rig, and we may assume that a schooner's rig was similar to a ship's. Spritsail yards were completely rounded and were identical in size to a fore topsail yard. With the largest diameter being $\frac{3}{4}$ inch for every yard of length ($\frac{1}{56}$ x yard length), the smallest was $\frac{3}{5}$ of the largest and the respective quarters between these extremes were $\frac{30}{31}$, $\frac{7}{8}$ and $\frac{7}{10}$ of the largest diameter.

Stop cleat dimensions were of a similar proportion to those for gaffs and sling cleats were placed on the yard's lower side at a distance of one diameter from the centre. Their length is given with one-and-a quarter times the yard's diameter, whereby one-quarter of the length was considered for width and two-thirds of the latter as height. Both yardarm ends were protected with iron ferules.

Lower yards

The hoisting of yards on topsail schooners has been explained in various ways by modern authors. Some presented the view that, because of the weight of the yards and the sails, those yards were only occasionally carried and then hoisted from deck, which is a method known as 'flying'. In the eighteenth century that term defined an infrequently hoisted square sail, whereby sheets, lifts, clue-lines, buntlines and bowlines were omitted. Darcy Lever remarked that such yards were sometimes also without braces[157]. When looking at contemporary illustrations of period schooners it is evident that marine artists were of a different opinion to the modern authors, particularly as yards on the fore mast usually appear fully rigged. Not only the artists, who were known to be astute observers, adhered to this, but also knowledgeable contemporaries such as Steel. In his rigging lists for schooners[158] Steel referred to ropes only fitted permanently to rigged yards, which may indicate the authenticity of the fully rigged foremast. Are descriptions of early schooner rigs mainly an interpretation of existing pictorial material? If so, the descriptions given by Fincham and Steinhaus during the nineteenth century are perhaps a confirmation of inferences made during the preceding century. Both authors shared the opinion that topsails on mainmasts were only set flying, whilst such on foremasts were fully rigged. It should again be made clear that the eighteenth century was a melting pot of new ideas in small craft rigging and pictures of schooners with fully rigged topsails on mainmasts were as well known as those in which only the mainmast had a topsail rig.

The foremost lower yard was also called fore spread yard or crossjack yard. A spread yard on topsail schooners usually spread a topsail's clues, while a crossjack yard, found on purely fore-and-aft-rigged vessels, was an irregularly used yard to which the crossjack or square sail was bent. On a topsail-rigged vessel the same yard was known as square sail yard. A fore spread yard was usually slightly longer than the main spread yard and occasionally fitted with studdingsail booms. Steel's yard dimensions for a 110-ton schooner from 1794[159] contradict Fincham and other sources, as he gives a longer length to the main spread yard. Since the square sail yard in that list is wrongly recorded under 'Main mast', there is a possibility that a number of printer's errors have occurred in the list. This confusion only proves that stringent rules cannot be applied to earlier schooner rigs.

With Steel's spar dimensions for schooners listed under vessels in the merchant service one has also to distinguish between the varying yard shapes of naval and commercial vessels. Such differences were most obvious at the yardarms. In the Royal Navy vessels were fitted with stop cleats and squared-off studding boom irons, while merchant vessels preferred boom irons fitted and cottered to iron yardarm extensions or, as in the French method, pressed on to the yardarm ends. Instead of stop cleats, yards on merchant vessels had squared sections at each end, with vertically inserted sheaves inside the yardarms replacing topsail sheet blocks.

Inner boom irons controlled the inner part of the studdingsail booms and were fitted to the yard at approximately one-third of boom length inside the outer boom iron. On naval vessels after 1775 the irons were hinged so that the upper half could open to provide easier access for boom fitting and removal. Merchantmen often had open timber boom saddles installed instead, a method favoured by smaller vessels according to Lever[160]. In English rigging studdingsail booms were placed at 45 degrees on a yard's upper face.

English yards were octagonal at the centre for a quarter of the yard's length, with the eight-part (or section of the octagon) nearest the mast extending to three-quarters of the yard's length and tapering out due to the reduction in yard thickness. Two-inch thick battens were nailed to all octagonal flats, except the front eight-part, to prevent friction damage of the mast and to protect against chafing from the shrouds. Prior to 1775 only one batten was in use, the one at the rear between yard and mast. The forward flat had the sling cleats nailed to it, dimensions of which have already been discussed in conjunction with the spritsail yard. Irrespective of the size or the type of a square-rigged yard, fractional diameters were always of similar proportions and can therefore be looked up under spritsail yard.

In contrast to English yards those on French vessels were frequently rounded over their full length, or had only a short octagonal centre section of one-tenth of the yard's length. The slightly enlarged sections for topsail sheet sheaves at the inner yardarms were not always squared, and could also have been rounded or octagonal. Outer boom irons pressed on to the yardarms faced forward (90 degrees) like on most of the continental vessels. Since studdingsails were usually only set to fully rigged yards, boom irons belonged mainly to the fore spread yard.

There is little difference between the known eighteenth-century yard dimensions and those of nineteenth-century schooners. Therefore, any dimension needed for an eighteenth-century schooner's yard can be taken from the dimension tables for masts and yards in Appendix 2, which partly belong to the nineteenth century.

Topsail yards

These were formed according to their size and place in a rigging concept either like a ship's topsail or topgallant yard. Larger yards had octagonal centres, whilst those on smaller craft were rounded over their full length. Iron ferrules driven on to each yardarm prevented splitting, and eyebolts in an axial extension were fitted to fore topsail yards for hanging jewel blocks.

Jackstays for bending the sails were introduced soon after 1810. Eyebolts were driven into the yard's topside 2½ to 3 feet apart and the jackstays were led through. Their outer ends were spliced round the yardarms and thimbles at the inner end lashed them together in the centre. It was recommended that jackstays should be made from rope so that they would not stretch. In 1719 Lever[161] wrote that cramps were driven into the yard's topside instead of eyebolts or, alternatively, thimbles were set into stirrups of plait or hide and then nailed to the yard 4 feet apart.

Topgallant yard

Relatively scarce in the eighteenth century, topgallant sails were mostly rigged in 'flying' mode. As already observed on the 1736 draught of the Portuguese schooner *St. Ann*, topgallant yards appeared more frequently during the last quarter-century, and with the increase in schooner size during the Napoleonic Wars became a permanent part of a larger schooner's rig by the early nineteenth century. Steel[162] underlined this in 1818 by providing all the essential ropes as braces, lifts, clue-lines etc, for a fore topgallant sail and yard of a 180-ton schooner. If a topgallant sail was not set flying but fully rigged then a second pair of yardarm-sheaves for topgallant sheets had to be fitted to the topsail yard in addition to those needed for reef-tackles. Stop cleats were nailed at a distance of 3 inches per yard length (¹⁄₁₂) away from the ends, while sling cleats followed those on spritsail yards. Fully rigged fore topgallant yards sometimes also carried studdingsails and then jewel block eyebolts were axially fitted. Another sail that sometimes made an appearance on a schooner's fore mast was a square sail or crossjack. Only used by wind from astern it could be hoisted in various ways, as discussed later.

Booms and additional spars

Although the principle schooner yards have now been covered, there are a few additional booms and infrequent spars still to discuss. With studdingsail booms, which had a length of 0.4 times yard length and a diameter of 0.017 times its own length, studdingsail yards were also required. With a length of four-sevenths of boom length, they had a diameter of 1 inch for every 5 feet of length (¹⁄₆₀). Yards for ringtail and water sails were in many ways similar to studdingsail yards.

Square sails were often, mainly on small vessels, hoisted to the crossjack yard on four halyards. Larger sails had to be slung to an additional yard, the square sail yard. These were of varying lengths, some covering only half or a quarter of that sail's head, and were termed 'club' yards. In his dimensions of a 110-ton schooner, Steel gives a slightly shorter length for the square sail yard when compared to the fore spread yard, but added ½ inch to its diameter. Antoine Roux sketched such a yard in his watercolour of an armed British cutter-schooner from 1801. Lowered to about 8 feet above deck the yard carries a furled square sail. The portrayal of studdingsail booms on this yard instead of the spread yard is remarkable. The yard was hoisted with a yard-tackle at the slings and two yardarm halyards. A short club yard would usually have two halyards at its arms and the sail an additional two at the earings. Halyards of a club yard were not always running through blocks on the spread yard but could also lead in front of that yard to blocks underneath the fore crosstree. This type of rigging called for a bib, an extension of the sail's middle top part, which reached up to the crosstree and filled the topsail roach, similar to the save-all-topsail used in combination with a normal squaresail to utilise every whisper of wind. With the bib hoisted to the crosstree, the halyards of the nock earings on that sail were rigged to the spread yard. The proportional diameter of a club yard was similar to that of a studdingsail yard.

A boomkin's function to spread a larger ship's fore course luff clew was taken up on smaller craft by a square-sail-boom. These booms had already been mentioned in the 1769 edition of Falconer's dictionary and according to various sources were either shorter or longer than the fore spread yard, with some contemporary illustrations indicating also a fitting of studdingsail booms. They fulfilled the same function as swinging studdingsail booms on larger ships. Dimensions are provided in Appendix 2.

Gaff topsail spars

A product of the later eighteenth century (about 1775) gaff topsail spars were rigged in several ways: a short topsail gaff could have spread the head of that sail; it could be bent to a longer, diagonally hoisted yard like a lugsail; fastened to a sliding boom it could become a sliding-gunter-sail; or it could be hoisted without any yard or gaff as a shoulder-of-mutton-sail. All these variations can be found on contemporary pictures but nothing much is known about proportional dimensions for these spars. Some are given in the table of US Navy Schooner dimensions (see Appendix 2).

Rigging

Any rig consists of two parts, the standing rigging and the running rigging. Standing rigging encloses any rope that has both ends durably fastened to a part of the vessel, for example the stays or shrouds. Ropes of running rigging have only one end fastened, whilst the loose end leads over the sheaves of one or more blocks to be hauled taut or slackened off as the need arises. The hauling part will then be belayed or stopped.

Standing Rigging

Bowsprit

After being stepped, the bowsprit was lashed to the stem with a gammoning of 3- to 4½-inch rope circumference, depending on the vessel's size. Slung around the bowsprit, the rope led either through an oval or triangular iron ring on the stem's face. On a stem with a small cutwater the gammoning followed round that protrusion, but with a larger cutwater went through a gammoning hole below the head's toptimber. This was repeated nine times, with each turn crossing the former, when possible, and being set taut and stitched together before the next was led around. Following the completion of the vertical turns they proceeded horizontally until the rope was spent and the end has been seized to the last turn. In his 'Proportions for the Lengths of the Standing and Running Rigging of all Ships' Steel spoke of a gammoning rope as one-and-a-half times the length of the bowsprit. By explaining in his preamble that the given rope measurements have all to be considered fathoms for feet (for example, 1π times bowsprit length equals 6 feet to a fathom on a 10-foot bowsprit 1.5 x 6 x 10 = 90 feet) so if we read fathoms for feet that makes it actually nine times the bowsprit's length.

While a gammoning connected bowsprit and stem, the task of a bobstay was to secure a bowsprit downward from the cap or fore stay collar position and to counteract headsail pressure. Again in accordance with size, a bobstay's circumference was 4 to 6 inches while the length was one quarter of the bowsprit's, reading fathoms for feet. An English bobstay was led through a hole in the cutwater above the water line, or sometimes a ring-bolt in the stem face, and spliced together to form a rope ring. Until 1770 a dead eye was seized into its upper bight but was later replaced with a heart and lashed to a corresponding dead eye or heart in the bobstay collar. Before 1720 bobstays were single. They were always serviced to include the collar, which could have been leather clad.

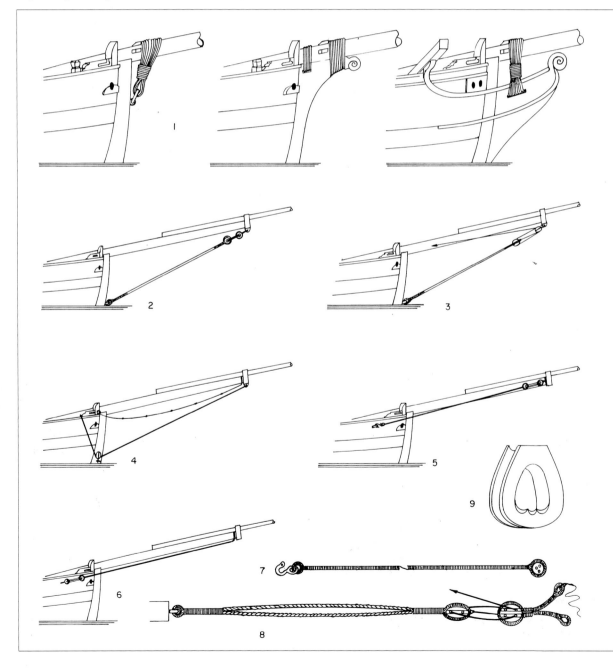

1. Three ways of fitting a bowsprit gammoning to smaller vessels
2. English type of bobstay
3. Continental bobstay generally preferred by merchant vessels
4. A bobstay according to FH af Chapman's schooner rig.
5. A bowsprit shroud, English fashion,
6. A bowsprit shroud doubled and seized to the bowsprit head. The dead eyes are fitted to the bow in Continental fashion
7. An English type bowsprit shroud with hook and dead eye
8. A bobstay with blocks. Continental fashion and merchant vessels
9. Heart for bobstays and bowsprit shrouds (English)

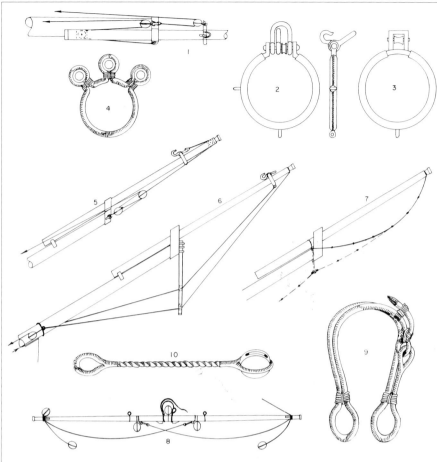

1. Jib boom outhauler and traveller inhauler
2. Traveller with hook and shackle
3. Traveller with a reel
4. Three thimble collar at jib boom's end; those outside were for topsail bowlines and the centre one for a topgallant stay
5. Traveller outhauler; jib stay fastened similar when led over traveler reel
6. Rigging of martingales
7. Jib boom horse; dashed line indicates a combined horse of bowsprit and jib boom
8. Rigging of a spritsail yard; an alternative with the right side fitted with a single lift
9. Spritsail yard sling
10. Brace pendant with block

Continental and English merchant vessels did not follow the naval method of using hearts for bobstay lashing. They replaced them with blocks, as can be seen on Chapman's schooner rig[163]. His drawing shows a single bobstay being led from the bowsprit through a block at the stem's starboard side, just above the water line, then over the gunwale, ending in a tackle on deck. The preference for block tackles is also stated by Lever[164] and again, as we see here, by Bobrik:

'Ships without a cutwater and whose cat-heads are placed very forward, set their bobstays like fig. 14 [with a tackle] to enable a loosening and tricing up, so that while weighing anchor the stock can stay clear of it.'[165]

Bowsprit shrouds were in use for side stabilisation. Literature infers that they were introduced in around 1706, but the St. Petersburg model of HMS *Royal Transport* implies an earlier dating of their use on bowsprit and jib boom. It appears that the seaman in Lord Carmarthen may

well have developed not only the schooner, but also provided incidentally a number of rigging innovations which, no doubt, made him *persona non grata* with the Lords of the Admiralty, yet revolutionised the head gear of all full rigged ships. The Admiralty's objection to his innovations can be read in a memorial to the Lords Justices, dated 25 May 1697:

'Such experiments ought not to be made on any of His Majesty's ships of War...building His Majesty's ships according to the fancy and humour of particular persons will break through those wholesome Rules and Methods which have been found absolutely necessary for the well performance of His Majesty's Service.'[166]

Bowsprit shrouds of English design were set up with hook and thimble and hooked to eyebolts in the bow. A dead eye, or later a heart, was seized into each fore end and lashed to a corresponding bowsprit collar. Continental bowsprit shrouds of twice the English length were doubled and went with their bight around the bowsprit head near the cap. Both ends were of equal length and seized beneath the bowsprit, led to eyebolts in the bow and set up with dead eyes or tackles. When continental bowsprit shrouds were fitted English fashion, they would hook to eyelets on an iron hoop near the bowsprit cap. The inner ends had a thimble spliced in and lashed with a lanyard to these eyebolts in the bow.

Although bowsprit shrouds remained part of a bowsprit rigging until the last days of sail, Röding notes their less frequent use in his time: 'In general are nowadays bowsprit shrouds nearly abolished because they create severe obstacles when weighing anchor, or running out the cables.'[167] His comments point to the prevailing ideas at the turn of the century in regard to small merchant vessels. Seen in the same light as the comments on bobstays made by Lever and Bobrik, this statement shows why the continental rigging tackles, which were close to the bow, were preferred over lashings close to the bowsprit head.

Horses or footropes could be rigged to one or both sides for access to the bowsprit. With the inner end spliced to an eyebolt in the knighthead, the outer went either with a bight around the bowsprit head, or was spliced or lashed to an eyebolt in the cap's side. Horses hung usually 3 feet below the bowsprit's upper and had diamond knots worked in for a safe foothold.

Jib boom

The boom outhauler hooked to the bowsprit cap's portside, passed through the sheave in the jib boom's heel, rove through a block at the cap's starboard side and returned to the fore deck. A traveller could shift the jib's position on the boom. When set 'flying' the sail tack fastened to the traveller's hook. A jib stay could also be fastened to a thimble next to the hook and a turning shackle on the same bolt served the outhauler. A simplified traveller, with only a reel at the top to guide the jib stay, appeared at the end of the eighteenth century. With this modified version the stay took over the function of an outhauler and the sail's tack bent simply to the traveller's ring.

In the earlier shackle-fastened concept the outhauler went

over the vertical sheave in the jib boom's head and ended in a tackle at the bowsprit cap's face to be belayed on fore deck. On small vessels, where a sheave would have severely weakened the jib boom head, a block was used instead. As an alternative the outhauler rove through a truck at cap side and the tackle hooked to an eyebolt at the bow below the gunwale.

With the function of a traveller's inhauler on a stay-hoisted jib taken up by the jib's downhauler, an extra inhauler was needed for the traveller when the jib was set 'flying' and not bound. Spliced or hooked into a cap eyelet, the inhauler went through a block at the traveller's side and returned to the fore deck to be belayed to a cleat at the bowsprit heel. Jib boom shrouds or guys worked in a similar way to these on the bowsprit. If a spritsail yard was rigged, these shrouds went through trucks on the upperside of the yard to avoid interference with the sail.

A martingale stay fulfilled the same function for a jib boom as a bobstay did for a bowsprit. Its earliest application can be traced to about 1782–84, while its official introduction to the Royal Navy dates to 1794. Spliced around the boom's rigging stop, the stay led via a notch in the martingale's (dolphin striker's) lower end to the fore side of the sling saddle, where it lashed to an eyebolt. By the turn of the century, at a time when the martingale made an entrance into schooner rigging, a second stay was introduced. This second stay ran from an eye at the bottom of the traveller through a hole or sheave in the vertical striker in a similar way to the first stay. Its function was to counteract the strenuous forces of a wind-pressed jib and the resulting strong arching of the jib boom. Since martingale stays on schooners were not hampered by spritsail yards, they rove through blocks at the inner bowsprit and ended in a tackle or girtline.

A rope-ring with three thimbles also formed part of the rigging stop. The centre thimble served an occasionally rigged fore-topgallant stay and the outer thimble was a lead for the topsail bowlines. A footrope was used to venture out on the jib boom. It was spliced round the rigging stop and bent behind the cap round the bowsprit, but could also have been a continuation of the bowsprit when it was run through stirrups behind the cap. Diamond knots were also worked into these ropes.

Spritsail yard

As mentioned earlier, these were part of some early Royal Navy schooner rigs dating from before the 1780s. Horses needed to be fitted before the yards could be rigged. With eyes spliced into both ends, the outer eye was lifted over the yardarm while the inner eye lashed to the yard at approximately 3 feet past the yard's centre. They hung about 3 feet below the yard's top surface to give a man on the yard the necessary balance. As a result of their modest length these horses were not led through stirrups. Once the horses were in place the brace pendants needed to be fitted. A block was spliced into the outer end of the pendants and an eye into the inner end, which then went over the yardarm. Outside the brace pendants strapped lift blocks were fitted. Clew-line blocks were placed at the lower rear (about 3 feet outside) of the yard's centre, while a block for the yard's outhauler was set at the centre's face.

A simple yard sling of a piece of rope with an eye spliced into one end, connected the yard to the bowsprit. The short end of the sling was seized to the yard slightly off centre with the eye, and the long end led over the bowsprit and around the yard again. Once more seized above the yard, it returned across the bowsprit and was fed through the eye to be reversed then seized to itself. Lead thimbles or trucks for the jib boom shrouds were placed at equal distances outside the yard sling and also on the yard's upper side.

Schooner mast

Rigging of the schooner mast commenced with mast tackles. Their pendants were entirely served over, laid around the masthead with a horseshoe splice and had a larger single block fitted to each end. These blocks were either hooked to thimbles or spliced directly into the pendants. Mast tackles on a mast with an uneven number of shrouds formed a pair with a single shroud, which was usually the last to be rigged. A tackle's runner, hooked with its standing part to a ringbolt in the chain-plate, passed through the pendant's block and its end was either fixed to a thimble to which a long-tackle block hooked, or a block was spliced directly into it. The lower block of that tackle was long-strapped and was hooked nearby to another ringbolt in the chain-plate. Mast tackles were not always hooked to chain-plates, but sometimes to similar bolts in the waterways. Hitched to the lower block, the fall rove through the blocks and belayed either to a cleat or was secured to the lower block's long strap. Small schooners were often without mast tackles.

Shrouds stabilised a mast laterally and, depending on a vessel's size or the type of schooner rig, between two and four pairs were fitted. Aftermost shrouds on fore-and-aft-rigged masts were serviced over their full length to prevent damage from the gaff sail's frequent chafing. Shrouds went in pairs over the masthead, with the first set up to starboard, the second to port and so on. Single shrouds were usually last and, as mentioned before, could form a pair with the mast-tackle pendant.

English warships and larger merchantmen had cable-laid shrouds, while those on smaller merchant craft were hawser-laid (shroud-laid). Hawser-laid shrouds were generally accepted in continental shipping. The strands of hawser-laid rope twisted right around and cable-laid rope left. The difference becomes obvious when fitting dead eyes. After turning a dead eye in, the short end of a cable-laid shroud was seized to the left side (on portside abaft and on starboard side forward), whilst a hawser-laid rope was seized to the right, therefore reversing this operation. The opposites to shroud dead eyes were channel (chain-wale) dead eyes, iron bound and linked to a chain plate.

Lanyards connected these opposing shrouds. With a Matthew Walker knot placed behind the hole offside the seized shroud part (cable-laid = right hole, hawser-laid = left hole) the lanyard went from the outside through the corresponding hole in the channel dead eye, and came up on the inside to the centre hole until all holes were connected. The hauling part was then pushed between dead eye and throat seizing and after a few turns round the seized section the end was stopped to the shroud.

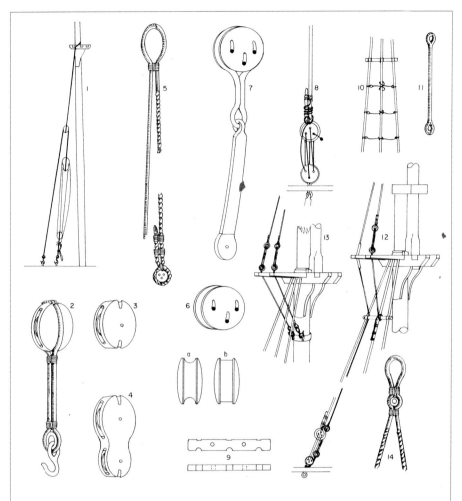

1. A mast tackle
2. A long strapped block
3. A single block
4. A long tackle block
5. A shroud pair: the left part is shown as an aftermost shroud, wormed, parcelled and served over its whole length
6. Dead eye: a) with a rounded groove for a shroud; b) with a flat groove for an iron band
7. Dead eye with chain-plate
8. Seizing of a dead eye, as seen from aboard
9. Wooden stretcher with belay pin holes
10. Futtock stave and ratlines
11. Catharpin
12. Topmast shrouds, the foremost before approximately 1780, the other from 1780 to 1815
13. Topmast shrouds after 1815
14. Lead thimble for topsail yard lift seized to the upper part of topmast shrouds, after about 1780

Ratlines made the task of entering a mast easier and were fitted to masts with three or more shroud pairs. Their distance apart varied between 12 and 16 inches, with 13 inches the most common. Fitted with eyes in their ends they were lashed to the outer shrouds while all inner shrouds were clove hitched.

Main topmasts without yard sails often did without shrouds as they just carried a pair of back-stays. The number of topmast shroud pairs was generally restricted to two. Having mostly thimbles turned into the ends, lanyards connected them to similarly fashioned futtock shrouds. During the larger part of the eighteenth century thimble-fitted futtock shrouds went through holes in the crosstree ends, slung once around the futtock stave and had the remaining piece seized to the nearest lower mast shroud. On English-rigged schooners this method of fastening ceased around 1780, but later pictures of continental schooners by artists such as Antoine Roux or Gerrit Groenewegen present vessels using the early method. Futtock shrouds were abandoned in the new technique and the extended topmast shroud length led through the crosstree holes, with the part exposed to rubbing clad in leather. The shroud passed then over the futtock stave, came down on the inside of the mast shroud and set up with thimbles to the channel dead eye. Futtock shrouds reappeared in around 1815, but were then being hooked with their lower ends to a futtock necklace, an iron strap around the upper part of the mast. In the late eighteenth century a thimble, or in large schooners a sister block, was seized into the upper part of topmast shrouds directly below their neck. These thimbles or blocks guided the topsail yard lifts and in case of reef tackles their tackle falls.

Backstays were common to all mast types. In their earliest form (for example, those on HMS *Royal Transport*) they went above the shrouds, round the pole-mast head and were set up to dead eyes behind the shroud channel dead eyes. Some later pictorial documentation points to extra chain plates and a set up with tackles.

Topgallant backstays of merchant vessels were mainly set flying. Therefore a block was turned into the lower end of the topmast backstay and a long-strapped double block hooked to a chain plate. The topgallant backstay passed first over one sheave of the long-strapped double block, then back over one sheave of the topmast backstay block, then to the lower block again and by passing for a second time the topmast backstay block formed the topmast backstay tackle. Its hauling part was then belayed to a deck cleat. In regard to back stays of smaller craft Steel reports that:

> '...standing back stays, if one pair, go over the mast-head with a cont-splice: if two pair, with eyes seized, and in the lower end a thimble, and set with a gun-tackle-purchase, hooked to a thimble of a strap round the lower dead-eyes, and sometimes with a lanyard and thimbles.' [168]

A top tackle was needed to raise or lower a topmast into position. Fastened at starboard to the lower mast's cap, it led over a sheave in the topmast's heel to which it was seized at intervals on portside. The tackle then went through a single block at the portside of the mast cap and came down to a

A wooden stretcher or squaring staff directly above the dead eyes was seized to the shrouds to prevent twisting of tensioned shrouds; it also often served as a belay rack. A second stretcher, the futtock stave, was fitted to the upper section of larger shrouds. This was usually a strong piece of serviced and tarred rope but could have been also made from timber. A futtock stave secured the futtock shrouds and was necessary for fitting catharpins and was therefore placed above the gaff jaws so it would not obstruct their movement. Fitting rules for ship-rigged masts suggested their placement at the same distance below the top as the cap was above. Catharpins connected the shrouds of both sides for improved shroud tension; they also counteracted the pulling force of topmast shrouds.

snatch block on deck, where the hauling part was laid with a few turns around the capstan. The topmast could then be wound into position, whereby each seizing was removed after passing the trestletrees. The rigging of top tackles was only temporary.

A grommet, or rope ring, was usually placed on to the mast's stop before rigging commenced to prevent damage to standing rigging from sharp edges. The grommet was made from unlaid strands of rope by placing one part over the other until it formed a ring. Another way to reduce rope chafing was the fitting of a paunch to the endangered section. As Falconer explains, a paunch, or mat, was:

'…a sort of thick and strong mat, formed by interweaving twists of rope-yarn into foxes, as close as possible. It is chiefly used to fasten on the outside of the yards or rigging, to prevent their surfaces from being chafed by the friction of some other contiguous object, and particularly when the vessel is rocked by a tempestuous sea.' [169]

Stays provided longitudinal forward stabilisation for a mast. The foremast's lower, the fore stay, was sometimes doubled with a fore preventer-stay, which was followed upwards by a jib stay and an outer jib stay, when this was not hoisted, and to a lesser extent by a fore topgallant stay. A schooner's fore stay was similar to a ship's, with an eye spliced into the stay's upper end. The eye was just large enough for the other end to run through but small enough to enclose the 'mouse', the pear-shaped stay enlargement that prevented the eye from slipping further. A dead eye or a heart turned into the lower end. With the part between eye and mouse serviced and the mouse itself pointed over to 1 foot below, the stay itself was 'wormed' over its whole length.

Worming was the act of filling the space between the strands of a thicker rope with one of lesser size, or with spunyarn. A wormed rope was nearly round and gained additional strength. Servicing a rope meant that a parcelling (tarred strip of old canvas) was laid around the wormed rope with spunyarn tightly wrapped around the canvas. Whilst the parcelling followed the direction of the strands, any service with spunyarn went against the lay.

Continental vessels very often rejected the English method of turning a dead eye or heart into the lower end of the stay in favour of a double block. Alongside the normal seizing of dead eyes, Steel also mentions[170] that cutters and other smaller vessels used a Flemish eye for their fastening. A Flemish eye was an eye splice made by unlaying one strand of the rope that formed the eye over a slightly longer distance than needed; the remaining strands formed then an eye against the single strand, which was put back into the lay to complete the task. The projecting ends were then thinned out and spun over with yarn. A running eye was made by bending the eye-forming strands round the rope itself to establish a noose into which the dead eye or a heart could be laid. The pulling lanyard of a tensioned stay kept the noose closed and the inlaid dead eye secured.

On vessels with a running bowsprit, like cutter-schooners, the fore stay's heart was lashed to holes in the stem's head or to an iron-bound opposing heart behind the stem. Schooners

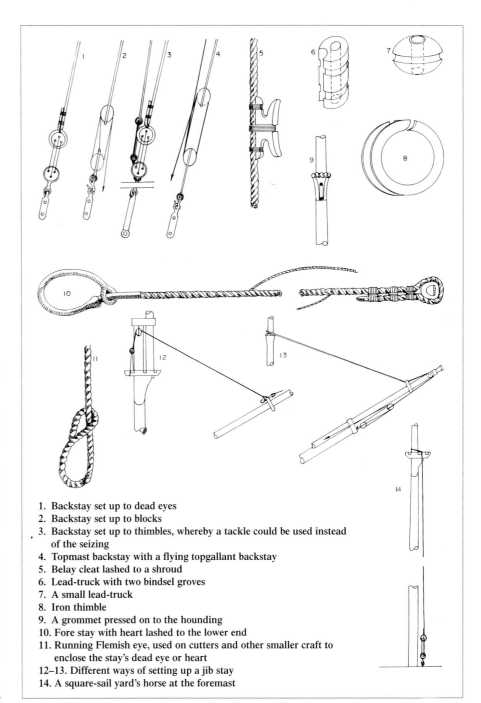

1. Backstay set up to dead eyes
2. Backstay set up to blocks
3. Backstay set up to thimbles, whereby a tackle could be used instead of the seizing
4. Topmast backstay with a flying topgallant backstay
5. Belay cleat lashed to a shroud
6. Lead-truck with two bindsel groves
7. A small lead-truck
8. Iron thimble
9. A grommet pressed on to the hounding
10. Fore stay with heart lashed to the lower end
11. Running Flemish eye, used on cutters and other smaller craft to enclose the stay's dead eye or heart
12–13. Different ways of setting up a jib stay
14. A square-sail yard's horse at the foremast

with a standing bowsprit above the stem had their counter dead eye seized to a stay collar, enclosing the bowsprit or leading through a hole in the head standard, as can be observed on the *Royal Transport* model. Stay collars were of a similar thickness to stays. Re-positioning of the fore stay from stem to bowsprit was part of a change in stay rigging on schooners that will be explained in detail later.

A preventer-stay was made similar to a fore stay but had only two-thirds of its thickness. Its dead eye was lashed to a corresponding one, either iron bound and bolted to the stem's face or seized to a collar.

The jib stay led from the same mast position as the fore stay to the bowsprit's outer end and was set up to dead eyes or thimbles. With the inner jib occasionally set flying a stay did not always exist. On a vessel with an outer jib stay (also called a flying jib stay) there were two options of setting that stay up. When spliced to the traveller's shackle, it ran on starboard through a block at the masthead or cap, and hitched directly to the rear crosstree (on smaller craft) or set up to a tackle (larger vessels). After introduction of the new traveller the stay was laid with an eye over the topmast's stop, rove down and passed below the traveller's reel forward over the jib boom sheave and set up with a tackle to the face of the bowsprit cap or alternatively at the bow.

Just below the mast's truck the fore topgallant stay spliced round the topmast's long pole. At the jib boom rigging stop it passed the centre thimble or centre sheave of a treble block and, with a thimble turned into the stay's lower end, was seized to a ringbolt near the stem. The stay could also have been lashed to the centre thimble.

The term 'horse' or jack stay was applied to a vertical stay in front or aft of a mast which had an eye over the masthead and was set up to dead eyes on deck. A schooner had such a horse rigged to the foremast (schooner mast):

> 'That on the fore-side, is for hoisting or lowering the square-sail, whose yard is attached to the horse by a traveller and slides up and down occasionally'. [171]

Modern authors usually name this yard the crossjack yard, probably because of this comment from Steel: 'The Cross-Jack-Yard is used to expand the foot of the mizen topsail; and the topsail, or square-sail, of vessels with one mast'[172]. The inclusion of square sail led to some initial confusion for historians. Steel[173] indicates in his tables for a schooner of 110 tons a spread yard and a square sail yard, but for a sloop of 60 tons a square sail- or crossjack yard. The spread yard only spread the clews of a topsail and was not used for the infrequent rising or lowering of a square sail, for which job, according to Falconer, an extra square sail yard was used. This extra yard could either be hoisted to below the spread yard or hoisted in front of the spread yard up to blocks below the trestletrees. The term crossjack yard usually applied only to a temporary square sail yard on purely fore-and-aft-rigged vessels.

The horse on topsail schooners would be rigged differently to fore-and-aft schooners in a number of ways. This is emphasised in Steel's tables[174] for ropes and blocks of a 180-ton schooner. The only reason for rigging a horse or jack stay was keeping an up-and-down running yard away from the gaff sail's mast hoops or lacing. A lower yard truss around the mast made the use of a jack stay superfluous in securing the yard's centre close to the mast. A truss also inhibited a jack stay's vertical movement, so the hoisting and lowering of a square sail yard on a topsail-rigged mast could only be achieved by running the jack stay clear (forward) of the yard.

Excellent examples of square sail yards can be noted in Antoine Roux's watercolours of the topsail schooner *Louisa*, dated 1826, and the British armed cutter-schooner, dated 1801. Both vessels are illustrated with their spread yards hanging in a sling. Whilst *Louisa* had her square sail bent to a short club-yard, the British vessel is seen with a full-length square sail yard, whereby both yards were lowered down to about 8 feet above deck and hanging in their halyards.

Falconer indicated that type of arrangement when he wrote, '...[that] which hauls out to the lower yard [is] called the square-sail-yard.' [175]

As previously mentioned, the practice of hoisting a crossjack yard on a horse could only be exercised on fore-and-aft schooners, where the yard merely carried the square sail and was not being used for spreading topsail clews. This application is visible on an illustration by Currier entitled 'An American Schooner from 1846'. The yard with a furled square sail is lowered and two gunwale-mounted spars replaced the square sail boom that usually lay athwart ship. Admittedly, these spars were vertically lashed to the shrouds and other conclusions have been drawn before about their usefulness. However, forward guys are drawn from the peak of these spars toward the bowsprit cap, which excludes any other utilisation.

Röding made some interesting comments regarding square sails[176]. This great collector of maritime information at the end of the eighteenth century described square sails as bent to the crossjack yards on purely fore-and-aft vessels. One should never confuse this yard with the similarly named yard on a full rigged ship and, as Röding continued, '...one uses the square sail when sailing before the wind, such is lowered down as soon as one sails close hauled'. By explaining the clew-line blocks on a cutter's crossjack yard, Steel expressed the same thoughts in a slightly different way: '...some sloops and light rigged vessels have no clue-line-blocks; they lower the yard'. Half a century prior to Currier's illustration of the American schooner, both authors interpreted that purely gaff-rigged vessels (like fore-and-aft schooners) moved their crossjack yard up and down.

Crossjack yard

To commence the rigging of the crossjack yard two thimble straps were seized or spliced around the yard's centre, with one pointing up and the other aft. Depending on the yard's application as square sail yard or spread yard, the upward-reaching thimble was used either for the halyard block's hook or for a sling to be attached. The aft-reaching thimble was either part of the truss or used as a traveller on the horse or jack stay of fore-and-aft-rigged vessels. A double-strapped double block was also lashed to the centre, but only to a topsail schooner's yard (spread yard) where the quarter block became necessary for leading the topsail sheets downward.

Parrels were used for the crossjack yard during the early schooner days and after 1760 were gradually superseded by trusses. A parrel consisted of a number of ribs and trucks alternately fitted on to the parrel ropes, which had an eye spliced into one end. According to yard size a rib had two or more holes for the parrel ropes. The eyes of these ropes went over and under the yard, to be seized together. The other ends were taken in turn above and below around the yard until extended. The crossing ropes at the back of the parrel were then marled together.

Trusses came in many variations and common to all was their ability to open and shut. In its most basic form a truss had a thimble spliced into one end, with that end laid round the yard near the centre to keep the thimble close to the rear. The long truss was then laid round the rear of the mast, the front of the yard and back across the rear to the thimble, from where it led downward to end in a tackle.

Foot ropes or horses were similar to those on larger ships, although the fore-and-aft schooner did not have use for them on the crossjack yard. A more detailed description is given under Spritsail yard. The use of stirrups depended on a yard's length and only one or two may have been necessary. Stirrups were vertical straps, made up of a thimble carrying a hanging part of three feet in length and a plaited part of such a length that it could be wound three times round the yard and nailed to it.

Placed with an eye splice over the yardarm, brace pendants had a single block spliced into the outer end. On topsail schooner yards and naval vessels this was followed by strapped sheet blocks with a single lift being spliced round the block strap's bight. Merchant vessels used an alternative arrangement with the leading of topsail sheets over sheaves in the squared yardarm stops. Lifts then went separately with an eye splice over the yardarms.

Halyard blocks for square sail nock halyards were fitted to yardarms like sheet blocks, but hanging down. Two similar blocks for the inner halyards were placed at about a quarter yard length away from the centre. An alternative place for these blocks was below the fore crosstree.

Topsail yard

A tye, fastened with a running eye round the yard's centre, led over a sheave in the topmast's hounding. The halyard tackle was formed by a double block, spliced into the downward end in combination with a fall and single-hooked block. The lower single block was strapped, long strapped or iron bound and either hooked to an eyebolt beside the mast or to an eyebolt in the chain-wale. The hauling part of the fall belayed either to a mast cleat or was led over a foot block and belayed to a cleat on the inner bulwark. If topsails carried horses they usually did not have stirrups. Clew-line blocks were stropped outside the yard cleats and up to a quarter of the yard's length away from the centre.

Buntlines were not often rigged, but can be seen on a watercolour of the American schooner *Baltick* from 1765, where a buntline block is shown above the yard at the hounding. According to the flags shown (ensign, jack and long pennant), the *Baltick* seems to have been a vessel under Royal Navy command.

Lifts were fitted similar to the lower yards on merchant vessels. During early years they rove through stropped blocks at the topmast hounding and later through thimbles in the upper part of the shrouds, belaying to lower shroud cleats (or more infrequently to a five-rail). William Ward's 1795 watercolour of the American schooner *Fame* indicates lifts fixed at both ends. These were described by Steel: '...[standing lifts] are made fast, and belong to yards that never require to be topped'.

Brace pendants belonged mostly to larger schooners; smaller vessels rigged their topsail braces single. They went with an eye directly over the yardarm.

Parrels of the last quarter of the eighteenth century were

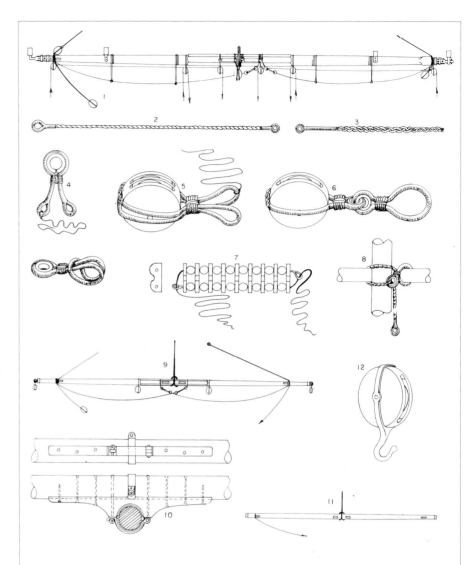

1. Lower yard: Left side indicates a Royal Navy yard with the horse leading to the outside of the opposite sling cleat. Right side shows a merchant vessel's yard with a dog & bitch brace block (around 1800) and a Continental foot horse, leading to the innermost sling cleat.
2. Horse or foot rope
3. Stirrup
4. Strapped thimbles.
5. Double strapped double block
6. Dog & bitch connected brace block
7. Parrel, English method
8. Simple truss
9. Topsail yard: left side with brace pendant and running lift; the right side with single braces and standing lift
10. Patent truss, in use after about 1830
11. Topgallant yard, rigged flying with halyard and sometimes single braces
12. Ironbound block with a hook

similar to those of a spritsail yard. A two-rowed rib-and-truck parrel was in use before 1830, after which a patent truss, made from timber and iron, superseded the earlier version on many vessels.

Topgallant yard

During the eighteenth century topgallant yards were generally set flying and rigged only with a halyard and occasionally single braces. The halyard went over a sheave in or through a block at the topmast's long pole head toward deck, while the sail's clews lashed to the topsail yardarms.

Gaffs

These were rigged according to their function as standing or hoisted gaff. Common to both was a single-stranded parrel to keep the gaff's jaws close to the mast. A gaff was usually slung or 'standing' when its sail was without a boom. The attachment was not dissimilar to that of a slung yard, or the sling was pulled with half its length through an eyebolt at the upper jaw's side and then seized. Both ends, about equal length with an eye spliced into each, were laid above the trestletrees round the masthead and seized together. But no rule is without exception and one cannot state that a slung gaff and a boom-less (loose-footed) sail were always used together.

If a gaff was rigged to hoist, a tackle was hooked into the eyebolt at the upper jaw's side and to another at the rear of the masthead. Instead of a tackle larger gaffs had a tye

hooked to the gaff's eyebolt leading over an iron-bound single block at the lower masthead. A double block was then spliced into, or hooked to, the lower end of the tye to form a tackle with a single block hooked to an eyebolt on deck. The former was known as throat halyard with the latter being a throat tye.

A slung gaff also had only a 'standing' peak tye hooked to a masthead eyebolt. This contrasted to a hoisted gaff's peak halyard, which led over one or more blocks at the masthead and gaff towards deck for the peak's height to be altered. Peak halyards were rigged in several ways. In one variation fitted with an eye over the gaff's peak, the halyard passed through blocks at the masthead, the gaff and the masthead again, leading downward. In a second hooked to the masthead, the halyard led toward a block at the gaff's peak, another at the masthead, again to the gaff's centre and

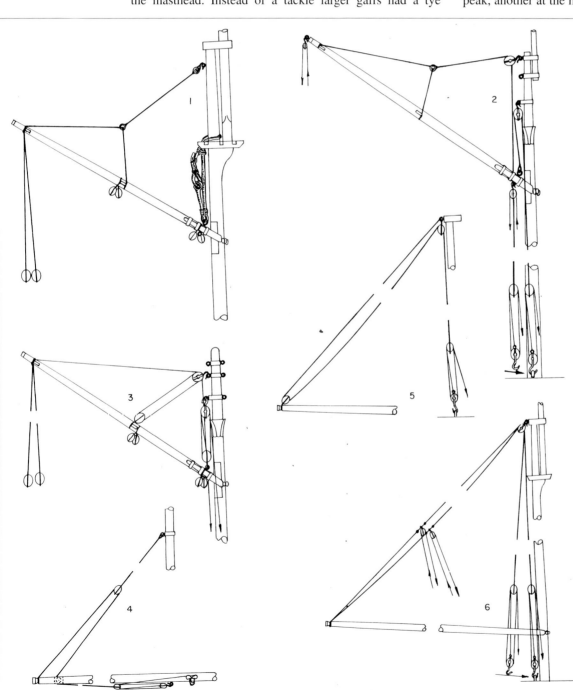

1. Slung gaff with standing peak tye, vangs and brail blocks
2. Hoisted gaff of a larger vessel's boom sail with peak tye; these ties were set up with tackles to both sides of the main mast; also visible are peak and throat-downhauler
3. Hoisted gaff with vangs and brail blocks
4. Single topping lift for smaller vessels
5. Topping lift by D Steel for cutters and other one-masted vessels
6. Commonly used double topping lift, set to tackles on both sides of the mast; this sketch also shows the use of crane-lines

finally through a fourth block, placed at the masthead, to be led downward as before. In a third way a leather-clad span fastened around the gaff's outer third, or third quarter, whereby the thimble of a tye ran along that span. Leading through a block at the upper masthead the tye came down towards deck similarly to the throat tye. The latter is known as a 'running' peak tye.

Although Lever[177] revealed that only slung gaffs were rigged with vangs, other authors did not differentiate. However, it becomes evident when studying contemporary artists' impressions that Lever's explanation was accurate. Vangs operated to regulate a gaff's peak position in similar ways as braces acted upon a yard, yet they would have obstructed a boom sail's movement severely. When rigging vangs, the rope was halved into pendants, seized to form an eye, which was pushed over the gaff's peak. Dependent on the size of the sail, the pendants were connected to eyebolts on deck by either a single block whip or tackles with double or long-tackle blocks.

Two pairs of brail blocks were seized to a gaff's lower side, with one placed close to the jaws and the other near the centre. Gaffs of boom sails did not normally rig brail blocks but had different furling arrangements: roving through a small block at the gaff's peak, both ends of a downhauler belayed to a boom cleat. Hooked to an eyebolt at the lower side of the jaws was a double block belonging to a tackle known as a throat downhauler. Its lower, single block hooked to a strapped thimble, which was lashed round the mast above deck level. Flag-line blocks seized or hooked only to a mainmast's gaff and then usually to a peak-extending eyebolt.

Boom

The rigging of the boom consisted of a single-strand truck parrel (as described in Gaff), a topping lift, a boom sheet and a boom guy. The rigging of a topping lift varied and could be set up according to several methods, none of which followed specific rules. For light rigging one usually had only one topping lift pendant hanging down from the masthead with a single block fitted to its end. The runner had its standing part spliced round the boom end, which went through the pendant block to a sheave in or to a block at boom's end. It belayed then to a boom cleat either directly, or by a larger sail with a tackle hooked into the hauling part.

One description of a boom for cutters and other one-masted vessels, mentioned that the standing part of the topping lift was hooked or clinched to an eyebolt at the masthead. Leading downward to a block at boom's end and returning to a block at the same eyebolt, it then came down on the starboard side. Ending in a double block/single block tackle, it hooked to an eyebolt at the rear section of the channel and belayed to a pin in the shroud rack. Occasionally a runner was added to this tackle.

A common method was to middle the topping lift to the bight, which was hitched and seized round the boom's end. Both ends of the lift rove through larger blocks, hooked or lashed to the upper part of the masthead or cap and came down at both sides of the mast, where tackles in their lower ends hooked to eyebolts on deck. A span was set up a few feet inside boom end, between topping lift and boom. With an eye spliced into both ends the span was under slight tension and being of lesser strength than the lift acted as safeguard. If the lift became overly strained, the span would brake first and preventive measures could be taken.

The foremost boom of two-masted merchant vessels in the North and Baltic Seas coastal trade was frequently fitted with topping lift pendant and tackle, which reached vertically upwards from a boom axis extending eyebolt and hooked to another at the face of the mast behind, just below the trestletrees. The tackle's fall belayed to the foot of that mast. That such an arrangement was not confined to North European coastal shipping alone but was also employed by North American east-coast traders is documented on Ward's watercolour '*Fame*' from Salem, Massachusetts. The advantages of this vertical lift over a single diagonal one was that the gaff's peak did not have to be dipped to get the lift to luff when the vessel was going about.

By using double-topping lifts the leeward lift was always kept slack. Crane line blocks, confined by two Turk's Heads, were often fitted to the lifts at half height. The crane line itself had a double-wall knot on one end and was stapled to a five-rail. After passing the lift block it belayed to a deck cleat. The purpose of that line was to maintain a certain distance between a lee topping lift and the sail, to prevent cutting in and chafing.

A double block for the boom sheet was found inside the taffrail strapped to the main boom and confined by stop cleats or a comb cleat, or to the end of a schooner sail boom. With a thimble running on a horse a further double or sometimes treble block was placed close to the taffrail, or for a schooner sail boom in front of the mainmast. Alternatively, the lower block of a schooner sail boom sheet was hooked, without horse, to an eyebolt at the partners. The sheet was belayed either to a deck cleat or to an extended axis pin of the lower block.

A strapped thimble sat inside the comb cleat confinement, next to the boom sheet block strap. A boom guy pendant supported the normal boom sheet with a luff tackle in an emergency or could be hooked into it in very bad weather. The luff tackle was hooked to the pendant, while its other block was hooked either to a chain-plate at the main channel (for a main boom), or was fastened to a bollard or an eyebolt near the windlass (for a schooner sail boom). Such tackle was naturally only set up to the weather side and belayed inboards. A footrope ran between the comb cleat and the boom's outer extremities to work the boom's extended length outside the taffrail.

Technical descriptions or drawings of square sail booms and dimensions are rare and the latter could only be found on a mast and spar table for US Navy schooners from 1826. Other details are taken from artists' impressions. The boom was positioned athwart ship in front of the fore mast and lashed either to timberheads or eyebolts. The only simple contemporary description is in the 1815 edition of Falconer's Dictionary: '…a boom lashed across the deck of a vessel with one mast, and used to spread the foot of the square sail.'

Square-sail sheet blocks were placed on the boom arms in a similar fashion to yards. If a square sail yard or spread yard carried studdingsail booms, the square sail boom would have

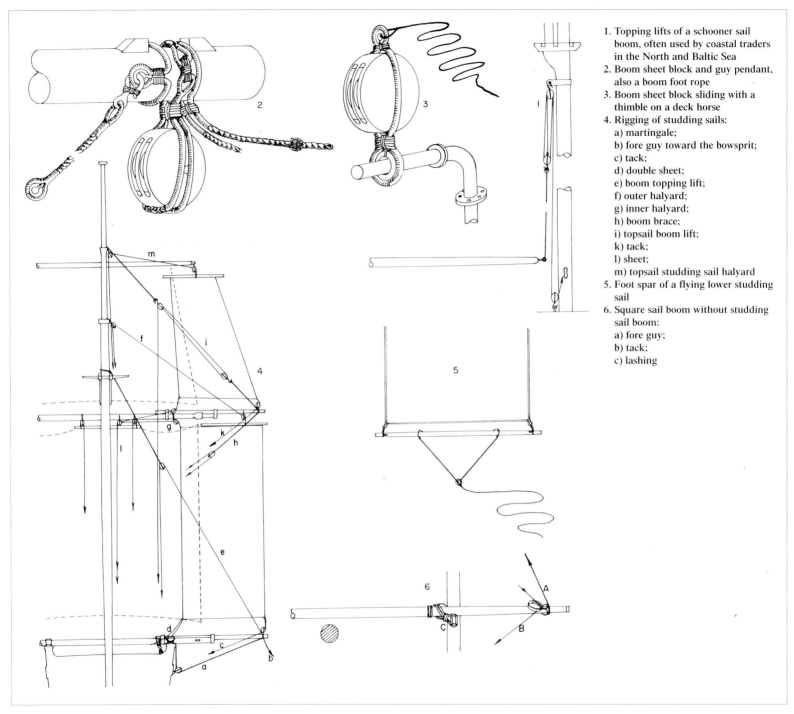

1. Topping lifts of a schooner sail boom, often used by coastal traders in the North and Baltic Sea
2. Boom sheet block and guy pendant, also a boom foot rope
3. Boom sheet block sliding with a thimble on a deck horse
4. Rigging of studding sails:
   a) martingale;
   b) fore guy toward the bowsprit;
   c) tack;
   d) double sheet;
   e) boom topping lift;
   f) outer halyard;
   g) inner halyard;
   h) boom brace;
   i) topsail boom lift;
   k) tack;
   l) sheet;
   m) topsail studding sail halyard
5. Foot spar of a flying lower studding sail
6. Square sail boom without studding sail boom:
   a) fore guy;
   b) tack;
   c) lashing

fitted these yards also. That mode was probably more preferred in English rigging than in rigs of other nations. On continental vessels the studdingsails were more frequently set flying and did not need their lower booms.

The use of studdingsail boom extensions on a square sail boom made it necessary for them to be rigged to withstand the sail's pressure. Fore-and-aft guys were used for horizontal stabilisation, with the forward guy going to the bowsprit, while a lift between trestletrees and the outer boom end counteracted the down-draft vertically. A bobstay or martingale was led from the outer arm through a block at an eyebolt in the wales and taken up to a timberhead to prevent any up-draft. A block for the studdingsail tack was also strapped to that outer point.

The type of studdingsail booms described here were gen-erally brought out without outhauler and finally lashed with their inner ends to the respective yard or the square sail boom. Fitted to the outer end of yard booms were single lifts, brace pendants and upward pointing blocks for the topsail studdingsail's tack. Slightly inward of that point a block hung for the lower studdingsail halyard. As a rule topsail yards did not carry studdingsail booms, they had only yard-extending eyebolts for the jewel blocks (halyard-blocks for the upper studdingsail). Studdingsail yards as well as square sail yards (club yards) were only rigged with their appropriate halyards.

Mainmast

Everything said under Foremast about mast tackles, shrouds and so on is also relevant for the mainmast, as only the stays were rigged in a different way.

Schooner stay

The main stay of a schooner was characteristic, particularly during the eighteenth and early nineteenth centuries. A schooner's main stay ran between the two mastheads above the gaff, so as not to inhibit fore gaff movement. That arrangement first appeared on the 1695 model of HMS *Royal Transport*. As can be ascertained from photographic reproductions of the St. Petersburg model, the stay was laid with an eye round the fore masthead and then led toward the main masthead where it passed through a block and came down before the mast. With a double block seized into the end, the tackle, of which the lower block was long strapped, hooked finally to an eyebolt on deck. As these inferences can only be drawn from photographs, it is probable that a visual examination of the model may lead to slightly different conclusions. Portuguese schooners (Yate Portugues and Lancho Do Alto) illustrated in Röding's work of 1794[178] provide us with a similar stay arrangement, although they are more identifiable as single stays. The painting 'English Yachts At Sea In A Fresh Breeze' from about 1704 by Willem van de Velde, the Younger, does not show a stay lead block at the masthead of these yachts. However, a diagonal stay from the taller main masthead down to the fore masthead points to a reversal of Osborne's method. The stay between the two mastheads later became known as the schooner stay.

An alternative to the schooner stay on American schooners dates from about 1790. The main stay was then doubled and rigged ship-like, with both sides leading past the foremast down to the fore deck where they ended in eye-bolt hooked tackles. The doubling of the stay was necessary to avoid constant lifting of the sail over a single stay when the vessel was going about. The leeward stay was always kept slack, like a leeward topping lift, so the sail was not hindered or chafed. The leeward stay was mainly an American phenomenon; it did not appear on European schooners before 1810 and so did not supersede the schooner stay, which could still be found on vessels in the middle of the nineteenth century.

The fore stay on schooner stay-rigged vessels originally acted as the principal stay until the introduction of dual main stays. In the dual rigging system the fore stay moved from its stem position to a more ship-like one at the middle of the bowsprit, making way for a larger fore stay sail. Modern rigging plans of pre-1790 American schooners are frequently drawn with a dual main stay, but contemporary artwork strongly suggests that the schooner stay was still very much in use before this date.

Although a 1765 watercolour by an unknown artist of the American schooner *Baltick* 'coming out of St.Eustatia ye 16th of Nov. 1765' shows the vessel rigged with a main stay sail, it cannot be concluded that this sail was hoisted on a main stay. No continuation of it toward the fore deck is visible and the height of the stay sail stay suggests that it would not have been possible: the stay would end up in the middle of the bowsprit, while a permanent lashing to the foremast at about one-third of its height would have totally impaired the movement of the schooner sail. Furthermore, the presence of a lee stay was not even considered. However, modern authors are still inclined to mention that vessel as being an

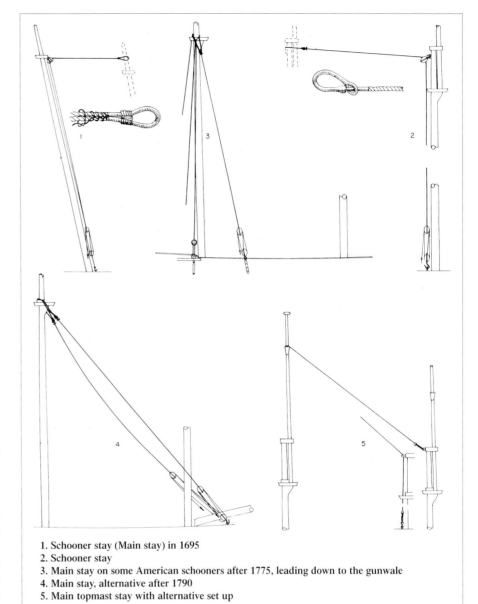

1. Schooner stay (Main stay) in 1695
2. Schooner stay
3. Main stay on some American schooners after 1775, leading down to the gunwale
4. Main stay, alternative after 1790
5. Main topmast stay with alternative set up

early example of the new schooner main stay, especially with a schooner stay not being shown and the appearance of a main topmast stay. A second watercolour by the same unknown artist 'This shows the Schooner *Baltick* in distress in 6 fathoms of Water on Nantucket Shoales with everything washed off the Decks & Two men Drounded. ye 19th Dec.' gives a clear view of the temporary main stay sail stay, but in this illustration it ran to a lower point at the foremast than in the first artwork. A schooner stay between the two mastheads can also be seen. A third picture by the same unknown sailor artist 'This Shews the Schooner *Baltick* On the Middle Ground going into Cape Fare in a Very hard Gale of Wind with the Pilot boat beating out to Her Feb. 15th 1766' illustrated the schooner stay as seen in the previous artwork but does not show the temporary stay sail stay. The story of the three pictures tells us of the rigging of a schooner stay on the *Baltick* and the use of a temporary main stay sail to goosewing the schooner sail when sailing before the wind, or – in a possibly more acceptable explanation – without the schooner sail to be rigged as a brigantine, since this is a typical brigantine sail[179]. The first watercolour provides us with all the sails that vessel was capable of carrying, but an early dating of the dual main stay cannot be concluded from the *Baltick*'s rig.

Forerunners of the dual main stay were carried on the American schooners *Revenge* and *Royal Savage*, both pictured in a primitive 1776 illustration of New England vessels at Valcour Bay[180]. A similar stay arrangement is also shown on a schooner in a harbour scene of Salem, Massachusetts in 1797. The featured dual main stays are identical with the mizzen stays on ketches, howker yachts, galiots and galeasses in North European waters. At about one-third of the length between the masts forward they were led to the sides to prevent interference with the swinging schooner sail boom.

Larger schooners also rigged a main topmast stay, which, according to a dimension table by Steel, was set up like the schooner stay but to thimbles. Its lead block was positioned

1. The rigging of spritsail and yard: on the left side is a double lift shows, as was in use on larger vessels
2. A fore staysail with alternative halyard arrangements
3. Iron hank of a staysail for fastening
4. A flying jib
5. A fore staysail's peak-spreader
6. Double sheet pendant of staysail clew
7. Two sheet blocks on one hook in a staysail's clew (D Steel)

on the fore masthead just above the schooner stay. During the nineteenth century a main topgallant stay could also be found on larger naval vessels.

Topsail yard

'In none of the other types of vessel are we confronted with such a great variation between each individual vessel as by those schooners who are preferably driven by gaff sails. It derives from the present utilisation of that type in a variety of sizes and for every possible purpose.' [181]

These words, by F L Middendorf in 1903, were not only true for the time they were written, but for the whole of the schooner era and had special validity for the rigging of topsail yards to schooner mainmasts. Even with Fincham and Steinhaus pointing explicitly to the flying nature of mainmast topsails, a matter underlined by a great number of contemporary artist impressions and rigging plan interpretations, we can probably find a similar number of contemporary sources that suggest that these sails were permanently rigged. For example, early Royal Navy schooners on 'A View of the Town of Boston with several Ships' by Revere, are shown with lifts fitted to their main spread and topsail yards as well as forward leading braces. The schooners *Peter & Mary* (1747), *Swallow* (1756) and *Sally* (1758), sketched by Ashley Bowen[182], had topsail yards hanging in lifts. Dominic Serres' 'Schooner With A View Of New York' from about 1780 shows a similar arrangement, along with footropes and a furled topsail. Other vessels equipped likewise included a British armed cutter-schooner from 1801 and the French schooner *La Favorite* from 1808, both of which were illustrated by Roux. Therefore, where it is proven that these yards were permanently rigged on a mainmast they would have been rigged like the foremast (except for studdingsail booms, which were usually not rigged to mainmast yards).

The expression 'flying' in regard to hoisting sails implied the simplest way possible, which meant that yard sails were without lifts, clew-lines, buntlines, sheets, bowlines, parrel and often also without braces, and stay sails were set without a stay or a stay sail stay. Yard sail clews were lashed to the yard below and with yard and sail being hauled up together, there was no need for any footrope.

Gaff topsail and other fore-and-aft topsails

Gaff topsails came increasingly into vogue from around 1775 and they could be set in a number of ways. They were laced to a short gaff, and placed above the main gaff and below the main topmast hounding. Fore-and-aft schooners could have gaff topsails set to both masts. The rig of a topsail gaff consisted of throat halyard and peak halyard. The former rove over a sheave in the topmast hounding on to deck, while the latter fastened to the topmast pole head and was led through a thimble at the gaff's peak, then through a block at the topmast pole head and from there downward. Instead of a gaff a small lug sail yard could be used, which only required a halyard.

The sliding-gunter pole provided another way of hoisting

a fore-and-aft topsail. Having been connected through two iron hoops forming a 'figure-of-eight', with the topmast pole head in such a way that an up-and-down movement was ensured, the pole halyard was fastened to its foot and rove over the sheave in the topmast hounding. The fourth possibility was a shoulder-of-mutton topsail. With no yard or gaff needed, the halyard was hitched to the sail's peak, then through a block at the topmast pole head and from there down on to deck.

Running Rigging

Spritsail yard

Information about the rigging of schooner spritsail yards is difficult to find in contemporary illustrative material and a great deal of research has still to be done to cover the subject thoroughly, as underlined by comments made to me by S M Riley from the National Maritime Museum in London: '…much work needs to be done to piece together the scraps of evidence, many of which can be found in our collections.'

A yard's running rigging would begin with its braces. Contemporary illustrative evidence suggests that they were single and went with an eye splice over the yardarms, as seen on Paul Revere's engraving 'Landing of troops in Boston, 30 September 1768'[183]. They are likewise only marked as a weak line on an illustration by Gwyn 'A topsail schooner c. 1780'[184], and the early Falconer schooner example[185] seems to corroborate that. Even the slightly misplaced spritsail yard on Baugean's etching of 'an armed schooner drying her sails' from 1814[186] has single braces. On all of the aforementioned pictures, apart from that by Falconer, the braces were led towards the foremost shrouds approximately at gaff level and then probably down to a shroud cleat or belay rack. Whether the brace lead-block was lashed to the shrouds (catharpins), or strapped to the mast cannot be ascertained. Falconer's schooner illustration in the 1780 edition had its braces leading about two-thirds of the way up a fore topmast stay and then to a slightly higher position at the shrouds. It also set the jib flying. The most common way of rigging spritsail yard braces on (larger) square-rigged ships was to hitch the standing part to the fore stay collar below the mast top, pass it through brace pendant blocks, lead it back to blocks on the collar and finally downward to be belayed.

A lift on Gwyn's watercolour fastened (hooked, spliced or hitched?) to the bowsprit cap, rove through the yardarm lift block and a cap lead-block toward the fore deck, where it probably belayed to a cleat on the inner bowsprit. Considering the size of a schooner's spritsail, clew lines usually ran single and hitched to the clews. Leading over clew-line blocks on the yard, they belayed to the same cleats as the lifts. A single buntline on the sail's face fastened to a span in the middle of the foot. Likewise single sheets were hitched to the clews and belayed to timberheads beside the foremast.

A spritsail yard usually also had an outhauler rigged, which could consist of a luff or a long tackle with the single block, either strapped or hooked, to the yard centre's face with a double or violin block at the bottom of the bowsprit cap. The tackle fall belayed to one of the fore timberheads.

Fore staysail

Connected to the fore stay with wooden or iron hanks, its halyard tackle hooked to the sail's peak. With the tack hitched to the stay's lower dead eye, the sheet belayed before the mast. A downhauler was hitched into the sail's peak, passing through a few hanks and a block strapped to the lower stay on its way down, and belayed to an inner bowsprit cleat. Fore staysails frequently had one or more reef bands to shorten that sail.

Jib

Set either to a stay or 'flying', the sail was fitted with a halyard tackle at its peak and a tack hooked or hitched to an eyelet on the bowsprit cap, or to the traveller when no outer or flying jib was carried. For a further control of the sail a pair of sheets, with or without pendants, were fitted to the clew. Their standing part spliced to a ring-bolt on deck, whilst the hauling part, or single sheets, fastened to belay pins in the windlass cross-piece. When hoisted on a stay, a jib had hanks and a downhauler, the latter being placed opposite to those of the fore staysail.

Outer or flying jib

The sail was rigged like the jib with its tack fastened to the traveller. The halyards of all staysails with blocks fastened to the stay collar at the mast usually had their falls belayed to the lower shrouds (cleats or pin rack).

Spread yard

This was permanently slung, contrary to a crossjack yard which was always hoisted on fore-and-aft-rigged vessels. Both methods are shown on the rigging plans of the 'Schooner For Port Jackson'. The terminology difference for the foremast's lower yard has been explained before under Masts and Spars and does not need repetition.

For a slung yard, a yard tackle would only be used initially to lift it into position and was then replaced with a sling. Slings were introduced to yard rigging during the 1760s. In the English naval method the sling was taken over the mast cap and lashed to the upward reaching thimble strap on the yard. The Continental method was different as the sling, which was similar to shrouds and stay, was placed around the masthead above the trestletrees.

Permanent halyard tackles were rigged in various ways. They could have been a double block tackle, with one end strapped round the masthead while the other hooked to a thimble strap and the fall belayed to a mast cleat. Or a tye was used, fastened with its standing part at portside to the masthead and rove as a whip through a block at the yard's centre, another at the starboard masthead. The running part ended in a luff tackle and hooked finally beside the mast to an eyebolt on deck.

The yard's braces led either forward or aft, with vessels of war preparing for combat carrying them both ways, the forward-leading brace considered a preventer brace. Fastened with its standing part to the bowsprit cap, the preventer brace returned through a forward-reaching block at the yard-arm to a lead block in the foremost part of the bowsprit and then towards fore deck. Spliced or strapped round the mainmast

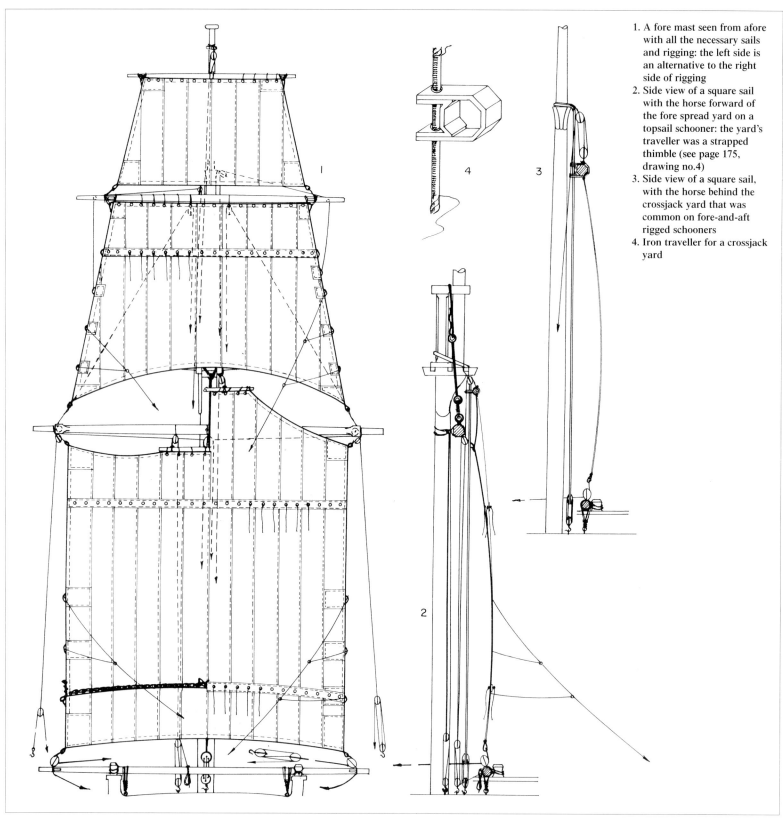

1. A fore mast seen from afore with all the necessary sails and rigging: the left side is an alternative to the right side of rigging
2. Side view of a square sail with the horse forward of the fore spread yard on a topsail schooner: the yard's traveller was a strapped thimble (see page 175, drawing no.4)
3. Side view of a square sail, with the horse behind the crossjack yard that was common on fore-and-aft rigged schooners
4. Iron traveller for a crossjack yard

below the mast hounding, the aft-leading brace was led via the brace pendant block at the yard-arm back to a lead block in the upper section of the foremost main shroud, came down and belayed to a shroud cleat. The watercolour by Gwyn from 1780 previously mentioned and a painting of a Flensburg schooner from 1843 reveal that these braces could also come from a gunwale position aft of the mainmast. The hauling part was thereby running over a snatch block on the

gunwale (as illustrated by Gwyn), or rove through a long strapped block (as on the Flensburg schooner) and led the brace ahead of the main shrouds inboard to a belay point.

Single lifts spliced either into the topsail sheet block strap, or went with an eye-splice over the yardarm. They rove through single blocks, hooked to the mast cap or seized to a span, and came down to cleats in the lower shrouds. In the case of a double lift the standing part was spliced to a becket on the cap block, passed the yardarm lift block, returned to the former and downwards, there sometimes through a foot block on deck, to be belayed as before.

Square sail

Contemporary pictorial evidence regarding square sails reveals again that no other rig was as individual as that of the schooner. Not only could a square sail yard be short, of medium size, or long enough to extend over the whole width of the sail, sometimes it did not exist at all and the sail was hoisted up on the spread yard or, on fore-and-aft schooners, bent to the crossjack yard. To fasten a square sail to the particular yard one used either a lacing or robands.

Square sail halyards were rigged accordingly and we distinguish between inner and outer halyards. Depending on sail volume, the inner halyards were either single or double tackles hitched at the outer quarters to a club yard. They hauled the yard to blocks vertically above, either fastened to the spread yard or to the mast cross trees. On sails without a yard these halyards were hitched to the sail's head-rope. On a full-length square sail yard the halyard tackle block was strapped to the middle, with the upper tackle block hanging beneath the sling of the spread yard.

All these variations shared outer halyards. They could either be hitched to the earrings or be put with an eye over the yardarms of a full square sail yard before being led over the respective blocks at the spread yardarms and coming down inboards to eyebolts in the waterways, with either a luff tackle or a whip. In some instances a halyard fall was hitched to the yardarm block and rove through another at the earing before coming down as before. On the Leith smack *Queen Charlotte*, painted in 1802 by J C Schetky[187], the halyard's standing part was fastened slightly inside the yardarm to the spread yard and led as a whip through earing and yardarm block to be secured as above.

Sheets were hitched to the clews in the usual manner. They rove through sheet blocks at the arms of the square sail boom and led aft, with luff tackles hooked to their ends and into eyebolts on deck. In such a way they acted concurrently with the boom's after guys and a counteracting guy was generally set forward to stabilise the gunwale-reaching boom in both directions.

Rigging normally identified with a fore course, like clew lines, buntlines and leech-lines, did not apply to square sails because of their occasional nature and their furling on deck. However, sreef bands were sewn to the upper and lower section of some sails, whereby the lower section was often substituted with a bonnet. In his description of a square sail for sloops David Steel pointed to the use of bowline cringles; bowlines therefore must be considered when rigging that sail.

In regard to reefing, words by Falconer are of interest:

'When a sail is reefed at the bottom, it is done by knittles, which being thrust through the eyelet-holes thereof, are tied firmly about the space of canvas of which the reef is composed, and knotted on the lower side of the bolt-rope. These knittles are accordingly removed as soon as the reef is let out.'

In the 1815 edition Falconer added these words:

'…it is generally done with knittles, in the room of points; or in large sails, such as the main-sails of armed cutters, pieces of line termed reef-hanks, are fixed in the eyelet-holes.'

Also in the 1815 edition reef-hanks are discussed:

'reef-hanks, short pieces of small line, sewed at certain distances on the reefs of boom-sails…'.[188]

Topsail

Permanently rigged topsails were comparable to those on smaller ships and had up to two reef bands. Clew lines were hitched to the clews and were usually single. Led through the clew-line blocks on the yard, they passed on their downward way through lead trucks in the upper section of the mast shrouds and were belayed to shroud cleats.

A buntline was only part of a larger schooner's topsail. That line was set up with an eye (thimble?) to a span, spliced at the face of the sail round the footrope (bolt-rope), and rove through a block at the topmast hounds to lead downward like the clew lines. In instances where a halyard block was strapped to the yard, the buntline block spliced to the top of the block's strap.

Reef tackles were an essential part of a sail that was fitted with reef bands. They enabled the leeches to be sufficiently hauled up to apply a reef with greater ease. Reef tackle cringles were fitted to the leech-rope (bolt rope) below the reef band cringles. On large schooners blocks were fastened to these cringles and the tackle fall, coming down from the yardarm as a whip, led through the block and a sheave in the yardarm to the sister block or thimble in the upper part of the topmast shrouds on deck. The forerunner of, and later an alternative to, the sister block was a long-strapped block at the topmast stop. The reef tackle was fitted to smaller topsails as a single line and was hitched directly to the reef tackle cringle.

Depending on sail size, single or double bridles were applied to topsail bowlines. They went forward to the outsides of the treble thimble strap, or in the case of a treble block to the outside sheaves at the jib boom stop; they belayed to cleats on the inner bowsprit. Lead blocks for bowlines on a permanently rigged main topsail were strapped to the foremast's rear cross tree. After 1775 embedded sheaves in the ends of the fore trestletrees became an alternative to these blocks. Main topsail bowlines belayed to fore shroud cleats.

Hitched to the topsail clews, sheets rove through the yardarm sheaves of the spread yard (or through sheet blocks), then via two singles or a double block (known as quarter blocks) near the yard's centre then downwards toward cleats on the lower part of the mast.

Braces were rigged fore or aft and, similar to the fore spread yard, one could find also a combination of both on the foremast. Illustrations of British naval schooners in Revere's engraving of 'Boston with British troops disembarking' from 1768 show braces leading to the same bowsprit position as those of the spread yard. The topsail schooner by Gwyn from 1780 show them going out to the jib boom rigging stop, which is identical to those on Plate XII, No 9 by Falconer from 1780. The braces always went through blocks toward the fore deck. Gwyn's topsail schooner indicated a combination of both braces, and forward-leading preventer braces as described by Steel:

'…a rope used in ships of war, to supply the place of a brace, should that be shot away or damaged. They are led the contrary way, to be less liable to detriment at the same time.'[189]

Rearward-leading single braces went through blocks strapped or hooked to the main masthead, and then via shroud lead trucks toward cleats at the foremost shroud. Dual braces were usually hitched to the main- or schooner-stay collar, and rove through the brace pendant blocks before going via shroud lead trucks towards the cleats.

Braces of permanent, sometimes also of flying, main topsail yards led to lead blocks at the fore masthead and via trucks in the fore shrouds to shroud cleats. The sheets of flying topsails were usually only bits of seizing, connecting the clews to the spread yard.

Topgallant sail

For most of the eighteenth century these sails were not a standard schooner feature and were predominantly rigged flying. They are already described under Standing Rigging.

Braces on fore topgallant yards were only rigged when, contrary to eighteenth-century custom, these were a permanent fixture and the sail fitted with lifts and sheets etc., as can be noted on the picture of schooner *Fame* from Salem by W Ward, dated 1795. This type of rigging is more applicable in the nineteenth century because royals were introduced to the sails of schooners and they took over the role of temporary flying sails. Fore topgallant sails were then rigged like topsails and their single braces rove either through blocks above, or over a second sheave in, the topsail brace blocks.

Gaff sail

When discussing the rigging of a gaff sail one must differentiate between gaffs with and those without a boom. The difference between the two becomes most obvious in the method of furling and in the sail's attachment to the mast. A gaff sail without boom was usually bent to a gaff, with the sail furled up to gaff and mast. If the gaff was lowered on a boom-sail and the sail was furled to it, the overshooting part was wound around itself and the clew pulled by the sail's sheet toward the boom's sheet sheave.

With the sail in the first method not being subjected to hoisting or lowering, a lacing to the mast was adequate, whereas the boom-sail was fitted with mast hoops to allow for an unhindered up-and-down movement. The fixing of the sail's head to the gaff was common to both methods. A lacing, spliced into the sail's peak, went spiralling round the gaff and through the eyelet-holes in the sail's head. On each of these eyelet-holes the lacing was stopped with a seizing to prevent lacing damage, which might result in the sail and gaff completely unravelling and parting. The connection between mast and mast leech was done in similar fashion, but another way to lace the mast was revealed by Lever. Instead of eyelet-holes, cringles were spliced into the mast leech's bolt-rope and the lacing spiralled not around the mast by going through the cringles, but returned always to the fore side, so that every turn of it was counter-rotating to the former. For safety that part of the lacing was also seized to each cringle. Mast hoops were lashed to dual eyelet-holes in the mast leech doubling. The inner diameter of the hoops had to be at least 1½ to 2 inches more than the largest of the mast to ensure that it could slide up and down smoothly.

Brails were required for a gaff sail without boom to bring the sail's aft leech closer to the gaff or mast (brailing up). Depending on the gaff's length and sail's size, the two or three needed were known as peak brails, middle brails and throat brails. Brails came in pairs and were spliced round the respective brail cringle. After passing through the corresponding brail blocks below the gaff, peak brails belayed to cleats inboard, middle brails (if present) rove through lead blocks at the hindmost shrouds and came down to shroud cleats, while the throat brails belayed to the middle pins at the windlass' cross-piece. Through one of his pictorial impressions Roux makes it clear that every rule has an exception. A coloured sketch from 1813 indicates two schooners with furled gaff sails and no differentiation between the sail without boom and that with a boom-sail has been attempted (could this be artistic licence?). For these schooners one would have to surmise brails even for the boom-sails.

A further variance between these two gaff sail types was the rigging of vangs. Being commonly only part of a standing gaff's sail, they incorporated pendants, like braces, and mostly a runner, hooked with one end to an eyebolt in the waterways. After passing the pendant block they came on to deck as a whip to belay directly, or after going through a foot block, to a cleat. Larger vangs had instead of a single block, a double or long-tackle block spliced or hooked to their pendants, which points to the use of stronger tackles then a whip. The sheet of such a gaff sail consisted of a tackle, hooked or hitched to the clew, and depending on the sail's mass was made up from a single/double block or a double/treble block combination. The larger, lower block hooked either to an eyebolt on deck or had a thimble seized to its strap, which ran on an iron horse. The sheet belayed to a deck cleat or alternatively to a belay-pin, being the extended axis of the lower block.

The sheet of a boom-sail was a single pendant spliced into the sail's clew. It went over a sheave in the outer boom and had a thimble turned into the lower end. A luff tackle was hooked into that thimble and another, which was strapped near the jaws to the boom. Once the sheet has been hauled taut, the clew was lashed thoroughly to the boom or to an eyebolt in the boom's outer end. Alternately the sheet could be lashed near the clew to the boom.

Peak and nock earings were lashed to the gaff's outer stop and to the eyebolt near the jaws. The tack tied to an eyebolt on deck, or in case of boom-sails the use of a luff tackle was preferred. The latter hooked to the tack's thimble and an eyebolt in the mast near the partners. A tack could also simply

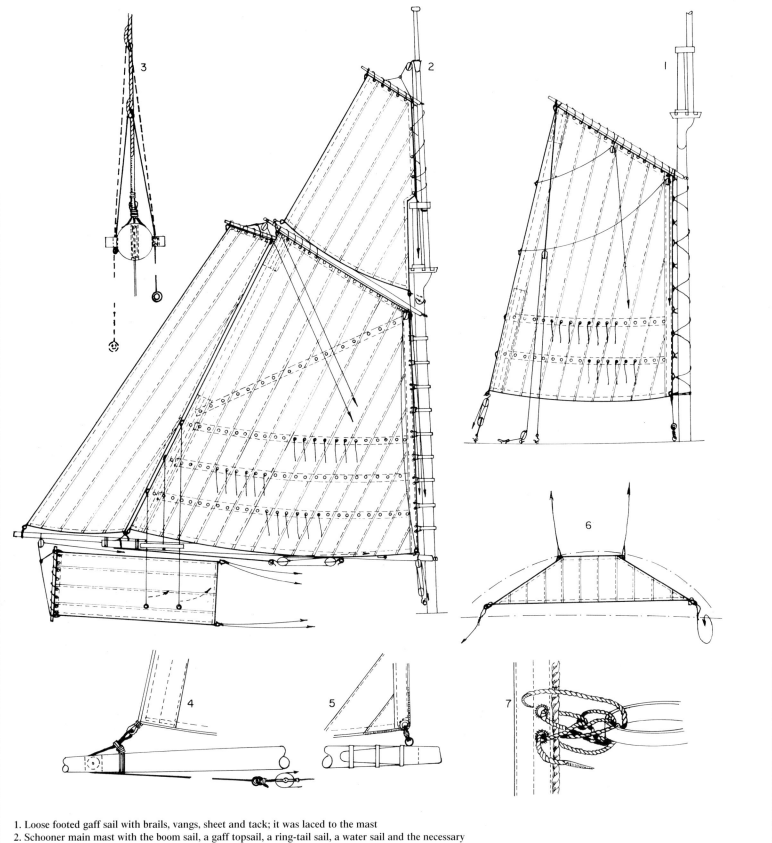

1. Loose footed gaff sail with brails, vangs, sheet and tack; it was laced to the mast
2. Schooner main mast with the boom sail, a gaff topsail, a ring-tail sail, a water sail and the necessary rigging of these sails; the doubled ropes at the foot of the water sail are both tack and sheet
3. Fastening of reef pendants seen from abaft: one side stopped with a stopper knot; the other, leading over a sheave, has a thimble spliced in for the tackle
4. Lashing of a main sail sheet
5. Alternate fastening of main sail tack to the boom
6. Save-all-topsail; fastening of a mast hoop

be seized to an eyebolt near the boom jaws.

A tricing line for the mast leech was only used on boom-sails. Being hooked to the tack thimble, it led upward to a block hooked to the throat-downhauler's eyebolt below the jaws. The tricing line belayed to a cleat at or near the mast.

Reef pendants or earings provided a similar function for the main gaff sail as a reef tackle would for a topsail. Steel mentions up to four pendants going through an equal number of holes in the outer end of the boom and with a thimble spliced in one end. They were almost completely wormed and served with spunyarn. The other end of the pendants rove through the respective reef cringle, then through the thimble at the lower side of the hole and was cats-pawed (hitched) on to the hook of a luff tackle to haul down the leech when a reef had to be taken in. Afterwards the pendant was frapped round sail and boom until expended, making fast with a hitch. To preserve the sail, it was common practice to put some old hammocks over it before frapping. After introduction of reef combs during the early days of the nineteenth century, one end of the pendants stopped with a knot below a comb hole, rove then through the reef cringle and down over a sheave in the opposite comb to have a thimble spliced into its end.

Gaff topsail

With throat and peak halyards already explained, only tack and sheet remain to be discussed. The tack, after being hitched to the sail, was attached to the mast above the main gaff's jaws. From contemporary pictures it can also be observed that the tack was not necessarily attached to the mast as mentioned, but was led down at the rear of the mast and belayed there. The sheet rove through a thimble on the gaff's peak down to the lower mast and was belayed to a cleat.

Studdingsails

When studdingsails were rigged on a topsail schooner, they would have been attached to their respective studdingsail yards with robands. With the help of two halyards the sail was then hoisted up to the spread yard's studdingsail boom. The outer halyard was hitched to the centre of the head-rope-covering yard, passed then through a block at the outer boom end and was led toward the mast cap, where a further block directed it on to deck. Hitched to the studdingsail's inner earing, the inner halyard went through lead blocks at the spread yard and followed the former downward.

The tack bent to the outer clew and went via a block at the outer end of the square sail boom's studdingsail boom inboard toward the rear. The sheet was doubled and its ends at the inner clew led fore and aft to be belayed to timber-heads.

A topsail studdingsail's halyard fastened to the middle of the respective yard, rove through the jewel block at the topsail yardarm and through another at the topmast pole head above the rigging upon deck.

A downhauler was hitched to the studdingsail's outer earing and led down passed a block and was seized to the outer clew to be led upon the fore deck. The sail's tack was also hitched to the same clew, went through a block at the spread yard's boom, through another block on deck and then to a cleat. One part of a double sheet led forward upon deck and the other aft to a lead truck in the shrouds, to be belayed. When the sheet was single, it was let through a block at the outer quarter of the spread yard, through another further in and then up on deck.

A ringtail sail can be described as a main gaff sail's upper studdingsail. The head, bent to a small yard, was hoisted into position with the gaff's peak downhauler. The clews were seized to a spar, which was lashed to the end of the boom to provide an extension.

If the ringtail sail was regarded as the upper sail, the water sail was the lower studdingsail. Also bent to a small yard, its halyard led through a block at the end of the boom or the lashed-on extension, to belay inboards to a taffrail cleat. Tacks and sheets, both doubled, were also belayed to cleats at the taffrail.

Save-all- topsail

The save-all-topsail was used only in very calm wind conditions and filled the gap between topsail roach and spread yard. The sheets were seized to the spread yard's lift block straps and the two halyards of that trapezoid sail rove through blocks at the inner quarter of the topsail yard on to deck.

From the early days of the nineteenth century it became more frequent to see a staysail between a fore-and-aft-rigged mainmast's topmast and the foremast-head. It was either triangular or four-cornered and was usually set flying.

A chapter dealing with Masting and Rigging would be incomplete without a discussion on sails.

Sail

This small excursion into the making of sails will describe to the sailing ship novice the various parts of the sail as well as its composition. Each sail incorporated a number of pieces of sailcloth, which when sewn together, make up the required shape and size, being triangular, trapezoid or rectangular. Sailcloth was canvas of a strong texture, produced from hemp or flax and sold in various quality grades, usually marked on every bolt of cloth. English bolts had a standard width of 2 feet and a length of 38 yards. The weight of a bolt determined its quality, graded from 1 to 10, whereby the first six grades were used for weather sails.

French cloth names were *toile à trois fils* (triple threat cloth), *toile à deux fils*, *toile de mélis double* etc., and a bolt measured 21 French inches (1 feet 10½ inches in English) in width and 50 French ells (about 65 yards) in length. Dutch named their cloth *kanefas* and the highest quality grade in Russia was the Best-blue-mark. Thus, every shipbuilding nation had its own sailcloth and quality grading. In the 1815 edition of his work Falconer remarked on the state of English sailcloth at that time:

'Although considerable quantities of this valuable article are annually manufactured in Britain, yet as they are not adequate to the demands of the navy, but being subject to mildew, are consequently less durable then the sail-cloth imported from North America.' [190]

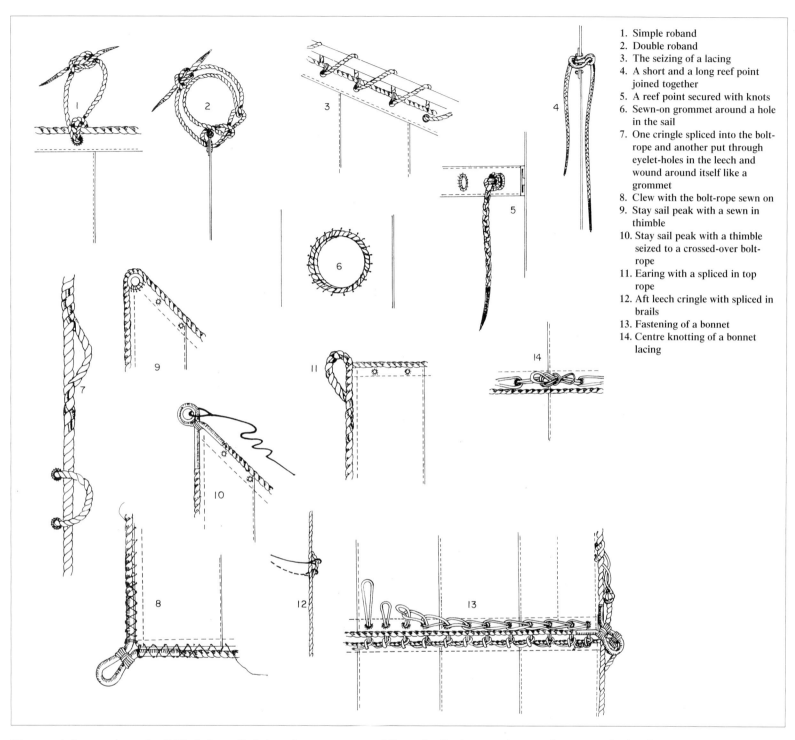

1. Simple roband
2. Double roband
3. The seizing of a lacing
4. A short and a long reef point joined together
5. A reef point secured with knots
6. Sewn-on grommet around a hole in the sail
7. One cringle spliced into the bolt-rope and another put through eyelet-holes in the leech and wound around itself like a grommet
8. Clew with the bolt-rope sewn on
9. Stay sail peak with a sewn in thimble
10. Stay sail peak with a thimble seized to a crossed-over bolt-rope
11. Earing with a spliced in top rope
12. Aft leech cringle with spliced in brails
13. Fastening of a bonnet
14. Centre knotting of a bonnet lacing

The search for a prolonged sail life led to sails being given a number of different preparations. The sails of some smaller merchant vessels were coated in a mixture of horse fat, tar and red or yellow ochre. In other cases a paste of seawater and ochre was rubbed into wet sails and once the sails were dry they were coated with linseed oil. Naval authorities did not approve of such treatment for their fleet sails. When sails were sewn for smaller vessels each cloth overlapped one inch and each cloth edge sewn on contained 108 to 116 stitches per yard length.

The nautical terminology of a sail is complicated and is best explained here in a short glossary.

Sail edges: Its perimeter had several names and, on a square or quadrilateral sail, the top edge was known as the head, while the bottom edge was the foot. The vertical or diagonal edges were leeches, and on fore-and-aft-rigged sails their location was specified as mast leech or aft leech. On triangular sails the large diagonal edge was the head or stay, the vertical the leech and the lower the foot.

Corners: Earings were the upper corners of a square sail, with the lower known as clews or clues. A triangular sail's top corner was the peak, the lower rear corner the clew and the forward pointing the tack. Quadrangular fore-and-aft sails had nock added for the upper forward corner.

Hemming: Hemming a sail's edges was known as tabling,

with the head tabling usually 3 inches wide, the leeches between 1½ and 3 inches, the mast leech generally 3½ inches and the foot between 1 and 3 inches.

Roaching and Goring: The edge of a sail was not always a straight line. If a sail was curved, concave or convex, the sail-maker would term it 'roaching' and when a sail was diagonally reduced the term was 'goring'.

Lining: Adding a lining strengthened sail parts exposed to increased wear and tear. A lining could have been sewn to the corners, to the mast leech, across the sail as reef bands and next to cringles. Linings on fore-and-aft sails were fitted to their portside and on square sails to their face, except for eventual top linings and mast cloths. Top lining was a doubling of a topsail around the trestletrees or a top with a mast cloth sewn on to prevent damage to the sail by chafing on the topmast. Reef bands in a schooner's suit of sails were mainly seen on gaff sails, topsails and the fore-staysail. There were between two and four reef bands on the lower half of each gaff sail, with an additional balance reef band sewn to the main gaff sail, reaching from the nock diagonally down to the rear above the uppermost reef band. In bad weather the sail could be reduced to its smallest effective size with the help of a balance reef. Reef bands of a fore stay sail were attached in such a way that a reef could be taken in or out from the safety of the fore deck. The reef bands of a topsail were, however, placed in the upper part of the sail since the reefs fastened to the yard. Square sails also frequently had reef bands sewn on, usually one at the upper and one at the lower part of that sail. The lower reef band was in some instances substituted with a bonnet.

Reef points: The number of reef points for each cloth varied. Although David Steel reported that there were two, some of his gaff sail illustrations only show one at the cloth overlap. By comparison, Darcy Lever presented on each of his sail illustrations one point at the middle of each cloth and another at the cloth overlap. Later pictures of merchant vessels often gave the impression of reef points only at the overlapping seam. Steel's gaff sail illustrations for a smack, a brig, a cutter and a sloop should be seen in the light of these pictures: while his words and some of his illustrations explained the reef point positioning on warship sails, the pictured gaff sails referred surely to merchant vessels.[191]

Holes: For the purpose of bending, reefing and so on, every sail was provided with a certain number of holes. They were marling-, reef-, head-, leech- and waterholes, and all of them had a small grommet sewn around to stabilise the edges.

Bolt ropes: Once a sail was prepared it would be provided with bolt ropes, which supported the sail like a frame. There were three kinds of bolt rope, the leech, foot or head rope, with the latter only 40 to 50 per cent as thick as the others. They were spun from the best clean hemp and soaked warm in Stockholm tar to obtain weatherproofing and flexibility. Bolt ropes also formed the clews and earings, which were originally loops outside the sail but by the end of the eigh-

teenth century were replaced with thimbles, sewn into the corners and at the outside enclosed by the rope.

Cringles: All necessary cringles for bowlines, brails and so on, were spliced into the bolt rope, with the cringle thickness usually ½ inch less than the rope itself.

Bonnets: Bonnets were removable lower attachments to certain sails. During the eighteenth century they remained only a part of smaller vessels and were used occasionally on fore stay sails and square sails on schooners. To fit a bonnet to a sail's foot a latching forming line was inserted and hitched to the holes in the bonnet's head tabling. These latchings were 6 inches long, except for the centremost two latchings, which were of double length; all were 6 inches asunder, which meant that four latchings were provided for each sail cloth. These latchings were placed into the corresponding holes of the sail's foot tabling from the outside inward, with the bight of the first being taken up by the second etc. until all the latchings connected. The two longer centre latchings were then joined together with two half hitches. By undoing the half hitches one could nearly instantaneously shorten that sail.

Drabler: The drabler should be mentioned in connection with the bonnet, as it was the name of a second bonnet. David Steel called it: '…an additional part of a sail, laced to the bottom of the bonnet of a square sail, in Dutch sloops etc….'[192]. Röding stated that it was: '…the lower bonnet in koffs and schooners, whose sails had double bonnets.'[193]

Notes:

[131] Röding, J H, *Allgemeines Wörterbuch der Marine*, Vol. 2 (Hamburg, 1794, repr. Amsterdam, 1969) p.521: '*Der Fockmast führt ein Gaffelsegel und der grosse Mast ein Giegsegel, die beyde eine beträchtliche Höhe haben*'.

[132] Edson, M A, Jr, 'The Schooner Rig, A Hypothesis', *The American Neptune*, Vol.XXV, No.2 (1969) pp.81–93

[133] Sutherland, W, *England's Glory, or Shipbuilding Unveiled* (London, 1717)

[134] Steel, D, *Elements of Mastmaking, Sailmaking and Rigging* (1794), repr. E W Sweetman Co (New York, 1932) p.105

[135] Röding, J H, op. cit., Vol.2, p.521: '*Eine zweymastige Takelasche die sich aber nur für lange schmale Fahrzeuge schickt.[…] Bey den Engländern, Amerikanern und überhaupt in Westindien werden die Schuner sehr häufig zur Handlung gebracht und führen 50 bis 100 und mehrere Lasten*.'

[136] Pâris, E, *Souvenirs de Marine* (Paris, 1882) Vol. 2, repr. Karl Butziger Verlag (Hamburg, 1972) p.108

[137] Fincham, J, *A Treatise on Masting Ships & Mast Making* (London, 1829), repr. Conway Maritime Press Ltd (London, 1982) p.72

[138] Steinhaus, C F, *Die Schiffbaukunst in ihrem ganzen Umfang*, Vol. 1 (Hamburg, 1858), repr. H Hamecher (Kassel, 1977) p.90

[139] Brady, W N, *The Kedge Anchor or Young Sailor's Assistant* (New York, 1879), repr. Macdonald and Jane's (London, 1974) p.322

[140] Lever, D, *The Young Sea Officer's Sheet Anchor* etc. 2nd edition (London, 1819), repr. E W Sweetman Co (New York, 1963) p.113

[141] Board of Navy Commissioners, *Tables showing the Masts and Spars, Rigging and Stores &c. of every Description allowed to the different Classes of Vessels belonging to the Navy of the United States* (Washington, 1826)

[142] Fincham, J, *A Treatise on Masting Ships & Mast Making* (London, 1829), repr. 3rd edition, Conway Maritime Press Ltd (London, 1982) p.278

[143] Steel, D, op. cit., p.39

[144] Jobe, J, ed. *The Great Age of Sail*, Edita (Lausanne, 1967) p.95

[145] Steel, D, op. cit., p.37

[146] Ibid., p.124

[147] Lever, D, op. cit., p.114

[148] Fincham, J, op. cit., 3rd edition, p.326

[149] Steinhaus, C F, op. cit., p.90

[150] Steel, D, op. cit., p.42

[151] Ibid., p.42

[152] Norie, J W & J S Hobbs, *Three hundred and six Illustrations of the Maritime Flags of all Nations, together with Regulations and Instructions relating to British Flags &c.* (London, 1848) repr.as *Flaggen aller seefahrenden Nationen*, Edition Maritime (Hamburg, 1987) p.XV: '7. With the foregoing exceptions, the Flags, Pendants, Ensigns, and Jacks, appointed to be worn by the Ships and Vessels of the Royal Navy, shall not be hoisted or worn on board any other Ship or Vessel whatsoever; nor shall the Masters of such other Ships and Vessels hoist or wear any Flags, Pendants Ensigns, and Jacks, made in imitation of, or resembling those appointed to be worn by Ships and Vessels of the Royal Navy (excepting as hereinbefore directed) nor any kind of Pendant whatsoever, nor what may be taken for such; and if they shall offend herein, and presume to hoist or wear any Flags resembling those worn by Her Majesty's Ships, or any other Colours than those hereinbefore specified, or any kind of Pendants whatsoever, it is Her Majesty's pleasure that the Captains, or any other Officers of Her Majesty's Ships of War, who shall see them, do seize such Colours, Flags, or Pendants, and report the Names of the Master, and of the Ship or Vessel, the Place to where she belongs, and the Merchants who are Owners of her, to the Secretary of the Admiralty, together with Affidavits of two Witnesses to the fact, in order that the person so offending, may be proceeded against according to law.'

[153] Falconer, W, *An Universal Dictionary of the Marine* (London, 1769) repr. 1780 edition David & Charles (Newton Abbot, Devon, 1870) p.213

[154] Falconer, W, op. cit., Plate XII, No.9

[155] Serres, D & J T, *Liber Nauticus and Instructor in the Art of Marine Drawing* (London, 1805), repr. Scolar Press (London, 1979) Plate 30

[156] Falconer, W A *A New Universal Dictionary of the Marine, improved and enlarged by W. Burney Li.D.* (London, 1815) repr. MacDonald and Jane's (London, 1970) Plate XXXIII

[157] Lever, D, op. cit., 2nd edition, p. 58

[158] Steel, D, *The Art of Rigging* (London, 1818), repr. Fisher Nautical Press (Brighton, Sussex, 1974) Appendix tables

[159] Steel, D, *Elements of Mastmaking, Sailmaking and Rigging* (London, 1794), repr. E W Sweetman Co (New York, 1932) p.56

[160] Lever, D, op. cit., 2nd edition, p.32

[161] Ibid. p.115

[162] Steel, D, *The Art of Rigging* 3rd edition (London, 1818), repr. Fisher Nautical Press (Brighton, Sussex, 1974)

[163] Chapman, F H af, *Architectura Navalis Mercatoria* (Stockholm, 1768) repr. VEB Hinstorff Verlag (Rostock, 1968) Plate LXII No.6

[164] Lever, D, op. cit., 2nd edition, p.21

[165] Bobrik, E, *Handbuch der praktischen Seefahrtskunde* (Leipzig, 1848) repr. H Hamecher (Kassel, 1978) p.401: '*Schiffe, welche kein Galjon haben, und deren Krahnbalken ziemlich weit nach vorne liegen, richten ihr Wasserstag wie in Fig. 14 ein, damit sie es beim Ankerlichten losmachen, und am Bugspriet aufholen können; der Ankerstock bleibt alsdann frei davon.*'

[166] PRO.Adm. 7/334, p.65

[167] Röding, J H, *Allgemeines Wörterbuch der Marine*, Vol.1 (Hamburg, 1794 repr. Amsterdam, 1969) p.227: '*Heutigen Tages wird das Backstag des Bugspriets, fast allgemein abgeschafft weil solches beym Lichten des Ankers, und Ausvieren des Taues viel Hinderniß verursacht.*'

[168] Steel, D, *Elements of Mastmaking, Sailmaking and Rigging* (London, 1794), repr. E W Sweetman Co (New York, 1932) p.188

[169] Falconer, W, op. cit., p.210

[170] Steel, D, *Elements of Mastmaking, Sailmaking and Rigging* (London, 1794), repr. E W Sweetman Co (New York, 1932) p.185

[171] Ibid., p.121

[172] Ibid., p.135

[173] Ibid., pp.56 & 287

[174] Steel, D, *The Art of Rigging* 3rd edition (London, 1818), repr. Fisher Nautical Press (Brighton, Sussex, 1974)

[175] Falconer, W A, *A New Universal Dictionary of the Marine, improved and enlarged by William Burney Li.D* (London, 1815), repr. MacDonald and Jane's (London, 1974) p.497

[176] Röding, J H, op. cit., Vol.1, p.385: '*Man gebraucht die Brefock wenn man vor dem Winde segelt, sobald man aber bey dem Winde läuft, wird solche wieder gestrichen.*'

[177] Lever, D, *The Young Sea Officer's Sheet Anchor* (London, 1819), repr. E W Sweetman Co (New York, 1963) p.44: '*When the Gaff is rigged to hoist, there are no Vangs, nor Blocks, for the Mizen Topmast and Mizen Top-gallant Braces…*'

[178] Röding, J H, *Allgemeines Wörterbuch der Marine*, Vol.4 (Hamburg, 1794, repr. Amsterdam, 1969) Pl. XXXIV f.263 & Pl. XXXVIII f.270

[179] *Nautical Research Journal*, Vol.35, No.2 June 1990 (Gloucester, MA) pp.102 & 103

[180] Chapelle, H I, *The History of the American Sailing Navy*, W W Norton & Co., Inc. (New York, 1959) p.136

[181] Middendorf, F L, *Bemastung und Takelung der Schiffe* (Berlin, 1903) repr. H Hamecher (Kassel, 1977) p.180: '*Bei keiner anderen Schiffsgattung tritt uns eine so große Verschiedenheit unter den einzelnen Individuen entgegen, wie bei den Schonern, die vorzugsweise durch Gaffelsegel fortbewegt werden. Es rührt dies daher, daß dieser Schiffstyp neuerdings zu allen möglichen Zwecken und in den verschiedensten Größen Verwendung findet.*'

[182] *Nautical Research Journal*, Vol.35, No.2, June 1990 (Gloucester, MA) p.101

[183] Hahn, H, *The Colonial Schooner 1763–1775*, Conway Maritime Press Ltd (London, 1981) p.24

[184] MacGregor, D, *Merchant Sailing Ships 1775–1815*, Argus Books Ltd (Watford, Herts, 1980) p.85

[185] Falconer, W, *An Universal Dictionary of the Marine* (London, 1769), repr. of 1780 edition by David & Charles (Newton Abbot, Devon, 1870) Plate XII No.9

[186] MacGregor, D, op. cit., p.156

[187] MacGregor, D R, *Fast Sailing Ships 1775–1875*, Nautical Publishing Co. Ltd. (1973) p.86

[188] Falconer, W A, *A New Universal Dictionary of the Marine, improved and enlarged by William Burney Li.D.* (London, 1815), repr. MacDonald and Jane's (London, 1974) p.588

[189] Steel, D, *Elements of Mastmaking, Sailmaking and Rigging* (London, 1794), repr. E W Sweetman Co (New York, 1932) p.117

[190] Falconer, W A, *A New Universal Dictionary of the Marine, improved and enlarged by W. Burney LL.D.* (London, 1815), repr. MacDonald and Jane's (London, 1970) p.424

[191] Reef point illustrations can be found in:
Steel, D, *Elements of Mastmaking, Sailmaking and Rigging* (London, 1794), repr. E W Sweetman Co (New York, 1932) Plates VIII–XIII, XX–XXI, XXIV–XXXIII, XXXVI–XXXVII; and in
Lever, D, *The Young Sea Officer's Sheet Anchor etc.* 2nd edition (London, 1819), repr. E W Sweetman Co (New York, 1963) pp.51, 54, 56, 58, 63, 66

[192] Steel, D, *Elements of Mastmaking, Sailmaking and Rigging* (London, 1794), repr. E W Sweetman Co (New York ,1932) p.62

[193] Röding, J H, *Allgemeines Wörterbuch der Marine*, Vol.1 (Hamburg, 1794, repr. Amsterdam, 1969) p.350: '*Nur blos Kuffen, Schmacken und einmastige Galioten haben dergleichen noch an ihren Segeln. etc.*'

Chapter 7

♦

Anchors, Boats and Other Furniture

A description of schooners would be incomplete without the accessories that were necessary to make the vessel a useful tool for trade, pleasure or war. This section discusses the means for warping or stopping, for moving goods, for orientation at sea and for departing from and to a vessel, plus the equipment necessary for turning a schooner into a fighting unit.

Anchors and fittings

An anchor is a heavy iron instrument used to stop and hold a ship at a fixed position in a harbour or roadstead. It consists of various parts. The long and vertical centre of a period anchor was known as the shank. Situated at the lower end of the shank were the arms, which were set to an angle of nearly 60 degrees and looked like opposing hooks. A flook, fluke or palm was fitted on to each upper side and a ring was set into the upper part of the shank. An oaken stock was located below the ring and right-angled to the arms. An anchor was a well-calculated device, since not only was its weight in proportion to the vessel's size, but also all parts were kept in proportion to each other. Röding remarked about the weight of anchors:

> 'We will take note that the weight of large ship anchors is equal to the square of a ship's breadth. ... The sheet anchor of a ship, which has a breadth of 49 French ft and of which the weight is 7653 Livres, shall here be used as an example to find the weight of any other anchor, e.g. for a ship with 20 ft breadth. $49^2 : 20^2 = 7653$ Livres : x Livres = 1331 Livres. This proportion, based on rational reasoning, is not only being followed by the French, but also by the English and by other Nations.' [194]

Röding's calculation should actually amount to about 1276 Livres if one considers Breadth 2 x 3.19 (3.18742), which was the underlying factor in his statement $49^2 = 7653$ Livres. With a Livre weight equal to 489 grams, the anchor's weight was 624 kilograms or nearly 12.3 cwt. He also quoted from English sources that an English ship of 49 feet breadth had a sheet anchor of 73 cwt, or in a conversion 7584 Livres.

Bearing in mind that 49 English feet equals approximately 46 French feet, English anchors weighed nearly 10% more than French anchors. Röding's statement can be corroborated if one takes the example of a ship of 20 French feet breadth (21ft 4in English), which would have been of about 170 to 180 tons, and compares it with an entry in Falconer's Dictionary of 1815. A table in Falconer's work 'Establishment And Value Of Anchors For Ships Of Each Class In The British Navy 1809' [195] (Brigs of 250 tons to Gun Brigs of 187 tons) provides for that class of vessels 3 Bowers of 14 cwt, 1 Stream anchor of 5 cwt and 1 Kedge anchor of 2 cwt. Falconer's table unfortunately did not record smaller vessels.

In nineteenth-century England another rule was often applied: ship's tonnage divided by 20 equals anchor weight in cwt (50.8kg = 1 cwt). It is however known from a table of anchor manufacturer Young & Thompson at Sutherland, reproduced in Steinhaus' work [196], that for vessels of 100 tons and smaller a sliding scale was applied.

Craft of 5 to 15 tons = vessel's tonnage divided by a factor of 10
Craft of 25 tons = vessel's tonnage divided by a factor of 12.5,
Craft of 40 tons = vessel's tonnage divided by a factor of 13.33
Craft of 60 tons = vessel's tonnage divided by a factor of 17
Craft of 100 tons = vessel's tonnage divided by a factor of 19
Craft of any size above 100 tons = vessel's tonnage divided by a factor of 20

Anchor weight was divided between shank and arms, inclusive of flukes, at a ratio of 8:7 and its proportional dimensions were as follows: a shank's length was ⅗ of a ship's breadth; its width was ½₇ the shank length for the smallest anchor and ½₄ shank length for the largest.

Depending on anchor size the upper width was between ½ inch and 2 inches less than the lower, with the smallest below the stock. To determine the length of anchor arms the shaft was divided into eight equal parts, a centre point was taken at three-eighths from the lower end and a circle drawn. From the lowest point, the crown was set up at an angle of 120 degrees equally on both sides, whereby the intersection of these angular lines with the circle determined the length of each arm. Flukes were half the arm's length and of a triangular shape, with the outside slightly rounded. The shank remained square at the anchor stock section, while the part below down to the trend, between the lower height of the flukes and the crown, was octagonal.

According to Röding and Pâris[197], small promontories, the nuts, protruded from the squared upper part of the shank in arm direction to localise the stock. Drawings of English anchors and comments by Brady[198] show the nuts in stock direction, which suggests that the first method was continental and the latter English/American. Anchor arms were predominantly straight during the eighteenth century and Falconer[199] reported that strengthening could be achieved by shifting the vertex from the crown or trend to a small angular break in the angled arm. The anchors illustrated by Röding, Pâris and Boudriot[200], are mainly continental and French anchors and have these angled arms mentioned by Falconer. Falconer continues with a description of anchor stocks:

'The stock of anchors consists of two beams of oak firmly united by iron bolts and hoops, two hoops being on each side of the middle, and one near each extremity. The length of the stock is equal to the length of the shank, and half the diameter of the ring. Its breadth and thickness in the middle are each one-twelfth of its length. At the extremities of the stock, the breadth and thickness is one twenty-fourth of its length. The upper surface of the stock next to the ring is always straight, or forms one continued plane. The under surface is composed of three planes. The central one extends to half the breadth of the stock, on each side of the middle, and from that place the surface descends to each extremity. Lest the wood should shrink, an opening of an inch and a half is generally left between the two beams of oak, that the hooks (hoops) which bind them together may be driven nearer the middle.' [201]

Steinhaus provides us with further details[202]: the stock's upper surface was slightly curved upward and the oaken stock pieces were connected by treenails rather than by iron bolts. According to Steinhaus, the gap between these two pieces near the shank was ½ to ¾ inch wide and that two hoops at each side of the stock were only used for anchors of less than 4000 lbs, those larger than this had three hoops. While Falconer described an English anchor, Steinhaus was more familiar with the continental style. An early reference to an iron anchor stock can be found on a drawing of anchors for an English 74-gun ship from 1800[203]. The iron stock illustrated is part of a small kedge anchor. However, it took another 30 years for the iron stock to be accepted into general shipping.

Anchor sizes and the number carried depended on a vessel's tonnage and purpose, as Röding explains:

'Every man-of-war carried four to five large anchors. As much as the Number of small anchors is concerned, it

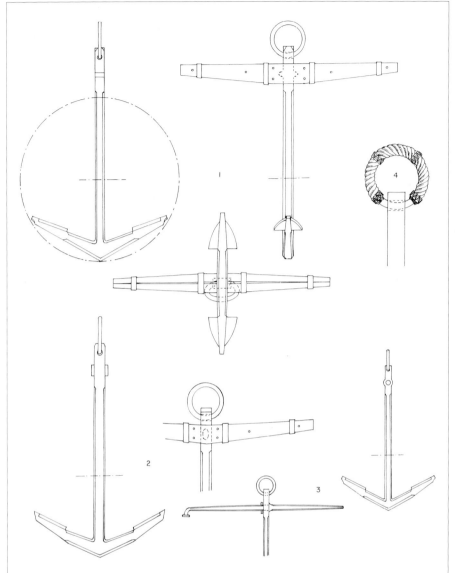

1. English anchor until about 1840; nuts on the shank are in stock direction
2. Continental anchor according to J Röding and E Pâris with slightly angled arms and the nuts in the direction of the arms
3. English kedge anchor with an iron stock, from around 1800
4. The puddening of an anchor ring

depended generally on time and circumstance, but usually every man-of-war is furnished with two to three kedge anchors.' [204]

Steinhaus noted that two anchors were used on merchant ships of less than 70 lasts or 200 tons, with three anchors for larger vessels. The weight of a best bower was about nine-tenths that of a sheet anchor, whilst a smaller stream anchor was one-third and a kedge anchor one-seventh the weight of the largest, the sheet anchor.

The diameter of the anchor ring was approximately one-eighth the shank's length on a small vessel and one-sixth of shank length on larger vessels, with its thickness one-ninth of its diameter. The hole in the squared part of the ring was located at one-and-a-half times the thickness of the ring below the upper end. Anchor rings were cladded, a procedure known as 'Puddening the Anchor', which counteracted cable chafing. A strip of tarred canvas was first laid round the ring and a number of lengths of spun yarn, three times the diameter of the ring, were temporarily fastened to the middle. These yarns went side by side, counter-rotating in the opposite direction and each one had a snaked seizing clapped on at one-eighth of the ring's circumference. The spun yarn covered approximately three-quarters of the ring and a further snaked seizing on each secured the ends. The ends of the yarn were then opened out and well tarred. There were no rules to govern the number of seizings on a ring and sometimes they filled the whole upper quarter of the ring.

Cable

These are the most important ropes on board as Röding explains:

'The cable's purpose is to enable a ship to ride before her anchor in a roadstead or harbour, it is therefore a thick and strong rope.' [205]

In the classification of ropes a cable is the strongest, with the thinnest being the rope yarn. A number of the latter formed a strand and three strands laid right-handed (termed 'with the sun') were known as a hawser-laid rope. Four strands laid the same way made it a shroud-laid rope. When three hawser-laid ropes (nine strands) were combined and turned left-handed they became a cable-laid rope and three shroud-laid ropes (12 strands) became a four-stranded cable.

Falconer stipulated the length of a cable as 120 fathoms, with which Steel agreed but only for ships of 300 tons and more; for smaller vessels Steel provided a figure of 90 fathoms. Röding commented on the length of cables:

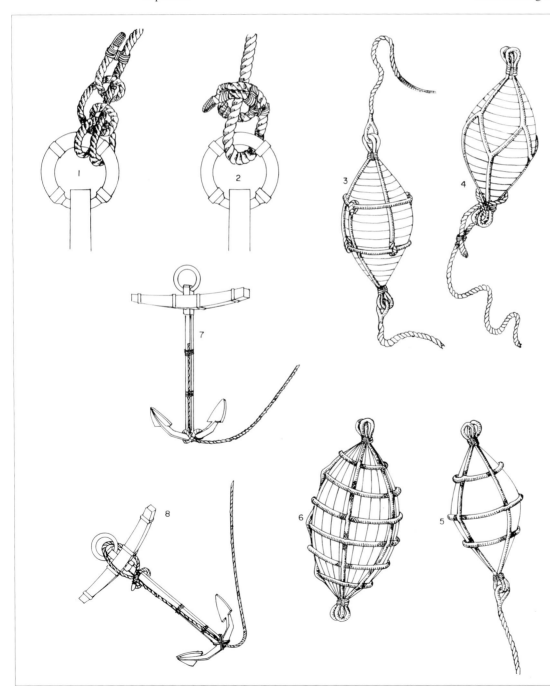

1. Fisherman's bend used on cables for smaller anchors
2. Cable clinch to fasten thicker cables to larger anchors
3. Cork buoy with rope and lanyard rigged 'Spanish Fashion' (used on English ships)
4. Cork buoy in 'Dutch Fashion'; the buoy rope made fast with a sheet bend
5. Wooden buoy in 'French Fashion'
6. A nun buoy
7. Buoy rope fastened to the anchor's crown with two half hitches and then seized to the shank
8. Securing a buoy rope to a smaller anchor (alternative)

'Nearly all cables are of 150 fathoms or 900 feet length including such for merchantmen, except those who sail as whalers to Greenland because they use cables of 120 fathoms length. It is not common to make cables longer than 150 fathoms notwithstanding that one repeatedly may have to use longer ones, but then two were spliced together.' [206]

When comparing Röding's figures one has to take into consideration the different metric values of Imperial (1828.8mm) and Hamburg fathom (1719.00mm).

Röding also provides the rule of thumb for sheet anchor cable thickness, which is measured as circumference, not as diameter: ½ inch for every foot of a vessel's extreme breadth. The sizes of anchor chains on larger English ships in the second decade of the nineteenth century are given on the earlier table of anchor sizes from Young & Thompson. The diameter of chain links for a vessel of 5 tons was ⁵⁄₁₆ inch and increased gradually to 1⅛ inch for vessels of 250 tons, with the weight of each fathom increasing from 5½ lbs to 70 lbs.

A cable was fastened to the ring of a kedge anchor with a fisherman's bend. For this two turns of the cable were laid round the ring and one around the cable and through the turns, the end half-hitched to the cable and seized. Fisherman's bends were too difficult to anticipate for heavier cables on larger anchors and bowers and so a clinch was applied: the cable was brought through the ring with its end turned around the cable and then was seized at several places. A shackle connected anchor ring and chain.

Buoy

The anchor and anchor buoy were also essential to every vessel, as Röding again makes clear:

'Coming to anchor in a harbour or roadstead, all ships must be provided with a buoy since it is not only extremely hazardous to neglect such but also forbidden by pain of punishment, as it could lead to damage of other vessels.' [207]

Buoys had to be large enough to be seen in the water and were either made from cork or timber. Those made from timber were called wooden buoys or nun buoys, the latter being egg-shaped and staved like a casket. Normal anchor buoys had a length of 4 feet 6 inches and a diameter of 2 feet 6 inches. Slices of cork for buoy construction were approximately 1 inch thick. Buoys used for smaller anchors were of smaller dimensions or were half-buoys, which only had one cone.

A net of ropes, known as slings and hoops, surrounded all buoys to provide stability. The application of these varied from country to country but the most common examples are explained on the illustration on page 192. Eyes spliced in at both buoy ends were common to all variations, with the lower used for connecting the anchor's buoy-rope. That was also achieved in a number of ways, all of which are shown on page 192. The minimum length for a buoy-rope was 18 fathoms for smaller vessels and 25 fathoms for larger. When a ship anchored in great depth the rope had to be extended in such a way that the buoy could be seen in the close vicinity of the dropped anchor. The upper eye in the buoy end

secured a short rope, the buoy-lanyard, which served as a fishing line to haul the buoy into a boat and to tie it into the shrouds.

Before the ropes for anchor catting and stowing are discussed we shall follow the course of a chain cable inside the hawse hole. Darcy Lever[208] gave an excellent description of the early stages of this: 'An iron roller [is] fixed before the Hawse-hole where the Chain-Cable enters and another of the same kind is fixed within board.'

Windlass

The next station was the windlass, where some changes took place with the introduction of chain, but we begin with hemp cables. As previously mentioned, capstan-operated cables ran over anchor bits, with stoppers preventing them from running out as well as relieving strain on the bits. This applied also to cables heaved in by a windlass. Stoppers rove through strong ringbolts on deck and were seized to the cable.

A windlass was a long, usually octagonal, timber shaft, rotating horizontally behind the foremast in the windlass' bits and served as a machine for heaving strong ropes and anchor cables. This contrivance was mainly used on merchant vessels, as warships preferred the use of a capstan. The reasons for this difference were saving space and manpower. On a man-of-war a large crew could easily work the vertical capstan, which also saved space, while on a merchantman the unwieldy windlass could be operated with only a few deck hands, as described by Röding:

'Considering that, because of the windlass' horizontal position, the full weight of a man presses on to the end of a lever or hand spike, he has thereby far more power to wind than on a capstan. Regardless of that however, this work requires a specific skill, consisting mainly of a co-ordinated down pressing of the spikes by all hands with one jerk.' [209]

The length of a shaft was nearly identical to the width of the particular deck section on which it was situated, while its diameter was between one-and-a-half and two times the circumference of the anchor cable. At a distance from both ends (between a tenth and a sixth of the total length) and over the width of the bits the shaft was reduced to half its thickness and rounded, which was known as trunnions. The barrel was situated between the trunnions and the ends outside of these were the heads. The diameter of the outer head was two-thirds of the centre barrel, with the barrel turning free above deck by at least 9 inches.

Shaft rotation holes for spikes and pawls were cut into the barrel and heads. These spike sockets were square openings, not less than 2½ feet apart and placed alternately into the eight shaft faces to obtain evenly balanced turning. To prevent reverse thrust each of these faces had two pawl notches at the centre for the dropping pawls. Iron pawl plates were inserted at the engaging side of the notches for stability. Windlass shafts were usually made from softer timber with battens or whelps nailed near the edges of each face to prevent the cables from cutting into the shaft. Although usually made from the same type of timber as the windlass, oak was preferred for whelps on smaller windlasses. The outer bits for the shaft to rest and turn in were composed of three parts. Their major part, bit pins, were vertically standing strong oak beams, twice as wide as thick, which led down into the hold to be placed, like those for anchor bits, in steps and bolted to crossing deck beams. At the necessary height above deck, semicircles of an appropriate size were cut into each aft side to accommodate the trunnion. The bit pinhead was shaped

like a bollard or carried in the older fashion of a knight's head.

Standards of similar thickness to the bit pins were placed in front of them, with their sleeping arms reaching over to be bolted to two to three deck beams. Bit cheeks, made from timber identical in size to the bit pins, were situated to the rear of the pins. The cheeks were furnished with another semicircle to enclose the shaft's trunnion and they also sometimes carried a bollard-head similar to the pins. Above and

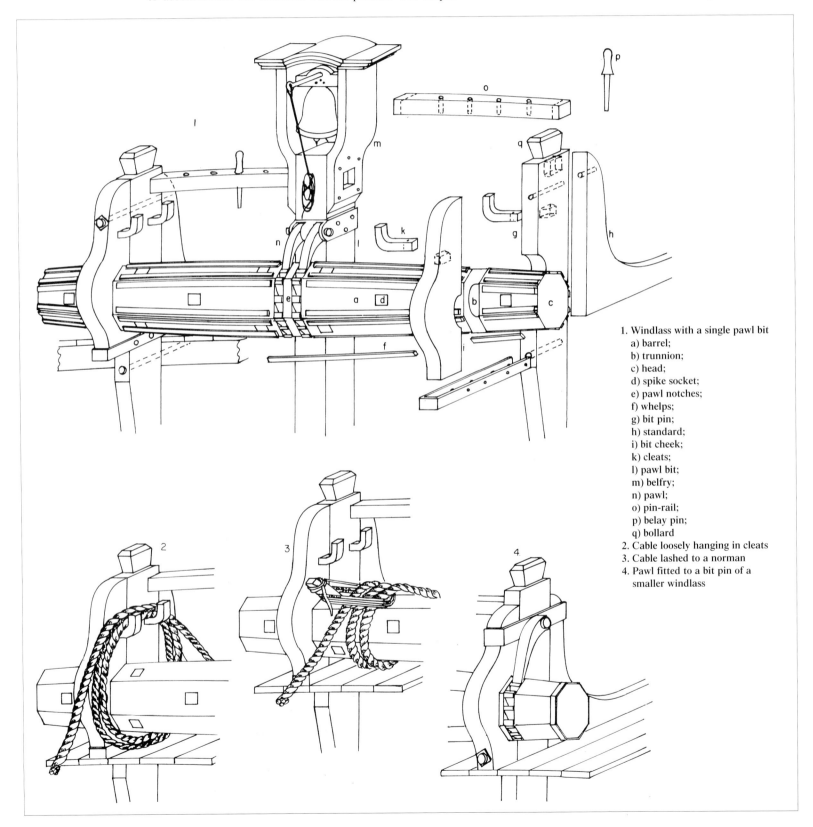

1. Windlass with a single pawl bit
   a) barrel;
   b) trunnion;
   c) head;
   d) spike socket;
   e) pawl notches;
   f) whelps;
   g) bit pin;
   h) standard;
   i) bit cheek;
   k) cleats;
   l) pawl bit;
   m) belfry;
   n) pawl;
   o) pin-rail;
   p) belay pin;
   q) bollard
2. Cable loosely hanging in cleats
3. Cable lashed to a norman
4. Pawl fitted to a bit pin of a smaller windlass

below the trunnion strong bolts connected the cheeks, bit pins and standing standard arms, to which the bolt ends were fore-locked. On the bit's inner face above the barrel there were two square sockets, half the thickness of the pin in depth, in which timber cleats were inserted to hang the second cable loosely when the first had to be taken in. One or two pawl bits stood in front and at the centre of the barrel; reaching down into the hold they fastened in a similar way to bit pins. Single or double pawl bits usually formed the foundation for a belfry. In pawls set up as doubles, side by side or one upon the other, the upper part was hinged to the bit or bits and was used to stop any reverse thrust of the barrel. On smaller windlasses without pawl bits the pawls were occasionally fitted to the rear of the foremast or to the outside of bit pins, which are also known as carrick bits. Pin-rails were placed at a sufficient distance above the barrel between bit pins and pawl bit to provide about eight pins on which to belay some running rigging. A pin-rail fitted between bit pins without break at a pawl bit was named 'strong back', being slightly curved for increased stability. Bollard-shaped bit pinheads were used to belay warp lines and the like.

The windlass was rotated by handspikes, which were rounded levers with squared feet made from tough hardwood. The squared part was slightly tapered toward the end for ease of fitting and removal of the spike from the similarly shaped shaft socket. If it became too hard to take an anchor in by normal action, a break boom was applied. This was a longer, stronger spike with a tackle set up to its outer end to turn the windlass with increased leverage.

When a vessel was at anchor in a harbour or safe roadstead, the cable was generally laid with two or three turns around the barrel, with each of these turns seized to itself and to a norman to prevent slipping. A norman was a stout, short, square peg thrust into a shaft socket for that special purpose. If a cable was expected to undergo greater strain, an extra turn was laid around the bit and over the head.

During the first half of the nineteenth century many alterations were made to the windlass. The first change occurred during the time that the chain was introduced as a replacement for cable. In 1819 Darcy Lever described the change: 'The Windlass and Stopper were drawn from those on board the *St. Patrick* Indiaman, Capt. Ferrier, of Hull' [210].

In the 1820s an English patent windlass appeared, which was rotated with crank-handles instead of handspikes. This type was installed on the 1829 *Hornet* class of 6-gun schooners or brigantines designed by Seppings, the 1832 *Dolphin* class of 10-gun brigs designed by Symonds, and on other ships like HMS *Beagle*.

A chain passed over the windlass, over a chain stopper and was then led like a cable through a hollow cleat at the edge of a fore hatch-cover into the cable store or tier.

Cat-tackle, cat-head stopper, shank painter and voyal

When an anchor was taken up to an a-peak position, a cat-tackle (or fish-tackle) would be employed for further lifting.

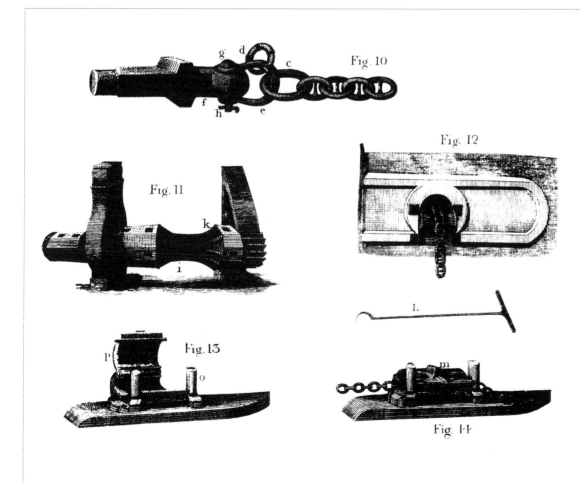

Drawings of chain windlass from about 1818
Fig. 10 represents part of a chain cable bent to the anchor. These cables are now in general use. A stout ring (c), and a smaller ring (d) for the buoy rope, are passed over the shackle (e); this shackle is attached to the end of the shank (f) by the bolt (g), which is secured by the forelock (h). To every link of the chain, a bar is placed across, to prevent them from being drawn together; at every seventh fathom, a shackle and swivel are placed. Thus it may be used as a mooring chain. This cable may be used with either a windlass or a capstern. When the former is carried, the part (i) Fig. 11, is entirely cased with iron; it rises gradually on each side and on the starboard side it has projections (k) raised something in the manner of thumb cleats. These prevent the chain from riding, and always keep it in its place. An iron roller like Fig. 12 is fixed before the hawse-hole where the chain enters; another of the same kind is fixed within board. The cable abaft the windlass passes through an iron stopper, Fig. 13; the horns (o) keep it from slipping out. It is held on by iron hooks (L), which are from two to three feet in length. When necessary, the upper part, or lid, of the stopper (p) is let down and appears as in Fig. 14. An iron bar, or crow, is put into the hollow of a raised strap (m), and pressed down to completely jamb the chain.

The next plate (on page 196) shows another improvement of the traditional windlass, as indicated in 1835 by Klawitter in his textbook for shipbuilders (see Bibliography, page 235).

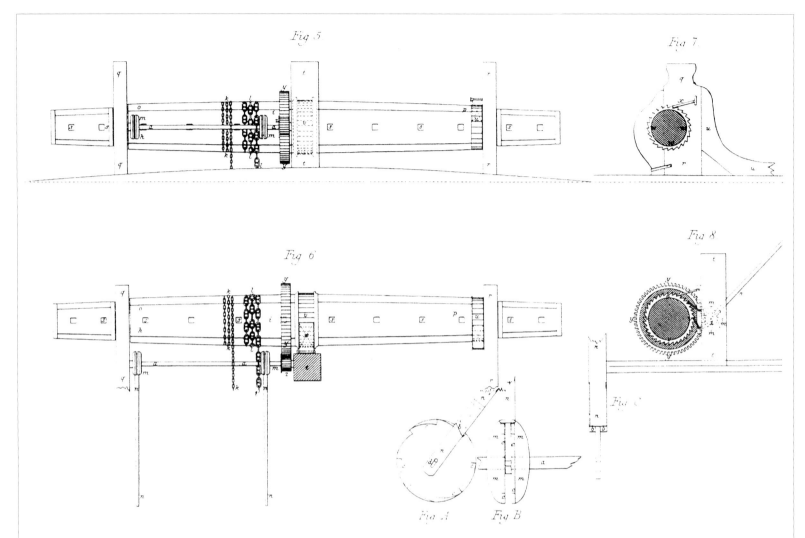

Fig. 5

Fig. 7

Fig. 6

Fig. 8

Fig. C

Fig. A   Fig. B

'An improvement has lately been fitted to the windlass, which comes especially into use when the power of a normal hand-spike, inserted into a shaft socket (ss), is not sufficient. This improvement consists mainly of the two wheels (y&z), whose cogs gear into each other. The wheel (y) is fastened to the shaft, just beside the pawl ring, while the wheel (z), sitting on a parallel iron axis (aa), can be engaged or disengaged, depending on the need for employing these. The metal bearings for the axis (aa) are fitted to the pawl bits and the bit-pins. To rotate the wheels and with them the windlass shaft, a few men are ordered on to each of the two levers, Figs. 6 & 8 (n & n), which when pressed down rotate the pinion (z) and also the large wheel (y), and therefore the shaft. The lever (nn), of which the iron lower ends are shown in Fig. C, has a shoulder or heel (b) which engages with the cogs of the two iron disks (cc), fitted in timber cheeks (mm) and sitting on the same axis as the pinion (z). These levers can not be detached from axis (aa) which is rounded, but embrace a part of it, since the hole (d), Fig. A, in each lever is oblong. After it is pressed down the lever can be pulled back and reset to one of the upper cocks to continue with the rotation. It seems at first glance that this may be a very slow action but with a bit of training one man can work both levers (one in each hand) to bring an anchor in by himself. For that reason this invention is well received, especially since it is very useful for smaller merchantmen with a crew of only a few men. When taking in the anchor chain (ll), it regularly winds itself up toward (i) and if it moves close to the cheek of the upper lever (mn), it has to be pushed back. Thereby the chain loosens and slips back in part and has to be wound in again. The thinner chain (kk), which like the larger (ll) is fastened on the ring of the anchor in the ground, is there to prevent this. If the larger chain has to be pushed back it will be first done with the smaller, then hauled tight before the larger (ll) is moved. Another device is used on English ships to prevent the running up or stopping of the anchor chain. For this, two axis or windlass shafts lie horizontally side-by-side and turn with the help of cogwheels in one direction. The chain, without the help of a small chain, runs over both shafts in fitting tracks, which it cannot leave, and since a chain coming from the anchor lays always in the same track, it cannot stop itself however long the shaft rotating will last. This arrangement can also be fitted to capstans and is very much to be recommended.'

A cat-tackle consisted of sheaves in the cat-head, a heavy cat-block with a large hook and a similar sheave arrangement, and the connecting cat-fall. Vessels without cat-heads used a fish-tackle, which incorporated a pendant around the fore mast-head and a runner tackle with a strong hook. When not in use the tackle was either hooked to an eyebolt inboard the stem or was seized to the lower fore stay. Fish-tackles were not only utilised in lieu of a missing cat-head, they also often replaced a davit when the anchor had to be stowed. The long davit, which in the later years of the eighteenth century was surpassed on larger ships by a channel davit, was still employed on smaller vessels right into the nineteenth centu-

ry. As Lever comments: 'Smaller Ships, which carry Davits, have them run out over the Gunnel athwart Ships, the inner end resting on the Forecastle.'[211]

Once the anchor was closely hoisted up, the cat-head stopper was run through the anchor ring and then either over a cleat at the side of the cat-head or over a vertical notch in the face of it. The stopper was set into a vertical hole aft of the sheaves, with a double walled knot securing its upper end, and was belayed to a timberhead nearby. A shank painter was used to stow an anchor to the outside of the vessel. With one end fastened to the channel or to a ring bolt outboards, it was then slung a few times round the anchor

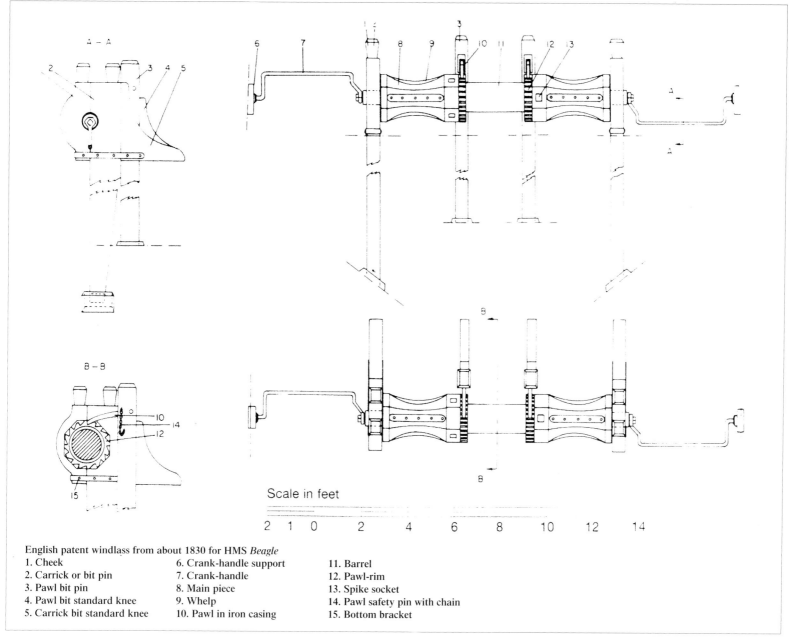

English patent windlass from about 1830 for HMS *Beagle*

1. Cheek	6. Crank-handle support	11. Barrel
2. Carrick or bit pin	7. Crank-handle	12. Pawl-rim
3. Pawl bit pin	8. Main piece	13. Spike socket
4. Pawl bit standard knee	9. Whelp	14. Pawl safety pin with chain
5. Carrick bit standard knee	10. Pawl in iron casing	15. Bottom bracket

shank and arm and was finally belayed securely to an appropriate timberhead.

To heave an anchor with a capstan the cable, which was usually too thick and unwieldy to be wound directly around the capstan whelps, was substituted with an endless thinner cable. At every five feet of the voyal (also known as messenger) a mouse was set as a stop for the nippers, which were short ropes that temporarily connected the voyal and cable during heaving.

Capstan

The double capstan was mainly used on warships for the heaving of anchors, while the single capstan on smaller vessels and merchantmen was used for moving heavy goods and for warping inside the harbour. As schooners only carried the single capstan, this is the only one discussed here.

A single capstan was composed of a vertical cylindrical barrel, with a drumhead, whelps and pawls and a cone-shaped spindle extension below deck. When searching for proportional barrel dimensions Duhamel's 'Alphabetic Specifications for Men of War'[212] provides a satisfactory answer. Duhamel includes data for 12 ships the largest being 176 by 48 feet, while the smallest is 96 by 24 feet. Ships above a breadth of 30 feet had a barrel diameter of $\frac{1}{24}$ of breadth, while ships of lesser width increased it gradually to $\frac{1}{20}$ of breadth. Other sources speak of a diameter of five times cable thickness. Shaft or barrel length above deck was for all sizes approximately 3½ feet. The complete length can be calculated by adding the length of the spindle between its step and deck above with the length of the deck itself. The spindle, cone-shaped between deck and step, had a pointed iron peg inserted into its lower end and turned in an iron saucer imbedded in the capstan's step.

The smallest capstans rested only with an iron spindle on extra supported partners, securely fore-locked beneath the support beam. That particular type was called a crab and was merely used for lighter work, with heavy duties being completed on the windlass.

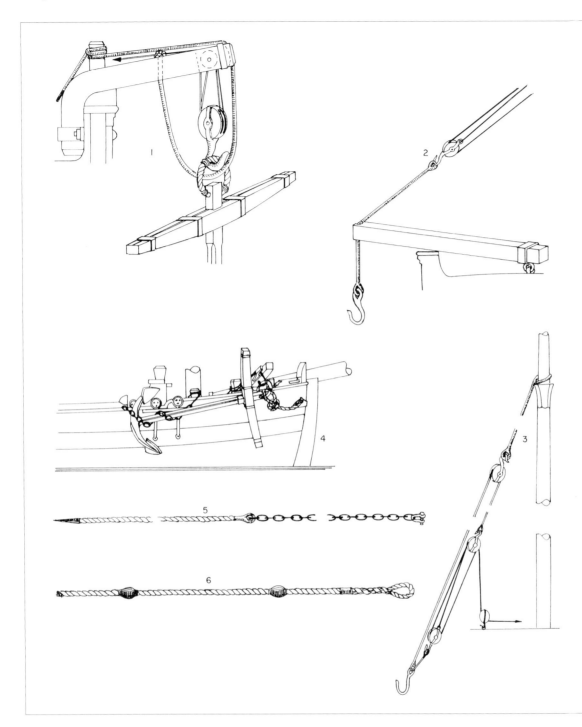

1. Anchor hanging on a cat-block and secured by a stopper
2. Davit sitting in an iron clamps on deck, a method still used on smaller ship during the early nineteenth century for the fishing of anchors
3. Runner and tackle of fishing tackle on ships without a davit
4. Securing an anchor with a stopper and a shank painter
5. Shank painter with a chain; also used without chain
6. Part of a voyal; each mouse was five feet apart and eye splices at each end were seized together to a continuous (endless) rope

The drumhead above the barrel was made from two cylindrical pieces of elm bolted to the barrel. The diameter of a drumhead was supposed to be twice the barrel's diameter, with a height of three-quarters barrel diameter plus 2 inches. Hand-spike sockets were cut into the side of the drumhead (six for smaller ones, and eight to ten for larger), with iron bands above and below providing extra strength. Iron bolts on light chains were fastened to the upper side of the drumhead to secure the handspikes in the sockets. Sockets on smaller vessels were about 3½ inches square and tapered along the sides and upper face by 1 inch for each foot in depth. The depth was usually one-and-a-half times socket height, with half of every socket being worked into each of the two drumhead parts. The barrel's head was octagon-shaped and tenoned into the underside of the drumhead.

Whelps were oak pieces bolted vertically to the barrel. At the lower end their depth measured half the barrel diameter and their width half the depth. The whelp was tapered by 9 degrees up to two-thirds of its height, and then protruded by 50 per cent so that a wound-up voyal could only run up to that point. Horizontal chocks with a width of one-third the whelp's depth were fitted between the whelps at one-quarter and three-quarters of barrel height.

'Still below the whelps sits a kind of locking wheel with about eight stops into which the arresting levers, termed PAWLS, fall to prevent a reverse thrust by the capstan.'[213]

This remark by Röding was only slightly altered by Duhamel, who added that the arresting levers were wooden.

Wooden pawls, still in operation by the middle of the eighteenth century were, by 1800, widely superseded by iron pawls. According to a reference from Falconer in his 1815 edition, the iron pawls were about 2 feet in length and had a thickness of 4 by 4 inches at capstan end, while the other end was prepared with a hole and bolted to the partners for the pawl to rotate. A capstan had two pawls with the pawl cleat, a piece of timber, bolted to the deck behind these as a safety measure. Cast-iron pawl rims appeared during the eighteenth century on English men-of-war, but were not used on smaller ships, particularly not on merchant vessels. They were mounted on deck below the capstan and engaged by pawls at the lower, widened chocks. Contemporary authors did not consider that method as being used on single capstans.

The length of a capstan's handspike was three-and-a-half times the diameter of the drumhead. The handspike was squared at one end, with three sides tapered according to the socket and the rest of its length rounded, and there was a groove at the other end to secure a safety line, which helped to contain men working the capstan in rough sea.

Pumps

Ship pumps were mainly used to remove water from the bilge. Deck wash pumps, as on larger men-of-war, were not necessary on smaller vessels, as the deckhands used (as they have since time immemorial) draw-buckets – buckets with a hand rope to scoop water from outboards.

The simplest and most preferred pump for this class of vessels was the suction pump, manufactured mostly from a bored elm tree trunk and set up to both sides of the main mast. The pump well, a boxed-in enclosure around mast and pumps, should have prevented any damage to the pumps, but not all vessels had these, as Duhamel du Monceau attests:

'Smaller ships usually have no well. One finds in such the pumps without a boxed in enclosure but with a rope woolding, or in tightly around the pumps fitted square trunks.' [214]

Röding described the pump's shaft as consisting of three main parts[215]. The lower pipe, the suction, was made from elm and went down beside the keelson into the bilge. Over its lower end fitted a copper strainer, the basket, to hinder any blocking flotsam from entering the system. Bolted to the head of the suction pipe was the pump chamber. It was completely made from copper, or at least provided with a copper insert. The third and upper, or raising, pipe did not differ in its inner diameter too much from the lower and was likewise made from elm. This kind of pump was fitted with two valves, the lower box or pump bucket was directly placed above the suction pipe, while the upper box or pump shoe was connected to the pump's spear and went up and down inside the chamber. Vertical movement of a pump's spear could be achieved by several methods. The Venetian pump was a type generally preferred on French warships. Falconer[216] described in detail the brake-operated or common pump, which Röding remarked was the most common pump on merchant vessels, and there was also the hand pump. Balance and wheel-operated pumps were not part of smaller craft and are not considered here.

The handle or brake of a Venetian pump was hooked to a mast strop at one-third of its length and another strop connected the brake's head with the pump spear. Several hand lines at the longer end enabled a group of men to work the pump by pulling these lines downward. The brake on common pumps revolved in a forked stanchion on the raising pipe. The fork itself was commonly known as ears or cheeks. The brake's head linked with a bolted joint to the pump spear and pumping action resulted from pressing and lifting the brake's longer lever. A common pump variation was the hand pump, which instead of a brake had a handle (the crutch) fitted directly across the spear; pumping took place when the crutch was pushed up and down. The tube of a hand pump was constructed in one piece and usually made from metal. Small common pumps did not differ in that

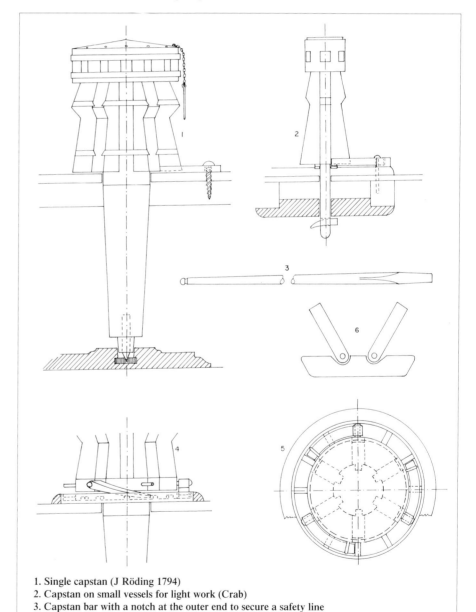

1. Single capstan (J Röding 1794)
2. Capstan on small vessels for light work (Crab)
3. Capstan bar with a notch at the outer end to secure a safety line
4. English pawl rim after about 1790; the projecting pins were only loosely fitted to keep disengaged pawls up
5. Pawl rim in plan view, three pawls, the barrel and whelps are indicated; a timber waterway was fitted around the rim
6. Wooden or iron pawls on deck, which were used generally up to the early nineteenth century on continental and merchant shipping

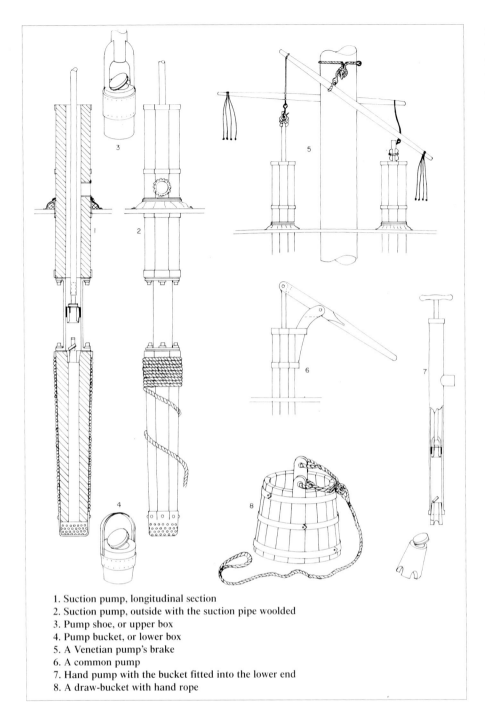

1. Suction pump, longitudinal section
2. Suction pump, outside with the suction pipe woolded
3. Pump shoe, or upper box
4. Pump bucket, or lower box
5. A Venetian pump's brake
6. A common pump
7. Hand pump with the bucket fitted into the lower end
8. A draw-bucket with hand rope

form of propulsion. The use of oars on schooners goes back to the very first vessel of this kind, HMS *Royal Transport* from 1695. That fore-and-aft schooner-rigged vessel was fitted with nine rowlocks to each side. Use of oars was not restricted to smaller vessels alone as Röding explains:

'The oar's length depends on a vessel's size; for sloops and boats they are 9 to 18 ft long. When in use, they are fastened in France with a strap to a thole. Englishmen and other nationalities lay them into rowlocks and on small sloops only against tholes. On frigates, privateers and other ships fitted out for war one can find oars of 30 to 45 feet length, partly to enable them to move into a most favourable position against the enemy, partly also to have an opportunity of escaping a superior enemy when becalmed or to get closer to an inferior one. These oars are thrust through row-ports in the ship's sides of which, according to the space between guns, one or two are placed between two guns.' [218]

Most contemporary works provide only very general information on oar sizes, as indicated by Röding. David Steel breaks down that generalisation and contributes tables with all the necessary dimensions for oars from a 100-gun ship down to boats of four feet in width – 'The Art of making Masts, Yards, Gaffs, Booms, Blocks and Oars as practised in the Royal Navy and according to the most approved Methods in the Merchant Service, London 1816' [219]. The dimensions in the tables presented in Appendix 4 (see pages 230–233) are an extract of this work. According to information from Röding oars were made from ash or beech, but Falconer disagrees:

'The oars for ships are generally made out of fir timber, those for barges are made of New England, or Dantzic rafters; and those for boats, either out of English ash, beech, or fir rafters from Norway.' [220]

Steel agrees with Falconer, but states that the larger sweeps had oak handles. An oar consisted of the following main parts: the flat blade, a rounded and tapered shank, a squared loom leading through the rowlock and finally the rounded handle. A boat oar's loom was also often rounded. Thin pieces of timber were nailed to the two faces of a squared loom most prone to wear and tear, while rounded looms received a leather cuff. A vessel's oars or sweeps were frequently bundled and stowed outboards to both sides of the quarter deck. Oars were also stored in iron forks on deck or above the gunwales.

Binnacle

The binnacle was a wooden box usually with three compartments, each of which closed with a sliding shutter. The centre section held an oil lamp with the two outside compartments holding two different compasses – a log glass and a watch glass. The walls of the centre section were paned with glass so that light from the lamp could shine on to the compasses in the outer compartments. The binnacle stood in front of the tiller or steering wheel to give the helmsman at one side and the watch officer at the other easy access to a

respect from the hand pump and in both types their lower valve, the pump bucket, was fitted into the pump pipe's foot. The woolding around pumps was not only thought of as protection from outside damage, it was also there to prevent bursting and was known by seamen as pump's service.

A remark by Röding gives specific details, which may be of interest to the model maker:

'At the place in the well where the suction pipe is situated, an extra layer of timber planks is laid because of the pump's suction being so strong that it pulls the oakum out of the seams and the ship will spring a leak.' [217]

Oars

It often remains unnoticed that during the period of sailing, smaller warships like armed schooners also had an auxiliary compass. Röding remarked that, for reasons of reciprocal interference, compasses should have been placed at least 7 feet apart, otherwise it would be better to have only one[221]. Compasses were usually portable, hung in gimbals and were fitted in a wooden box. If there was no room for a binnacle on the deck of a small craft, the compass box had to be located in a secure place in front of the tiller.

Beside the binnacle, compartments for flags and paint would have been normal parts of quarterdeck furniture. These could have been side extensions of the companion capping, or boxes on the inside of the taffrail.

Lantern

Lanterns were essential on every vessel, although stern lanterns were only fitted on vessels up to the end of the eighteenth century and only a minority of smaller craft carried them even then. Yet lights needed to be seen during darkness and to prevent collision, so lanterns on smaller craft were probably hoisted into the masthead. Lanterns were also useful for signalling as Röding remarks:

'With these lanterns, hung to various places in the ship and her rigging, signals are given during the night and such lanterns are then called signal lanterns.' [222]

Special battle lanterns were used on vessels engaged in night fighting. They were hung between two guns with their flat back against the bulwark to provide light for the gunners. A sailor negotiated his way through a dark lower deck with a hand lantern or with a dark or thief's lantern, which directed a negligible glimmer of light to one point so it was not spotted by the enemy. The powder room lantern was also particularly useful on warships. This was usually surrounded with horn and a wire netting and placed in a wooden, lead-sheathed and water-filled container.

Galley

No specific information can be found on the galleys or cabooses of small vessels. All pictorial evidence, which in itself is vague, relates to much larger ships than schooners. Of galleys Röding stated that: 'Such is usually a portable machine, constructed either totally from iron, or from lime, stones and ironwork.'[223] Falconer commented that the galley:

'Somewhat resembles a sentry-box, and generally stands against the barricade on the fore-part of the quarter-deck. It is the place where victuals are cooked on board merchant-ships.' [224]

Ordnance

There were several types of guns aboard smaller warships such as schooners. Armed schooners were equipped, according to their size or task, with swivel guns of ½-, ¾-, 1- or 2-pdr calibre, 3- to 4-pdr howitzers and/or 3- to 9-pdr carriage guns. During the last two decades of the eighteenth century carronades of 12- to 24-pdr calibre were introduced. Gunboats carried two or three 18- or 24-pdr long guns, either

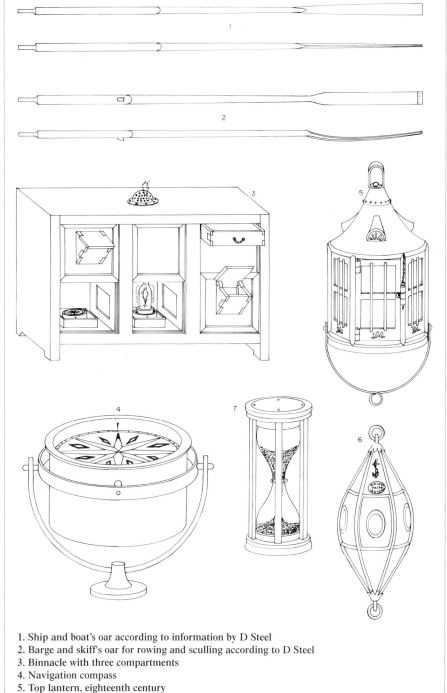

1. Ship and boat's oar according to information by D Steel
2. Barge and skiff's oar for rowing and sculling according to D Steel
3. Binnacle with three compartments
4. Navigation compass
5. Top lantern, eighteenth century
6. Brine's Patent lantern as used during the early nineteenth century in the Royal Navy
7. Sand hour-glasses in various sizes (for ½ hour, ½ minute and ¼ minute) were in use for measuring the ship's speed and the length of a watch.

mounted on carriages or on skids. Skids slid on a turntable, enabling them to turn full circle.

Swivel guns

The smallest swivel gun was set with its trunnions into the eyes of an iron fork to allow for vertical directing. The fork's shaft stood and pivoted in a vertical timber mount bolted to the side or in the upright arm of a standard fitted inboard for horizontal aiming. Trunnions of the swivel gun were placed below the centre line, although this did not always apply to larger guns. The main characteristics of a swivel gun were its

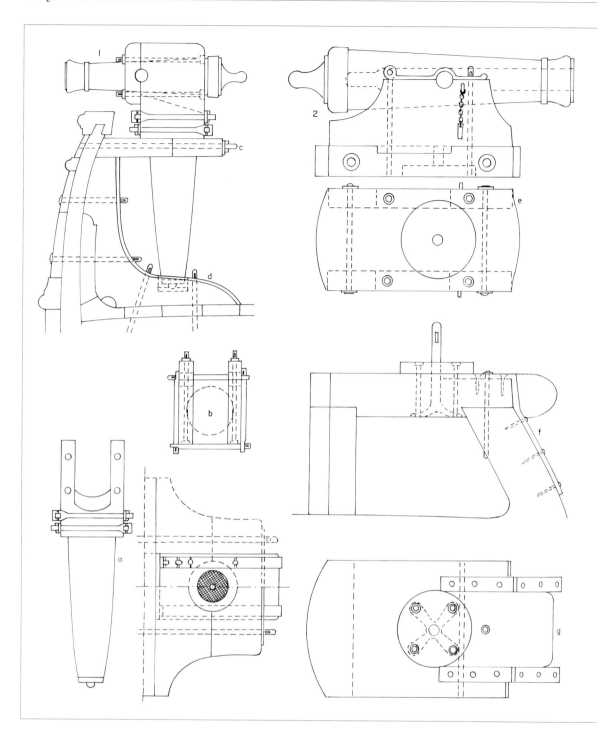

1. Three-pdr howitzer mounted like a
   swivel gun in a wooden fork:
   a) Fork as seen from the rear with a
      girdle of iron staves ;
   b) Plan view;
   c) Turn plate bolted to frames and
      planking;
   d) Standard with inserted iron saucer
2. Similarly sized howitzer imbedded in a
   revolving mounting:
   a) Base plate from below;
   b) Bedplate bolted to the frames and
      secured to the deck;
   c) Bedplate plan view with pivot bolt

Both mountings were developed by FH af
Chapman (Röding).

mounting in an iron fork and its cascable-fitted handle for aiming. Swivels were usually placed into timber stocks outside the fore and quarterdeck rails and to long boats for landing parties. Certain dimensions for swivel guns have been compiled from various sources:

English iron ½- and ¾-pdr		2ft 10in
English bronze ¾-pdr (1790)		3ft 6in
French bronze 1-pdr (1770)		3ft 1½in
The bore of an	*English ½-pdr*	40.13mm
	French 1-pdr	53mm

Heavier swivel guns were known as howitzers, which mostly had a shot weight of three pounds and were mounted to a more solid timber, pivoting base at the bulwark. They gener-

ally had no handle for aiming and their length was less than that of a 3-pdr carriage gun. Chapman's dimensions for the heavier gun were between 3ft 9in and 4ft 3in. An English carriage gun of three pound shot weight (from 1753) in comparison was: bronze gun – 6ft 5in; iron gun – 4ft 6in. Howitzer trunnions were at centre line level and the bore of an English 3-pdr was 74mm.

Röding outlined the howitzer mounting presented in Chapman's work (Plate XXXVI No 5). It consisted of sides bolted to a base plate, with the gun barrel resting in it as on a carriage and the trunnions secured with iron cap-squares:

'Mister Chapman invented also a kind of carriage mounting
for swivel guns.... That mounting revolves around a pin and
can carry a three pdr swivel gun, which can be as accurately

aimed as a carriage gun and much easier than those goose-neck mounted swivel guns.' [225]

The sides of the carriage were two-thirds the howitzer length, a height one-third the length and a depth of approximately one-third the height. The depth of the base plate was approximately half the side height, its width was half the length and its length was slightly longer at the centre line than the sides. Underneath the base plate there was a round recess of three-quarters plate width by one-third of plate thickness. A hole for the pivot bolt was drilled into the recess centre. Its counterpart was a strong bedplate, fastened with heavy iron bands to the rails and supported vertically on deck. A disk of recess dimensions, with the pivot bolt at its centre, was connected through the bedplate with four bolts and four forged tonques at right angles to the pivot bolt. The length of the bedplate was about six-sevenths gun barrel length, with its width half of that length and its thickness one-third.

In the second type of mounting shown a standard was bolted to the spirketting and reinforced inside with an iron band. A turntable was bolted above the upright arm inside the frames and parallel to the deck. The pivoting mount with its forked top was a massive piece of tough hardwood, with the conical pivot pin of a larger diameter than the gun barrel. An iron shoe with a hemisphere welded on was fitted to its foot so the gun mount could rotate like a capstan in an iron saucer, imbedded in the standard's sleeping arm. The sides of the fork extended above the gun barrel with trunnion beds worked into half of the front face. The other half of the face was cut into strong timber cleats, which were bolted with two bolts each to the sides after the gun was placed. Iron bolts or bands, forelocked to each other, strengthened the mounting at the square part between fork and pivot pin to prevent splitting.

Carriage guns were found on schooners and similar smaller craft in the range of 3 to 9 pounds, although gunboats were an exception being equipped with heavier guns of between 18 and 24 pounds shot weight. Information on carriage-gun dimensions can be more easily found than on swivels and howitzers and a few of these are mentioned here. (B) is for bronze and (I) is for iron ordnance:

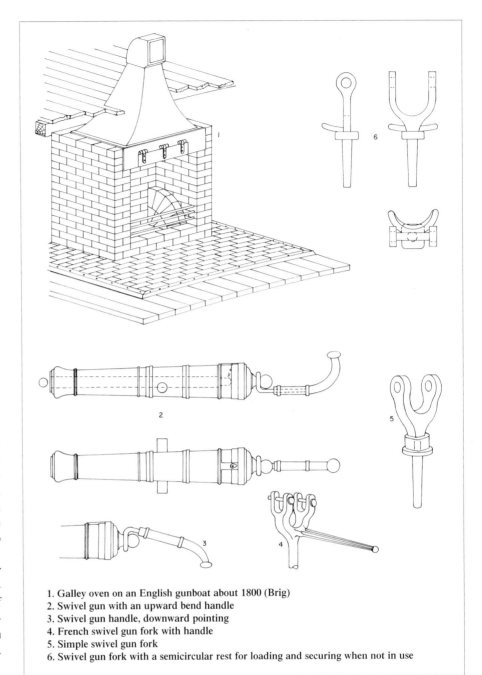

1. Galley oven on an English gunboat about 1800 (Brig)
2. Swivel gun with an upward bend handle
3. Swivel gun handle, downward pointing
4. French swivel gun fork with handle
5. Simple swivel gun fork
6. Swivel gun fork with a semicircular rest for loading and securing when not in use

Size	Falconer 1753 [226]	Röding [227]	Bobrik [228]
3-pdr (B)	6ft 5in		
3-pdr (I)	4ft 6in		
4-pdr (I)	6ft	5ft 6in French	
6-pdr (B)	8ft		
6-pdr (I)	7ft	6ft 2in French	5ft 8in to 7ft 6in French
8-pdr (B & I)		6ft 10in French	
9-pdr (B)	8ft 5in		
9-pdr (I)	8ft 5in		
18-pdr (B)	9ft	8ft French	7ft 6in to 8ft 5in French
18-pdr (I)	9ft	8ft French	7ft 6in to
24-pdr (B)	9ft 5in	8ft 6in French	8ft 5in French 8ft 5in to 8ft 11in French
24-pdr (I)	9ft 5in	8ft 6in French	8ft 5in to 8ft 11in French

Dimensions of English iron guns in the Royal Navy according to a 1782 Artillery Memorandum:

3-pdr	4ft 6in	bore 2.91in
4-pdr	5ft 6in	bore 3.21in
6-pdr	6ft to 7ft 6in	bore 3.66in
18-pdr	8ft 6in to 9ft 6in	bore 5.29in
24-pdr	9ft to 9ft 6in	bore 5.83in

A gun barrel was divided into three main sections, with the length of the gun measured from its breech and not the cascable. The hindmost of the three sections was the first reinforce, taking up $\frac{5}{17}$ of barrel length, followed by the second reinforce with $\frac{3}{17}$ of length, with the last, the chase, $\frac{9}{17}$ of length. Each of these sections ended with a reinforcing ring. The base ring and ogee were at one end of the barrel, with ring and ogee also at the first and second reinforce, while at the fore end they were replaced by the swelling and muzzle moulding. The trunnions were placed in the second reinforce. Apart from reinforcing rings the gun also had three ornamental bands. The hindmost defined the vent field forward and was called the vent astragal and fillets. The chase

astragal and fillets marked the forward border of the chase girdle and the muzzle astragal and fillets marked the rear of the neck. The distance between mouth and muzzle astragal was $\frac{2}{17}$ of the gun's length, the muzzle itself being $\frac{1}{17}$ gun length. Breech thickness was measured from the vent's rear and counted for one-and-a-quarter of bore diameter, with the cascable three-quarters of that diameter. Trunnion length and diameter equalled the bore diameter.

Röding[229] provides specifications for the reducing dimensions toward the muzzle on iron guns used by the French Navy. The dimensions are gun wall thickness times bore.

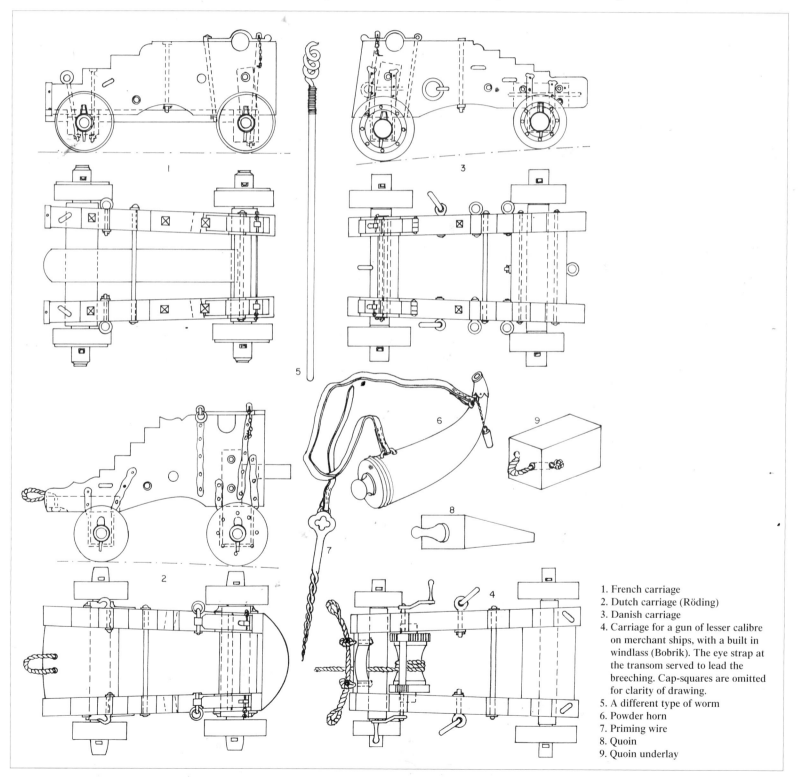

1. French carriage
2. Dutch carriage (Röding)
3. Danish carriage
4. Carriage for a gun of lesser calibre on merchant ships, with a built in windlass (Bobrik). The eye strap at the transom served to lead the breeching. Cap-squares are omitted for clarity of drawing.
5. A different type of worm
6. Powder horn
7. Priming wire
8. Quoin
9. Quoin underlay

Thickness according to calibre	24-	18-	6- + 4-pdr
At breech and vent	$^{24}/_{21}$ X	$^{24}/_{20}$ X	$^{24}/_{19}$ X
At the first reinforce	$^{22}/_{21}$ X	$^{22}/_{20}$ X	$^{22}/_{19}$ X
At the second reinforce	$^{19}/_{21}$ X	$^{19}/_{20}$ X	$^{19}/_{19}$ X
At the beginning of the chase	$^{17.5}/_{21}$ X	$^{17.5}/_{20}$ X	$^{17.5}/_{19}$ X
At the neck between muzzle and muzzle astragal and fillets	$^{11}/_{21}$ X	$^{11}/_{20}$ X	$^{11}/_{19}$ X
At the muzzle	$^{18}/_{21}$ X	$^{18}/_{20}$ X	$^{18}/_{19}$ X

Bronze guns were not so prone to bursting as iron guns and so were not as thick. Their circumference at the vent was 9⅔ of the bore, while at the trunnions the circumference was 7⅔ of bore, and at the muzzle astragal and fillets it was 5½ of bore. The diameter of the shot was always slightly less then the calibre bore of the gun and the difference between these measurements was known as play of the gun. On a 24-pdr that difference was 1 line (½in or about 2mm).

A carriage was the most common gun mounting during the period covered in this book. Their design differed according to the country of construction, although all had cheeks or brackets, axtrees and trucks. In the English design

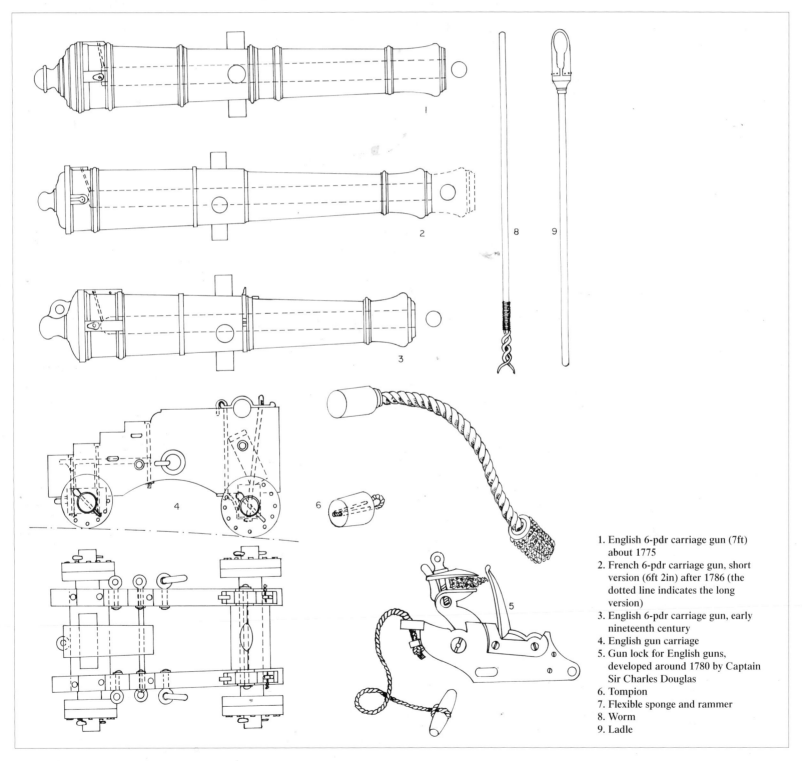

1. English 6-pdr carriage gun (7ft) about 1775
2. French 6-pdr carriage gun, short version (6ft 2in) after 1786 (the dotted line indicates the long version)
3. English 6-pdr carriage gun, early nineteenth century
4. English gun carriage
5. Gun lock for English guns, developed around 1780 by Captain Sir Charles Douglas
6. Tompion
7. Flexible sponge and rammer
8. Worm
9. Ladle

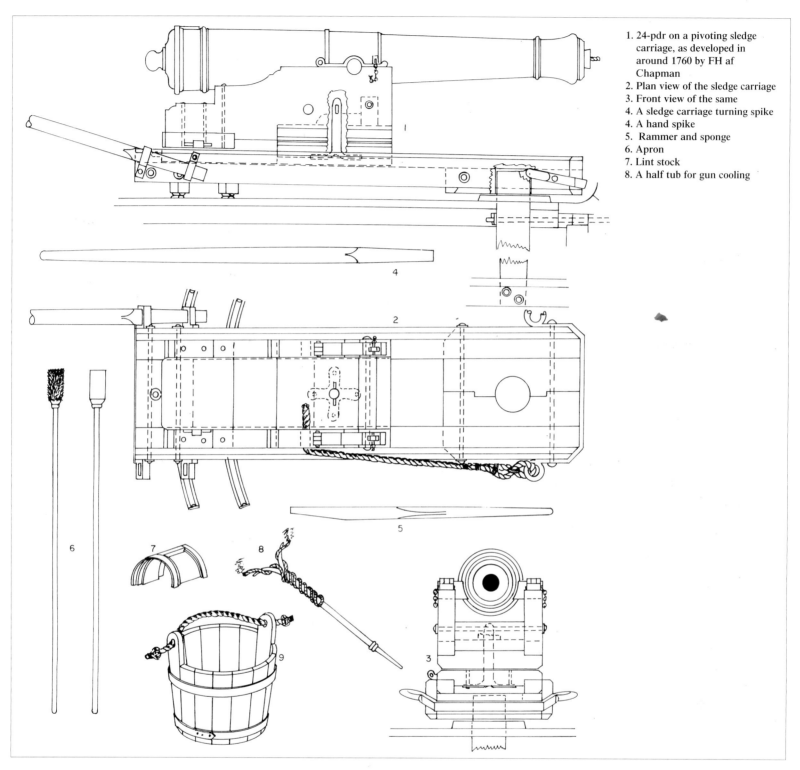

1. 24-pdr on a pivoting sledge carriage, as developed in around 1760 by FH af Chapman
2. Plan view of the sledge carriage
3. Front view of the same
4. A sledge carriage turning spike
4. A hand spike
5. Rammer and sponge
6. Apron
7. Lint stock
8. A half tub for gun cooling

the brackets were bolted to axtrees and a transom was tenoned diagonally to the inside of the bracket above the fore axtree. The transom was situated between the brackets semi-circular trunnion recesses and the axtree and had a half-round indentation at the top edge to make room for the motion of the gun barrel. A strong bolt, the transom, connected both brackets and the transom horizontally. A second bolt, the bed bolt, was placed lower and further back and carried the stool bed, with extra support provided by a bolster on top of the rear axtree. According to English references the stool bed was a timber plank but Röding called it 'a sort of iron bench'. The purpose of the stool bed was to provide a

base for the quoin. Located at and bolted through the brackets outside were strong breeching rings and slightly lesser eyebolts for the port tackles. Another eyebolt was fastened to the centre of the rear axtree for the train tackle, and semicircular iron clamps, the cap-squares, secured the trunnions in their beds. The bracket steps in the upper rear half were needed for handspikes or crowbars when pointing the gun.

French carriages differed from the English design in that the stool bed was replaced with a bed base of twice the length, and instead of breeching rings holes were drilled into the brackets for the breeching to pass through. A French carriage usually had two train tackles, with the eye-

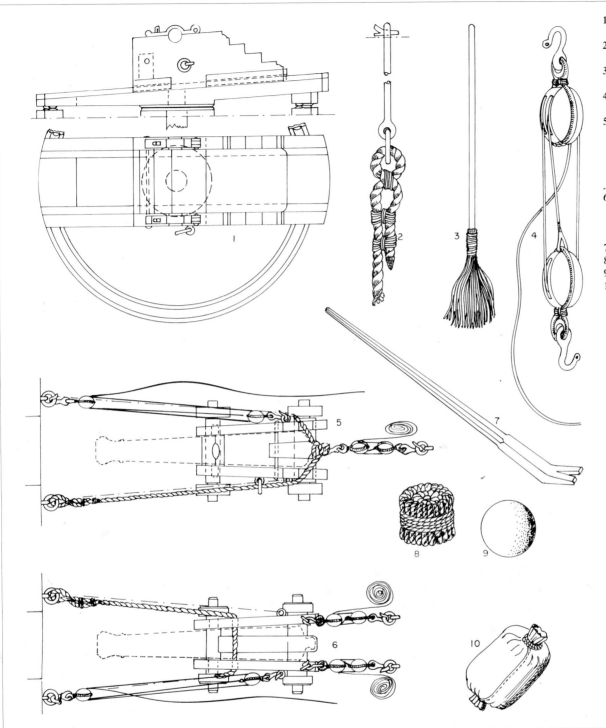

1. Simplified drawing of a turntable skid carriage
2. Breeching seized to a ringbolt at the ship's side
3. A swabber, made from short ends of old rope
4. Tackle employed as port- or train tackle
5. English gun: breeching is indicated on the lower (left) and the port tackle on the upper (right) side of the carriage; only one train tackle hooked to the centre of the rear axtree
6. French gun: breeching and port tackles are shown at opposite sides; two train tackles are hooked to the carriage
7. Iron crowbar
8. Wad
9. Round shot
10. Cartridge bag

bolts anchored vertically into the lowest bracket step.

The Dutch design, as illustrated by Röding[230], differed in a number of ways. Iron bands rather than long bolts were used to connect axtrees and brackets. The trunnion beds were cut deeper and therefore had flat cap-squares, which were not fastened with bolts like English and French designs, but with iron bands. Horizontal breast pieces were fitted between the brackets at the transom's front face. The train tackle was also different: rather than an eyebolt, a rope strap was inserted and fastened to two holes at the rear of the base plate. The base plate was located between the rear axtree and the end of bracket. Danish carriages were in many ways an amalgam of English and Dutch designs. Details not

mentioned in this short description can easily be taken from the accompanying illustrations. Another carriage, remarked on by Bobrik, was equipped with a small windlass for reeling and unwinding a single port rope, which was designed for easy handling of a lesser gun on an undermanned merchant vessel.

Proportional carriage dimensions are available from Röding and to a certain extent from Falconer, while Bobrik provides actual measurements. Another source for this information is John Robertson's *Table of General Dimensions of the Parts of a Ship Gun Carriage in Calibres of the Respective Shot*[231], published in 1775. As a rule of thumb carriage length was approximately the length of the gun from the muzzle to the centre of the trunnion plus half of the fore truck's diameter. The overall height was the height of the lower gun-port sill plus two-fifths of the gun-port height. Bracket thickness varied according to calibre between 3 and 6 inches, being apart from each other by the gun barrel's diameter plus ½ inch.

The trucks and the rounded parts of the axtrees were of equal thickness to the brackets. Axtrees were 1 inch higher and their width was twice their height. Truck diameters have not been provided in any of the sources, but it has been noted that those at the rear were of a slightly narrower diameter than those at the front. A transom was of equal thickness to the brackets and its height reached from the front axtree to below the trunnions, where a segment was cut out to prevent interference with the gun barrel. The transom was mortised with 1-inch deep swallowtails into the interior of the bracket.

The bed bolt was located vertically below the uppermost bracket step and at one-fifth of the height from the lower edge. Transom bolt position was one-third of the height below the trunnions and the port tackle eyebolts were below the second step at one-third of height. The breeching ring-bolt was level with the bed bolt at the middle of the bracket, while holes for the same rope were placed at two-fifths the length from the rear and at half the height of a continental carriage's brackets.

Extract from Bobrik's 'Main Dimensions and Weights of English Ship Gun Carriages' (1848)
Calibres in English pounds and Dimensions in French inches

Calibre	24	18	6
Name of part	*Dimensions in French inches with ¹⁄₁₀₀'s*		
Length of bracket	67.56	64.75	56.30
Their foremost height	22.52	20.64	15.02
Their thickness	5.16	4.69	3.28
Thickness of transom	5.16	4.69	3.29
Length of fore axtree	51.61	47.86	37.53
Width of fore axtree	9.38	9.38	8.45
Thickness of fore axtree	6.33	5.63	4.69
Length of rear axtree	51.61	47.86	37.53
Width of rear axtree	11.26	11.26	11.26
Thickness of rear axtree	6.33	5.63	4.69
Foremost width of carriage	15.95	14.08	11.26
Rear width	21.58	19.71	15.95
Diameter of front trucks	16.89	16.89	13.14
Thickness of front trucks	5.16	4.89	3.28
Diameter of rear trucks	15.02	14.08	11.26
Thickness of rear trucks	5.16	4.69	3.28
Distance of the trunnion hole fore edge from the front	7.51	7.51	6.22
Highest point of trunnion	29.09	28.15	22.53
Weight in lbs of carriage including quoin	830	727	285

Carriages on skids were frequently used for heavy ordnance on schooners. They were more or less mobile being either fixed in one position, set up to a semicircular segment of various degrees or set to a full circle. Developed from Chapman's invention, the advantages of these gunboat carriages were outlined by Röding:

'These carriage types are in some ways beneficial, in others not. They can be moved much more rapidly with far less hands: One single man can aim an eighteen pdr forward, to the rear or side of a hostile ship and can fire two shots for one in a given time. However, and that is why they are not much in use, their shortcomings are obvious in regard to their far heavier weight than normal carriages and the excessive space taken up on deck.' [232]

In their fixed design these carriages went back to forward gun mountings on galleys, with their essential parts consisting of a bed and a strong, sliding wooden frame without axtrees and trucks. They could not be turned to the sides and were employed on rowing craft whereby the vessel was steered in the direction of the target.

Chapman's improvements to this basic design incorporated bed rotation and an additional circling provision for the sledge carriage itself. The bed revolved around a strong oaken post anchored either to the deck beams or to stem- or sternson. The gun-barrel carrying body stood on a vertical iron pivot bolt in the sliding base and could rotate on itself. This had the advantage of serving the gun inboards without moving the bed from its action position. A spring between both carriage parts, tensioned and cocked with the upper part in service position, was ready to spring into action when released. Iron brackets bolted to the rear of the bed were used to house the turning spike for carriage mobility. An iron band with two large eyes was also laid across and bolted to the bed's face to accommodate the breeching of the fore ends of the skid carriage. An iron plate covered the deck around the turning post and semicircular iron rails were bolted below the bed's rear to the deck.

A 360-degree turntable carriage design followed the same principle, except that the turning post was placed in the centre and not at the fore end of the bed. That extra swivel action of the skid carriage could also be disregarded, since a full circle movement made it unnecessary. Skid-carriage dimensions do not appear in the researched material, but they would not have varied a great deal from normal carriage proportions and can easily be established from drawings, as seen on a drawing of a Norwegian gunboat's turntable gun carriage from 1823.

In 1779 a new page was turned in the development of the ship gun. During June of that year the carronade became a standard weapon in the Royal Navy, or as Falconer's Dictionary (of 1815) declared, the carronade was 'instituted by the King and Council'. This new gun very soon had tremendous appeal for smaller ships such as brigs and schooners, since it was lighter, a larger calibre and needed less manpower to operate.

Carronade

Development of this gun began in 1747 with a much discussed article by Benjamin Robins, explaining the advantages of large-calibre short guns during naval engagements, which were usually carried out at close quarters. These arguments impressed General Robert Melville who, by 1774, had developed a short gun of 31 cwt with 8-inch bore, capable of firing a 68-pound shot into a target. The gun, named The Smasher, was cast in the foundry of the Carron Iron Works at Falkirk, Scotland. Melville's successful gun became the prototype for all the new and variously calibrated weapons, which were named carronades after their birthplace. In 1778 the Carron Company armed their own merchant ships with these new guns, which resulted in them winning, in May 1779, an engagement with a hostile and superior man-of-war. The new weapon's popularity grew very rapidly and in January 1781 the Royal Navy already had 429 ships fitted with carronades, not counting privateers or merchant vessels. Carronades revealed their greatest advantage over normal carriage guns during close fighting 'at yard-arm's length', but were inferior to long guns in long-distance encounters.

Dimensions of Carronades of all calibres

Calibres in lbs	bore	length	weight
68	8.05in	5ft 2in	36 cwt
		4ft	29 cwt
42	6.84in	4ft 3½in	22 cwt
32	6.35in	4ft ½in	17.14 cwt
24	5.68in	3ft 7½in	13 cwt
		3ft	11.72 cwt
18	5.16in	3ft 3in	9 cwt
		2ft 4in	8.48 cwt
12	4.25in	2ft 2in	5.85 cwt

Direct comparison of two equally calibrated weapons, a 12-pdr carriage gun and a 12-pdr carronade provides a better understanding of the savings in weight, deck space and gun crew of a carronade over a long gun.

	bore	length	weight	
12-pdr long gun	4.63in	9ft 6in	32 cwt	8 men
shorter long gun		8ft	27.5 cwt	8 men
12-pdr carronade	4.52in	2ft 2in	5.85 cwt	3 men

Conventional guns and carronades were not only different in length and weight but also in appearance. Carronades did not have trunnions, but instead had an integrated solid eye beneath the barrel hinged in an iron mounting. However, trunnions were for a while still part of Danish carronades as a draught from 1795 indicates[233] and part of an *obusier*, the French answer to the new carronade. Both types of gun were developed from the English method.

While the Danish still aimed with crowbar and quoin, the English carronade and the French *obusier* had a vertically pointing screw fitted to the cascable. The carronade carriage followed Chapman's principle in its basic design. It consisted of a timber skid with a mounting body bolted on and a bed with a turning bolt through the fore end and small wheels at the rear for pivoting.

For effective gun service further items were needed. Port tackles used to haul the gun out were hooked to eyebolts in the gun brackets and to similar bolts in the spirketting beside the gun-port. Train tackles (which varied nationally) hooked to one or two ringbolt(s) in the binding strakes and to either an eyebolt in the middle of the rear axtree, a strap in the bed, or to two eyebolts in the lower steps of the carriage brackets. A plug for closing the muzzle, a tompion, was made from cork and at sea was carefully prepared with tallow or putty to prevent water penetration into the bore. A thick rope, the breeching, controlled the gun's recoil and its length was supposed to be sufficient to bring a gun's muzzle at least 2 feet inboard for reloading. On English and Danish guns the breeching was laid around the cascable with a turn or a horseshoe splice. After gun improvements were made early in the nineteenth century the breeching only rove through an eye above the cascable. The breeching then went through strong ringbolts at each side of the carriage, to be fastened to ringbolts solidly mounted in the spirketting. French and Dutch gunners did not apply the breeching in the same way and instead the breeching rope led through a special hole in each bracket and went directly to the ringbolts in the spirketting.

Circumference and Lengths of Tackles and Breeching[234]

Calibre (pdr)	Length (ft)	Breeching Circum-ference (in)	Breeching Length (ft)	Tackles Circum-ference (in)	Tackles Length (ft)
24	9½	6½	32	3	54
24	8	6½	22	2½	42
24	6½	6½	20	2½	40
18	9	5½	28	2½	48
18	8	5½	25	2½	42
6	6	4½	23	2	30
4	5½	3½	21	1½	26
3	4½	3½	21	1½	26

For each tackle there was a single and a double block with hook and thimble. On 24-pdrs, it was 8 inches, on 18-pdrs it was 6½ inches and on 3- to 6-pdrs it was 5 inches.

Dimensions of Breechings For Carronades (same source)

	Circumference (in)	Length (ft)	Circumference (in)	Length (ft)
68	9	21	2	30
42	8	20	2	30
32	8	20	2	30
24	6½	20	2	24
18	5½	16	1½	20
12	5½	15	1½	20

The following tools were used to load, unload and clean the guns. The rammer was a cylindrical piston on a stick, which was used to press the load home. When confined space made

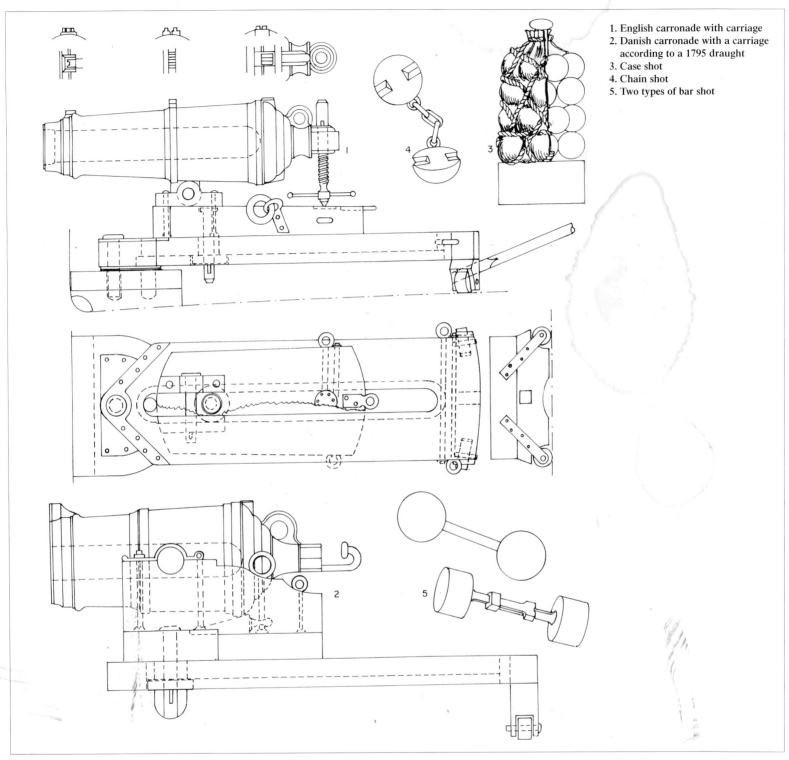

1. English carronade with carriage
2. Danish carronade with a carriage according to a 1795 draught
3. Case shot
4. Chain shot
5. Two types of bar shot

loading difficult another rammer was sometimes fitted to a stiff piece of rope on which a sponge was attached at the other end. A sponge was either a round brush or a timber piston with a piece of sheepskin nailed to it and was used to extinguish smouldering powder residues after firing. The gunner used a worm – two spiralling hooks on a stick – to remove the wad and unload the shot. A ladle was used to insert the powder cartridge into the bore. This rounded, long-stemmed, copper shovel was the same size as the bore.

The next group of instruments was used to aim and fire a gun. A wedge-shaped piece of timber, the quoin, was used to keep a trained gun pointed. One or two men trained the gun,

following orders from the gun trainer, using crowbars or handspikes placed between the bracket steps and the gun breech. The quoin was then, with or without a quoin underlay, placed between breech and stool. Handspikes were lifting booms with their front tapered and iron shoed to reach under the breech for training. An apron covered the touchhole around the gun when it was not in use to prevent moisture from entering the bore. Tied down at its corners to the port tackles, the apron was a 1-foot-square sheet of lead formed to fit the gun. Copper or iron needles, priming wires, of about 10 to 12 inches long penetrated the touchhole and pierced the cartridge to let some powder run out. A number

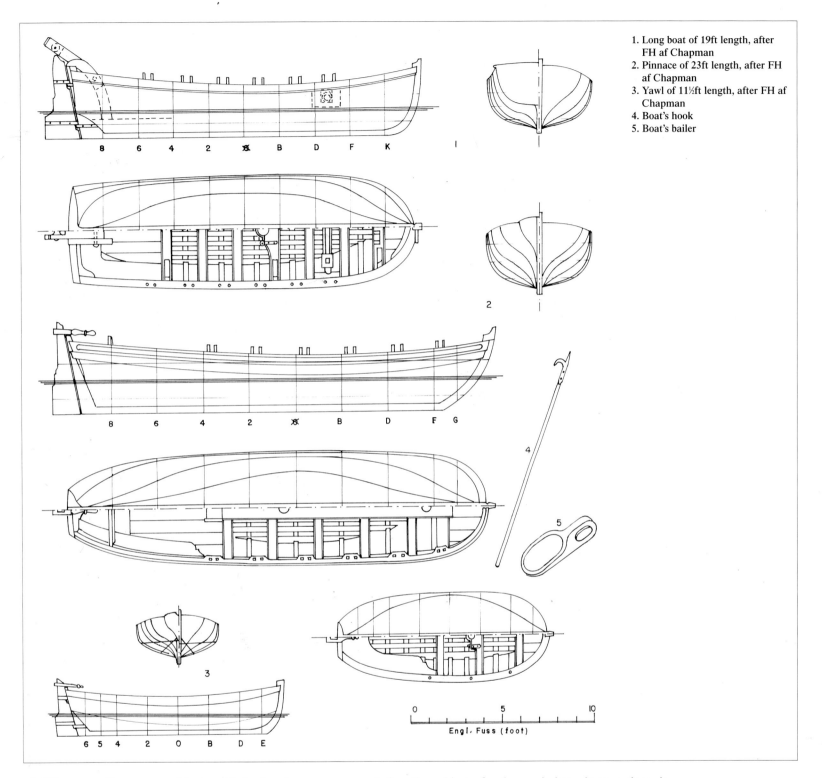

1. Long boat of 19ft length, after FH af Chapman
2. Pinnace of 23ft length, after FH af Chapman
3. Yawl of 11½ft length, after FH af Chapman
4. Boat's hook
5. Boat's bailer

Engl. Fuss (foot)

of different needles were used for touchhole cleaning.

The list of essential instruments also includes the cartridge box, powder horn, lint-stock and lints, a crowbar, swabbers, cooling buckets and tools for measuring calibre, not to mention the load or charge. The charge was composed of a cartridge, the shot and a wad. Shot existed in various shapes such as round shot, bar shot, chain shot, case shot and so on. Finally, a number of men were necessary to serve the gun – that number related to its calibre: 24-pdr long gun required 11 men; 18-pdr long gun required 9 men; 6-pdr long gun required 5 men and on smaller carriage guns 3 or 4 men were required.

Before the subject of ordnance is brought to a close, it should not be forgotten that in around 1780 Captain Sir Charles Douglas perfected the flint-lock, known on muskets since the early sixteenth century, for ship's guns. This new invention was officially introduced in 1790 to the Royal Navy, although there is no evidence that it was used on French ships any earlier than about 1800.

Boats

In a modern landlubber's mind ship's boats are generally thought of in terms of life saving but this was not the main reason for carrying boats aboard ships during the period under consideration – they were substitute crafts for a multitude of operations that one could not execute with a larger ship.

To berth on a wharf after entering a harbour was rather an exception than the rule; ships usually anchored either inside a harbour, in a roadstead or were moored to a buoy. Therefore it was necessary to transport people or goods between ship and land by boat. If an anchorage was too shallow to be safely navigated by a ship, a longboat was used to lay out or weigh the anchor. Uncharted waters that were deemed too risky to approach were first approached in the

boat. Boats could also be employed to tow the ship when becalmed, or be used for painting or repairing the hull. These are some of the many reasons that a boat was carried aboard, and rescue is not one of them – a boat was only a doubtful bonus for the crew of a distressed ship.

The number of boats aboard a ship depended not only on the size but also on the type of vessel. Merchant ships, with the exception of whalers, usually carried no more than two boats: a long boat, launch or cutter and a pinnace or gig. Smaller vessels frequently carried only a multipurpose boat for transport as well as for work. Survey ships also carried an extraordinary number of varying boat types for charting.

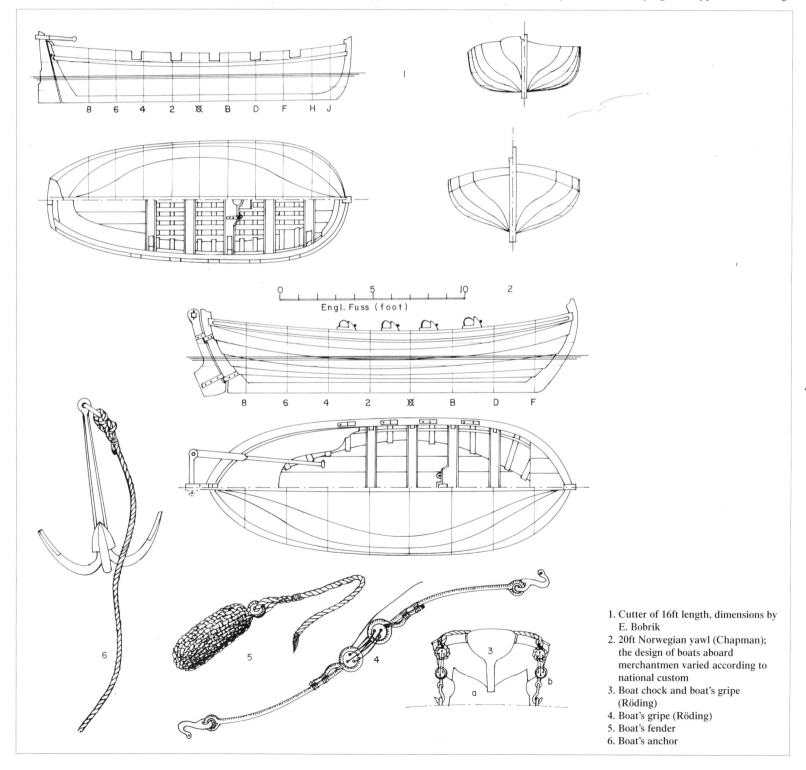

1. Cutter of 16ft length, dimensions by E. Bobrik
2. 20ft Norwegian yawl (Chapman); the design of boats aboard merchantmen varied according to national custom
3. Boat chock and boat's gripe (Röding)
4. Boat's gripe (Röding)
5. Boat's fender
6. Boat's anchor

Warships had more boats aboard than merchantmen and the types carried were sub-divided into two groups. The first group, used for work and transport of low-ranking personnel, was commonly known as boat, whilst the second, used to convey officers and guests, was a pinnace. These boats and pinnaces, most of which were not used on schooners, consisted (in rank order): admiral's barge, captain's pinnace or gig, officer's yawl; followed by the working boats – longboat, launch, cutter, wherry and whale boat.

One of these terms is confusing. Yawls were described in 1750 by Blanckley as 'the inferior and smallest Boats allowed Ships'[235]. Falconer spoke of a yawl as 'a wherry or small ship's boat, usually rowed by four to six oars'[236]. Yawls were clincher-built but by the end of the century, they were no longer an inferior boat. The standard yawl in the Royal Navy around 1800 was 26 feet long, cravel-built and two-masted. The boats could be propelled with four, six or eight oars and often replaced the longboat or launch.

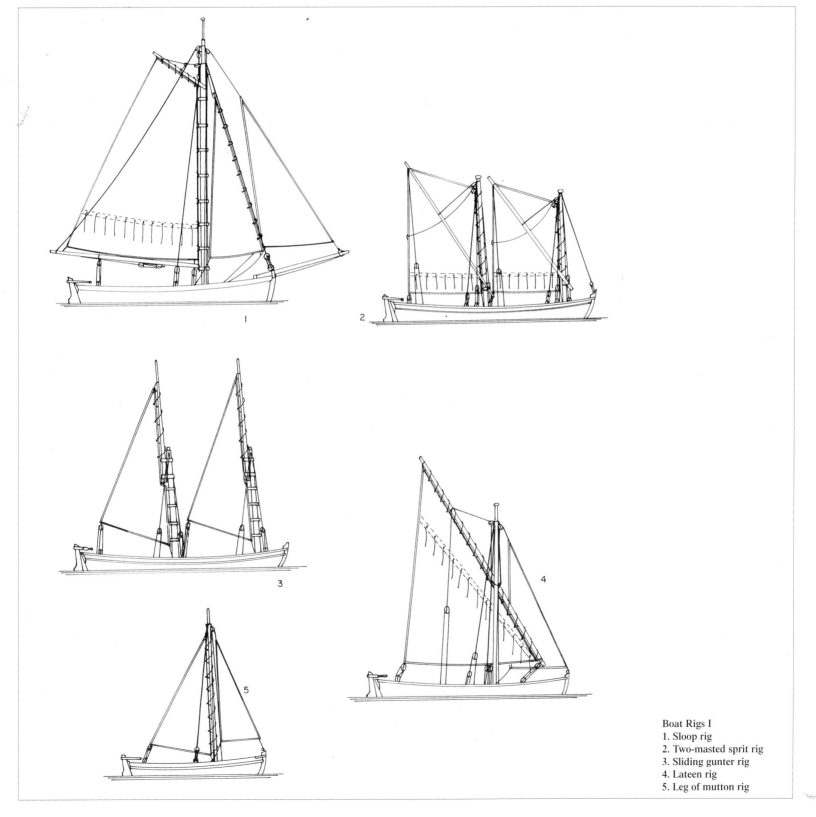

Boat Rigs I
1. Sloop rig
2. Two-masted sprit rig
3. Sliding gunter rig
4. Lateen rig
5. Leg of mutton rig

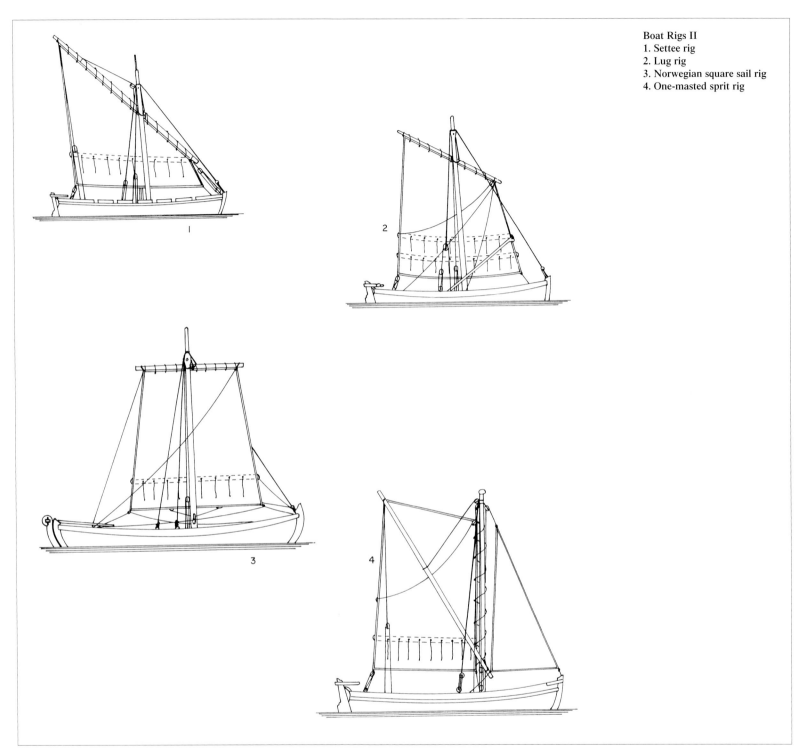

Boat Rigs II
1. Settee rig
2. Lug rig
3. Norwegian square sail rig
4. One-masted sprit rig

Admiral W Smyth commented in 1867 that the yawl was 'a man-of-war's boat, resembling the pinnace, but rather smaller; it is carvel-built, and generally rowed with twelve oars'[237].

The longboat was not only the largest but also the strongest boat, and equipped with masts and sails. It was employed for laying out anchors, transporting water casks and so on, and therefore the boat was fitted out with a small windlass in the fore section and a curved davit with built-in reel at the stern. In case of shipwreck the longboat was the safest in which to be, as it was built with wales, in contrast to the next largest boat, the launch, which only had a rail plank. Being flatter and wider than a longboat, the launch

was frequently the largest boat aboard. Although better adapted to rowing, she could also carry sails when the need arose. Her distinguishing features included a broader stern than the longboat's and chocks for a stern davit.

In size (although not in status) the launch was followed by the admiral's barge. The barge was the noblest of all the ship boats and her work was restricted to the transportation of Admirals and persons of high rank. Lighter built and more elegant in her lines she was often three-masted and rowed with 12 oars. A captain's pinnace was similarly built but was smaller and carried no more than eight oars. Lighter, and narrower still, the gig was really a rowing, rather than a sailing, boat. The yawl was a similar design to the pinnace but much smaller, with no more than six oars, and was used for officers below the rank of captain and also on merchant vessels. With the exception of the gig's clincher planking, all these conveyances were cravel-built. Cutters served as utility boats for work and transport of non-commissioned personnel. Being shorter and wider in proportion, they were also rigged with mast and sail. A wherry was smaller than a cutter but similarly constructed, did not very often carry a mast and sail and was rowed with two to four oars. The rigs of each boat type could have come from a variety of sail arrangements; rules did not exist. Boat rigs in use were sloop rig, sliding gunter rig, sprit, lateen and settee rig as well as lug and leg-of-mutton rig. Each of them could have been applicable to any of the boats. Bobrik provides tables of dimensions for boats (see Appendix 4, pages 230–233).

When stowed on deck during a voyage boats stood in chocks placed over deck beams usually mid-ships above the main hatchway. Boat chocks were timber pieces, shaped on their upper side like a negative to the particular frame sections to ensure a close fit when the boat rested in them. Once a boat was sitting in the chocks, rope straps (gripes) secured it to the deck. These straps had a hook and thimble spliced into one end and a dead eye fitted to the other. Hooked each side to a ringbolt on deck, they reached over the gunnel to near the centre of the boat, where both dead eyes were seized together by a lanyard. When a second boat was aboard it was placed inside the first (nested) and secured adequately in similar fashion.

Boat thwarts in general, with the exception of those holding a mast, were only loosely fitted and could be removed when transporting bulky goods like casks and boxes. Iron bands were usually used to fasten mast thwarts to the sides. Pinnaces and related boats contained seats for officers and travellers of rank fitted to the cockpit. The floor space around these seats (and sometimes of the whole boat) was covered with a loose floor of thin planks, nailed slightly open together.

Tholes for rowing were placed into the gunnels, with either iron bolts or wooden dowels set up in pairs or singly. Oars rested between pairs but were laid against single bolts, in which case attached eye straps hooked over the thole dowel. Alternately, rowing cleats were nailed to, or rowlocks cut into, the gunnel.

Steinhaus' proportional dimensions indicate masts and spars for the boat rigs shown here (see Appendix 4, pages 230–233). The dimensions deviate only slightly from those given by Steel and Fincham[238].

Other implements besides oars and rigging were needed in a boat: fore-and-aft lines (known as painter and sternfast), one or two plaited fenders, a boat's hook, a bailer (a kind of wooden shovel to remove overcoming water), sometimes a grapnel or grapling (a small boat anchor with four or five flukes) and, for certain voyages, swivel guns.

Schooners for all Reasons

In this attempt to describe a small ship's principal pieces of equipment in more detail it is inevitable that some items could be overlooked and that others have been reduced to a short mention. The description of a multipurpose vessel type is always prone to remain incomplete, even by limiting the era of reference. It is hoped that this effort has told the story of development and has given ship-lovers a deeper insight into a type of vessel commonly known as the Schooner.

———— ♦ ————

Notes:
[194] Röding, J H, *Allgemeines Wörterbuch der Marine*, Vol.1 (Hamburg, 1794, repr. Amsterdam, 1969) p.83: '*Wir wollen noch bemerken, daß das Gewicht der schweren Schiffsanker sich verhält wie das Quadrat von der Bfreite des Schiffes selbst.[..] Es soll uns hier der Pflichtanker von einem Schiffe, welches 49 Fr. Fuß Breite hat und wovon derselbe 7653 Liv. Wiegt, zur Vergleichung dienen, um das Gewicht von jedem andern Anke zu finden. Z.E. von einem Schiffe, welches 20 Fuß Breite hat. 49² : 20² = 7653 Liv. : x Liv. = 1331 Liv.. Dieses Verhältniß, welches auf vernünftigen Gründen beruhet, wird nicht allein von den Franzosen, sondern auch von den Engländern und andern Nationen befolgt.*'
[195] Falconer, W A, *A New Universal Dictionary of the Marine, improved and enlarged by William Burney Li.D.* (London, 1815), repr. MacDonald and Jane's (London, 1974) p.14
[196] Steinhaus, C F, *Die Schiffbaukunst in ihrem ganzen Umfang*, Vol.2 (Hamburg, 1858) repr. H Hamecher (Kassel, 1977) p.168
[197] Pâris, E, *Souvenirs de Marine* (Paris, 1882) Vol.2, repr. Karl Butziger Verlag (Hamburg, 1972) p.105.
[198] Brady, W N, *The Kedge Anchor or Young Sailor's Assistant* (New York, 1879) repr. Macdonald and Jane's (London, 1974) p.291
[199] Falconer, W A, op. cit., p.11
[200] Boudriot, J, *The Seventy-Four Gun Ship*, Vol.2, Author publication (Paris, 1986) p.102
[201] Falconer, W A, op. cit., p.11
[202] Steinhaus, C F, op. cit., Vol.2, p.167
[203] Lavery, B, *The Arming and Fitting of English Ships of War 1600–1815*, Conway Maritime Press Ltd. (London, 1987) p.32.
[204] Röding, J H, op. cit., Vol.1, p.83: '*Jedes Kriegsschiff führt vier bis fünf schwere Anker, Was die Zahl der kleinen Anker anbetrifft, so hängt solche mehrentheils von Zeit und Umständen ab; gemeiniglich ist aber jedes Kriegsschiff mit 2 bis 3 Wurfankern versehen.*'
[205] Ibid., p.98 '*Das Ankertau oder Kabel dient dazu, die Schiffe auf einer Rhede oder in einem Hafen vor Anker zu halten, und ist ein dickes und starkes Tau…*'
[206] Ibid., p.99 '*Fast alle Ankertaue werden 150 Faden oder 900 Fuß lang gemacht, und dieses findet auch auf Kauffahrthey-Schiffen Statt, doch diejenigen ausgenommen, welche auf den Wallfischfang nach Grönland fahren, denn diese gebrauchen nur Ankertaue von 120 Faden Länge.Es ist nicht üblich, die Ankertaue länger als 150 Faden zu machen, ungeachtet man oftmals längere gebrauchen muß, sondern man splitset alsdenn zwey zusammen.*'
[207] Ibid., p.90: '*Alle Schiffe, welche in Häfen oder auf Rheden ankern, müssen mit einer Boye versehn seyn, weil es höchst gefährlich ist solches zu unterlassen; auch ist es wegen des Schadens welchen andere Schiffe darüber leiden können bey Strafe verboten.*'
[208] Lever, D, *The Young Sea Officer's Sheet Anchor* (London, 1819), repr. E W Sweetman Co (New York, 1963) p.116
[209] Röding, J H, op. cit., Vol.1, p.383: '*Da wegen der horizontalen Lage des Bratspills die ganze Schwere des Mannes auf das Ende des Hebels oder der Spake würkt, so hat solcher hiebey weit mehrere Kraft zu winden, als by dem Gangspill. Demungeachtet erfordert die Arbeit eine besondere Geschicklichkeit, welche hauptsächlich darinn besteht, daß alle Arbeiter zu gleicher Zeit ihre Spaken mit einem Ruck niederdrücken.*'
[210] Lever, D, op. cit., p.116
[211] Ibid., p.69
[212] Duhamel du Monceau, H L, *Anfangsgründe der Schiffbaukunst oder Praktische Abhandlungen über den Schiffbau* (1752) translated with annotations by Christian G D Müller (Berlin, 1791), repr. H Hamecher (Kassel, 1973) p.57
[213] Röding, J H, *Allgemeines Wörterbuch der Marine*, Vol.2 (Hamburg, 1794, repr. Amsterdam, 1969) p.656: '*Unter den Klampen oder Ausfutterungen ist noch eine Art von Sperrad von etwa 8 Sperren, in*

[214] Duhamel du Monceau, H L, op. cit., p.37: '*Kleinere Schiffe haben gewöhnlich gar keinen Pumpsoo. Man findet in denselben die Pumpen ohne alle Bekleidung mit Tauwerk bewuhlt, auch in blossen viereckigten dich um die: Pumpen zusammengeschlagenen Kasten.*'

[215] Röding, J H, op. cit., Vol.2, p.656

[216] Falconer, W, *An Universal Dictionary of the Marine* (London, 1769) reprint of 1780 edition by David & Charles (Newton Abbot, Devon, 1870) p.221

[217] Röding, J H, op. cit., Vol.2, p.302: '*Ueber die Stelle des Pumpsoods worauf das Saugrohr steht, wird eine Bekleidung von Holz gelegt, weil die Würkung der Pumpe so stark sit, daß das Werk aus den Nathen gezogenn und das Schiff dadurch leck werden kann.*'

[218] Ibid., p.333: '*Die Länge der Riemen richtet sich nach der Größe der Fahrzeuge, bey Schlupen und Böten sind sie 9 bis 18 Fuß lang. In Frankreich befestigt man sie, wenn sie dienen sollen, vermittelst eines Stropps an einen Dullen. Bey den Engländern und andern Nationen legt man sie in Rojeklampen und auf kleinen Schlupen nur blos gegen die Dullen. Auf Fregatten, Kapern und andern zum Kriege ausgerüsteten Schiffen, findet man auch wol Riemen die 30 bis 45 Fuß lang sind, theils um dieselben fähiger zu machen, während einem Gefecht die vortheilhafteste Lage gegen einen Feind anzunehmen; theils aber auch Gelegenheit zu haben bey Windstillen einem überlegenen Feind leichter zu entfliehen, und einen schwächern einzuholen. Diese Riemen fahren durch an den Seiten der Schiffe befindliche Rojepforten deren man nach der Grösse des Zwischenraums zwischen dem Geschütz, zwischen zwey Kanonen, eine bis zwey anordnet.*'

[219] Steel, D, 'Oar-Making', *Nautical Research Journal* 25/2 (Washington DC, 1979)

[220] Falconer, W A, *A New Universal Dictionary of the Marine, improved and enlarged by W. Burney LL.D.* (London, 1815), repr. MacDonald and Jane's (London, 1970) p.322

[221] Röding J H, op. cit., Vol.2, p.203

[222] Ibid., p.26: '*Vermittelst der Laternen die an verschiedenen Stellen des Schiffs und der Takelasche gehänkt werden, geschehen auch bey Nacht die Signale und diese Laternen heissen alsdann Signal-Laternen.*'

[223] Ibid., Vol.1, p.897: '*Es ist solche gewöhnlich eine bewegliche Maschine, die entweder ganz von Eisen oder auch von Kalk, Steinen und Eisenwerk zusammengesetzt wird.*'

[224] Falconer, W A, *A New Universal Dictionary of the Marine, improved*

[225] Röding J H, op. cit., Vol.2, p.349: '*Herr Chapman hat auch eine Art Rapert zu Drehbassen erfunden. [...] Dieses Rapert drehet sich um die Pfanne und kann eine dreypfündige Drehbasse tragen, die eben so genau gerichtet werden kann als eine Kanone und weit leichter als die auf Schwanenhälsen stehenden Drehbassen.*'

[226] Falconer, W, *An Universal Dictionary of the Marine* (London, 1780) repr. David & Charles (London, 1970) p.66P

[227] Röding, J H, op. cit., Vol.1, p.783

[228] Bobrik, E, *Handbuch der Praktischen Schiffahrtskunde* (Leipzig, 1848), repr. H Hamecher (Kassel, 1978) p.480

[229] Röding, J H, op. cit., Vol.1, p.782

[230] Ibid. Vol.4, pl.LI, fig.525

[231] Edson, M, ed. *Ship Modeller's Shop Notes*, Nautical Research Guild (Washington DC, 1979) p.126

[232] Röding, J H, op. cit., Vol.2, p.349: '*Diese Arten Raperten sind in einigem Betracht vortheilhaft, in andern aber nicht. Sie können geschwinder und mit weit weniger Mannschaft bewegt werden: ein einziger Mann kann einen 18 Pfünder nach vorne, nach hinten oder nach der Seite des feindlichen Schiffs richten, und in einerley Zeit zwey Schüsse für einen thun. Ihr Fehler aber und weswegen sie eben nicht gebraucht werden, besteht darin: daß sie weit schwerer sind als die gewöhnlichen Raperten und auch auf dem Deck weit mehr Platz einnehmen.*'

[233] Howard, Dr F *Sailing Ships of War 1400–1860*, Conway Maritime Press Ltd (London, 1979) p.213

[234] Atkinson & Clarke, *Naval Pocket Gunner* (London, 1814)

[235] Blanckley, T R, *A Naval Expositor* (London, 1750), repr. J Boudriot Publications (Rotherfield) p.14

[236] Falconer, W, *An Universal Dictionary of the Marine* (London, 1769), reprint of 1780 edition by David & Charles (Newton Abbot, Devon, 1870) p.328

[237] Smyth, W. H. *Sailor's Word Book*, London (1867), repr. Conway Maritime Press London (1991) p. 741

[238] Steel, D, *Elements of Mastmaking, Sailmaking and Rigging* (London, 1794), repr. E W Sweetman Co (New York, 1932) pp.47 & 48
and
Fincham, J, *A Treatise on Masting Ships & Mast Making* (London, 1829), reprint of 3rd Edition by Conway Maritime Press Ltd (London, 1982) pp.45–55

Appendices

Appendix 1: **TIMBER DIMENSIONS BETWEEN 1768 AND 1858**

SPECIFICATIONS OF OAK TIMBERS FOR LIGHT BUILT PRIVATEERS

Frederic H af Chapman, 1768

(Swedish measure 1ft = 296.9mm, 1in = 24.7mm)

Length of ships between pp (ft)	*110*	*100*	*90*	*80*	*70*	*60*	*50*
Extreme Breadth of ships (ft)	*29*	*27*	*25*	*22*	*19*	*17*	*15*
Name of parts							
The width of keel	11¾	11	10	9	8	7	5½
The width of the sternpost at the wing-transom	12½	11¾	10½	9¼	8	7	5½
The width of the stem at the wales	11¾	11	10	9	8	7	5½
The head of the stem, wide	15¾	14¾	13¾	12½	11¼	9½	7
The floor-timbers and futtocks, wide	8½	7⅞	7¼	6⅝	6	5½	5
The other frame parts are wide	8	7⅜	6¾	6⅛	5½	5	4½
The thickness of all frame-timbers							
At the floor-heads	7⅜	6¾	6⅛	5½	5	4½	4
At the lower deck	5⅛	4⅝	4⅛	3¾	3½	3¼	3
At the top below the gunwale	3¾	3½	3¼	3	2⅞	2¾	2¼
Thickness of the wales	5	4½	4¼	3⅞	3½	3¼	2¾
Thickness of the floor-planks	2¾	2⅝	2½	2⅜	2¼	2	1½
Thickness of side planks							
above the wales	2⅝	2½	2⅜	2¼	2⅛	1⅞	1⅜
below the gunwale	2⅛	2	1⅞	1¾	1½	1⅜	1¼
Thick-stuff at the floor-heads	3½	3¼	3	2⅞	2½	2	1¾
Orlop-beams	6½	–	–	–	–	–	–
Planks of the orlop-deck	2⅜	2¼	2⅛	2	1⅞	1½	1¼
Clamps of the first deck	4⅛	3¾	3⅜	3	2¾	2½	2
Deck beams, thick	9	8¾	7½	6¾	6	5	4
wide	10½	9¾	9	8¼	7½	6¼	5
The knees	5¾	5¼	4⅞	4½	4	3¼	2¾
The waterways	3¼	3	2¾	2½	2¼	2	1½
The clamps for the quarter-deck and forecastle	2⅞	2¾	2⅝	2½	2¼	2	1½
The deck beams for forecastle and quarter-deck, thick	5	5	4¾	4¼	4	3½	3
The knees of these beams	4	3¾	3½	3¼	3⅛	3	2¾
The head of the rudder athwart ship, is wide	15¾	14¾	13½	12	11	9¼	7
The rudder stock is wide	7¼	6½	5⅞	5⅜	4¾	4¼	3½
The thickness of the bit-pins	10¼	9	8	7½	7	6½	5

FRAME AND PLANK DIMENSIONS FOR VARIOUS MERCHANT SHIPS

Gustav David Klawitter, 1835

(Stettin measure: 1ft = 282.5mm, 11in = 23.5mm)

Normal lasts of 4000 pounds	*200*		*100*		*60*	
Length of keel (ft)	*100–90*		*85–70*		*70–60*	
Breadth extreme (ft)	*28–26*		*25–23*		*22–18*	
	Dimensions in inches					
Name of parts	*wide*	*thick*	*wide*	*thick*	*wide*	*thick*
The keel	11½	16	10½	14	9	11
The stem	16	10	14	9	13	8
The sternpost	12–16	10	11–15	9	10–14	8
The floor-timbers above keel	12	11½	11	11	10	9½
The floor-timbers at the bilge	–	10	–	10	–	8
The futtocks above the bilge	12	9	11	8½	10	8
The futtocks below the wales	–	8	–	7½	–	7
The futtocks above the wales	10	7	9	6½	7	6
The futtocks at the gunwale	--	5½	–	5½	–	4¾
The first futtocks	11	10¾	10	9	9	8
The keelson	15	18	13	16	11	14
The lower deck beams	12	11	12	10	–	–
The upper deck beams	12	9	12	8	10	8
The wales	10	4	10	4	10	3
The planks of the floor-heads	10	4	10	4	10	3
The waterway	10	5½	10	5	10	4
The planks above the wales	10	3	9	3	9	2½
The varnished planks	5	2½	5	2	4½	2
The painted plank	–	3	–	3	5	2½
The gunwale	12	3	12	2½	11	2½
The planks below the wales	10	3	10	2½	10	2½
The floor planks	–	3	–	2½	–	2½
The flat clamps (knees)	10	5	10	5	10	4
The ordinary clamps	10	3	10	3	10	3
The ceiling planks below clamp	10	2½	10	2½	10	2
The thick-stuff of the floor-head	10	4	10	4	10	3
The floor planks	10	2½	10	2½	10	2
The deck planks	8	2⅝	8	2	8	2

SPECIFICATIONS OF OAK TIMBERS FOR MERCHANTMEN

F H af Chapman, 1768

(Swedish measure 1ft = 296.9mm, 1in = 24.7mm)

Length of ships between pp (ft)	*110*	*100*	*90*	*80*	*70*	*60*	*50*
Extreme breadth of ships (ft)	*30¾ to 29¼*	*28½ to 27*	*26¾ to 24¾*	*24 to 22½*	*21½ to 20¼*	*19 to 18*	*16½ to 15½*
Name of parts							
The width of keel	13½	12½	11½	10½	9½	8	6
The width of floor-timbers	10½	9½	8¾	8	7½	6⅜	5½
The futtocks	9¾	9	8¼	7½	6½	5½	5
The top-timbers	9½	8½	7¾	7	6	5¼	5
The height or thickness of these frame pieces							
At the floor-heads	9¼	8½	7¾	7	6	5	4¾
Below the wales	7½1	6⅞	6⅛	5½	4⅞	4¼	3½
Below the gunwales at the top	4¼	4	3¾	3½	3¼	3	2½
Thickness of the wales	5½	5	4½	4	3⅝	3¼	2¾
Thickness of the floor-planks	3	2⅞	2¾	2⅝	2⅜	2	1½
Thickness of the waist rail	3⅞	3½	3¼	3	–	–	–
Thickness of filling planks	3	2⅞	2¾	2⅝	2⅜	2	1½
Thickness of planks above waistrail	2½	2⅜	2¼	2⅛	2	1¾	1¼
Keelson, square	13	12	11¼	10¼	9½	8	6
Thickness of thick-stuff at floor-heads	4¼	3⅞	3½	3¼	3	2¾	2¼
Thickness of foot-waling and thick-stuff in the hold	2¾	2⅝	2½	2⅜	2¼	1⅞	1½
The thickness of clamps at lower deck	5⅛	4¾	4⅜	4	3⅝	3¼	2¾
The deck beams of lower deck, thick	12¾	11¼	10	9	8	7	5½
Wide	13¾	12¼	11	10	9	8	6
The standard knees, as much as the timber provides, taper to	7⅞	7¼	6⅝	6	5¾	4¾	4
The deck's ledges	4	3⅝	3¼	3	2⅞	2¾	2½
Thickness of carlings	3½	3¼	3	2¾	2½	2¼	2
Thickness of binding strakes	4¾	4½	4¼	4	3¾	3½	3
Thickness of deck planks (fir)	2⅞	2¾	2⅝	2½	2¼	2	1½
Thickness of waterways	4⅛	3⅞	3⅝	3⅜	3⅛	2¾	1¾
The upper deck clamps	4⅛	3⅞	3⅝	3¼	3	2¾	1¾
The beams of the upper deck thick	8⅞	8¼	7½	6¾	6	5	4
wide	10	9¼	8½	7⅜	7	6	5
The knees are tapering to	5½	5	4⅝	4¼	4	3¾	3¼
The thickness of the ledges, upper deck	3½	3¼	3⅛	2⅞	2¾	2½	2
Thickness of carlings	2⅞	2¾	2⅝	2½	2¼	2	1½
Thickness of deck planks (fir)	2¾	2⅝	2½	2¼	2	1¾	1½
Thickness of the waterways	2⅞	2¾	2⅝	2½	2¼	2	1¾
The clamp thickness of forecastle and quarter-deck	3	2⅞	2¾	2⅝	2⅜	2⅛	1⅞
The beams below quarter-deck and forecastle	6⅛	5¾	5¼	4¾	4¼	3⅝	3
The knees taper to	4⅜	4	3¾	3½	3¼	3	2¼
The deck planks on forecastle and quarter-deck	2	2	2	2	1¾	1¾	1¼
The stern-timbers taper to	7½	7	6½	6	5½	5	4
The head of the rudder, wide	17⅜	15⅞	14⅞	14	12	11	8
The width of the stock	7½	7	6½	6	5½	5	4
Thickness of rudder at heel	6¾	6¼	5¾	5¼	4⅞	4½	3

DIMENSIONS OF THE MAIN-COMPONENTS FOR ALL KINDS OF SHIPS

C F Steinhaus, 1856

(Hamburg measure: 1ft = 286.5mm, 1in = 23.9mm)

Ship length at w/line (ft)	*40–50*		*50–60*		*60–70*		*70–85*		*85–100*		*100–115*	
w = wide, th = thick	*w*	*th*	*w*	*th*	*w*	*th*	*w*	*th*	*w*	*th*	*w*	*th*
Keel	12	7	13	8	14	9	15	11	16	13	17	13½
Stem in the waterline	–	7	–	8	–	9	–	11	–	13	–	14
Sternpost outside rabbet	–	7	–	8	–	9	–	11	–	13	–	14
Frames above the keel	9	6½	10	7	10½	7½	11	8	11½	8½	12	9
Frames at the floor-head	6	–	6½	–	7	–	7½	–	8	–	8½	–
Frames at the gunwale	4	–	4¼	–	4½	–	4	–	5	–	5¼	–
Wing-transom	–	9	–	10	–	11	–	12	–	13	–	14
Transoms	–	6½	–	7	–	7½	–	8	–	8½	–	9
Keelson	12	10	13	11	14	12	15	13	16	14	17	15
Clamps for upper deck	9	5	9	5½	10	6	10½	6½	11	7	11½	7½
Thick-stuff	10	5	10½	5½	11	6	11½	6½	12	7	12½	7½
Deck beams	5½	9	5¾	9½	6	10	6½	10½	7	11	7½	11½
Beams for lower deck	–	–	–	–	8	10	8½	10½	9	11	9½	11½
Waterway	10	6	10½	6	11	6½	11½	7	12	7½	12/8	
Gunwale	–	2½	–	2½	–	3	–	3	–	3	-	3½
Wales	8	3	8	3½	9	3½	9	3¾	9	4	9	4
Outside planks*)	–	2	–	2½	–	2½	–	3	–	3	–	3
Thick-stuff at floor-head	8	3	8	3½	9	3½	9	3¾	9	4	9	4
Ceiling	–	2	–	2½	–	2½	–	3	–	3	–	3
Rails	–	3	–	3	–	3	–	3	–	3½	–	3¾
Deck planks	–	2	–	2½	–	2½	–	3	–	3	–	3
Pawl-bits	11	13	12	14	12½	14½	13	15	14	16	15	17
Bits	–	5	–	6 ¼	–	6½	–	6¾	–	7	–	7½

* Garboard strakes are 1 inch thicker

Appendix 2: MAST AND SPAR DIMENSIONS BETWEEN 1735 AND 1858

DIMENSIONS OF MASTS AND SPARS FOR BRIGANTINE (1) AND TOPSAIL SCHOONER (2)

C F Steinhaus, 1858

		(1)	(2)
Main mast including head	B	x 3.2	x 3.1 = MM
Length of head	MM	x 0.106	x 0.106
Fore mast including head	MM	x 0.944	x 0.958 = FM
Length of head	FM	x 0.106	x 0.106
Main topmast to first stop	MM	x 0.325	x 0.325 = MTM
between first and second stop	MTM	x 0.42	x 0.435
Fore topmast to first stop	FM	x 0.333	x 0.294 = FTM
between first and second stop	FTM	x 0.4	x 0.5
Bowsprit outside stem	B	x 0.739	x 0.654
Jib-boom outside bowsprit			
to first stop	B	x 0.652	x 0.619
between first and second stop	B	x 0.5	x 0.429
Fore yard, whole length	L	x 0.609	x 0.6 = FY
Yard-arms	FY	x 0.05	x 0.05
Topsail yard	FY	x 0.705	x 0.717 = TY
Yard-arms	TY	x 0.078	x 0.078
Topgallant yard	TY	x 0.648	x 0.621
Yard-arms	TY	x 0.083	x 0.083
Main yard, whole length	L	x 0.565	– = MY
Yard-arms	MY	x 0.054	–
Main topsail yard	MY	x 0.705	– = MTY
Yard-arms	MTY	x 0.079	–
Main topgallant yard	MTY	x 0.648	– = MTGY
Yard-arms	MTGY	x 0.083	–
Main boom	L	x 0.511	x 0.55 = MB
Main gaff	MB	x 0.708	x 0.65 = MG
Fore gaff	MG	x 0.722	x 0.679
Peak	MG	x 0.148	x 0.148
Fore boom		as long as circumstances allow	
Lower studding sail yard	FY	x 0.2	x 0.2
Upper studding sail yard	TGY	x 0.5	x 0.5
Studding sail boom	relevant Y	x 0.5	x 0.5

Diameter of lower masts	
Largest	every 5ft length x 1½in = D
Heel	⅝ D
Head	½ or ⅓ D
Topmasts	
Largest to first stop	every 4ft length x 1in = D
At the first stop	⅞ D
At the second stop	⅝ D
At the truck	⅓ D
Bowsprit	
Largest	similar to lower masts = D
At the inner end	1 D
At the outer end	⅔ D
Jib-boom	
Largest	every 4ft length x 1¾in = D
At the inner end	1 or ⅞ D
At the outer end	⅔ D
Flying jib-boom	
Largest	every 3ft length x 1½in = D
At both ends	⅔ D
If jib- and flying jib-boom are made from one piece, they are the same	
At the stop	⅔ D
At the outer end	½ D
Yards	
Largest	every 4ft length x 1 in = D
Arms of lower yard	½ D
Arms of topsail yard	½ D
Arms of topgallant yard and studding sail yard	⅓ to ½ D
Booms	
Largest	every 4ft length x 1in = D
At the inner end	⅔ D
At the outer end	¾ D
Gaffs	
Largest at the throat	every 4ft length x 1in = D
At the outer end	⅜ to ⅝ D
Studding sail booms	
Largest	relevant yard-arm = D
Both ends	⅔ D

MAST AND SPAR DIMENSIONS OF THE SCHOONER ST. ANN 1735

according to the contemporary draught, entitled:
'The St. Ann A Portugal Scooner That Arriev'd Wth. A Packet From Lisbon In July 1736 And Was Taken Off At Portsmouth In August Following.'

(English measure)

Masts and Spars	Length (ft & in)	
Main Mast From Deck to the Hounds	44	3
Pole Head	5	9
Whole length	56	2
Gaff	10	1
Fore Mast From Deck to hounds	41	10
Pole Head	6	5
Whole length	54	10
Gaff	10	1
Bowsprit Before the Stem	15	10
Whole length	20	9
X jacke y. (Crossjack yard)	29	10
Top's y. (Topsail yard)	26	4
Top gall. or (Topgallant yard)		
Pidgeon each	13	0
Flying Gibb (Jib boom)	13	0
Boom	30	8

DIMENSIONS OF MASTS AND YARDS FOR A SCHOONER OF 110 TONS

David Steel, 1794

(English measure)

Mast and yards	Length (ft)	Diameter (in)
Main mast	75	15
Top gallant mast	32	7½
Topsail yard	38	6
Spread yard	47	7
Top gallant yard	27	5½
Square sail yard	38	7½
Fore mast	66	15
Top gallant mast	26	6½
Topsail yard	30	6½
Top gallant yard	25	5
Spread yard	40	7
Gaff	22	6½
Bowsprit	50	14½
Boom	47	10½
Gaff	28	7

VARIOUS PROPORTIONS FOR THE MASTING OF SCHOONERS

C F Steinhaus, 1858

Length in the water-line (L)
Breadth (B)

Position of masts	
For topsail schooners:	
Fore mast	0.256 L aft of stem perpendicular
Distance between fore and main mast	0.348 L
For fore and aft schooners:	
Fore mast	0.250 L aft of stem perpendicular
Distance between fore and main mast	0.375 L
Rake of masts:	
Fore mast	10–11°
Main mast	11–12°
Angle of bowsprit against the horizon	19–22°

DIMENSIONS OF MASTS AND SPARS FOR THE SCHOONER *SULTANA*

American schooner, built after 1760 and bought for the Royal Navy in 1767. Dimensions taken after purchase, according to a Navy Board report.

(English measure)

Masts and spars	*Length (ft*	*& in)*	*Diameter (in)*
Main Mast	54	7	13¾
Polehead	6	0	6 upper part; 8½ lower part
Boom	37	3	7¾
Gaff	17	5½	4¾
Fore Mast	53	4	13⅞
Polehead	5	7	5½ upper part; 8 lower part
Gaff	15	0	4½
Cross-jack Yard	23	3	5
Bowsprit	27	8	11¾
Flying jib-boom	21	2	4¾

FRENCH EIGHTEENTH-CENTURY SCHOONER SPECIFICATIONS

E Pâris, *Souvenirs de Marine*, Vol. 2 /112

1.) Schooner From Brest Harbour 1769 (fore-and-aft schooner)

(feet and inches are in English measure)

	(m)	*(ft)*	*(in)*
Length between perpendiculars	15.727	51	4½
Extreme breadth	3.333	10	11
Length/Breadth ratio	4.7 : 1		
Armament	6 x 4-pdr.		

Name	*Length (m)*	*(ft)*	*(in)*	*Diameter (m)*	*(ft)*	*(in)*
Main Mast	15.180	49	9½	0.215	0	8½
Masthead	1.220	4	0			
Fore Mast	13.700	44	11⅓	0.200	0	8
Masthead	1.850	6	0			
Main Boom	9.630	31	5½			
Main Gaff	3.700	12	1⅔			
Fore Boom	5.180	17	0			
Fore Gaff	2.960	9	8½			
Boom (Bowsprit?)	5.100	16	8¾			

2.) Masting of other eighteenth-century schooners of 21 metres length, according to a contract

Breadth = 0.266 x length = 5.586m

Masts and spars	*Length (x breadth)*	*Diameter*	*Masthead*
Main mast	3.00 x breadth	1/46	⅛
Fore mast	2.91 x breadth	1/45	⅛
Bowsprit	1.50 x breadth	1/27	
Main topmast	1.60 x breadth	1/53	¼
Fore topmast	1.54 x breadth	1/52	⅛
Jib boom	1.00 x breadth	1/50	
Boom	0.66 x ship's length	1/57	
Gaff	0.34 x ship's length	1/52	
Gaff	0.29 x ship's length	1/50	
Fore spread yard	0.464 x ship's length	1/50	
Topsail yard	0.352 x ship's length	1/56	
Mainmast position	0.024 x ship's length aft of centre		
Fore mast position	3.720m forward of centre		
Rake of masts	1/12 (7–8°)		
Angle of bowsprit	⅓ (30°)		

The proportional dimensions in direct measurements
(those in brackets differ from measurements by E Pâris)

Name	*Length (m)*	*(ft)*	*(in)*	*Diameter (m)*	*(ft)*	*(in)*
Main mast	16.758	55	0	0.364	1	2⅓
	(16.710)			(0.350)		
Masthead	2.095	6	10½			
	(3.090)					
Fore mast	16.255	53	4	0.361	1	2⅙
	(16.260)					
Masthead	2.032	6	8			
	(2.020)					
Bowsprit	8.379	27	6	0.310	1	0
Main topmast	8.938	29	4	0.169		6⅔
	(8.950)					
Masthead	2.236	6	9¾			
	(2.240)					
Fore topmast	8.602	28	2⅔	0.165		6½
	(8.910)			(0.160)		
Masthead	2.150	7	½			
	(2.230)					
Jib boom	5.586	18	4	0.112		4⅓
(5.580)				(0.110)		
Boom	13.860	45	5⅔	0.243		9½
	(13.260)			(0.230)		
Gaff	7.140	23	5	0.137		5⅓
				(0.130)		
Gaff	6.090	20	0	0.122		4¾
(0.120)						
Fore spread yard	9.744	32	0	0.195		7⅔
	(9.740)			(0.180)		
Topsail yard	7.392	24	3	0.132		5¼
	(7.390)			(0.150)		

The mast positions given by Paris are incorrect. 0.024 x length between perpendiculars would be 504mm. By adding 3.720m for the fore mast position, the distance between both masts would only amount to 4.224m, however the fore gaff's length alone is 6.090m. Distance between masts is by Steinhaus 7.308m and by Fincham 8.064m.

TABLE OF THE MASTS AND SPARS ETC. FOR A US NAVY SCHOONER FROM 1826

Prepared by the Board of Navy Commissioners and approved by the Secretary of the Navy.

The second dimensions are minor differences between the 1826 figures and 'A Table Of Spars &C. For All Classes Of Vessels, USN' by W N Brady (1876), while varying dimensions for USN schooner *Grampus* of 10 guns from 1821 are recorded below the Brady figures.

Hull dimensions of the schooner in question were not provided. A comparison with dimensions by Steinhaus led to an approximate length between perpendiculars of 85–90ft and a width of 25ft. USN schooners of that size were the Alligator class of 1821 with a length between perpendiculars of 86ft and a moulded beam of 24ft 9in.

USN schooner *Grampus* of 10 guns from 1821

Length between pp.	92ft 6in
Breadth	24ft 6in
Depth	9ft 6in
(English measure)	

Name	Length (ft)	Length (in)	Diameter (in)	Masthead/Yard-arm (ft)	Masthead/Yard-arm (in)
Main mast	78	8	20.5	8	
Brady			20. 3		
Grampus			18. 5		
Main topmast	26	2	7. 5		
Main topgallant mast	13	1	5		
Main flag pole	3		2. 5		
Brady	6				
Grampus	1				
Fore mast	75	8	22	8	
Brady			21. 3		
Grampus			20		
Fore topmast	26	2	8. 5		
Brady			7. 5		
Fore topgallant mast	13	1	5. 5		
Brady			5		
Fore flag pole	3		2. 5		
Brady	6				
Grampus	1				
Fore yard	50		11.5	2	6
Brady			11. 3		
Fore topsail yard	33	4	7. 5	2	6
Brady			7. 4		
Grampus				3	
Fore topgallant yard	22	2	5	1	
Brady			4. 5		
Grampus	22				

Name	Length (ft)	Length (in)	Diameter (in)	Masthead/Yard-arm (ft)	Masthead/Yard-arm (in)
Bowsprit	29	1	18		
Jib boom	37		11		
Grampus			9		
Main boom	50		11. 5		
Brady			11		
Grampus	54	9	12		
Main gaff	25		8		
Brady			8. 5	5	
Grampus	27	4			
Fore gaff	25		8. 5		
Brady			8		
Grampus	27	4			
Ring-tail boom	25		6. 5		
Ring-tail yard	8	4	3		
Lower swinging boom	22		5		
Brady			4. 6		
Grampus	31	6	7		
Lower studding sail yard	8	8	3		
Brady	11		2. 6		
Fore top studding sail boom	26	6	5. 5		
Brady	25		5. 3		
Fore top studding sail yard	12		3. 5		
Brady	14	2	3		
Fore topgallant studding sail boom	17	6	4		
Brady	16	8	3. 6		
Fore topgallant studding sail yard	6	3	2. 5		
Brady	10	1	2. 2		
Square-sail boom	45		9. 7		
Grampus			9		
Square-sail yard	22	8	5		
Grampus	13	11	4. 5		
Gaff topsail yard	22	8	4. 5		
Jack gaff (Brady)	9		3		

Dolphin Striker (Brady) length for schooners is governed by steeve of bowsprit

PROPORTIONS FOR MASTS, YARDS, BOOMS &c. OF SCHOONERS

J Fincham, 1854; 1st edition 1829

(English measure)

	Length	*Breadth*
1.) Common Schooner	90ft 0in	24ft 0in
2.) Bermuda Schooner	95ft 0in	24ft 7in
3.) Bermuda Schooner	94ft 7in	24ft 0in
4.) Three-masted Schooner	78ft 7in	21ft 6in

Masts or spars	*Known quantity x*	*1.)*	*2.)*	*3.)*	*4.)*
Main-mast hounded	Breadth	2.61	2.75	2.83	2.78
Main-mast headed	Hounded length	0.12	0.13	0.13	0.10
Fore-mast hounded	Main-mast hounded	0.92	0.97	0.91	0.95
Fore-mast headed	Hounded length	0.12	0.13	0.13	0.10
Mizen-mast hounded	Main-mast hounded	–	–	–	0.74
Mizen-mast headed	Hounded length	–	–	–	0.10
Main-top-mast hounded	Breadth	0.83	1.00	0.99	0.25
Main-top-mast pole	Hounded length	0.50	0.50	0.52	0.31
Fore-top-mast hounded	Main-top-mast hound	1.00	0.90	1.00	0.92
Fore-top-mast headed	Hounded length	0.50	0.50	0.54	0.31
Mizen-top-mast hound	Main top-mast hound	–	–	–	0.90
[Pole dimension not provided but probably similar to Main topmast pole]					
Bowsprit	Fore-mast	0.49	0.45	0.50	0.35
Fore-yard	Length	0.572	0.48	0.56	0.50
Fore-top-sail-yard	Fore-yard	0.71	0.747	0.585	.70
Fore-top-gallant-yard	Ditto	0.458	0.483	0.422	0.48
Square-sail-yard	Length	0.52	0.44	0.47	0.50
Main-top-sail-yard	Square-sail-yard	0.77	0.75	0.64	0.607
Main-top-gallant-yard	Ditto	0.50	0.48	0.46	–
Main-boom	Length	0.70	0.66	0.68	0.226
Main-gaff	Boom	0.53	0.44	0.48	–
Fore-gaff	Main-gaff	0.73	1.00	0.10	1.06
Mizen-gaff	Ditto	–	–	–	0.90
Mizen or driver boom	Length	–	–	–	0.39
Jib-boom	Bowsprit	0.87	1.30	1.20	0.97
Flying jib-boom	Jib-boom	–	–	–	0.40
Swinging boom	Fore-yard	–	–	–	0.50
Ring-tail boom	Length	–	–	–	0.21
Square-sail-boom	Ditto	0.40	0.37	0.44	0.22
Main-mast from the middle (abaft)	Length of water-line	0.046	0.108	0.084	0.033
Fore-mast before the middle	Ditto	0.338	0.279	0.31	0.295
Mizen-mast abaft the middle	Ditto	–	–	–	0.366
Main-mast to rake	In 12 feet	24in	24in	33in	27in
Fore-mast to rake	Ditto	15in	16in	36in	24in
Bowsprit to stive	Ditto	34in	24in	32in	22in
Main-mast below load-waterline	Breadth	0.26	0.31	0.31	0.277
Fore-mast ditto	Ditto	0.22	0.27	0.21	0.17
Centre of effort from middle of length of water-line	Length on water-line	0.02	0.023	0.025	0.065
Height of centre of effort above load-water-line	Breadth	1.50	1.50	1.56	1.539
Area of sails	Area of load-water Section	3.63	3.54	3.61	4.944
Moment of sails	Ditto	138.00	128.60	132.50	164.40
Bowsprit housed from the fore part of the stem	Breadth	0.46	0.448	0.45	0.32
Difference of draught of water excess aft		12in	24in	48in	36in

Tables in Fincham's *Treatise On Masting Ships & Mastmaking*, pages 73, 76 and 77, about schooner mast and yard lengths are only a mathematical adaptation of the afore specified proportions for vessel from 50–98ft length and 12–25ft breadth. Dimensions prepared in additional tables on pages 171–72 are based on the following proportions:

Breadth (B)
Length (L)

Main-mast hounded	2.56	B
Main-mast headed	0.165	Main-mast hounded
Main-mast housed	0.2	Main-mast hounded
Main-top-mast to stops	0.51	Main-mast hounded
Main-top-mast pole	0.11	Main-mast hounded
Fore-mast hounded	2.465	B
Fore-mast headed	0.173	Fore-mast hounded
Fore-mast housed	0.193	Fore-mast hounded
Fore-top-mast to stops	0.375	Fore-mast hounded
Fore-top-gallant pole	0.19	Fore-mast hounded
Sky-sail pole	0.065	Fore-mast hounded
Bowsprit, whole length	0.62	Fore-mast hounded
Bowsprit housed	0.225	Fore-mast hounded
Jib-boom whole	0.56	Fore-mast hounded
Main-gaff	0.35	L
Main-boom	0.654	L
Fore-yard	0.55	L
Fore-yard-arm	0.04	Fore-yard
Fore-top-sail-yard	0.45	L
Fore-top-sail-yard-arm	0.08	Fore-top-sail-yard
Fore-top-gallant-yard	0.32	L
Fore-top-gallant-yard-arm	0.04	Fore-top-gallant-yard
Fore-gaff	0.317	L

Largest diameters:

Lower masts	0.025	Length of mast hounded
Main-boom	0.0175	Length of boom
Bowsprit, common schooner	0.046	Length of bowsprit
Bowsprit, Bermuda schooner	0.05	Length of bowsprit
Top-mast	0.025	Length of top-mast
Gaffs	0.021	Length of gaff
Lower yard	0.019	Length of yard
Square-sail-yard	0.013	Length of yard
Top-sail-yard	0.017	Length of yard
Top-gallant-yard	0.017	Length of yard
Royal-yard	0.015	Length of yard
Jib-boom	0.025	Length of jib-boom
Flying jib-boom	0.015	Length of flying jib-boom
Swinging studding-sail-boom	0.017	Length of swinging studding sail boom
Square-sail-boom	0.017	Length of square-sail boom
Ring-tail-boom	0.015	Length of ring-tail boom

The Proportion that the small diameter commonly bears to the large:

Lower Mast	hounds	⁹⁄₁₀ or ¾
	head	½ or ⅔
	heel	⅚
Top-masts	hounds	¹⁰⁄₁₃ or ⅚
	head	½ or ³⁄₇
Bowsprit	heel	1
	head	⅔
Lower yard yard-arm	½	
Square-sail yard-arm	½	
Top-sail yard-arm	¾	
Top-gallant and royal	³⁄₇ or ½	
Main-boom	outer end	¾
	inner end	⁵⁄₇
Jib-boom	outer end	⅔ or ¾
	inner end	1
Jib and flying jib-boom in one	at the stops	⅔
	the outer end	½
Studding-sail-boom, swinging or lower	outer end	⅔ or ¾
	inner end	⅔ or ¾
Gaffs	outer end	⅜ or ⁵⁄₉

Appendix 3: RIGGING DIMENSIONS 1818–1864

TABLES OF THE LENGTHS AND DIMENSIONS OF THE STANDING AND RUNNING RIGGING, WITH THE SPECIES, SIZE, AND NUMBER, OF BLOCKS, HEARTS, DEAD-EYES &C.

Schooner of 180 tons
David Steel, 1818

(English measure)

Names of the standing rope and running rigging	in	fthm	Blocks type	size	number
Bowsprit					
Woolding	4	36	–	–	–
Shrouds	4	12	*H	7	2
Collar	4	3	H	7	2
Seizing	1	6	–	–	–
Lashing	1½	4	–	–	–
Lanyard	2	4	–	–	–
Bobstay, cabled	5	10	H	7	2
Collar	5	3	H	7	2
Seizing	¾	12	–	–	–
Lashing	1½	4	–	–	–
Lanyard	2	5	–	–	–
Jib					
Horses	2	16	–	–	–
Guy-pendent	3	16	–	–	–

Names of the standing rope and running rigging	in	fthm	Blocks type	size	number
Fall	1½	18	D	8	2
			S	8	2
Strapping	2½	2	–	–	–
Out-Hauler	3	6	–	–	–
Tackle-Fall	1½	10	S	6	*2
Martingale-Stay	3	20	T	–	2
Stay	4	17	–	–	–
Tackle-Fall	1½	10	S	6	2
Strapping	2	1	–	–	–
Haliard	2½	36	S	8	*2
Strapping	2½	1	–	–	–
Down-Hauler	1½	14	S	6	1
Sheets, single	2	18	–	–	–
Pendents	3	6	S	7	2
Flying Jib					
Guys	2	15	–	–	–
Martingale-Stay	2	14	–	–	–
Stay	2½	20	–	–	–
Haliard	1½	24	S	6	1

Names of the standing rope and running rigging	in	fthm	Blocks type	size	number
Down-Hauler	1½	14	S	6	1
Sheets	1½	18	–	–	–
Strapping	1½	1	–	–	–
Foremast					
Girtlines	2	28	S	7	1
Strapping	2½	2	–	–	–
Tackle-Pendent	4	5	T	–	2
Runner of Tackle	3½	28	S	11	*2
			D	8	*2
Fall of Tackle	2	60	S	8	*2
Strapping	2½	3	–	–	–
Shrouds, cabled 4 Pair	5½	72	D.E.	8	8
Seizing, Eye	¾	12	–	–	–
Throat	¾	12	–	–	–
End	¾	12	–	–	–
Lanyard	3	40	–	–	–
Ratline	1	85	–	–	–
Stay, 4 Strands, cabled	7	17	D.E.	7	1
Seizing	¾	10	–	–	–
Lanyard	3	5	–	–	–
Preventer-Stay, 4 Strands, cabled	5½	17	D.E.	6	1
Lanyard	2½	4	–	–	–
Seizing	¾	8	–	–	–
Forestay-Sail Haliard	3	36	S	10	2
Sheets	3	22	–	–	–
Down-Hauler	2	12	S	6	1
Catharpin-Legs	3	4	T	–	2
Seizing	¾	12	–	–	–
Lanyard	1	3	–	–	–
Fore-yard					
Jears	2½	55	D	8	2
Strapping	3	4	–	–	–
Seizing	¾	6	–	–	–
Lashing Mast Head	1½	3	–	–	–
at the Yard	1½	2	–	–	–
Horses	2½	9	–	–	–
Stirrups	3	2	–	–	–
Braces	2½	54	D	7	2
			S	7	2
Strapping	3	3	–	–	–
Seizing	¾	12	–	–	–
Lashing	1	3	–	–	–
Lifts	3½	44	S	11	2
Short Span	3½	3	–	–	–
Seizing	1½	4	–	–	–
Truss-Pendents	3½	16	–	–	–
Bowlines	2	30	S	7	2
Bridles	2	2	–	–	–
Strapping	2	1	–	–	–
Sheets, cabled	3	44	S	8	4
Strapping	3	2	–	–	–
Seizing	¾	4	–	–	–
Jackstay	3½	11	D.E.	7	2
Lanyard	1½	3	–	–	–
Studdingsail Haliard	2	50	S	7	4
Sheets	2	8	–	–	–
Tack	2	40	S	7	2
Strapping	2	3	–	–	–
Gaff					
Throat Haliard	3½	50	D.I.bd.	11	2
Peek Haliard	3	48	D	9	1
			S	9	2

Names of the standing rope and running rigging	in	fthm	Blocks type	size	number
Sheets	3	52	S	9	*4
Vang-Pendents	3	10	S	7	2
Falls	2½	28	S	7	*2
Lacing Mast	1½	12	–	–	–
Gaff	1	20	–	–	–
Peek-Brails	1½	35	S	6	4
Throat-Brails	2	32	S	6	2
Middle-Brails	1½	22	S	6	2
Foot-Brails	1½	38	S	6	2
Throat Down-Hauler	1½	20	S	6	2
Peek Down-Hauler	2	26	S	6	1
Strapping	3½	2½	–	–	–
	2½	8	–	–	–
Fore-Topmast					
Shrouds, 2 Pair	3	44	T	–	8
Seizing	¾	4	–	–	–
Lanyard	1	6	–	–	–
Ratline	1	20	–	–	–
Standing Backstays, 1 Pair	3½	22	T	–	4
Tackle	1½	14	S	6	*4
Strapping	1½	2	–	–	–
Stay, 4 Strands, cabled	3½	22	T	–	2
Lanyard	1½	4	–	–	–
Fore-Topsail					
Tye	3	10	S	8	2
Strapping	2½	2	–	–	–
Haliards	2	55	D	6	1
			S	6	1
Strapping	2	1	–	–	–
Horses	2	7	–	–	–
Braces	2	50	S	6	2
Strapping	2	1	–	–	–
Lifts	2½	42	Sis.	12	2
Seizing	¾	5	–	–	–
Clueline	2	48	S	6	2
Strapping	2	2	–	–	–
Buntline	1½	17	S	6	2
Strapping	2	½	–	–	–
Bowlines	1½	46	S	6	2
Bridles	1½	2	T	–	2
Reef-Tackle Pendent	2	26	S	6	2
Strapping	1½	1	–	–	–
Sheets	3	40	D	9	1
			Sho.	9	2
Strapping for Sheet Blocks	3	4	–	–	–
Studdingsail Haliard	2	56	S	6	2
Sheet	1½	22	S	6	2
Tack	2	18	S	6	2
Fore-Topgallant-Mast					
Shrouds, 2 Pair	2	26	T	–	8
Lanyard	1	8	–	–	–
Standing Backstay, 1 Pair	2	38	T	–	4
Lanyard	1	8	–	–	–
Stay, cabled, 4 Strands	2	24	–	–	–
Fore-Topgallant Yard					
Tye	2	38	D	7	1+T3
			S	7	1
Strapping	2½	1	–	–	–
Horses	1½	6	–	–	–
Braces	1	46	S	4	4
Strapping	1	1½	–	–	–
Lifts, single	1½	14	T	–	2

Names of the standing rope and running rigging	in	fthm	Blocks type	size	number
Cluelines	1	50	S	4	2
Strapping	1½	2	–	–	–
Bowlines	1	50	S	4	2
Bridles	1	1½	T	–	2
Earing and Lacing	¾	3	–	–	–
Sheets	1	40	Sho.	4	2
			S	4	2
Strapping	1	1	–	–	–
Main-Mast					
Girtlines	2½	30	S	7	1
Strapping	2½	2	–	–	–
Tackle-Pendents, cabled	6	5	S	11	*2+T2
Runner of Tackle	3½	28	D	8	2
Falls of Tackle	2	62	S	8	*2
Shrouds, cabled 3 Pair	5½	54	D.E.	8	6
Seizing Eye	¾	12	–	–	–
Throat	¾	12	–	–	–
End	¾	12	–	–	–
Lanyard	3	30	–	–	–
Ratlines	1	70	–	–	–
Stay, cabled, 4 Strands	5½	11	–	–	–
Luff Tackles, 2	1½	36	D	9	*2
			S	9	*2
Strapping	2½	3	–	–	–
Main-Topmast					
Shrouds, 2 Pair	2½	44	T	–	8
Standing Backstay, cabled, 2 Pair	3½	24	T	–	4
Stay, cabled, 4 Strands	3½	16	T	–	2
Lanyard	1½	3	–	–	–
Staysail Haliard	1½	27	S	6	1
Strapping	1½	½	–	–	–
Sheet	1½	24	–	–	–
Tack	1½	22	–	–	–
Down-Hauler	1½	20	S	5	1
Strapping	1½	½	–	–	–
Main-Topgallant-Mast					
Staysail Sheets	1½	28	S	5	2
Tack	1½	10	T	–	2
Down-Hauler	1	20	S	4	1
Strapping	1½	2	–	–	–
Studdingsail Haliard	1½	40	S	5	6
Sheet	1½	16	–	–	–
Tack	1½	26	S	5	4
Boom-Tricingline	1½	10	S	5	2
Strapping	2	1½	–	–	–
	1½	6	–	–	–

Names of the standing rope and running rigging	in	fthm	Blocks type	size	number
Necessary Ropes					
Cat-Fall	2½	24	D.I.bd.	12	2
Fish Tackle Fall	2	25	D.do.sc.	10	*1
			S.do.sc.	10	1
Strapping	3	3	–	–	–
Seizing	¾	5	–	–	–
Stopper, Sheet Anchor	3½	4	–	–	–
Stopper, Bower	3½	4	–	–	–
Shank Painter, cabled, Sheet Anchor	2½	2½	–	–	–
Bower	2	2	–	–	–
Buoy-Rope, cabled, Sheet Anchor	3	24	–	–	–
Bower	3	24	–	–	–
Ropes, Entering 4	3	8	–	–	–
Slings, Buoy	2½	16	–	–	–
Lanyards	1½	4	–	–	–
Seizing	¾	15	–	–	–
Cable Bends	1½	28	–	–	–
Haliard, Ensign	¾	12	–	–	–
For fitting Ensign, Jack, Signal Flags	¾	18	–	–	–
For different uses of the Ship	–	–	Sn.I.bd	10	1
	–	–	Sn.I.bd.	11	1
	–	–	S.I.bd.	9	*4
Gig					
Main and Fore Haliard	1	8	–	–	–
Main and Fore Sheet	1	4	–	–	–
Life Boat					
Fore Haliard and Sheet	1	4	–	–	–
Main Haliard and Sheet	1	4	–	–	–
Brails	¾	5	–	–	–

Steel did not mention boom topping lifts and boom sheets in these tables, and certain ropes, such as the gaff, are referred to only once under **Foremast** and not repeated under **Mainmast**.

Abbreviations
D = Double Block
D.E. = Dead Eyes
do.sc .= double scored
H = Hearts
I.bd. = Iron bound
S = Single Block
Sho . = Shouldered Block
Sis. = Sister Block
Sn = Snatch Block
T = Thimbles
* = with hook and thimble

STANDING RIGGING DIMENSIONS

C F Steinhaus, 1856

(Hamburg measure)

Loading capacity in Hamburg	Schooner	
Commerce lasts to 6000 pounds	50	40
Circumference	(in)	(in)
Main and fore shrouds	6	6
Number of shrouds on each side	4	4
Ratlines	1	1
Main and fore stay	6	6
Main and fore topmast standing back stays	5	4½
Jib stay sail stay (Jib guys ? in more)	3½	3¼

Commerce lasts to 6000 pounds	50	40
Circumference	(in)	(in)
Main and fore topmast shrouds	3¼	3
Main and fore topgallant mast standing back stays	3¼	3
Main and fore topgallant shrouds	2¾	2½
Main topgallant stay	3	3
Fore topgallant stay	3	2¾
Flying jib stay sail stay and flying jib guy	3	2¾
Fore royal stay	1¼	1⅛
Main and fore yard lifts	3	2¾
Main and fore topgallant yard lifts	2¾	2½
Boom topping lifts	3¾	3½

Commerce lasts to 6000 pounds Circumference	*50 (in)*	*40 (in)*
RUNNING RIGGING DIMENSIONS		
Fore braces and clew garnet lines	2	1¾
Fore sheets	2¾	2½
Fore buntlines	1½	1½
Fore tacks	3	2¾
Fore topsail tye	3¼	3
Fore topsail braces, halyard, clew-lines, buntlines	1¾	1½
Fore top-stay sail halyard and sheet pendants	1¾	1½
Reef tackle pendants	1⅛	1
Reef tackle falls and fore top-stay sail downhauler	1⅛	1
Jib and upper studding sail halyard	2	1¾
Jib downhauler and sheets, sheet pendants 1 in more	1¾	1½
Schooner sail sheets	2¾	2½
Peak and throat halyards	1¾	1¾
Main a. fore topgallant yard halyard	1¾	1½
Main tackle runner, halyard,	1	1
Clew-line, braces and buntlines	1	1
Topgallant sail sheets	1¾	1½
Cat-fall	2½	2¼
Shank-painter	4	3½
Cat-head stopper	4½	4¼

SOME LINEAR MEASUREMENTS AND WEIGHTS AS USED IN THIS BOOK

1ft = 12in = 12 lines
1ft = 11 thumbs (Amsterdam)

French ft = 324.9mm, in = 27.1mm, fathom = 5ft
English ft = 304.8mm, in = 25.4mm, fathom = 6ft
Swedish ft = 296.9mm, in = 24.7mm, fathom = 6ft
Stettin ft = 282.5mm, in = 23.5mm, fathom = 6ft
Hamburg ft = 286.6mm, in = 23.9mm, fathom = 6ft
Danish (& Rhineland) ft = 313.9mm, in = 26.16mm, fathom = 6ft
Norwegian ft = 313.7mm, in = 26.15mm, fathom = 6ft
Amsterdam ft = 283.13mm, thumb = 25.74mm, fathom = 6ft

English ton = 1016kg = 2240lbs to 453.6g
French ton = 978kg = 2000 livres to 489g
Swedish Last = 2448kg = 5760lbs to 425g
Stettin Last = 1874.4kg = 4000lbs to 468.6g
Hamburg Commerce Last = 2906.4kg = 6000lbs to 484.4g

A TABLE SHOWING THE LENGTH AND SIZE OF STANDING AND RUNNING RIGGING FOR ALL CLASSES OF VESSELS IN THE US NAVY

Schooner extract
W N Brady, 1876

The size (circumference) is measured in inches and the length in fathoms

Name of Rigging	*No*	*Size*	*Length*
BOWSPRIT GEAR			
Gammoning (iron for all classes of vessels)			
Shrouds (pairs)	1	5½	8
Collars for Shrouds	1	4¾	2
Lanyards for Shrouds (four-stranded)	2	2¼	8
Bobstays (pairs)	1	6	7
Collars for Bobstays	1	6	2
Lanyards for Bobstays (four-stranded)	1	3	7
JIB-BOOM GEAR			
Jib Stay	1	5	28
Jib Guys (pairs)	1	5	16
Foot Ropes	2	2½	9
Martingale Stay	1	5½	4½
Martingale Back ropes (pair)	1	3½	8
Halliards	1	2¾	26
Downhaul	1	2	21
Sheets	2	2¾	40
Pendants	2	4½	6
FLYING JIB-BOOM GEAR			
Flying-Jib Stay	1	3½	27
Flying-Jib Guys	2	2¾	24
Foot Ropes	2	2¼	6
Martingale Stay	1	3¾	10
Halliards	1	2	33
Downhaul	1	1¾	26
Sheets	2	2	24
Heel-rope	1	1½	14

Name of Rigging	*No*	*Size*	*Length*
FORE-MAST AND YARD GEAR			
Pendants (pairs)	1	6	4
Shrouds (pairs)	4	6	88
Stays	1	10½	19
Futtock Shrouds	Iron		
Slings Proper (to go over Cap) Chain for all vessels			
Pendant Tackle Falls	2	2¾	90
Foot Ropes	2	3	11
Stirrups	4	2	4
Truss	Patent		
Lifts	2	4	36
Braces	2	2¾	90
Tacks (tapered)	2	3½	90
Sheets (tapered)	2	2¾	20
Yard Rope	2	3¼	58
Lift Jiggers	2	2	20
Fore Storm Stay Sail Stay	1	7½	14
Halliards	1	3	33
Downhaul	1	2¾	15
Lower Studding-sail Halliards	2	2¾	58
Lower Studding-sail Sheets	2	2½	12
Lower Studding-sail Outhaul	2	2¾	36
Swinging-boom Topping-lifts	2	3½	36
Falls & Lizard for Topping-lifts	2	2¼	30
After Guys	2	3	36
Forward Guys	2	3	36
FORE TOP-MAST AND YARD GEAR			
Shrouds and Pendants (pairs)	2	3¾	24
Stays	1	4½	24
Standing Back stays (pairs)	1	4½	28
Cat-Harpen Legs	2	2½	2
Mast Rope	1	4	34
Jackstays (bending)	Iron		
Foot Ropes	2	2½	8

Name of Rigging	*No*	*Size*	*Length*
Stirrups	2	2	4
Flemish Horses	2	2	3
Parrel	1	3½	3
Top-sail Ties (all hide)	1	4½	7
Halliards for Top-sail Ties	1	2¾	41
Rolling Tackle	1	2	5
Lifts	2	4	20
Braces	2	2½	64
Sheets	2	3¾	46
Clew-lines	2	2¼	56
Bow-lines	2	2	52
Bunt-lines	2	2¼	44
Reef Pendants (all hide)	2	3	7
Whips for Reef Pendants	2	2	50
Clew Jiggers	2	1½	46
Lift Jiggers	2	2¼	12
Boom Tricing-lines	2	1¼	14
Studding-sail Halliards	2	2½	66
Studding-sail Tacks	2	2¼	72
Studding-sail Sheets	2	2½	32
Studding-sail Downhauls	2	1½	40
FORE TOP-GALLANT MAST AND YARD GEAR			
Shrouds (pairs)	1	2½	15
Stay	1	2½	28
Standing Backstays (pairs)	1	3	34
Long Yard or Mast Rope	1	3	35
Jackstays	Iron		
Foot Ropes	2	2	6
Parrel	1	2	2
Lifts	2	2	28
Braces	2	2	52
Sheets	2	2	44
Clew-lines	2	1¼	48
Bow-lines	2	1	54
Tripping-line	1	1½	18
Studding-sail Halliards	2	2	70
Studding-sail Sheets	2	2	36
Studding-sail Tacks	2	1¾	32
FORE TRY-SAIL, MAST AND GAFF GEAR			
Peak Halliards	1	3¼	55
Throat Halliards	1	3¼	40
Vangs	2	2¾	58
Peak Brails (pairs of)	2	1¼	80
Throat Brails (pairs of) Pendants	1	3½	16
Whip	2	2¾	40
Middle Brails (pairs of)	1	2¼	28
Foot Brails (pairs of)	1	2½	36
Sheets	2	4¼	54
MAIN-MAST AND YARD GEAR			
Pendants (pairs)	1	6	4
Shrouds (pairs)	3	6	66
Stays	2	6½	30
Futtock Shrouds	Iron		
Slings Proper (to go over Cap) Chain for all vessels			
Pendant Tackle Falls	2	2¾	90
Foot Ropes	2	3¼	9
Stirrups	4	2	4
Truss	Patent		
Lifts	2	3	34
Braces	2	2½	66
Reef Pendants	2	5	13

Name of Rigging	*No*	*Size*	*Length*
MAIN TOP-MAST AND YARD GEAR			
Shrouds and Pendants (pairs)	2	3	24
Stays	1	3	10
Standing Back stays (pairs)	1	3	30
Cat-Harpen Legs	2	2½	2
Long Mast Rope	1	4	34
Jackstays	Iron		
Foot Ropes	2	2¾	7
Stirrups	2	2	2
Flemish Horses	2	2	4
Parrel	1	4	3
Top-sail Ties (all hide)	1	4⅟	7
Halliards for Top-sail Ties	1	2½	34
Rolling Tackle	1	2	5
Lifts	2	3½	18
Braces	2	2¼	64
Sheets	2	3½	46
Clew-lines	2	2	50
Bow-lines	2	2	42
Bunt-lines	1	2	22
Lift Jiggers	2	2	16
MAIN TOP-GALLANT MAST AND YARD GEAR			
Shrouds (pairs)	1	2¼	15
Stay	1	2½	12
Standing Back stays (pairs)	1	2¾	34
Main-boom Topping-lifts	2	5	40
Falls for Main-boom Topping-lifts	2	3	36
MAIN TRY-SAIL MAST AND GAFF GEAR			
Peak Halliards	1	3¾	54
Throat Halliards	1	3¼	38
Vangs	2	2½	30
Peak Brails (pairs)	1	2	40
Throat Brails (pairs)	1	3¼	38
Middle Brails (pairs)	1	2	34
Foot Brails (pairs)	1	2½	36
Sheets	1	4	35
Outhauler	1	4	25
Boom Tackle for Outhauler	2	2¾	60
Reef Pendants for Outhauler	2	5½	6
Reef Tackle for Outhauler	1	3	18
GAFF TOP-SAIL GEAR			
Halliard	1	3	34
Outhauler	1	3	26
Sheets	2	2¾	26
Downhaul	1	2¼	18
MISCELLANEOUS GEAR			
Braces, Preventer (Lower Yards)	1	2½	45
Braces, Preventer (Top-sail Yards)	1	2¼	42
Cleets, Iron, for Tops	12		
Chain Slings for Top-sail Yards	2		
Chain Slings for Gaff	4		
Falls, Cat	2	3¼	40
Falls, Fish Pendants	2	4	6
Falls, Stern Boat	2	2½	40
Falls, Quarter Boats	4	2¾	112
Falls, Deck Tackle	1	3¼	50
Falls, Stock and Bill Tackles	2	2½	42
Falls, Luff Tackles	12	3	120
Falls, Stay Luff Tackles	2	3	50
Falls, Jiggers	6	2¼	120

Name of Rigging	No	Size	Length
Fenders, Boat (Stuffed Leather)	one set for each boat		
Futtock Staves (Iron)	8		
Gripes, Launch	1	4½	18
Girt-lines, Fore Mast-head	2	2½	70
Girt-lines, Main Mast-head	2	2½	92
Girt-lines, Hammock	3	2½	120
Hooks, Can (Iron)	1	1	1
Halliards, Signal (set)	1		
Hooks, Fish (franch.)	2		
Jacks, Iron (sets)	1		
Lines, Clothes (Manila)	12	2	300
Lines, Tricing, Hammock	4	2½	85
Rungs for Jacob Ladder (set)	1		
Ropes, Buoy	2	4	40
Ropes, Ridge, Awning (set of)	1		

Name of Rigging	No	Size	Length
Ropes, Old (for lashings)	as much as may be required		
Rudder Pendants and Chains	as may be required		
Stopper, Cat-head	2	5	3
Stoppers, Ring	2	3½	8
Stoppers, Deck (chain claw)	4	4ft	
Stoppers, Boats	4	2¼	20
Stoppers, Fighting, doz	2	3¼	60
Stoppers, Bit	3	6	7
Strap Sevagees (doz)	2		
Swabs (dozens)	2		
Seines	1	35	
Shank Painters (a part Chain)	2	4½	2

Schooner dimensions are not available but would probably be similar to those assumed for USN Schooners in A TABLE FOR MASTS AND SPARS.

'A Table Showing The Size And Description Of The Different Blocks Of All Classes Of Vessels, U.S.N.'

W N Brady, 1876

Schooner: Block sizes are in inches

Name of Block	No.	Size	Swallow	Description
FLYING JIB-BOOM				
Downhaul	1	5	0.8	S
Halliards Fore Top-gallant mast-head	1	6	1.1	S
JIB-BOOM				
Downhaul	1	6	1.0	S
Brails on Stay	2	5	0.8	S
Brails leading on Boom-end	2	5	0.8	S
Martingale back ropes	2	7	1.2	D
	2	7	1.2	S
Top-gallant Bow-lines	2	5	0.7	S
Guy Tackles	4	8	1.0	D
	4	8	1.0	S
Jib-stay Tackle	1	8	1.0	D
	1	8	1.0	S
Sheets in Clew of Sail	2	8	1.0	S
Halliards in head of Sail	1	7	0.9	S
Halliards on top-mast Trestle-trees	1	10	1.0	S.I.bd.
BOWSPRIT				
Fore-top Bow-lines	2	8	1.2	S
FOREMAST AND YARD				
Pendant Tackles	2	10	1.2	D
Truss Tackles	2	10	1.2	D
Clew Garnet	2	9	1.4	S.I.bd.
Clews of Sail	2	8	1.1	S
Braces on Yard-arms	2	9	1.1	S
Braces leading under Main Trestle-trees	2	9	1.1	S
Lifts on Cap	2	8	1.2	S
Lift Jiggers	2	7	0.8	D
	2	7	0.8	S
Swinging-boom Topping-lift	2	8	1.2	Cl.
Swing-boom Topping-whips	2	7	0.8	D
	2	7	0.8	S
Pendants f.out. Halliards	2	9	1.1	S
Outer Studding-sail Halliards on Boom	2	7	1.1	S
Inner Studding-sail Halliards on Yard	2	7	0.9	S
Inner Studding-sail Halliards on Quarter	2	7	0.9	S
Tripping-line	2	7	0.8	S
After Guys	2	8	1.0	S.I.bd.

Name of Block	No.	Size	Swallow	Description
Forward Guys (Cheek on Bowsprit)	2	8	1.0	S
Tacks on Boom-end	2	8	0.9	S
FORE TOP-MAST AND YARD				
Top Blocks	1	10	1.5	S.I.bd.
Top Runners	2	8	1.2	S
Breast Back stays	2	10	1.2	D
	2	10	1.2	T.I.bd.
Fly Blocks	1	10	1.2	D
	1	10	1.2	S
Leader for Fly Blocks	1	10	1.2	S
Braces on Yard-arms	2	8	1.0	S
Braces under Main Trestle-trees	2	10	1.2	S
Sister	2	10	1.4	D
Leader of Lifts	2	7	1.4	Cl.
Lift Jiggers	2	7	0.8	D
	2	7	0.8	S
Quarter Blocks	2	8	1.2	D.I.bd.
Clew-lines in Clew of Top-sail	2	8	1.2	S
Rolling Tackle	2	8	1.2	D
	2	8	1.2	S
Bunt-lines at Mast-head	2	8	1.2	S.I.bd.
Reef Tackle Whips	2	8	1.2	S
Bunt-runner	1	6	0.9	S
Jigger for Bunt-runner	1	6	0.9	D
	1	6	0.9	S
Clew Jiggers	2	6	0.9	S
Span for Studding-sail Halliards	2	9	1.4	S
Jewel Blocks	2	9	1.4	S
Studding-sail Tacks on Boom-ends	2	5	0.8	S
Studding-sail Downhaul in Sails	2	6	0.8	S
Leaders for Boom-braces in Main Rigging	2	6	1.0	S
FORE TOP-GALLANT MAST AND YARD				
Breast Back stays	2	7	0.9	S
Breast Backstays in Channels	2	7	0.9	D.I.bd.
Halliards	2	7	1.0	D
Braces on Main Top-mast-head	2	5	0.9	S
Sister	2	5	1.2	S
Span Blocks Top-gallant				
Studding-sail Halliards	2	6	0.9	S
Jewel Blocks	2	6	0.9	S
Studding-sail Tacks on Boom-ends	2	5	0.8	S

Name of Block	No.	Size	Swallow	Description
FORE TRY-SAIL MAST AND GAFF				
Peak Halliards	1	14	1.7	D.I.bd.
	2	14	1.7	S
Throat Halliards	1	14	1.7	D
	1	14	1.7	S
Peak Brails	Cheek			
Throat Brails	2	9	1.2	S
Middle Brails	2	7	0.9	S
Foot Brails	2	9	1.5	S
Sheets	4	13	1.1	S
Vangs	2	8	1.2	S
MAIN MAST AND YARD				
Pendant Tackles	2	10	1.3	D
	2	10	1.3	S
Truss	Patent			
Braces on Yard-arms	2	8	1.0	S
MAIN TOP-MAST AND YARD				
Top Blocks	1	10	2.0	S.I.bd.
Fly Blocks	1	12	1.3	D
	1	12	1.3	S
Leaders for Fly Blocks	1	10	1.2	S
Braces on Yard-arms	2	10	1.2	S
Bunt-runner	1	6	0.9	S
Jigger for Bunt-runner	1	6	0.9	D
MAIN TRY-SAIL MAST AND GAFF				
Peak Halliards	1	14	1.6	D.I.bd.
	2	14	1.6	S
Throat Halliards	1	14	1.6	D
	1	14	1.6	S.I.bd.
Peak Brails	Cheek			
Throat Brails	2	8	1.2	S
Middle Brails	2	8	1.2	S
Foot Brails	2	8	1.2	S
Sheets	2	12	1.5	S
Sheets on Booms of two-masted vessels	2	12	1.5	D
Vangs	2	6	1.0	S
SPANKER BOOM AND GAFF				
Topping-lifts	2	11	2.0	S
Tackles f. Topping-lifts	4	11	1.2	D
	2	11	1.2	S
Dasher Block (Ensign Hall)	1			D

Name of Block	No.	Size	Swallow	Description
MISCELLANEOUS BLOCKS				
Cat Blocks	2	11	1.5	D
Clear Hawse Pendants	1			S
Bull's Eyes for Clothes-lines	20			T
Cap Bobstay Hearts	2			H
Middle and Inner Hearts	2			H
Bowsprit Shroud Hearts	4			H
Iron-strapped Bull's Eyes (in head)	size and number as required			
Luff Tackle Blocks	20	9	1.1	S
Luff Tackle Blocks for Stays	4	10	1.2	D
Five-rail Leaders	20			S.d.sc.
Side Leaders	20			T
Snatch Blocks	8	Assorted		Sn.
Hammock Girtlines	8	9	1.1	S
Hammock Tricing-lines	8	7	1.1	S
Relieving Tackles	2	9	1.2	D
	2	9	1.2	S
Awning Jiggers	6	6	0.8	D
Lower Yard Whips	2	6	0.8	S
Crow-foot Halliards	4	5	0.7	S
Stern, Quarter and Waist Davit Blocks	10	8	1.0	D.I.bd.
Leading Trucks	12			D
	12			S
Fore Yard	1	20	1.3	F
	1	10	1.1	S
Main Yard	1	20	1.3	F
	1	10	1.1	S
Dead Eyes (set)	1			
Trucks for Jaws of Gaff (set)	1			
Mast-head Trucks (set)	1			

Explanation of abbreviations used in Brady's tables

Cheek = Cheek Block
Cl. = Clump Block
D = Double Block
F. = Fiddle Block
H = Heart
I.bd. = Iron bound
S = Single Block
S.d.sc. = Single Block double scored
Sn. = Snatch Block
T = Thimble
Tr. = Treble Block

Appendix 4: FURNITURE ETC.

ANCHOR MEASUREMENTS FOR SMALLER VESSELS

W A Falconer, 1815

(English measure)

Weight	Length of the shanks		Length of the flooks		Breadth of the palms		Thickness of the palms
(cwt)	(ft)	(in)	(ft)	(in)	(ft)	(in)	(in)
1	5	8	1	10	0	9	¾
2	6	6	2	2	0	11	¾
3	7	0	2	4	1	0	⅞
4	7	6	2	6	1	1	⅞
5	8	0	2	8	1	2	1
6	8	6	2	10	1	3	1
7	9	0	3	0	1	4	1
8	9	6	3	2	1	5	1⅛
9	10	0	3	4	1	6	1⅛
10	10	4	3	5	1	7	1⅛
11	10	8	3	7	1	8	1¼
12	11	0	3	8	1	8¼	1¼
13	11	4	3	10	1	8½	1¼
14	11	8	3	11	1	8¾	1¼
15	12	0	4	0	1	9	1⅞

Weight	Size of the trend	Size of the small round	Outer Diameter of the ring		Thickness of the ring
(cwt)	(in)	(in)	(ft)	(in)	(in)
1	2½	2	0	9	1
2	2¾	2¼	0	11	1⅛
3	3	2½	1	0	1¼
4	3¼	2¾	1	1	1⅜
5	3½	3	1	2	1½
6	3¾	3¼	1	3	1⅝
7	4	3½	1	4	1¾
8	4¼	3¾	1	5	1⅞
9	4⅜	3⅞	1	6	1¹⁵⁄₁₆
10	4½	4	1	7	2
11	4⅝	4⅛	1	8	2¹⁄₁₆
12	4⅝	4⅛	1	8¼	2¹⁄₁₆
13	4¾	4¼	1	8½	2⅛
14	4⅞	4⅜	1	8¾	2³⁄₁₆
15	5	4⅜	1	9	2π

Anchor dimensions by Bobrik (1848) largely correspond with those above.

DIMENSIONS OF OARS FOR SLOOPS, BRIGS, BARGES, LIGHTERS & SHIPS' BOATS

Excerpt from 'The Art Of Making Masts, Yards, Gaffs, Booms, Blocks And Oars As Practised In The Royal Navy And According To The Most Approved Methods In The Merchant Service', Steel & Goddard, 1816

(English measure)

Number of tons	Lengths Sweep	Handle		Loom		Body or Shank		Blade		Loom Thick	Deep	Blade inn. Broad out.		inn.	Thick out.	Handle Diameter
	(ft)	(ft)	(in)	(ft)	(in)	(ft)	(in)	(ft)	(in)	(in)	(in)	(in)	(in)	(in)	(in)	(in)
Sloops & Brigs	28	1	6	10	3	7	0	10	0	4	4	4	7	3⅛	1	1¾
130	27	1	3	11	0	6	0	9	0	4¼	4¼	4	7	3½	1	1¾
100	26	1	2	10	6	5	9	8	9	4¼	4¼	3¾	6½	3⅛	1	1¾
80	25	1	2	10	0	5	6	8	6	4¼	4¼	3½	6½	3	1	1¾
70	24	1	1	9	9	5	3	8	0	4⅛	4⅛	3½	6⅜	3	1	1¾
50	23	1	1	9	3	5	0	7	9	4⅛	4⅛	3½	6⅜	3	1	1¾
30	22	1	0	8	9	4	9	7	6	4⅛	4⅛	3¼	6¼	3	⅞	1¾
20	21	1	0	8	6	4	6	7	0	4	4	3⅛	6¼	2⅞	⅞	1¾
Boats in breadth																
(ft) (in)																
7 0	20	0	10	6	0	6	10	6	4	4	4	3⅛	6⅛	2⅞	⅞	1¾
6 0	19	0	10	5	0	7	2	6	0	3⅞	3⅞	3	6	2¾	⅞	1¾
5 0	18	0	10	4	0	7	6	5	8	3⅞	3⅞	3	6	2¾	⅞	1¾
4 6	17	0	10	3	6	7	4	5	4	3¾	3¾	2⅞	5¾	2⅝	⅞	1½
4 0	16	0	10	3	0	7	2	5	0	3½	3½	2¾	5¾	2½	¾	1½

DIMENSIONS OF OARS & SKULLS FOR BARGES, WHERRIES & SKIFFS

Breadth		Lengths Sweep	Handle		Loom		Body or Shank		Blade		Loom Thick	Deep	Blade inn. Broad out		inn	Thick out	Handle Diameter
(ft)	(in)	(ft)	(ft)	(in)	(ft)	(in)	(ft)	(in)	(ft)	(in)	(in)	(in)	(in)	(in)	(in)	(in)	(in)
5	9	20	0	11	4	6	8	11	5	8	4	4½	2½	6½	3½	¾	1⅝
5	6	19	0	11	4	4	8	5	5	4	3¾	4¼	2¼	6¼	3	¾	1⅝
5	0	18	0	10	4	0	8	0	5	0	3½	4	2	6	2¾	¾	1⅝
4	9	17	0	10	3	10	7	7	4	8	3¼	3¾	1¾	5⅞	2½	⅝	1⅝
4	6	16	0	10	3	6	7	4	4	4	3	3½	1½	5¾	2⅜	½	1⅝
4	3	15	0	10	3	3	7	0	4	0	2¾	3¼	1⅜	5½	2¼	½	1⅝

SKULLS

Breadth		*Lengths*									*Loom*		*Blade*				*Handle*
		Sweep	*Handle*		*Loom*		*Body or Shank*		*Blade*		*Thick*	*Deep*	*inn.*	*Broad out*	*inn*	*Thick out*	*Diameter*
(ft)	*(in)*	*(ft)*	*(ft)*	*(in)*	*(ft)*	*(in)*	*(ft)*	*(in)*	*(ft)*	*(in)*	*(in)*	*(in)*	*(in)*	*(in)*	*(in)*	*(in)*	*(in)*
5	6	14	0	4½	2	4	7	9	3	6	3	3½	2	5½	2¼	½	1¾
5	3	13	0	4½	2	2	7	2	3	3	2¾	3½	1⅞	5⅜	2½	½	1¾
4	9	12	0	4	2	0	6	8	3	0	2½	3	1¾	5¼	2⅛	½	1¾
4	6	11	0	4	1	11	6	0	2	9	2½	2¾	1⅝	5⅛	2⅛	½	1¾
4	3	10	0	4	1	9	5	5	2	6	2⅛	2⅝	1½	5	2	⅜	1¾
4	0	9	0	3½	1	7	4	10	2	3	2	2½	1⅜	4¾	2	⅜	1¾

The looms of boat oars are frequently rounded. Oars and sculls are made of ash (and sometimes of fir). A leather button is nailed on the foreside, about 2 inches from the loom, and that edge is rounded to work easily in the row-lock: tin is strapped around the lower end of the blade to prevent splitting. Oars or skulls made of fir exceed the dimensions in the above tables by ⅛in.

BUILDING DIMENSIONS FOR BOATS

Long boat, Launch, Barge, Pinnace, Cutter and Yawl

E Bobrik, 1848

Part	*Long boat*		*ι*				*Launch*	
	26ft		*22ft*		*19ft*		*24ft*	
	(ft)	*(in)*	*(ft)*	*(in)*	*(ft)*	*(in)*	*(ft)*	*(in)*
Moulded breadth	8	9	7	6	7	1	7	10
Depth middle	3	8	3	6	2	10	3	3
bow	4	9	4	2	3	3	3	9
stern	4	10	4	3	3	4	3	9
Keel, not the moulded side								
middle	0	4¾	0	4⅜	0	3¾	0	5½
height below the rabbet	0	5¾	0	5½	0	5	0	4½
above the rabbet	0	⅞	0	¾	0	¾	0	1
Stem, not the moulded side	0	3⅞	0	3¾	0	3½	0	3
afore the rabbet	0	6	0	5½	0	5	0	4½
behind the rabbet	0	1⅝	0	1⅜	0	1⅓	0	2
Transom, wide	5	3	3	9	3	4	6	6
thick	0	3½	0	3	0	2¼	0	3
knee	0	3¼	0	2¾	0	2	0	3
Sternpost at the stern	0	3¾	0	3¼	0	3	0	4¾
at the keel	0	2¾	0	2⅝	0	2½	0	4¾
wide, or fore and aft at the keel	1	1	1	0	0	10	0	10
at the transom	0	6¾	0	5	0	4½	0	5¼
Floor timber at the side	0	2¾	0	2½	0	1¾	0	2¼
moulded at the top	0	2½	0	2¼	0	1⅝	0	2¼
at the neck	0	4½	0	4½	0	3¾	0	4½
Futtocks at the side near the heel	0	2½	0	2⅛	0	1¾	0	2
at the top	0	2	0	1⅞	0	1½	0	1½
moulded at the top	0	2	0	1⅞	0	1½	0	1½
Frame scarfs	2	4	2	0	1	10	2	2
Keelson, wide	1	0	0	11	0	10½	0	10
thick	0	2½	0	1¾	0	1½	0	2
Foot-waling, thick	0	1	0	1	0	1	0	1
Thwart-waling, wide	0	9	0	8	0	6½	0	7
thick	0	1⅛	0	1⅛	0	1	0	1

Part	*Long boat*		*ι*				*Launch*	
	26ft		*22ft*		*19ft*		*24ft*	
	(ft)	*(in)*	*(ft)*	*(in)*	*(ft)*	*(in)*	*(ft)*	*(in)*
Thwart, middle, wide	0	11	0	10	0	10	0	10
thick	0	3½	0	3¼	0	3	0	3¼
after, wide	0	9	0	9	0	9	0	9
thick	0	2½	0	2¼	0	2	0	2
foremost, wide	0	10	0	10	0	10	0	9
thick	0	2¾	0	2½	0	2¼	0	2
loose, wide	0	8	0	8	0	8	0	9
thick	0	2	0	1¾	0	1½	0	2
Thwart knees, not moulded side	0	2¾	0	2½	0	2⅓	0	3
Seats at rear of the boat, wide	1	0	0	11	0	11	1	0
thick	0	1½	0	1¼	0	1¼	0	1½
Deadwood, not at the moulded side	0	2¾	0	2¼	0	2	0	3
Garboard-strake, thick	0	1⅛	0	1	0	⅞	0	⅞
The next plank at the bottom, wide	0	9½	0	9	0	8¾	0	8
The uppermost plank, wide	0	10	0	9	0	8	0	9
Gunnel, deep	0	3	0	2½	0	2¼	0	3
Breasthook, not the moulded side	0	2½	0	2¼	0	2	0	3
long	3	6	3	3	2	10	3	0
moulded at the neck	0	5	0	4½	0	4	0	5
Knighthead knee, n.a. moulded								
side	0	3¼	0	3	0	2½	0	3
long	1	6	1	4	1	2	1	6
Chock, thick	0	2¾	0	2½	0	2	0	2
long	1	4	1	2	1	1	1	2
Washboard, wide, bow	0	7	0	6	0	5¼	0	6
rear	0	7	0	6	0	5¼	0	6
Bowsprit step, thick	0	2		iron		iron		
wide	1	0						
Windlass, diameter	0	9	0	8	0	7	0	8
Bits, thick	0	5	0	4½	0	4	0	5
wide	0	10	0	9	0	9	0	11
Rudder, wide at the heel	1	8	1	7	1	6	1	7
at the counter	1	2	1	1	1	½	1	1½
at the head	0	8	0	7½	0	7	0	8
thick	0	1½	0	1¼	0	1¼	0	1½

Part	Pinnace				Cutter			
	25ft		17ft		25ft		21ft	
	(ft)	(in)	(ft)	(in)	(ft)	(in)	(ft)	(in)
Moulded breadth	6	0	5	9	6	10	6	7
Depth middle	2	7	2	5	2	8	2	6
bow	3	2	2	11	3	3	3	1
stern	3	5	3	2	3	4	3	1
Keel, not the moulded side middle	0	3¾	0	3½	0	3¾	0	3½
height below the rabbet	0	4	0	4	0	3½	0	3¼
above the rabbet	0	⅞	0	¾	0	⅞	0	¾
Stem, not the moulded side	0	3½	0	3¼	0	3¼	0	3
forward of rabbet	0	3¼	0	3	0	4¾	0	4½
behind the rabbet	0	2¼	0	2⅛	0	2⅜	0	1¼
Transom, wide	3	6	3	0	3	1	2	10
thick	0	2	0	1¾	0	1½	0	1
knee	iron		iron		0	1	0	1½
Sternpost at the stern	0	3	0	2¾	0	2⅞	0	2¾
at the keel	0	2½	0	2⅜	0	2½	0	2⅜
wide, or fore and aft at the keel	0	9¼	0	8½	0	9	0	8½
at the transom	0	2¼	0	2	0	4	0	3¾
Floor timber at the side	0	1½	0	1⅜	0	1½	0	1⅜
Moulded at the top	0	1⅜	0	1¼	0	1¼	0	1¼
at the neck	0	3⅝	0	3½	0	2¾	0	2⅜
Futtocks at the side near the heel	0	1⅜	0	1¼	0	1⅜	0	1¼
at the top	0	1¼	0	1⅛	0	1⅛	0	1
moulded at the top	0	1¼	0	1⅛	0	1⅛	0	1
Frame scarfs	1	8	1	7	1	10	1	9
Keelson, wide	0	10½	0	10	0	9½	0	9½
thick	0	1⅛	0	1⅛	0	1⅛	0	1
Foot-waling, thick	0	¾	0	⅝	0	¾	0	¾
Thwart-waling, wide	0	4⅛	0	4	0	4	0	3¾
thick	0	⅞	0	⅞	0	⅞	0	⅞
Thwart, middle, wide	0	9½	0	9	0	9	0	8
thick	0	1½	0	1½	0	1½	0	1½
aftermost, wide	0	8½	0	8	0	8	0	8
thick	0	1⅝	0	1½	0	1¾	0	1¾
foremost, wide	0	7½	0	7	0	10	0	10
thick	0	1⅜	0	1⅜	0	2	0	2
loose, wide	0	7½	0	7	0	8	0	8
thick	0	1⅜	0	1¼	0	1½	0	1½
Thwart knees not moulded side	iron		iron		0	1⅛	0	1⅛
Seats at rear of the boat, wide	0	11	0	10	0	11	0	11
thick	0	1⅛	0	1¼	0	1¼	0	1¼
Deadwood, not the moulded side	0	2½	0	2½	0	2½	0	2½
Garboard-strake thick	0	⅞	0	⅞	0	¾	0	⅝
The next plank at the bottom,								
wide	0	6½	0	5	0	5	0	4½
The uppermost plank, wide	0	6½	0	5½	0	6	0	5
Gunnel, deep	0	3½	0	3¼	0	1¾	0	1½
Breasthook, not the moulded side	0	1½	0	1⅜	0	2	0	1¾
long	2	0	1	8	1	8	1	7
moulded at the neck	0	3½	0	3	0	3	0	2¾
Knighthead knee, n.moulded side	0	1½	0	1½	0	1½	0	1¼
long	0	10	0	10	1	2	0	11
Chock, thick	0	1¼	0	1¼	0	1¼	0	1¼
long	1	0	0	11	1	2	1	0
Washboard, wide, bow	0	4	0	3½	0	1¼	0	1¼
rear	0	5	0	4	1	2	1	0
Bowsprit step, thick	0	5	0	4¾				
wide	0	5	0	4¾				
Rudder, wide at the heel	1	3	1	1	1	4	1	2
at the counter	1	0	0	10	1	1	1	0
at the head	0	7½	0	7½	0	7	0	6½
thick	0	1	0	⅞	0	1	0	⅞

Part	Cutter		ι Yawl			
	16ft 26ft		16ft			
	(ft)	(in)	(ft)	(in)	(ft)	(in)
Moulded breadth	6	0	6	8	5	6
Depth, middle	2	3	2	11	2	3½
bow	2	9	3	6	2	9
stern	2	9	3	9	2	11
Keel, not the moulded side						
middle	0	3	0	3¾	0	3¼
height, below the rabbet	0	2¾	0	3	0	2¾
above the rabbet	0	¾	0	¾	0	¾
Stem, not the moulded side	0	2¾	0	3¼	0	2¾
afore the rabbet	0	4	0	4½	0	4
behind the rabbet	0	1¼	0	1¼	0	1⅛
Transom, wide	2	4	3	8	2	7
thick	0	1¼	0	1¾	0	1½
knee	0	1¼	iron		iron	
Sternpost, at the stern	0	2½	0	2⅝	0	2¼
at the keel	0	2	0	2¼	0	1¾
wide, or fore and aft at the keel	0	7	0	8¾	0	7
at the transom	0	3	0	2	0	1½
Floor timber at the side	0	1¼	0	1¾	0	1½
moulded at the top	0	1⅛	0	1⅝	0	1½
at the neck	0	2	0	3½	0	3
Futtocks at the side near the heel	0	1⅛	0	1½	0	1½
at the top	0	⅞	0	1¼	0	1⅛
moulded at the top	0	⅞	0	1¼	0	1⅛
Frame scarfs	1	7	1	10	1	8
Keelson, wide	0	8	0	10	0	9
thick	0	⅞	0	1⅛	0	1
Foot-waling, thick	0	⅝	0	¾	0	¾
Thwart-waling, wide	0	3½	0	6	0	5
thick	0	¾	0	1	0	1
Thwart, middle wide	0	7	0	10	0	7
thick	0	1½	0	1½	0	1½
foremost, wide	0	9	0	7½	0	7
thick	0	1¾	0	1½	0	1½
loose, wide	0	7	0	7½	0	7
thick	0	1½	0	1½	0	1½
Thwart knees, not moulded side	0	1	iron		iron	
Seats at the rear of the boat, wide	0	10	0	11	0	10
thick	0	1⅛	0	1¼	0	1⅛
Deadwood, not the moulded side	0	2	0	2¼	0	2
Garboard-strake, thick	0	⅝	0	⅞	0	⅞
The next plank at the bottom, wide	0	4	0	8	0	7½
The uppermost plank, wide	0	4½	0	8	0	7½
Gunnel, deep	0	1½	0	2½	0	2¼
Breasthook, not the moulded side	0	1½	0	2	0	1¾
long	1	6	2	4	2	2
moulded at the neck	0	2½	0	3½	0	3
Knighthead knee, n. moulded side	0	1¼	0	2	0	1¾
long	0	9	1	0	0	11
Chock, thick	0	1¼	0	1¾	0	1½
long	0	11	1	1	1	0
Washboard, wide, bow	0	4½	0	4½	0	4¼
rear	0	4½	0	5½	0	5½
Rudder, wide at the heel	1	1	1	5	1	3
at the counter	0	10	1	½	0	11
at the head	0	6	0	7	0	6
thick	0	⅞	0	⅞	0	⅞

MAST AND SPAR DIMENSIONS FOR BOATS

C F Steinhaus, 1858

B = Breadth   L = Length of the boat

Part	Gaff sail	Lug sail	Sprit sail
Length of:			
mainmast (MM)	B x 2.87–3.50	2.40–2.70	2.40–2.70
fore mast (FM)	MM x 0.96	0.90–0.92	0.90–0.92
mizzen or jigger mast (JM)	MM x –	0.60	0.60
main gaff (MG)	L x 0.26–0.34	–	–
fore gaff	MG x 0.90	–	–
boom	L x 0.56–0.60	–	–
bowsprit outside stem	B x 1.0	1.0	1.0–1.25
main yard (MY)	L x –	0.38–0.50	–
fore yard	MY x –	0.86–0.90	–
mizzen yard or jigger yard	MY x –	0.50–0.55	–
outrigger	L x –	0.30–0.32	0.28
main sprit	MM x –	–	0.90
fore sprit	FM x –	–	0.90
mizzen or jigger sprit	JM x --	–	0.90
main sliding gunter	MM x –	–	–
fore sliding gunter	FM x –	–	–
jigger sliding gunter	JM x --	--	–
MM behind boat centre	L x 0.031	0.015–0.034	–
afore the centre	L x –	–	0.066
FM afore the centre	L x 0.34	0.287–0.281	0.33
jigger mast at the stern	no	yes	yes
mast diameter (1" for ? feet)	4–5	4½	4½
of gaff, sprit, yard and			
sliding gunter	3	5	9
of boom and outrigger	5½	3	3
of the bowsprit	2½	2½	2½

Part	Settee sail	Sliding gunter	Lateen sail
Length of:			
main mast (MM)	B x 2.15	2.20	1.40–1.76
fore mast (FM)	MM x 0.93	0.93	0.98
mizzen or jigger mast (JM)	MM x 0.43	0.53	0.67
main gaff (MG)	L x –	–	–
fore gaff	MG x –	–	–
boom	L x –	–	–
bowsprit outside stem	B x –	–	L x 0.19–0.25
main yard (MY)	L x 0.83	–	0.90–1.16
fore yard	MY x 0.95	–	0.80–0.90
mizzen yard or jigger yard	MY x 0.56	–	0.50–0.53
outrigger	L x 0.38	–	0.31–0.34
main sprit	MM x –	–	–
fore sprit	FM x –	–	–
mizzen or jigger sprit	JM x –	--	–
main sliding gunter	MM x –	0.83	–
fore sliding gunter	FM x –	0.83	–
Jigger sliding gunter	JM x –	1.0	–
MM behind the boat's centre	L x 0.037	–	–
afore the centre	L x –	0.053	0.018
FM forward of centre	L x 0.312	0.328	0.370
Jigger mast at the stern	yes	yes	yes
Mast diameter (1" for ? feet)	3½	4	3½
of gaff, sprit, yard and			
sliding gunter	5	5½	5
of boom and outrigger	3	3	3
of the bowsprit	–	2½	–

The length of mast heads and gaff outer arms weas arbitrary, the main mast's rake for lateen sails was 1–2°, while the fore mast leaned forward by 19–20°. The gaffs, the gore of a spritsail head and lug yards inclined by approximately 25–30°, but settee and lateen sails inclined 45–50°. The suspension point on lug yards was 0.33 x length aft of the fore end, on settee yards 0.58 for the main and 0.45 that length for the fore yard, while on lateen yards these figures were 0.54 and 0.42 respectively. The suspension of a sliding gunter boom has been explained in Masting and Rigging (Chapter 6). Jigger masts could also be omitted from any boat. The largest diameter of any mast and yard was at their point of fastening, but on sprits this point was at one-third from their lower end.

Differences between the largest and smallest diameter:
D = largest diameter

Mast at the hounds	= 0.45 D	at the heel = 0.90 D
Boom at the outer end	= 0.75 D	at the inner = 0.55 D
Yard at the arms	= 0.60 D	
Bowsprit at the outer end	= 0.75 D	at the inner = 0.80 D
Gaff at the outer arm	= 0.50 D	
Sprit at the outer end	= 0.70 D	at the heel = 0.90 D

Bibliography

Anderson, R and R C, *The Sailing Ship*, G G Harrap & Co (London, 1926)

Anderson, R C, *Oared Fighting Ships*, Percival Marshall (London, 1982)

Archibald, E H H, *The Fighting Ships In The Royal Navy 897–1984*, Blandford Press (Poole, Dorset, 1984)

Archibald, E H H, *Dictionary Of Sea Painters*, Antique Collectors' Club Ltd (Woodbridge, 1982)

Baker, W A, 'Fishing under Sail in the North Atlantic', in *The Atlantic World Of Robert G. Albion*, ed. B W Labaree, Wesleyan University Press (Middeltown, Conn., 1975)

Baker, W A *The Mayflower And Other Colonial Vessels*, Conway Maritime Press Ltd (London, 1983)

Bateson, C, *Australian Shipwrecks 1622–1850*, A H & A W Reed (Sydney, 1972)

Biddlecombe, G, *The Art Of Rigging 1848*, Marine Research Society (Salem, Mass., 1925)

Blanckley, T R, *A Naval Expositor* (London, 1750), repr. J Boudriot Publications (Rotherfield, 1988)

Bobrik, E, *Handbuch Der Praktischen Seefahrtskunde* (Leipzig, 1848), repr. H Hamecher (Kassel, 1978)

Boudriot, J, *The Seventy-Four Gun Ship*, J Boudriot (Paris, 1987)

Brady, W N, *The Kedge Anchor Or Young Sailor's Assistant* (New York, 1876), repr. Macdonald and Jane's (London, 1974)

Bracker, J, M North and P Tamm, *Maler Der See*, Koehler (Herford, 1980)

Brown, D K, *Before The Ironclad*, Conway Maritime Press Ltd (London, 1990)

Cannenburg, W V, *Beschrijvende Catalogus Der Scheepsmodellen En Scheepsbouwkundige Teekeningen 160 –1900*, Nederlandsch Historisch Scheepvaart Museum (Amsterdam, 1943)

Chapelle, H I, *The Baltimore Clipper*, Marine Research Society (Salem, Mass., 1930)

Chapelle, H I, *The History Of The American Sailing Ship*, W W Norton & Co. Inc. (New York, 1935)

Chapelle, H I, *The History Of The American Sailing Navy*, W W Norton & Co Inc. (New York, 1949)

Chapelle, H I, *The Search For Speed Under Sail*, W W Norton & Co Inc. (New York, 1967)

Chapman, F H af, *Architectura Navalis Mercatoria* (Stockholm, 1768), repr. VEB Hinstorff Verlag (Rostock, 1962)

Chatterton, E K, *Fore & Aft Craft And Their Story*, Seeley, Service & Co. Ltd (London, 1927)

Clark, A H, *The History Of Yachting*, G P Putnam's & Sons (London, 1904)

Congreve, W, *An Elementary Treatise On The Mounting Of Naval Ordnance* (London, 1811), repr. Museum Restoration Service (Ottawa, Ontario, 1970)

Crone, G C E, *De Jachten Der Oranjes*, N V Swets & Zeitlinger Boekhandel & Uitgevers-Mij (Amsterdam, 1937)

Davis, C, *Ships Of The Past*, Bonanza Books (New York, 1929)

De Groot, I, and R Vorstman, *Sailing Ships*, Viking Press (New York, 1980)

Duhamel du Monceau, H L, *Anfangsgründe Der Schiffbaukunst Oder Praktische Abhandlung Über Den Schiffbau* (German translation of *Elemens De L'architecture Navale Ou Traité Pratique De La Construction Des Vaisseaux* with enlarging annotations by C G D Müller, Joachim Pauli (Berlin, 1791, repr. Kassel, 1973)

Edson, Jr M A, 'The Schooner Rig, A Hypothesis', in *The American Neptune* Vol.XXV, No.2 (1965)

Edson, Jr M A, ed. *Ship Modellers Shop Notes*, Nautical Research Guild (Washington DC, 1979)

Falconer, W A, *An Universal Dictionary Of The Marine* (London, 1769/80), repr. David & Charles (Newton Abbot, Devon, 1970)

Falconer, W A, *A New Universal Dictionary Of The Marine, improved and enlarged by William Burney LI.D.* (London, 1815), repr. Macdonald and Jane's (London, 1974)

Færöyvik, B and O, *Inshore Craft Of Norway*, Conway Maritime Press (London, 1979)

Fincham, J, *A Treatise On Masting Ships & Mast Making* (London, 1829), 2nd edition 1854, repr. Conway Maritime Press Ltd (London, 1982)

Fincham, J, *A History Of Naval Architecture* (London, 1851), repr. Scholar Press (London, 1979)

Furttenbach, J, *Architectura Navalis* (Frankfurt, 1629), repr. Schiffbautechnische Gesellschaft (Hamburg, 1968)

Goodwin, P, *The Construction And Fitting Of The Sailing Ship Of War 1650–1850*, Conway Maritime Press Ltd (London, 1987)

Government of Commonwealth Of Australia *Historical Record Of Australia 1788–1805*, National Library (Canberra A C T)

Greenhill, B, *The Merchant Schooners*, David & Charles Ltd (London, 1968)

Groenewegen, G, *Verzameling Van Vier En Tachtig Stuks Hollandsche Schepen*, J van den Brink (Rotterdam, 1789)

Hahn, H M, *The Colonial Schooner 1763–1775*, Conway Maritime Press Ltd (London, 1981)

Hall, H, *Report On The Shipbuilding Industry In The U.S.*, Dept. of The Interior, Census Office (Washington DC, 1884), repr. Macdonald and Jane's (London, 1974)

Harland, J, *Seamanship In The Age Of Sail*, Conway Maritime Press Ltd (London, 1985)

Harris, D G, *F. H. Chapman, The First Naval Architect And His Work*, Conway Maritime Press Ltd (London, 1989)

Henderson, J, *Sloops And Brigs*, Adlard Coles Ltd (London, 1972)

Hogg, I and J Batchelor, *Naval Gun*, Blandford Press (Poole, Dorset, 1978)

Holck, P, *Lists Of Men-Of-War 1650–1700, Part III, Danish-Norwegian Ships* S.N.R. Occasional publications No. 5 *The Mariner's Mirror* (Greenwich, 1936)

Höver, O, *Von Der Galiot Zum Fünfmaster*, Angelsachsen Verlag (Bremen, 1934)

Howard, F, *Sailing Ships Of War 1400–1860*, Conway Maritime Press Ltd (London, 1979)

Hutchinson, W, *A Treatise On Naval Architecture* (Liverpool, 1794), repr. Conway Maritime Press Ltd (London, 1969)

King, I H, *The Coastguard Under Sail, The U.S. Revenue Cutter Service 1789–1865*, Naval Institute Press (Annapolis Ml., 1989)

Kemp, P, ed. *The Oxford Companion To Ships And The Sea*, Granada Publishing (London, 1979)

Kerchove, R de, *International Maritime Dictionary*, Van Nostrand Reinhold Co. (New York, 1961)

Klawitter, G D, *Vorlegeblätter Für Schiffbauer* (Berlin, 1835), repr. H Hamecher (Kassel, 1978)

Korth, J W D, *Die Schiffbaukunst* (Berlin, 1826), repr. H. Hamecher (Kassel, 1980)

Laing, A, *The American Sail*, E P Dutton & Co. Inc. (New York, 1961)

Lásló, V, and R Woodman, *The Story Of Sail*, Chatham Publishing (London, 1999)

Lavery, B, and S Stephens, *Ship Models, Their Purpose And Development from 1650 to the present*, Zwemmer, an imprint of Ph. Wilson Publishers Ltd (London, 1995)

Lawson, W, *Blue Gum Clippers And Whale Ships Of Tasmania*, D & L Book Distributors (Launceston, 1949)

Lever, D, *The Young Sea Officer's Sheet Anchor* (London, 1819) repr. E W Sweetman Co. (New York, 1963)

Lyon, D, *Sailing Navy List, All The Ships Of The Royal Navy – Built, Purchased And Captured – 1688-1860*, Conway Maritime Press (London, 1993)

McCalip, D L, 'Some Thoughts on the Rigging of Colonial Schooners' in *Nautical Research Journal* 32/1 (Washington DC, 1986)

MacGregor, D R, *Schooners In Four Centuries*, Argus Books Ltd (Watford, Herts., 1982)

MacGregor, D R, *Fast Sailing Ships 1775–1875*, Nautical Publishing (Lymington, 1973)

MacGregor, D R, *Merchant Sailing Ships 1775–1815*, Argus Books Ltd (Watford, Herts., 1980)

McKay, L, *The Practical Shipbuilder* (New York, 1839), repr. Macdonald and Jane's (London, 1974)

Marquardt, K H, *Schoner In Nord Und Süd*, Hinstorff Verlag (Rostock, 1988)

Marquardt, K H, E*ighteenth Century Rigs & Rigging*, Conway Maritime Press (London, 1992)

Marquardt, K H, 'The Fore and Aft Rigged Warship & Rigs and Rigging', in *The Line Of Battle*, ed. R Gardiner, Conway Maritime Press (London, 1992)

Marquardt, K H, *HMS* Beagle*, Survey ship extraordinary*, Conway Maritime Press (London, 1997)

Marquardt, K H, 'The Origin of Schooners', *The Great Circle*, Vol. 10/1 (Toronto, NSW, 1988)

Marquardt, K H, 'Schooner for Port Jackson – again', *Nautical Research Journal*, Vol. 32/4 (Silver Spring, Ml., 1988)

Marquardt, K H, '*Das erste Jahrhundert der Schonerentwicklung und deren Auswirkung auf den Schiffbau des Ostseeraumes*', *Daslogbuch*, Vol 31/1 (Hamburg, 1995)

Marquardt, K H, '*Seiner Majestät bewaffneter Schoner Berbice* 1789/96', Special Edition *Das Logbuch* (Neuwied, 1999)

Marquardt, K H, 'The Schooner Enterprize 1830–1847', *Model Shipwright*, No. 97, Conway Maritime Press (London, 1996)

Marquardt, K H, 'H.M. Armed Schooner *Berbice* 1789', *Model Shipwright*, No. 101, Conway Maritime Press (London, 1997)

Menzel, H, *Smakken, Kuffen, Galioten*, Schriften des Deutschen Schiffahrtsmuseums, E Kabel Verlag (Hamburg, 1997)

Middendorf, F L, *Bemastung Und Takelung Der Schiffe* (Hamburg, 1903) repr. H. Hamecher (Kassel, 1977)

Norie, J W and J S Hobbs, *Three Hundred And Six Illustrations Of The Maritime Flags Of All Nations Etc.* (London, 1848), German repr. Edition Maritim (Hamburg, 1987)

Ozanne, P, *Auf See Und Vor Anker*, Edition Maritim (Hamburg, 1986)

Padfield, P, *Guns At Sea*, H Evelyn (London, 1973)

Pâris, E, *Souvenirs De Marine* (Paris, 1882), repr. Verlag K H Butziger (Hamburg, 1972)

Paasch, H, *Illustrated Marine Encyclopedia* (London, 1890), repr. Argus Books Ltd (Watford, Herts., 1977)

Paasch, H, *From Keel To Truck*, Eckardt & Messtorff (Hamburg, 1901)

Petrejus, E W, *Das Modell Der Brigg Irene*, German translation of *Model Van De Oorlogsbrik Irene*, Delius, Klasing Verlag (Bielefeld, 1988)

Rees, A, *Naval Architecture 1819/20*, David & Charles reprints (London, 1970)

Röding, J H, *Allgemeines Wörterbuch Der Marine* (Hamburg, 1794), repr. Uitgeverij Graphic Publisher (Amsterdam, 1969)

Robertson, F L, *The Evolution Of Naval Armament* (London, 1921), repr. H T Storey (London, 1968)

Ryan, W F, 'Peter the Great's English Yacht', *Mariner's Mirror*, Vol 69/1 (London, 1983)

Serres, D, and J T, *Liber Nauticus* (London, 1805), repr. Scolar Press (London, 1979)

Sleeswyk, A W, 'The Origin and Development of the Triangular Sail and the Gaff Sail in Seventeen Century Holland', *Mariner's Mirror*, Vol 73/4 (London, 1987)

Smith, G, *King's Cutters*, Conway Maritime Press Ltd (London, 1983)

Smyth, W H, *Sailor's Word Book*, Conway Maritime Press (London, 1996)

Steel, D, *The Elements Of Mastmaking, Sailmaking And Rigging* (London, 1794), repr. E W Sweetman (New York, 1932)

Steel, D, *Art Of Rigging* (London, 1818), repr. Fisher Nautical Press (Brighton, 1974)

Steel, D, 'Oar-Making', *Nautical Research Journal*, Vol 25/2 (Washington DC, 1979)

Steinhaus, C F, *Die Schiffbaukunst In Ihrem Ganzen Umfange* (Hamburg, 1858), repr. H Hamecher (Kassel, 1977)

Szymanski, H, *Deutsche Segelschiffe*, E S Mittler & sohn (Berlin, 1934)

Szymanski, H, *Die Segelschiffe Der Deutschen Kleinschiffahrt*, Hansischer Geschichtsverein (Lübeck, 1929)

Unknown *Der Geöffnete See-Hafen* (Hamburg, 1705–06, repr. E Kabel Verlag (Hamburg, 1989)

Index

♦